Great City Parks

In memory of Martin Spencer Jones (1949–2000)
– friend, colleague and fine photographer

Great City Parks Alan Tate

SPON PRESS
Taylor & Francis Group

London and New York

First published 2001
by Spon Press
11 New Fetter Lane, London EC4P 4EE

Simultaneously published in the USA and Canada
by Spon Press
29 West 35th Street, New York, NY 10001

Spon Press is an imprint of the Taylor & Francis Group

Typeset in Weiss by M Rules
Colour separation by Tenon & Polert Colour Scanning Ltd
Printed and bound in China

British Library Cataloguing in Publication Data
A catalogue record for this book is available
from the British Library

Library of Congress Cataloging in Publication Data
A catalog record has been applied for.

ISBN 0–419–24420–4

Contents

List of Drawings

Introduction

Parks are generally defined as enclosed pieces of land stocked with 'beasts of the chase'. City or urban parks are areas specifically allocated for public recreation. They are often enclosed but they are rarely stocked with 'beasts of the chase'. Urban parks are one of the principal products of the design discipline known as landscape architecture. It has even been suggested that the title landscape architect was first used with respect to the work of Frederick Law Olmsted (1822–1903) and Calvert Bowyer Vaux (1824–95) on Central Park, New York. The development of urban parks began in the mid-nineteenth century and led to the growth of the profession of landscape architecture in Europe and North America. The development of parks presaged two major changes in the character of Western cities. First, it led to the allocation for public use of large tracts of land in or close to rapidly growing cities – and, in Europe, also to the transfer of areas of royal land to public use. Second, it led to the creation of non-productive, vegetated scenery in urban areas.[1]

Urban parks of different shape, size, type and purpose can now be found in cities and towns throughout the world. Nineteenth-century parks in most Western cities were based on primarily pastoral models developed first in Germany and England. Danish-born Christian Cay Lorenz Hirschfeld (1742–92), Professor of Philosophy and Aesthetics at Kiel University, wrote about the provision of public parks in 1785. His doctrines were adopted by Peter Joseph Lenné (1789–1866), principal designer of the Tiergarten in Berlin, and Lenné's pupil, Gustav Meyer (1816–77). Humphry Repton (1752–1818), whose work was interpreted by John Nash (1752–1835) at Regent's and St

James's Parks in London and adapted by Joseph Paxton (1803–65) at Birkenhead, developed the English pastoral urban park. The model was further adapted and applied by practitioners like Olmsted, Vaux and H. W. S. (Horace William Shaler) Cleveland (1814–1900) to the specific conditions of the rapidly expanding cities of the United States – which I refer to as 'American Pastoral' – and by Jean-Charles Adolphe Alphand (1817–91) and his team of municipal designers in Paris.

Towards the end of the nineteenth century, the pastoral model for the public park gave way to symmetrical, geometric layouts. These were typified by the Beaux-Arts Grant Park in Chicago; by the axial Stadtpark in Hamburg, forerunner of the modernist Volkspark, and by the Parque de María Luisa in Seville. Galen Cranz described the period from 1900 to 1930 as the era of the Reform Park. The ensuing period – Cranz's era of the Recreation Facility (1930–65) – was typified by function-led designs like the Amsterdamse Bos and functionalist management like the 'efficient' treatment of Central Park under New York Park Commissioner Robert Moses. Aspects of the Open-Space System (from 1965) are revealed in a number of the cities whose parks are examined in this study. Latterly, relatively small parks have been created, and more private funding and business-derived management techniques have been applied to parks in North America. Meanwhile in mainland Europe numerous new parks have been developed – particularly on derelict industrial sites in Germany, France and the United Kingdom.[2]

Every city park has a history. But this is not an historical study. It is based on the principle that parks, like cities, are constantly developing and are never completed. It is a comparative study of twenty parks in Western Europe and North America. A fundamental concern of this study has been the question of whether there are discernible criteria for the 'successful' planning, design and management of urban parks. Jane Jacobs contended in 1961 that 'every city park is a case unto itself and defies generalizations. Moreover, large parks . . . differ much within themselves from part to part, and they also receive differing influences from the different parts of their cities which they touch'. There are, however, many bases for the comparison of parks of whatever age, size or location. These include questions like why the parks were created, how they were designed, how they are managed and what plans are being made for them at the beginning of the twenty-first century.[3]

The idea of writing 'a book about parks' arose in the early 1980s when the firm that I was running for Brian Clouston in Hong Kong was designing the town park for Sha Tin – the first of a number of major 'new towns' being developed in the Territory. Brian Clouston and I recognized that, at that time, there was little documentation of urban parks. I resolved that, once the construction of the Sha Tin park was completed, I would write a book about what makes a 'successful' park. The study started to take shape when I spent six months during 1986 as an Academic Visitor at University College London under the direction of Professor Michael Ellison. I was persuaded at that time by my former tutor, Ian Laurie, then Director of Landscape Studies at the University of Manchester, to think in terms of a world-wide comparative study. Laurie had been considering a similar project – looking only at large parks – with American academic Jere S. French. I also met with Sir Geoffrey Jellicoe to discuss the study. He suggested, with his characteristic acuity, that the continuing purpose of public parks 'should be to lift people out of their everyday lives'. He also told me – for better or worse – that it took he and Susan Jellicoe seventeen years to complete their research for the first edition of *The Landscape of Man*.[4]

I filled the fourteen years following my meeting with Jellicoe by continuing to work on the design of urban parks in Hong Kong and, from 1992 to 1997, as a consultant for Greenwich Royal Park in London. I ran the landscape consultant's team for the early design stages of Disneyland Paris and subsequently ran two other landscape consultancies and served as President of the United Kingdom Landscape Institute from 1995 to 1997. The Landscape Institute was particularly vocal in its call for greater government attention to the plight of urban parks in the United Kingdom and was proactive in bringing together park advocates, politicians

and funding agencies. The writing-up of the research began in 1998 when I took up a teaching position at the University of Manitoba.

At that time the study was intended to cover forty parks in fifteen different countries. Criteria for inclusion were that the parks had been specifically designed – or substantially redesigned – for public use; they had to allow free admission, and they had to be significant examples in the development of park planning and design. After a year of writing it became clear that this volume would have to be restricted to parks in North America and Western Europe. The number of parks was reduced to twenty-five. All twenty-five were written up but a further reduction to twenty was made shortly before submission to the publisher. The intention throughout this process has been to maintain a balance between parks of differing sizes, of differing ages and demonstrating a wide range of characteristics.[5]

Since this is neither an historical study nor a geographical study, the parks are ordered according to size – ranging from smallest to largest. This is done on the basis that the character of a park is heavily influenced by its size. Size, in turn, is heavily influenced by age and location. On the one hand this ordering creates some apparent anomalies – like Prospect Park appearing before Central Park, and Birkenhead Park appearing before Regent's Park. On the other hand, it results in four North American parks with high levels of private involvement in their designation, management or funding coming together at the beginning. These are followed by four Paris parks then Parque de María Luisa – designed by French landscape architect, Forestier. The two examples in the United Kingdom – Birkenhead and Regent's Parks – appear consecutively, and then the two early twentieth-century parks – Hamburg's Stadtpark and Grant Park, Chicago appear together. They are followed by the Landschaftspark Duisburg-Nord – one of the late twentieth-century examples. Prospect Park – widely considered Olmsted and Vaux's most accomplished design – comes before the Tiergarten, Berlin's 'central' park, and before New York's Central Park. Stanley Park, Vancouver, the single example of 'trapped wilderness', is followed by another forest park – the Amsterdamse Bos. The final example, the Grand Rounds in Minneapolis, was commenced in the late nineteenth century and was still being added to at the beginning of the twenty-first.

It has often been remarked that only sites with limited commercial potential are allocated for development as parks. The examination of each park therefore looks at the size and condition of the sites at the time of designation. It then looks at the reasons for their designation and at the key figures behind the decisions to build them. The principal designers are also profiled. The profiles look at their backgrounds and the values that they brought to the projects. Each park is then examined in terms of its planning and design – looking at its location in the city, and the shape, size and existing landform of the site. The original design concept is reviewed in terms of spatial structure, circulation systems and intended character. The examinations then review the current status of the parks, looking at the organizations that manage them – how they are appointed, how they canvass their users' views, how the parks are funded – and at patterns of use. The final section of the examinations looks at current plans for each of the parks. The study concludes by considering whether there are clear planning, design and management criteria for 'successful' city parks.

The principal sources of information for the study were published material, questionnaires in 1987 and again in 1998 to the managers of the respective parks and follow-up interviews with

them. Each of the parks was visited at least once between October 1998 and July 2000. Many were visited on more than one occasion. Regularly consulted publications, particularly for the histories of the parks, were George F. Chadwick's *The Park and the Town* (1966), Norman T. Newton's *Design on the Land* (1971), Galen Cranz's *The Politics of Park Design* (1982), Georges Teyssot and Monique Mosser's *The History of Garden Design* (1991), Alexander Garvin's *The American City – What Works, What Doesn't* (1996), Gayle Berens and Alexander Garvin's *Urban Parks and Open Space* (1997), and *Landscape Architecture* magazine. This study would have been far more difficult without those works.

The book reflects a belief that well-planned, well-designed and well-managed parks remain invaluable components of liveable and hospitable cities. It is primarily directed at students, practitioners and politicians with an interest in the planning, design and management of urban parks. I hope that the book will also prove valuable to park users; to people who travel to the cities in which the parks are located, and to the people who live in those cities.

Metric/Imperial conversion table

Imperial	Metric	Metric	Imperial
1 inch	25.40 millimetres	1 millimetre	0.039 inches
1 foot	0.3048 metres	1 metre	3.281 feet
1 mile	1.609 kilometres	1 kilometre	0.621 miles
1 square foot	0.929 square metres	1 square metre	10.766 square feet
1 acre	0.405 hectares	1 hectare	2.471 acres

Dimensions for all parks in the United States are given in Imperial measurements; dimensions for all parks in Canada and Europe are given in Metric measurements.

Location of New York
parks

1 New Jersey
2 Central Park
3 Paley Park
4 Bryant Park
5 Manhattan
6 Long Island
7 Prospect Park

1 km

1 Paley Park, New York

4200 square feet (390 square metres)

INTRODUCTION

Paley Park was completed in 1967 and completely rebuilt to the same design in 1999. Privately owned, privately built and privately run for free public use, it is the model pocket park. Located on the north side of East 53rd Street in midtown Manhattan, between Fifth Avenue and Madison Avenue, Paley Park is the product of a concept promoted by landscape architect Robert Zion (1921–2000) and taken up by William S. Paley (1901–90). Paley, the founder and Chairman of the Columbia Broadcasting System (CBS), established the park as a memorial to his father, Samuel Paley (1875–1963). It was not a result of 'Incentive Zoning', a policy commenced in 1961 that permitted developers 'to install paving around their buildings, call them plazas, and collect their 10:1 or 6:1 floor area bonus as of right'. Paley Park was a philanthropic donation to the people of New York. Few human-made places provoke such unequivocal praise. It 'has become one of Manhattan's treasures,

Paley Park and 53rd Street from above (October 1999)

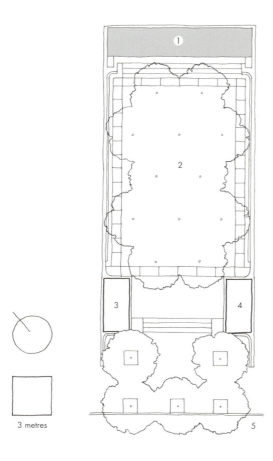

Paley Park, New York

1 Waterfall
2 Honey Locust Grove
3 Gatehouse/Pump Room
4 Gatehouse/Kiosk
5 East 53rd Street

3 metres

a masterpiece of urbanity and grace . . . memorable because it makes no effort to be so'; 'an oasis in the city's heart'; 'visiting Paley Park affects me as much as going to Yosemite'.[6]

HISTORY

Designation as a Park

The concept of the pocket park was demonstrated by Zion in May 1963 at an exhibition, 'New York Parks for New York', organized by the Park Association of New York and staged at the Architectural League of New York. He showed prototypical designs for parks 'as small as 50 by 100 feet between buildings where workers and shoppers could sit and find a moment's rest'. The sites that Zion used were vacant lots on 40th, 51st and 56th Streets. Such proposals caused controversy between their advocates, Mayor John Lindsay (elected 1965) and his Park Commissioners Thomas Hoving and August Heckscher on the one hand, and Robert Moses, New York Park Commissioner from 1934 to 1960, on the other. Moses argued that open

spaces of less than 3 acres (1.2 hectares) would be 'very expensive and impossible to administer'.[7]

William S. Paley would have been aware of the exhibition and of the controversy surrounding pocket parks. In a statement issued shortly after the opening of the park in May 1967, he stated that 'as a New Yorker, I have long been convinced that, in the midst of all this building, we ought to set aside occasional spots of open space where our residents and visitors can sit and enjoy themselves as they pause in their day's activities. When I was casting about for an appropriate way to create a memorial to my father . . . it occurred to me that to provide one such area in the very center of our greatest city would be the kind of memorial that would have pleased him most'. Paley formed The Greenpark Foundation in 1965 to acquire a site close to CBS headquarters and build the park. Construction began on 1 February 1966. The park opened on 23 May 1967.[8]

Size and Condition of the Site at the Time of Designation

The site had been occupied by a seven-storey building housing the Stork Club, an infamous New York nightspot, from the 1930s to 1965. It is 42 feet wide by 100 feet deep (12.8 metres by 30.5 metres). In line with the Manhattan street grid, it is oriented to the south-west – optimal for sun pockets. Although the sidewalk in front of the park belongs to the City of New York, it is a visual extension of the park.[9]

Key Figures in the Establishment of the Park

William S. Paley's father was a Russian immigrant who became a successful cigar merchant. William S. joined his father's company after graduating from the Wharton School of Finance at the University of Pennsylvania. He developed an interest in broadcasting after buying advertising time on a Philadelphia radio station. Described as 'fabulously wealthy and notoriously despotic', Paley had an uncanny ability to succeed with projects that others treated more cautiously. This led him, first, to buy an unprofitable chain of radio stations and later, to invest in television broadcasting 'when skeptics were denouncing the new medium'. He was 'an intensely private man with patrician tastes'.[10]

Zion obtained masters' degrees in Business, Industrial Administration and Landscape Architecture from Harvard University. In 1957 he went into business with fellow Harvard-trained landscape architect Harold Breen. Zion's aggressive marketing included writing letters to newspaper and magazine editors about the firm's work and an article in the *AIA Journal* about ways to make New York City more habitable. The latter proposed galleries, parklets and zoolets — ideas eventually presented at the Architectural League exhibition in 1963. Zion and Breen moved their office from Manhattan to rural New Jersey in 1973. This enabled Zion to combine running the practice with management of his rural estate – including an extensive plant nursery. Zion was, by all accounts, as demanding a person as Paley. He died in a traffic accident in April 2000.[11]

PLANNING AND DESIGN

Location

'Midtown, roughly 14th to 59th Streets, is the city's engine room, powered by hundreds of thousands of commuters who pour in each day'. The park is in the middle of a concentrated area of stores, offices and hotels – and just the other side of Fifth Avenue from the perennially popular Museum of Modern Art.[12]

Original Design Concept

The pocket park concept demonstrated at the 1963 exhibition showed a prototype 'based on the concept of a small outdoor room . . . with walls, floors and a ceiling'. It dealt with *size* – as small as 50 by 100 feet (15.2 by 30.4 metres); *enclosure* – removed from the flow of traffic and sheltered from noise; *purpose* – for adults to rest; *furniture* – movable, comfortable, individual seats; *materials* – rugged; *walls* – neighbouring buildings, covered with vines; *floor* – with textural interest and pattern; *ceiling* – dense canopy from trees 12 to 15 feet (3.7 to 4.6 metres) apart; *waterworks* – bold and simple; *kiosks* – with vending machines or cafés. 'Food', as William H. Whyte noted, 'draws people, and they draw more people'.[13]

Layout and Materials

The trees in Paley Park – honey locusts – were planted in a 12 foot (3.6 metres) quincunx rather than the square grid shown in the 1963 exhibition. This looser layout of trees, their continuation onto the sidewalk and the long, low steps at the entrance all contribute to the ordered casualness in the park. The shelter from surrounding buildings and the orientation create a comfortable microclimate. In line with one of Jane Jacobs' criteria for the success of neighbourhood parks, the site can be bathed in sunlight at lunchtime from spring to fall. But the single most alluring feature in Paley Park is the 20-foot-high (6-metres) waterfall that thunders down the full width of the back wall. The loud but somehow soothing roar dulls the sounds of the surrounding city. The steps, outer paving and planter walls are stippled pink granite – smooth but not too slick. The central paving is of 4-inch (100-millimetres) red–brown granite setts in a square grid – controlled but not too stiff. The movable white-painted metal lattice chairs and rather frail-feeling marble tables add to the sense of informality. The mono-specific tree planting and ivy on the walls complement the almost Zen-like restraint of the hard materials. The year-round cycle of herbaceous plants includes characteristic yellow tulips each spring.[14]

MANAGEMENT AND USAGE

Paley Park is owned and operated by The Greenpark Foundation. This is a private foundation wholly funded from the Paley Park Fund of the, also private, William S. Paley Foundation – an endowment established under his will. The total operating budget for the park in 1998 was around $225,000. In 1989 it was around $150,000. In 2000 the park had three full-time attendants overseeing its use; in 1980 there were only two. There are no formal channels of communication between users and operators although comments are passed back to The Greenpark Foundation by the attendants. There is virtually no vandalism.

The Foundation does not undertake user surveys. But two informative statistics were recorded in the early years of the park. First, in January 1969, that 'ever since its opening, between 2,000 and 3,000' people visited the park 'every sunny day'. Second, William H. Whyte recorded in 1980 that 'the two places people cite as the most pleasing, least crowded in New York – Paley Park and Greenacre Park are by far and away the most heavily used per square foot'. Whyte recorded 35 people per 1000 square feet (93 square metres) in Paley Park and 25 in Greenacre – and concluded that sensitive design increases the carrying capacity of small urban spaces. If the park were full to this carrying capacity for its entire 12 hours of opening and the average length of stay were half an hour, the number of daily visits would be nearly 3500. Given that the park is closed each January, it is reasonable to speculate an average of more than 500,000 visits per year.[15]

PLANS FOR THE PARK

The firm intention for the park is to retain it exactly as it was originally designed. To this end it was

Park from the north-west
corner (October 1999)

Annual display of yellow
tulips (April 2000)

closed to the public from 1 January to 21 June 1999 for complete reconstruction at an overall cost of around $700,000. The original cost of the park, including land acquisition, had been about $1 million. The only element that was not replaced were the three trees in the 53rd Street sidewalk. The reconstruction works included replacement of the waterfall pumps and of the underground irrigation system; replacement of all soils and planting; lifting, cleaning and reinstallation of all hard materials and replacement of all site furniture. The works were designed and overseen by restoration architects Beyer Blinder Belle. The Greenpark Foundation did not go back to Zion primarily because they wanted faithful restoration without any reinterpretation.[16]

CONCLUSIONS

Subtle and sophisticated, Paley Park is a carefully conceived adult retreat from the bustle of midtown Manhattan. Its Zen-like restraint contrasts with its hyper-urban setting. The park is an object lesson in the use of orientation to create optimal microclimate; in the use of flexible seating to accommodate dense crowds; in the use of white noise to obscure street noise; in the attraction of outdoor food outlets in urban locations, and in the value of human surveillance. The scale and function of Paley Park are a specific response to Manhattan conditions. Its impact has been as potent in its own way as the impact of Central Park.

Park from 53rd Street
(July 1989)

2 Village of Yorkville Park, Toronto

0.36 hectares (0.9 acres)

INTRODUCTION

The Village of Yorkville is an upmarket commercial and residential district in downtown Toronto. Yorkville Park occupies a 150 by 30 metre strip of land directly above a subway line, just north and one block west of the intersection of the city's two major streets – Yonge and Bloor. It is designed as ten individual gardens each representing a different type of natural Canadian landscape. The gardens are aligned north–south and interspersed with three pathways between Yorkville and Bloor Street. The design was prepared by San Francisco-based landscape architects Schwartz/Smith/Meyer in collaboration with Toronto-based architects Oleson Worland, winners of an international competition launched in July 1991. Construction commenced in spring 1992 and was completed in spring 1994. It

cost C\$3 million. Creation of the park reflects the emergence of Toronto, the fifth largest city in North America, as a place that is committed to investment in its public realm. First the city had the integrity to proceed with the construction of the competition-winning design. Then it withstood a barrage of scathing comments in the local and national press. The hiatus revolved around the cost of cutting and transporting to site the natural granite rock that is now the focal point of the park.[17]

HISTORY

Designation as a Park

The Village of Yorkville developed in the 1830s on 'Farm Lots' north of Bloor Street. The village was incorporated in 1853 and annexed to the City of

Village of Yorkville Park, Toronto

1   Cumberland Street
2   Amelanchier Grove
3   Herbaceous Border Garden
4   Rock in Canadian Shield Clearing
5   Water Curtain
6   White Alder Grove
7   Ontario Marsh/BC Douglas Fir Boardwalks
8   Crab Apple Orchard
9   Fragrant Herb Rock Garden
10 River Birch Grove
11 Prairie Wildflower Garden
12 Scots Pine Grove/ Fog Emitters
13 Bellair Street

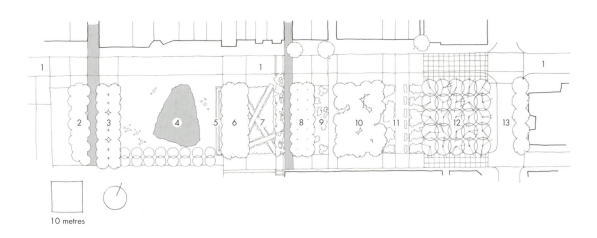

10 metres

Toronto in 1883. By 1930 the village had become a centre for business and entertainment. Yorkville was known in the 1960s 'for its cafés and hippie culture; the atmosphere of the village past can be found in the narrow tree-lined streets, Victorian mews houses and picturesque gardens'. The row of brick-built houses on the south side of Cumberland Street was demolished in 1954 to make way for Toronto Transit Commission's Bloor subway line. An entrance to its Bay station is located in the park. Following construction of the subway, the site was acquired by the city for use as a parking lot. Local residents did, however, exact a promise from the City Council in 1973 that the land would, eventually, be designated as a park.[18]

In 1974 a small area was designated as public open space. But the short-stay car park was lucrative for the council and some traders feared that its closure would harm their businesses. Formation in 1985 of the Bloor–Yorkville Business Improvement Area (BIA) helped to sustain demand for the park. The mandate of the BIA was to 'develop, implement and maintain streetscape beautification and promotional programs with a view to increasing business revenues and tourism in the twenty-seven block area'. And although money for acquisition of the site and for construction of the park had been approved in 1983/84 it took until July 1991 for the launch of the design competition.[19]

The competition was organized in two stages. First as an international call for expressions of interest and then as a limited competition between eight shortlisted applicants. The brief for the competition stressed that the park was 'an opportunity to create a new *natural oasis*' and to 're-establish a foothold for nature in this vibrant neighbourhood . . . to contribute to the *Greening* of Toronto and to implement the City Council's environmental and urban forestry initiatives'. The brief called for an 'ecosystem approach . . . resulting in local and regional ecosystems remaining intact' – a reflection, perhaps, of the *zeitgeist*, more than of the scale of the park. The brief also called for a park that encouraged 'use in all seasons, daytime and nighttime' and created 'a sense of quietitude [*sic*] distinct from the surrounding uses and activities'. It called for competitors to 'consider how the beauty and phenomena of natural processes can be articulated

Crab Apple Orchard and Pergola (October 1999)

through design' and encouraged exploration of 'qualities of seasonality, colour, texture, fragrance, sound, form and the process of natural decay . . . in temporal and spatial terms'.[20]

Condition of the Site at the Time of Designation

The site is almost entirely located above the subway tunnel. The park is, to all intents and purposes, a ground level roof garden. Competitors had to deal with toxic soils that contained concentrations of spilled oil residues, heavy metals and de-icing salt. They also had to bear in mind that air quality studies showed pollution levels that would 'inhibit the ability of trees and other plant material to grow', and that existing building shadows across the park were anticipated to remain and to increase as a result of further development on the north side of Bloor Street. Designers were required to consider ways of achieving zero per cent stormwater runoff from the site.[21]

Key Figures in the Establishment of the Park

The park was instigated by Toronto City Council. Park Commissioner Herb Pirk and his staff are to be admired for the way they withstood the barrage of criticism that the project provoked. But the principal campaigner on the part of Yorkville residents, businesses and (latterly) the Bloor–Yorkville BIA was Budd Sugarman. Interior designer Sugarman consistently and persistently goaded the City Council into agreeing to build a park on the site after the construction of the subway line in the 1950s. He helped to elicit the council's commitment in 1973 to build it as soon as the parking garage was completed and he eventually sat on the panel that judged the design competition in 1991.[22]

In the 1960s Toronto Mayor Phil Givens had campaigned for the purchase and placing of a Henry Moore sculpture, *The Archer*, outside the new City Hall. Givens' proposal became the subject of heated political debate. He launched an appeal to raise the money from private sources; Moore agreed to reduce the price of the piece; Givens lost the subsequent mayoral election; Toronto got the sculpture. *Toronto Star* columnist Pierre Berton suggested that 'the city hall competition and the purchase of *The Archer* marked a turning point for a city just emerging from its anal-retentive past'. He also suggested that Yorkville Park was 'exactly the sort of thing we need if we're going to boast about being a world class city'. Berton reflected the view of architect and *Globe and Mail* columnist Colin Vaughan

that the debate over *The Archer* led to 'an election lost, maybe, but a giant gain in civic pride and maturity'.[23]

The Yorkville competition was won by San Francisco-based landscape architects Schwartz/Smith/Meyer working with Toronto-based architects Oleson Worland. By all accounts the joint venture for the competition was instigated by Oleson Worland. They contacted Martha Schwartz at the practice she had formed in 1990 with Ken Smith and David Meyer, fellow designers from the office of Peter Walker. The agreement for detailed design of the park was made with Oleson Worland conditional on them retaining the services of Schwartz/Smith/Meyer. Credit for the design of the park is often accorded to Martha Schwartz – perhaps because of the notoriety of many of her other projects. Discussions with Ken Smith and David Oleson suggest that if any individual is to be singled out as author of the design it should be Smith himself. The detailed design, writing of specifications, testing of prototypes for installation in the park and inspection of work on site were, however, very much a collaborative exercise.[24]

PLANNING AND DESIGN

Location

The Bloor–Yorkville BIA claims that it is Canada's 'most fashionable commercial district' – a point that did not go unremarked upon by the press when the rock was being transported to site during an economic recession in 1993. The park marks a transition between high-rise buildings to the south and high-culture businesses to the north. The influence of the park has 'migrated outward and now goes up and down the subway as well as north to the rest of the village and south to Bloor. It has contributed to the rise in real estate values in the immediate vicinity'. In official terminology, 'the land between Cumberland Street and Bloor Street is designated as high density, mixed commercial/residential. Land to the north of Cumberland Street, west of Bellair Street, is designated as low density, mixed commercial/residential'.[25]

Original Design Concept

The ten gardens in the park each represent a different type of Canadian landscape. They are interspersed with three cross walks. The gardens and cross walks follow the property lines of the nineteenth-century buildings that previously occupied the site. Smith described the design objectives for the park as being to:

*Ontario Marsh, Pergola
and Crab Apple Orchard
(October 1999)*

*Water Curtain between
White Alder Grove and
Canadian Shield
Clearing (October 1999)*

- *reflect, reinforce and extend the scale and character of the original village*. This had to be done in the face of very different scales of development on either side of the park and is achieved particularly through aligning the gardens with the previous property lines
- *provide unique inner-city ecological opportunities for the introduction and display of native plant species and communities.* Smith continued the nineteenth-century symbolism by likening the diverse individual gardens to the specimen trays in a Victorian 'collection box'
- *provide a variety of spatial and sensory experiences, landscape qualities and park functions.* Pergolas, trellises, the climate-sensitive Water/Ice Curtain and the fog emitters supplement the high density of vegetation in closing out the surroundings and heightening the experiential qualities of the park
- *link the park to existing pedestrian walkways and adjacent areas.* The north–south alignment of the park – the 'collection boxes' – are the key to its diversity and to its integration with wider patterns of pedestrian circulation.[26]

Design Review

The park is like a striped scarf with a non-repeating pattern unfurled along the length of Cumberland Street; one park but many gardens. The design is a strong response to context and setting. It is particularly successful in relating the contrasting scales of surrounding buildings and reflecting the history of the site. It introduces to downtown Toronto a high-density distillation of the landscapes of this huge country. It uses seasonal changes of climate to dramatic effect. Unlike most other urban spaces that use the name 'park', Yorkville Park is remarkably unenclosed. It is open, permeable and visible from all sides and from above. It is 'the post-Olmstedian opposite of that iconic anodyne, a park that screens everything out'. The park remains, to all intents and purposes, an island in a sea of roads. It has busy streets on two sides and private accesses along the other two sides. The only ways across the island are the north–south pedestrian ways. The detailing of the park demonstrates a delicate balance between robustness and lushness. The galvanized steel beams of the Pergola; the stainless steel cables on the Water Curtain; the massive re-assembled rock and the hewn granite benches all project a powerful, rugged, assertive presence.[27]

The tree groves – the pine, the birch and the alders – have the same sort of presence. They are powerful ecological abstracts. They are made more powerful by their contrast with the wildness of the prairie garden, the fragrance of the herb garden,

the various greens in the marsh garden and the lushness of the herbaceous border garden. The park contains an astonishingly dense collection of visual images, historical references and representational landscapes. At first these can seem too dense; too clever and too self-referential and the north–south alignment can seem too rigid and too restricting. But, with a site that is so narrow and so visible and which is perched like a roof garden on the surface of a subway tunnel, perhaps it is appropriate to espouse opacity. Otherwise the village of Yorkville might have little more than a small, transparent, token open space. And the site might as well be a car park again.[28]

MANAGEMENT AND USAGE

Yorkville Park is managed by the Parks and Recreation division of the City of Toronto – one of six divisions in the Department of Economic Development, Culture and Tourism. The Parks and Recreation division is organized into five geographically defined operational districts – North, South, East, West and Central/Waterfront. Yorkville Park is in the Central/Waterfront district. As a matter of policy the division tries to run its operations and maintenance programmes with a minimum of outsourcing. This applies to Yorkville Park where the City has worked on the basis of having one horticulturist based there full-time. This ensures continuity of care. It also provides a source of information for users and a form of policing. Yorkville is, in any case, a part of the city with minimal vandalism. There are limited controlling regulations for the park. This is reflected in the use of movable seats – the first example in Toronto parks. Representatives from other areas of the city might regard the attention devoted to central parks like Yorkville as an expensive luxury. But there is a counter argument that the rise in real estate values resulting from the presence of the park repays the cost of this level of attention.

The BIA, having been instrumental in the establishment of the park, projects a strong sense of ownership towards it and retains a watchful interest in its well-being. The BIA often rectifies minor problems faster than the city can. The city's Department of Public Works is responsible for maintenance of highways – including the strips of paving that run out from the park across Cumberland Street. They maintain the road with the same paving materials – and cross charge the Park and Recreation division the extra cost of doing so.

Funds for maintenance of Yorkville Park all derive from the general revenues of the City of

*Rock seats in the Prairie
Wildflower Garden
(October 1999)*

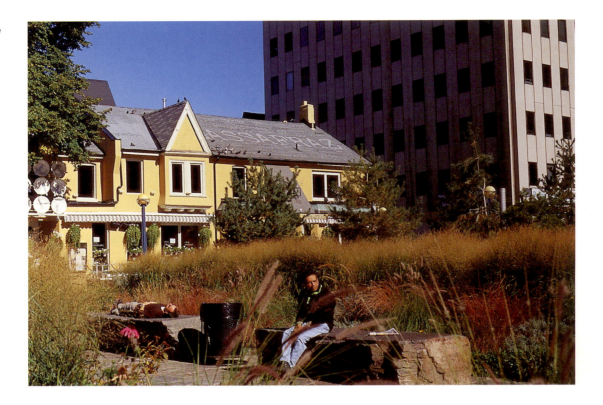

Rock seats in the Prairie Wildflower Garden (October 1999)

Toronto. No separate breakdown is kept by the Parks and Recreation division of the cost of maintaining individual parks within each of the five operational districts. Observations have been made that the park – and particularly the rock – has drawn children to an otherwise adult part of town, but no formal surveys of park usage have been conducted to date. The BIA and the resident horticulturist do, however, provide channels for the feeding back of comments and suggestions to the Council.

PLANS FOR THE PARK

The principal aim for Yorkville Park is to ensure that it fulfils the objectives established by its designers. This means having to make adaptations in response to adjacent changes like eventual construction of the high-rise buildings on the north side of Bloor and the proposed redevelopment of the entrance to the Bay subway station. It also means having to respond to the growth and development of the plant material in the park.

CONCLUSIONS

Yorkville Park won the President's Award of Excellence from the American Society of Landscape Architects in 1996. The citation in *Landscape Architecture* magazine described the collection of landscapes as 'a perfect concept for an urban park that places nature in a heavily human context'. The park is an object lesson in 'placemaking' through response to context. It draws on the history of the site with wit and sincerity and introduces cameos of the landscape of this vast country into the heart of its largest city. Development of the park was a demonstration of courage on the part of the council. It showed commendable integrity in staging the competition and following through with construction of the winning scheme. One day perhaps, like Paley Park, it too will merit complete reconstruction. In the meantime it is appropriate to consider the words of one of the many journalists who wrote about the park during its design and construction. 'Cities that don't nurture such ideas aren't very interesting. They aren't the kind of place people talk about or want to visit. Or even want to live in.'[29]

3 Freeway Park, Seattle

5.2 acres (2.1 hectares)

INTRODUCTION

Freeway Park, like Yorkville Park, is primarily a roof garden over a transport route. It spans the Interstate 5 (I-5) highway as it passes directly east of downtown Seattle, the largest city in the Pacific Northwest of the United States. The I-5 runs from the US–Canadian border 110 miles (176 kilometres) north of Seattle to the US–Mexican border, more than 1300 miles (2000 kilometres) to the south. The park covers most of a 460-metre-long, ten-lane-wide stretch of the highway at its closest point to the downtown. The highway was constructed through Seattle between 1959 and 1965. The park is a prime example of the exploitation of 'air-rights' over a highway. It was built in three stages during the 1970s and 1980s. Two of these stages involved the construction of substantial buildings.

Numerous freeways were built to and through the hearts of urban areas in the United States in the twenty-five years after the Second World War. Freeway Park set a precedent as a noise-reducing

Freeway Park and Interstate Highway 5 from Eighth Avenue (November 1999)

Freeway Park, Seattle

1   Convention Center
2   East Plaza
3   I-5 Freeway South
4   I-5 Freeway North
5   Pigott Memorial Corridor
6   First Hill District
7   Eighth Avenue
8   Parking Garage
9   Apartment Builidng
10 Park Place
11 Concrete Canyon
12 Seneca Street
13 Naramore Fountain
14 Sixth Avenue
15 Spring Street

25 metres

'lid' over a small section of one of them. It embodied principles proposed by San Francisco-based landscape architect Lawrence Halprin in his 1966 book *Freeways*. Its centrepiece is a concrete canyon where water thunders into a deep void over the median of the highway. This was designed by Halprin's associate Angela Danadjieva. It was a development of her earlier work with Halprin on 'Ira's Fountain' (the Auditorium Forecourt), a one block water feature in downtown Portland, Oregon, whose iconic design was inspired by the cliffs and mesas of the American West. With its angular, blocky, board-marked concrete forms and its regularly replicated palette of primarily evergreen plants, Freeway Park clearly reflects the age in which it was conceived and built. It is an essay in late modernism. In some respects it is little more than a Band-Aid over the deep gash of the I-5. In a broader perspective it signalled the start of an urban revival in the United States after a post-war orgy of highway construction.[30]

HISTORY

Designation as a Park

The I-5 through Seattle was planned and constructed during the 1950s and early 1960s. Environmentally concerned citizens conducted a forceful campaign for a lid over the downtown portion of the freeway, and for a park to be built on that lid. Their call was initially rejected: 'the freeway was costing enough money without adding any frills'. Floyd A. Naramore of Seattle architects Naramore, Bain, Brady and Johanson (latterly NBBJ) continued to campaign for a park over the freeway. He also donated in 1967 the fountain by sculptor George Tsutakawa that stands by the freeway off-ramp at the corner of Sixth Avenue and Seneca Street. But the real impetus for creation of the park did not develop until a number of forces came together in 1968.[31]

In that year Seattle voters approved a 'Forward Thrust Program' with bond resolutions for $334 million and including $65 million for park facilities. The principal advocate of that programme was Seattle attorney James R. Ellis. The State Highway Department had finally agreed to provide the 'lid' on which the park would be built. At the same time the City of Seattle was looking for a site on which to build a parking garage that would intercept downtown traffic leaving the freeway. Also at that time, property developer R. C. Hedreen was looking for a site for a twenty-one-storey office building. He was proposing to develop the land fronting Seneca Street west of the freeway – the place where the Highway Department wanted to

locate the footings for one of the spans across the freeway. The outcome was an agreement whereby Hedreen located his building (Park Place) at the north-west corner of the lot and his parking garage to the east. This ensured that the heart of the park (as then conceived) would not be in the afternoon shade of Park Place and that the park could extend over the roof of the parking garage. The park was to continue over the roof of the city's East Plaza Garage – further north, on the east side of the freeway.

Construction began in 1972 and the park was ceremoniously opened on the bicentennial Independence Day – 4 July 1976. The total cost of the project was $13.79 million. The bridges cost $5.53 million derived from federal and state funds. The parking garage cost $4.2 million raised through city council bonds but was expected to pay for itself. Construction of the park itself cost $4.07 million. The majority of that ($2.8 million) came from the Forward Thrust bonds. The remainder was largely drawn from various federal and city funds. The American Legion donated $35,000 for a play area on the East Plaza. As James Ellis pointed out, constructing the park in the air space above the freeway cost about $45 per square foot at a time when the purchase price of land in the downtown was about $50 per square foot. Moreover, the annual property tax on the Park Place building was $175,000 compared with $50,000 for the previous buildings on that site.[32]

Freeway Park was extended twice during the 1980s. First, in 1984, the city extended it eastward into the First Hill residential neighbourhood – the Pigott Memorial Corridor. This linked a retirement community with the original park. Then, in 1988, the park was extended northward over the freeway as part of the construction of the 370,000 square foot (49,000 square metres) Washington State Convention Center – another project inspired by Ellis. This led to an increase from 400 feet (120 metres) to 1500 feet (460 metres) in the overall length of freeway spanned by the park.

Key Figures in the Establishment of the Park

Clearly, the key figure in the initial establishment and subsequent extension of the park was James Ellis (b. 1921). The Forward Thrust Program that Ellis inspired led to the involvement, in turn, of architects NBBJ, of landscape architects Edward McLeod and Associates, of urban designer Lawrence Halprin (b. 1916) and of his associate, Angela Danadjieva (b. 1931). Writing in 1986, Charles Moore noted that for Ira's Fountain – designed in 1965 – and for Freeway Park,

Danadjieva took on the role that Moore himself had played on the adjoining Lovejoy Plaza in Portland. Moore noted Halprin's 'powerful presence' and suggested that 'some future architectural historian will have fun analysing the differences in these works' or perhaps not, 'since the expectations of a solo performance from the historian are at some odds with the realization that the design process is seldom, if ever, a solo flight'. Peter Walker and Melanie Simo noted that 'as Halprin confronted problems of urban landscape design in cities . . . he began to focus on process rather than immutable product'. They suggest that 'he discovered a new role for the artist – not the solitary hero but the person who choreographs . . . activities . . . for and with the community'. Walker and Simo identified Lovejoy Plaza as 'perhaps Halprin's masterpiece' but state that Ira's Fountain, where 'Danadjieva made important contributions . . . seems melodramatic, its expression in concrete somewhat raw and thin'.[33]

Their view contrasts with Ada Louise Huxtable's description of Ira's Fountain as 'one of the most important urban spaces since the Renaissance'. In any event, we have a picture of Halprin as the facilitator; the catalytic choreographer working with individuals like Moore and Danadjieva who, in turn, gave physical form to his dance scores. Halprin has been compared with Frederick Law Olmsted in that 'his singular achievements rest on his unusual skill at harnessing the efforts of others'. Danadjieva confirms that she was given 'all the opportunities you can ever imagine for creativity' and that 'her imagery came from a month long tour of western canyons she took while working for Halprin'. Danadjieva trained as an architect in Sophia, Bulgaria and Paris. She moved to the United States after winning an international design competition in 1965 for a new civic centre plaza for the City of San Francisco. She left Halprin's office in 1977 to establish a partnership with Thomas Koenig. Danadjieva and Koenig Associates designed the Pigott Memorial Corridor (1984) and Convention Center (1988) extensions to the park and the interior landscape of the Center.[34]

Part of the original park directly above the freeway (November 1999)

PLANNING AND DESIGN

Location

The entry of the I-5 Freeway to Seattle from the north meets Halprin's call for 'understanding of the great possibilities of aesthetic impact inherent in the act of approaching a great city'. As it descends into the city it offers stunning panoramas across Lake Union to Gasworks Park and the more distant Space Needle and downtown Seattle. It heads directly towards the downtown, curving around the foot of First Hill before veering away onto a north–south alignment between Sixth and Seventh Avenues, parallel with the grid of downtown streets. First Hill is a residential neighbourhood. Although the park creates a physical link between the downtown and First Hill, it is an extension of the downtown. It is located at the junction of the commercial and government 'quarters' of the downtown – which makes it difficult to get people to go there.[35]

Shape and Natural Landform of the Site

The site is, unsurprisingly, a long, thin strip. Initially it covered 400 feet (120 metres) of freeway. It is now nearly 1200 feet (460 metres) long overall. Seattle is 'characterized by strong changes in elevation, both natural and man-made' – including hills, freeway cuttings and high-rise buildings. There is a change in grade of 50 feet (15 metres) between the park and 9th Avenue and a 90 foot (27-metres) difference between the highest and lowest points of the park itself. This difference is largely taken up by the central waterfall that plunges into Danadjieva's canyon between the carriageways below.[36]

Design

The canyon, clearly, is the focal point of the park. It exploits the change in level between the deck and the highway below. The noise of 28,000 gallons (100,000 litres) per minute of water thundering into the canyon helps to drown out the roar of the traffic. Danadjieva herself explained the design from three perspectives – first in terms of microclimatic imperatives; second in terms of the metaphor of natural canyons and third in terms of motion through and within the site. She exploited the siting of Hedreen's Park Place to arrange the park elements so that 'the most exciting areas (the canyon, the cascade) are oriented towards the south'; she composed these elements 'to allow the fresh breeze from the waterfront to enter the park', and she 'designed walls and berms to block the penetration of the fumes from the freeway'. The walls and planter boxes on the edges of the park are also designed to act as sound barriers. The blocky concrete forms in the park (and latterly inside the Convention Center) reflect Danadjieva's fascination with replication of natural canyons – a fascination that emerged earlier in the design of Ira's Fountain. But equally significant was her interest in motion. Reflecting both Halprin's interest in choreography and prefiguring Tschumi's design for Parc de la Villette, she wrote about her experience as an art director for movies, observing that 'motion changes the perception of the scale of the city texture' and that 'scale appears different from a driver's viewpoint than from that of a pedestrian'. She sought to relate these two different impressions of scale by making the 'frame of the park' particularly heavy and by making the interior elements smaller in scale.[37]

This intention is also reflected in the planting. Larger trees are planted in higher areas and on made ground. They have grown to dominate the view of the park from the road. Particularly visible are native Western Red Cedar, liquidambar and maples that colour-up strongly in the fall. These are augmented by trailing ivy hanging from stacks of planter boxes facing the freeway. The park was 'significantly over planted for early impact'. Two major thinning operations have been carried out since the original planting – in 1985 and 1995 – and more than one hundred trees had been removed by 1999. These operations sought to respect the original intention of designing the park as a series of 'rooms' that visitors could walk through. Danadjieva was invited to advise on both thinning operations in order to ensure that the principle of interconnecting rooms remained – even if the walls between some of them had to be removed.[38]

Despite these thinning operations, it has been suggested that 'the park is little more than a forest within the city'. This might be true of the driver's view of the park but planting of the pedestrian 'rooms' of the park is less overpowering. Here the original palette was an austere mix of lower-growing, predominantly evergreen material including azaleas, cotoneasters, Boston ivy, evergreen ivy and laurels. These interplay with the alternating vertically and horizontally board-marked concrete structures to create a consistent characteristic of the park. The predominantly evergreen planting and the concrete structures contrast with the more florid planting around Park Place and the city's own twice-yearly herbaceous plant-outs. There is also a continuously visible flow of grass through the original part of the park. This combines with the structures and the woody planting to create 'rooms' within the 'building' – or 'glades' within the 'forest'.[39]

Futagawa summarized Freeway Park as 'a sculpture for people to move in and through' and as a 'stage set for people's creative involvement'. Lyall described the park as 'an episodic design' noting that this is inevitable given 'the way the whole design evolved as a process of taking opportunities as the possibilities of using more pieces of land emerged'. Both these comments reflect Danadjieva's intention of creating a park that might provide an unfolding series of experiences to people walking through it. Walker and Simo described the park as 'more refined and complex' than Ira's Fountain and 'perhaps overly melodramatic' with planting that is 'opulent, recalling the ancient forests of the Pacific Northwest'. They describe it as 'a place of great beauty . . . tinged with terror – the sublime' where 'the concrete forms are heroic'. The park overall – and particularly the concrete forms – are, certainly, iconic. So is Ira's Fountain. But the fountain is a Zen-like abstract of landscape elements – landform, water and a single species of tree – Freeway Park is a subtler synthesis. And melodrama was certainly an appropriate response on such a hostile site. The power of the original design did, after all, give sufficient impetus for the park to be successfully extended northward over the freeway and eastward up First Hill.[40]

MANAGEMENT AND USAGE

Freeway Park is managed by the Seattle Department of Parks and Recreation in concert with the owners of Park Place and the Board of the Convention Center. The Department is run by a Superintendent who acts on the direction of the Seattle Board of Park Commissioners. That Board is a volunteer advisory organization whose members are appointed by the Mayor of Seattle for 3-year terms. In 1999 it had seven members who met twice monthly. The Board 'consults and makes recommendations to the Superintendent of Parks and Recreation regarding that department's policies for the planning, development and use of the city's park and recreation facilities'. The park is entirely maintained by staff who are directly employed by the department. Park Place and the Convention Center Plaza and Walkway are maintained by private maintenance contractors.[41]

Emergency alarm buttons to call guards, and gates to close off the plaza at night were installed when the Convention Center was built. It was reported in 1993 that 'homeless people and drug addicts occasionally use the park after dark' and that 'panhandling is routine and assaults have been reported'. A neighbourhood group – the Friends of Freeway Park – became particularly active at that time in an attempt to address the perceived lack of safety in the park. They met monthly and exhorted the Department of Parks and Recreation to develop a policy of Crime Prevention Through Environmental Design (CPTED).[42]

The Friends also contributed $60,000 towards installation of additional lighting in the park in 1994 and the widening of the Eighth Avenue underpass in 1995. Nevertheless, the labyrinthine design of the park contains many concealed corners and the ever-thriving vegetation makes these difficult to police. Another commentator noted that 'a couple of nasty criminal acts occurred in broad daylight, and the place began to acquire a reputation as being less than desirable'. He suggested that, despite the thinning of trees, the park is a 'somewhat scary forest' that 'still seems forbidding and spooky' but does admit that 'contrary to popular perception, Freeway Park is relatively safe according to city statistics. Perhaps this is reflected in the fact that by the end of 1999 the Friends were far less active and were playing a participatory role towards the management of the park – particularly in the organization of events – rather than a proactive one. The Department of Parks and Recreation has never done any user surveys of the park but is well aware that the heaviest usage is around weekday lunchtimes, particularly by 'brown baggers'. One-off events also draw people to the park – but these had become less frequent by the end of the 1990s.[43]

PLANS FOR THE PARK

The principal plan for the park is to pursue management and maintenance practices that will ensure the continuity of the original design. There is also a desire, consistent with the CPTED policy, to ensure that the park is as widely used as possible. To this end the Department of Parks and Recreation entered a partnership in 1999 with the recently expanded Seattle Downtown Business Improvement Area to promote 'twenty-four/seven' use of the downtown generally. Measures being considered included a wider range of events in public places and keeping all downtown water features – including the thundering cascade into the Freeway Park canyon – running year-round.[44]

CONCLUSIONS

Seattle is renowned as the base for enterprises like Boeing and Microsoft – and for its rainy coastal climate. It is also becoming renowned as one of the most 'liveable' cities in the United States. The forces – orchestrated by people like James Ellis – that led to its earning this sobriquet were also instrumental in the establishment of Freeway Park. Ellis commented in 1977 that the park was 'a joint project by imaginative private owners, by sensitive highway officials and by a city determined to stay livable' and that 'the result was a successful private investment, a successful public investment and a demonstration of use to other cities'. Halprin commented in 1993 that air rights development 'can become heavy-handed' and that 'just because it's been shown to work in one place doesn't automatically mean it ought to be allowed to happen everywhere'. There is little question, however, that measures like the removal of San Francisco's elevated Embarcadero Freeway following the 1989 earthquake and Boston's 'Big Dig' to bury its Central Artery before the end of the twentieth century contribute a great deal to the quality of life in the downtowns of those cities. Admittedly, Freeway Park continues to present many management challenges. But it also demonstrates what can be achieved by pro-active citizens and by designers who can turn adversity to advantage.[45]

4 Bryant Park, New York

6 acres (2.43 hectares)

INTRODUCTION

Bryant Park shares two midtown Manhattan blocks with the New York Public Library. Located between 40th and 42nd Streets and Fifth and Sixth Avenues, it is the largest public open space in this part of the island. (see location plan on page 4). There have been four distinct phases in the history of the park. It began life in 1842 as Reservoir Square; it was reshaped following demolition in 1899 of the reservoir to allow construction of the Library; it was completely redesigned in the 1930s, and completely refurbished between 1988 and 1992. That refurbishment followed transfer of the park to private management and transformed it from a forbidding haven for drug dealers – referred to as 'Needle Park' – into the most intensively used public open space in midtown Manhattan. The recovery of Bryant Park symbolized the revitalization of New York in the 1990s. The park was refurbished according to principles developed by William H. (Holly) Whyte (1919–99) – an urbanist who spent much of the 1970s analysing how people in New York used urban spaces. He noted in 1980 that 'Bryant Park is dangerous. It has become the territory of dope dealers and muggers because it was relatively underused

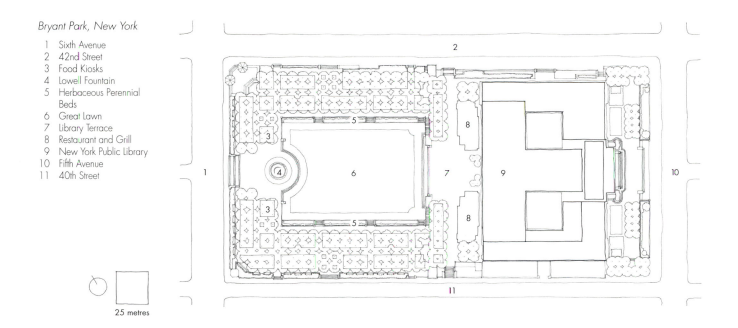

Bryant Park, New York

1　Sixth Avenue
2　42nd Street
3　Food Kiosks
4　Lowell Fountain
5　Herbaceous Perennial
　　Beds
6　Great Lawn
7　Library Terrace
8　Restaurant and Grill
9　New York Public Library
10　Fifth Avenue
11　40th Street

25 metres

*South west corner of
library and offices on
40th Street
(October 1999)*

by other people. Bryant Park is cut-off from the street by walls, fences, and shrubbery. You can't see in. You can't see out. There are only a few entry points. This park will be used by people when it is opened up to them'. The 'opening-up' of the park was engineered by the Bryant Park Restoration Corporation under Executive Director Daniel Biederman (b. 1954), a disciple of Whyte and an advocate of highly attentive, event-driven management. Where Paley Park became a prototype for the private pocket park made available to the public, Bryant Park has become a model for the private funding and management of the small public park.[46]

HISTORY

Designation as a Park

The land now occupied by the Library was acquired in 1842 for construction of a reservoir. The adjacent land was designated as a public space named Reservoir Square. It was renamed in 1884 for *New York Post* Editor William Cullen Bryant (1794–1878), a leading advocate for the creation of Central Park. The reservoir was made redundant by the construction of the Central Park reservoir. It was demolished in 1899 to make way for the Library. The park was already neglected by the time it was used in the 1920s as a dump for excavate from the Sixth Avenue subway. 'More than a hundred plans for the rehabilitation of Bryant Park were proposed' during the 1920s and early 1930s.[47]

In 1934 Robert Moses became the first Parks Commissioner to oversee the unified New York City Department of Parks covering the five boroughs of Manhattan, Brooklyn, Queens, Staten Island and The Bronx. Moses excelled at tapping into federal funds made available under Franklin D. Roosevelt's 'New Deal'. Reconstruction of Bryant Park was one of the many projects that he initiated that year. The designers were Lusby Simpson, winner of a design competition open to out-of-work architects, and landscape architect Gilmore Clarke, a friend of Moses who went on to do vast amounts of work for the Department of Parks. The Simpson/Clark design produced the Great Lawn and the promenades of London plane trees. It was also the source of many of the park's subsequent problems. Moses required that the subway excavate remain on site – elevating it above the surrounding sidewalks – and called for railings and a thick hedge around the edges. There were only 'five skinny, steep entry staircases at its perimeter'.[48]

Refurbishment of the Park

Bryant Park was designated a Scenic Landmark in 1974 – the same year as Central Park. But by then it was already in severe decline – again. In 1979 the Rockefeller Brothers Fund was considering support for renovation of the New York Public Library. The Fund was not prepared to support that project unless the park was also renovated. The Library and the Fund went for advice to Whyte and the Project for Public Space. They reported in November 1979 that the critical issue was access. They recommended removal of the iron fences; removal of the shrubbery; cutting openings in the balustrades; improving visibility into the park from Sixth Avenue; providing a broad, shallow flight of steps between the two existing flights on 42nd Street, providing ramps, providing access to the terrace at the back of the Library, and restoring the Lowell Fountain.[49]

In January 1980 the Chairman of the Library, Andrew Heiskell, hired the then 26-year-old Daniel Biederman. They formed the Bryant Park Restoration Corporation (BPRC). The BPRC was established as a not-for-profit private management company. It was tasked with developing a viable plan for revival of the park. Biederman's strategy was 'to attack all the park's problems simultaneously rather than piecemeal, as had been tried previously'. The principal barrier to this type of approach was lack of funds. BPRC therefore established a Business Improvement District (BID). BID's are 'self-financed legal entities that allow local property owners . . . in commercial areas to provide common services beyond those that the city can provide'. Income is generated through an annual levy per square foot from commercial property owners in the District.[50]

Landscape architects Hanna/Olin Ltd were introduced to the project in 1982 through their work on redesign of the Fifth Avenue frontage of the Library. Design work almost came to a halt in 1985 when the Library announced that its shelves were full. It was considering vacating the building. The impasse was resolved by a decision to construct 84 miles (135 kilometres) of reserve stacks under the Great Lawn so that, in effect, it became a huge roof garden. Approval was granted in July 1988 for a relatively conservative rehabilitation of the park. Construction commenced that year, and was completed in 1991. The park was opened in three phases between 1991 and May 1995. The total cost of the works was $17.69 million. It was funded two-thirds by the City and one-third by the private sector.[51]

Key Figures in the Rehabilitation of the Park

'Many of those who have been intimately involved' in the rehabilitation of Bryant Park 'regard it as a monument to the vision of Holly Whyte'. Whyte has been described as 'something of a philosopher-king of open space'. Much as Zion had already developed the model that materialized at Paley Park, so Whyte had already developed the principles that determined the approach at Bryant Park. The extent to which those principles informed the final scheme is attributable in large part to their promotion by Biederman. He was an MBA working as a systems consultant and was chair of the local Community Planning Board when he helped to establish BPRC in 1980. He had been a volunteer assistant to Whyte's Street Life Project in 1975. Biederman has been immersed in managing the park for more than twenty years. In 2000 he still regarded it as 'a big deal to keep running it' and relished talking about the park to business people and to design students.[52]

PLANNING AND DESIGN

Location

When construction of the reservoir began in 1839 the site was on the edge of the built-up area of Manhattan. The northward development led to the park being subsumed by the city but not embraced by it. Even after the reservoir gave way to the Library, the park did not take on any great significance – until the Board of the Library insisted in 1979 that 'something should be done about it'. By then, Bryant Park was an island of open space in a sea of skyscrapers. In 1997, 7 million squre feet (650,000 million square metres) of office and retail space bordered Bryant Park and, a couple of years after the park reopened, 'leasing activity on Sixth Avenue had increased 60 per cent in the first 8 months of 1994 compared with 1993'.[53]

Shape and Natural Landform of the Site

The site is 560 feet (170 metres) by 470 feet (140 metres). The reshaped Great Lawn is 270 feet (82 metres) by 180 feet (55 metres). The lawn is the main feature of the park but occupies less than 20 per cent of its total area. The landform is largely the result of the filling that followed excavation of the Sixth Avenue subway in the 1920s. The site sits about 4 feet (1.2 metres) above the surrounding streets and the Library terrace is even higher than the tree-lined promenades. The lawn sits like a huge stage below the promenades.

Original Design Concept

The Simpson/Clark design was a Beaux-Arts layout organized around the axis of the Library. It reflected a predilection on Moses' part for treating parks as refuges cut off from the city. The park had fortress-like edges – walls, railings and shrubs under a canopy of large trees – and the open, herbaceous-edged lawn at the centre. Seating was all fixed benches rigidly aligned with the rest of the park.

Top: *Rear of the library
from south of the Great
Lawn (April 2000)*

*Tree-lined promenade to
north of the Great Lawn
(October 1999)*

And while Whyte provided the programmatic parameters for rehabilitation of the park, the itinerant Biederman was also impressed by Parisian precedents – particularly the Jardin des Tuileries. This manifest itself in the introduction of sealed gravel pathways and movable chairs. The large beds of ivy under the plane trees were retained and, like the birch trees and ivy in the courtyard of the Museum of Modern Art, remain something of a Manhattan motif.[54]

Federal landscape preservationist Charles Birnbaum accused Hanna/Olin of 'muddled articulation of a preservation philosophy'. The self-confessedly 'intemperate' Olin countered that there is not 'such a thing as landscape restoration'. This spat notwithstanding, the first part of Whyte and Biederman's concept was to make the park as accessible and unthreatening as possible – particularly to women. The second part was to provide facilities and events that would draw people to the park – and generate the revenue to sustain it. This led to installation of two kiosks at the Sixth Avenue end of the park and construction of the hard-fought-for Bryant Park Grill and Café at the back of the Library. Proposed in 1981, the Grill was eventually built by BPRC itself and opened in May 1995. In the meantime a massive schedule of events was developed – including major fashion shows and open-air film screenings. In the mid-1990s the BPRC was receiving five or six requests a year to stage events in the park. By the end of the decade they were dealing with ten requests a day. Although the pieces from the 1930s' layout and their locations remained largely the same, the refurbishment of Bryant Park was a rehabilitation in the spirit of its predecessor – not a restoration to a particular previous form.[55]

Design

The principal elements that remained in place during the refurbishment were the London plane trees and the ivy below them. Many elements were restored and returned to their original locations – including the Lowell Fountain; (most of) the outer wall and cast iron railing, and many of the pavings and balustrades. Five new entrances were cut into the wall and railing. Existing entrances were widened and flattened out. Bluestone paths under the trees were widened. A ramp was constructed at the Library terrace. A larger reincarnation of the Great Lawn was created on 6 feet (1.8 metres) of soil over the roof of the new Library stacks. The lawn was given a definitive granite edge – which now doubles as a seat when all others are occupied – and was surrounded by a sealed gravel walk. New, 300-feet-long (90 metres) beds for

Bryant Park and New York Public Library from west side of Sixth Avenue (October 1999)

herbaceous perennials were created either side of the gravel walk. These have become one of BPRC's motifs for distinguishing Bryant Park from other open spaces in Manhattan. But their main motif is the green, wood and metal, chairs imported from France. Movable chairs – providing flexibility and a sense of freedom for their users – were one of Whyte's ideas. Importing them from France was one of Biederman's. Initially 1100 were provided. By 2000 the number was 2000. The principal reason for replacements was damage through heavy usage – not theft or vandalism.[56]

MANAGEMENT AND USAGE

Managing Organization

Responsibility for management and improvement of Bryant Park was transferred to BPRC in 1988 under a fifteen-year agreement with the City of New York. BPRC shares its management team with the 34th Street Partnership – another BID also run by Biederman. The 34th Street Partnership completed the restoration in 1999 of two small triangles, Herald Square and Greeley Square, at the intersection of Broadway, Sixth Avenue and 34th Street. BPRC and 34th Street Partnership had an in-house team of fifteen office staff in 2000. Six members of the team were involved 'on the aesthetics side'; the

rest on marketing and administration. In summer there are more than fifty people working in the park. BPRC's mission is: to eliminate crime, litter and graffiti; to recruit the best tenants to the district; to aid troubled and poor citizens; to make street and park improvements 'of undisputed quality'; and to establish a diverse and stable revenue scheme. They aim to do this by, among other things, 'using the best techniques of private business; paying market prices, and paying attention to details'.[57]

In the 1970s there was an average of thirteen rapes and 150 robberies per year in the park. Murders were committed there in 1976 and 1977. The average number of people using the park at lunchtime in the late 1970s was 1000; Whyte's report in 1979 noted that use by women had fallen from 42 per cent in the early 1970s to 29 per cent. Since 1991 there has been less than one felony per year. This was achieved more through introduction of heavy usage than through heavier policing. After the re-opening the Police Department allocated four officers to the park. A few years later, BPRC and the Police Department agreed that the police presence would be reduced – since it implied danger and looked wasteful. Latterly there have been two security officers on patrol – mainly engaged in 'quality of life enforcement' – and police only visit the park occasionally.[58]

Lowell Fountain
(October 1999)

Funding

The BPRC budget for 2000 was $3.7 million inclusive of organizing events and administration. Of that, $1 million was allocated to day-to-day maintenance of the park; $0.6 million to deferred maintenance items like building repairs and $0.5 million to management costs. After the completion of the refurbishment, the city continued to contribute its previously budgeted maintenance for the park. In 1998 this was $0.2 million. In the late 1990s the city reneged on its annual contribution. (It has been suggested that Mayor Giuliani found the success of Bryant Park 'an active irritant'.) Income in 2000 was set to come from a wide range of sources. These included BID Assessments, 33 per cent; event fees, 30 per cent; restaurant, 30 per cent; sponsors, 3 per cent; concessions, 3 per cent, and 1 per cent from interest and other minor sources. Café receipts until 2006 were pledged to refinancing construction of the restaurant.[59]

User Characteristics

Biederman regards user counts as the 'only form of profit and loss account that exists in park management'. BPRC therefore does user counts by gender at peak time – 1:15 p.m. – every business day. Figures are tabulated alongside weather conditions, the events being staged and whether the lawn is open. The carrying capacity of the park according to Whyte's calculations and recorded figures is around 5000 visitors at any one time. The statistic that is still regarded as key to the success of the park – the proportion of women users – is sensitive to temperature; to the day of the week and to whether the lawn is open . . . and whether it is wet. The managers are surprised how many children use the park in what is essentially a commercial part of the city. The park is also used by some homeless people. Providing they obey the rules, they are not turned away. The BPRC does, however, take action to prevent them from colonizing any particular part of the park. They have noticed that homeless users tend to gravitate towards less active areas. They therefore relocate facilities – like chess tables – into those areas to bring enough activity to dilute the proportion of homeless users.

PLANS FOR THE PARK

Biederman lists ten factors that control the success of urban parks – security, sanitation, concessions, restrooms, chairs and tables, lighting, horticulture, programming, design, and management – plus, number eleven, details. The plan for Bryant Park is to perfect these factors. Priorities in spring 2000 were to build the budget; to stabilize the schedule of events; to renegotiate the 1988 agreement with the city; to provide food outlets closer to the most heavily used parts of the park; to put hanging baskets on the lamp standards; and to provide more planted urns. Horticultural expectations still run high in Manhattan. Public art, by contrast, is low on BPRC's wish list. They believe that people will only come to see 'legendary' pieces and they are highly selective about donated works.[60]

CONCLUSIONS

Inevitably, the revitalization of Bryant Park has been held up as an example both for and against 'privatization of the public realm'. Typical of the comments in the early 1990s about BPRC was that 'in the long run, the idea of maximum access to public parks may not be well served by city government turning over considerable control to private agencies'. Such comments should be balanced against the views of New York journalists at that time. Paul Goldberger, architecture critic for *The New York Times*, noted in May 1992 that 'the park has become a more truly public place than at any time in the last generation'. In November that year Eve Kahn, architecture critic for *The Wall Street Journal*, described a walk in Bryant Park as being 'like meeting a once-troubled friend who kicked all bad habits and found a great new job'.[61]

There remains a suspicion that private sector management practices will inevitably lead to reductions in public rights. It would be shameful if they did. But the role of BPRC has to be seen in the perspective of a park that has been transformed from public nuisance to public service. It also has to be seen in the perspective of electorates that empower politicians who promise tax cuts. The revitalized Bryant Park is an object lesson in the application of Whyte's observations on the use of small urban spaces. It is an object lesson in the patient, persistent and professional application of sound business principles in the public realm. It might be suggested that these lessons are only applicable in the commercial heart of a major city. Aspects of the rehabilitation of New York's Bryant Park are, of course, unique to that city and to that park. But many of its lessons are universally applicable.

5 Parc de Bercy, Paris

13.5 hectares (33 acres)

INTRODUCTION

Built between 1992 and 1997, Parc de Bercy was the third of three major new parks completed in the 1990s on former industrial sites in central Paris. The other two are Parc de la Villette, built by the French national government, and Parc André-Citroën, like Parc de Bercy, built by the City of Paris. They were the first major parks to be built in central Paris since the completion of Parc des Buttes-Chaumont in 1867. The designs for all three new parks resulted from open international competitions. The design and development of Parc de la Villette and Parc André-Citroën became something of a bragging match between leftist President François Mitterand (presided 1981–95) and rightist Mayor of Paris Jacques Chirac (mayor 1977–95 and Mitterand's successor as president). The design and development of Parc de Bercy were more low key. Architect Bernard Huet and his team of architects and landscape architects eschewed monumentalism in favour of smaller scale, site-derived proposals.[62]

HISTORY

Designation as a Park

Until the seventeenth century Bercy was part of the

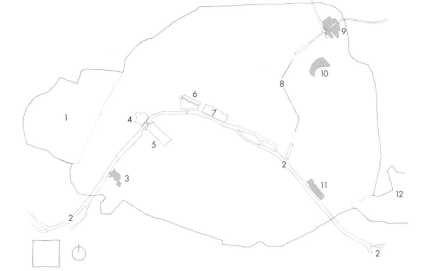

1 km

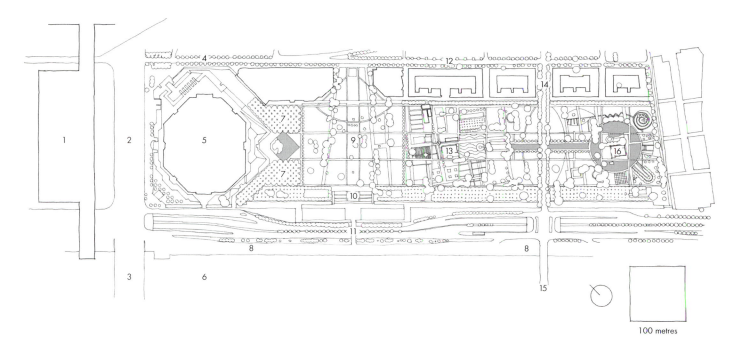

rural landscape of the Plain of Conflans in the Commune of Charenton to the east of Paris. During that century a number of private mansions were constructed along the Rue de Bercy with gardens running towards the banks of the Seine. These gardens were laid out perpendicular to the river – before it was straightened in the nineteenth century. The mansions and their gardens were followed by the development of timber yards and, from the beginning of the nineteenth century, wine warehouses. The Château de Bercy, the principal eighteenth-century building on the site, was abandoned after the French Revolution (1789) and demolished under Napoléon III (Emperor 1852–70). The mansions were sold and their sites taken over, little by little, by the buildings and warehouses of the wine trade. Wine was brought by boat from the Bourgogne region and unloaded at Bercy, which was outside the city – thereby avoiding city taxes – and then delivered by road or rail.[63]

By the beginning of the nineteenth century Bercy was one of the principal European markets for wines and spirits. The settlement was eventually annexed to the City of Paris in 1859 as part of its reorganization by Baron Haussmann (1809–91), Prefect of the Seine region under Napoléon III. The warehouses became liable for taxes. The government appointed architect Eugène-Emanuel Viollet-le-Duc (1814–79) to 'establish a rational plan for the warehouses'. Some official warehouses were built to Viollet-le-Duc's plan. But he made little change to the network of streets or to the diverse collection of picturesque buildings. The site contained remains of the earlier, now oblique, pattern and newer roads perpendicular to the realigned river – particularly the Boulevard and Pont de Bercy and the Rue de Dijon (now Rue Joseph Kessel) leading to the Pont de Tolbiac. The marks of each era of development were superimposed on the lines created by earlier eras.[64]

By the beginning of the 1970s wine trading had ceased and Bercy had become 'more than an old wine depot; it was a secret village of vintages'. The idea of creating a new quarter with a park at its heart emerged in that decade. It materialized in the Schéma de Secteur Seine Sud-Est (Plan for the south-east Seine area of the city) adopted by the Council of Paris in 1973. This was reiterated in 1977 by the Schéma Directeur d'Architecture et d'Urbanisme (SDAU; Plan of the Director of Architecture and Planning) for Paris. The SDAU contained the succinct statement that the area should comprise 'a park surrounded by housing and other activities, with the placing of a large public building in the area of the Boulevard de Bercy'. Also in 1977, a system of directly elected city government under a mayor was established for Paris. This led to a dramatic change in role for the Atelier Parisien d'Urbanisme (APUR; City Planning Authority). The APUR had been founded by the city, the Ile-de-France region and the state. In 1978 it changed from being 'an advisory body in charge of elaborating . . . general development and land use plans' to assuming 'control of various inner city schemes'. Suddenly the people who 'for years had been "thinking" the city now found themselves in charge of actually "making" it'. Pierre-Yves Ligen, then Director of the APUR, had all the Zones d'Aménagement Concerté (ZACs; comprehensive development areas) suspended. In the space of two years revised master plans were prepared for all eighteen of them.[65]

The ZAC de Bercy was established in 1979. The proposed park remained as the focus of the development area. The objectives for Parc de Bercy – and for the park in the ZAC Citroën-Cevennes in the south-west of the city – were:

- to contribute to the creation of new mixed 'quarters' with residential and other activities on former market or industrial sites close to the edge of the city
- to create spaces of a city-wide scale and that opened onto the Seine in the Parisian tradition
- to provide attractive open spaces giving distinct identity to the new neighbourhoods.[66]

Also in 1979 the competition was staged for the design of the Parc Omnisports de Paris Bercy (POPB) – the octagonal sports hall with a seating capacity of 17,000 characterized by its turfed 45-degree slopes – on the south side of Boulevard de Bercy. This was followed in 1983 by commencement

Community garden in the Parterres (June 1999)

of construction of the Ministry of Finance building on the north side of Boulevard de Bercy. These two major structures gave Bercy a new identity and launched it as a major development area. They presaged the inauguration by the Council of Paris in November 1983 of their Plan Programme de l'Est de Paris (Planning Programme for Eastern Paris). A major thrust of this programme was the creation and embellishment of major public parks and open spaces – including Parc de la Villette and Parc de Bercy.

Size and Condition of the Site at the Time of Designation

The ZAC de Bercy covered about 40 hectares. The park was broadly defined in the 1973 plan for the south-east Seine area as occupying 8–10 hectares. This eventually increased to more than 13 hectares. As well as the pattern of streets left by the wine trade, there was a mosaic of more than 500 mature trees, mainly planes and horse chestnuts, largely over a century old and mostly in good phytosanitary condition. Bercy was a 'world apart' from the rest of the city. Such 'romantic evocation of nature and the rural atmosphere of the site were exceptional in Paris'.[67]

Key Figures in the Establishment of the Park

Parc de Bercy was the second major new park in Paris inspired by Mayor Chirac. Whereas Parc André-Citroën was Chirac's direct response to President Mitterand's Parc de la Villette, the development of Parc de Bercy was less ostentatious. Chirac did, however, take a direct interest in the project. He imposed a decision, for instance, that the maximum possible number of existing trees be retained throughout the ZAC. The individual who commanded most publicity in the professional press was architect Bernard Huet (b. 1932). Huet was the leading figure in a tripartite team composed of architects FFL (Marylène Ferrand, Jean-Pierre Feugas and Bernard Le Roy) and landscape architect Ian Le Caisne. Le Caisne died in 1991 and was succeeded by Philippe Raguin. The members of FFL had all been students of Huet at the Paris-Belleville School of Architecture. Le Caisne and FFL had been shortlisted for the Parc André-Citroën competition in 1985.[68]

Meanwhile, Huet came to prominence with his restoration of Place Stalingrad at the western end of the Bassin de la Villette in Paris. In February 1992 he stated that he trained as an architect and used to hate landscape as much as he hated city planning. Huet went on to note, however, that 'a city is, in essence, a continuous process. And an urban project is totally different from architectural design, because time and space are totally different'. Displaying a conservative classicism, Huet argued that green spaces result from 'destruction of the city by modern, functionalist urbanization' but that 'you have to be very eclectic according to the problem you have to resolve'. He was characterized as regarding 'the park' as representing 'a nostalgic longing for Arcadia that justifies an autonomous position in the city'. Huet's work is pragmatic urban design.[69]

PLANNING AND DESIGN

Location

In September 1978 the Council of Paris approved a policy from the SDAU for improvement of the banks of the Seine and the canals in the city. The new parks at Bercy and Citroën-Cevennes were seen as reinforcing the axis of the river – Bercy near its entry to the city, André-Citroën at its exit. They were to become the central Paris counterparts to the two massive peripheral parks – the 845-hectare Bois de Boulogne to the west and the 995-hectare Bois de Vincennes to the east – that had been redesigned for mass recreation under Haussmann more than a century before. In 1981 the APUR conducted a strategic study of public open space in the city. That study established simple hierarchies of space on the basis of, first, quantity of space per inhabitant and, second, the quality and range of facilities in those spaces. It called for the creation of new parks which would 'provide an excellent service in poorly catered for riparian areas like the development areas at Bercy and Citroën-Cevennes'. They were envisaged largely as facilities for local inhabitants and also intended to serve the city as a whole and adjacent suburbs.[70]

A major influence on development at Bercy was its enclosure by railways on its north-eastern and south-eastern sides. The south-western side is defined by the right bank of the Seine. The left bank of the Seine opposite Bercy – the site for the French National Library – was also cut off from the rest of the city by railways. The response to this confinement was to introduce a range of activities intended to promote vitality. These included cultural facilities like the Frank Gehry-designed American Center and artists' studios; commercial developments including offices, hotels and restaurants and 1500 apartments. The POPB, opened in 1984, occupied the north-west side of the ZAC; retained wine warehouses ('Saint-Emilion Court') and closed off the south-east side. Architect Jean-Pierre Buffi was appointed to coordinate the design

of new development; architect Muriel Pagès was appointed to design the public spaces in the ZAC. Buffi's proposals included a series of openings between buildings to appear like extensions of the park.[71]

Shape and Natural Landform of the Site

The site was a 710 metre by 190 metre rectangle parallel to the Seine. The 13.5-hectare site was subdivided by the Rue Joseph Kessel (then Rue de Dijon) into 8.5 hectares to the north-west and 5 hectares to the south-east. The only significant level change across an otherwise effectively level site was the Rue de Dijon, which sat 2 metres higher.

Competition Brief

A policy launched in 1982 mandated the staging of design competitions for all public construction projects with a value in excess of FF180,000. The competition for Parc de Bercy was organized by the APUR for the City of Paris. It was announced in February 1987. Expressions of interest were invited from European teams comprising landscape and building architects. One hundred and six dossiers were received – sixty from France and forty-six from other countries. The jury shortlisted ten teams and called for their proposals by December 1987. The brief required competitors to:

- conceive of the park on the scale of Paris
- imagine a programme designed for daily routines rather than for spectacular activities
- resolve the question of the isolation of the site as a result of highways and railways
- draw on the individual character, heritage and history of the site.

The brief also drew attention to constraints within the site – in particular, the requirement to conserve the better existing large trees; the crossing of the site by the Rue de Dijon and the highness of the water table. Competitors were required to provide additional parking for the POPB and to take account of a future footbridge across the river.[72]

Original Design Concept

The entry from Huet's team was called Jardin de la Mémoire ('Garden of Memory'). It 'conformed with the terms of the brief and clearly expressed the history and morphology of the place. The composition was based on the idea of a palimpsest: writing over writing. In effect, the design proposed the

*Bridge over Rue Joseph
Kessel (June 1999)*

century mansion converted into a garden display and instruction centre
- steep, unramped embankments and two foot-bridges over the Rue Joseph Kessel link the Parterres to the Jardin Romantique (Romantic Garden). A symbolic link between the two areas is also created by a canal on the centreline of the POPB. The canal opens into a circle of water in the middle of the Romantic Garden
- the Grande Terrace – 7.5 metres above the level of the park; 8.5 metres above the Quai de Bercy – is a substantial but deceptively simple device running the entire length of the park. Planted with double lines of lime (basswood) trees it is redolent of the Jardin des Tuileries. Aligned with the river, it fulfils the mandate of relating the park to the scale of the city; it reduces the noise of the expressway; it encloses the park and it houses parking, storage and security facilities. It also supports the slightly sterile, slickly detailed cascade that runs down towards the Grande Prairie.

The park has an established verdant atmosphere from more than 200 mature trees that have been retained on site. These were augmented by more than 1200 newly planted trees and 30,000 shrubs. It is a tightly controlled composition of gridded gardens inserted between the existing tree canopy and the largely flat remains of the village of wine warehouses. Landscape architects decry the park on a number of bases – loss of rustic charm; directness and cost of paving materials; flatness; revivalist classicism and its planting combinations. Perhaps this is a customary reaction of landscape architects to architect-designed landscapes. But in this case it seems inappropriate. Parc de Bercy respects the 'genius of the place'; it feeds from the history of the area; it exploits existing tree cover and it relates the site to the city. The design reflects an emerging pattern in park design. This runs along the line that more users now visit parks alone or in smaller groups; that they want dispersed rather than centralized activities; that this increases the efficacy of grid pattern layouts since they are more polycentric, and that the smaller scale of such layouts favours more intimate garden-type facilities. It is also argued that, as at Bryant Park, the higher levels of intervisibility inherent in rectilinear layouts on level ground are conducive to a greater sense of security.[74]

superimposition of a new grid on top of the existing grid without either disturbing the other'. The new grid projected the geometry established by the Rue de Bercy and the Rue de Dijon into the site. This enabled the design to address the POPB and the new development to the east of the park. Retaining the old, oblique grid facilitated the protection of the existing mature trees as well as the 'network of rails, tanks, casks, warehouse foundations and piles of stone from the gardens of eighteenth-century mansions'. Huet himself commented that 'the grid gave continuity to the city. The continuity is very formal here, because it is in line with the street, the grid and so on, but the continuity is also in time . . . it is a piece of urban archaeology'.[73]

Spatial Structure, Circulation System, Landform, Materials and Planting

Parc de Bercy comprises five areas:

- a quincunx of tulip trees around the diamond-shaped fountain at the foot of the monstrous POPB
- the Grande Prairie (large meadow) mediating between the POPB and the Parterres (flat, formal plant beds at ground level) and between the entrance from Rue de Bercy and the cascade down the Grande Terrace. It too is virtually flat – a freely accessible lawn (uncharacteristic for Paris) punctuated with irregular lines of retained trees and a regular grid of nine new stone pavilions
- the Parterres are the heart of the park. They are a fenced-off grid of nine gardens – the eight outer squares are occupied by theme gardens that drip with symbolism (kitchen, orchard, perfume, rose and four colour-coded seasonal gardens). The central square is occupied by the retained Maison du Jardinage – an eighteenth-

Construction of Park de Bercy did not begin until December 1992 – five years after Huet and his team had won the competition. Completion of the succeeding phases ran from north-west to south-east. The final phase of the park – the south-eastern end of the Jardin Romantique and the terrace – was opened in September 1997.

Circle of water in middle of
Jardin Romantique (June 2000)

MANAGEMENT, FUNDING AND PLANS

Design and management of the City of Paris's parks are handled by two separate organizations. Design is undertaken by the project section of the Direction des Parcs, Jardins et Espaces Verts. Maintenance is divided by *arrondissement*. It is undertaken by directly employed staff. Management of parks by the City of Paris is highly centralized and does not lend itself to the establishment of 'friends' or other direct consultative groups. Funding for construction and management of the City of Paris's parks comes entirely from the Ville de Paris. The initial construction cost of Parc de Bercy was reported in 1994 to be FF390 million.[75]

The principal proposal affecting the park at the start of the twenty-first century is to create a footpath link along the banks of the river between Parc de Bercy and Parc André-Citroën, 12 kilometres to the west. The last part of this link – the Bercy-Tolbiac footbridge designed by architect Dietmar Feichtinger – was scheduled for completion in autumn 2001. This bridge will also create a direct link between the park and the new National Library on the left bank of the Seine.[76]

CONCLUSIONS

Cascade falling from Grande Terrace (June 2000)

The Parc de Bercy is tighter, less monumental and more gardenesque than the slightly earlier and slightly larger Parc André-Citroën on the other side of Paris. It reflects the more modest ambitions of the City of Paris for this peripheral enclave and the more pragmatic approach of designer Bernard Huet and his team. As Huet put it, 'the city is inhabited by many people, and you do not have to be aggressive with them'. They called their design *Jardin de la Mémoire*. They regarded it as a piece of urban archaeology. It is a pragmatic mediation between memory and modernity. The requirements of the brief are met through the careful combination of two orthogonal grids. These grids allowed the original street pattern and associated mature trees to be retained at the same time as responding to the new geometry of nineteenth-century highways and 1980s' buildings.[77]

The design is plan-form driven. The park remains remarkably flat until it meets an obstacle like the raised Rue Joseph Kessel or the riverside expressway. Huet and his team did, however, seek to treat both these obstacles as opportunities. They overcame the first with a dramatic sweeping hill and two footbridges; the latter with a massive terrace affording views across the city. The ornamental landforms in the Jardin Romantique are peculiarly contrived and the gridded gardens will require high levels of maintenance to operate effectively. But the park is a logical, legible, secure, place-derived response to an awkwardly located site. And its polycentric rectilinear layout successfully meets the emerging demand for parks to cater for solitary visitors and visitors in small groups.

6 Parc André-Citroën, Paris

14 hectares (35 acres)

INTRODUCTION

Named after the car manufacturer whose factory used to occupy the site, Parc André-Citroën is on the left bank of the River Seine in the south-western corner of central Paris (see location map on page 32). Launched in 1985 by rightist Mayor (later President) Jacques Chirac, it was to be a city-owned, landscape architect-designed park 'for the twenty-first century'. It was intended to stand in direct contrast to Parc de la Villette, located in the north-eastern corner of central Paris and one of leftist President François Mitterand's *Grands Projets* – a multicultural national urban park – also 'for the twenty-first century'. The final design for Parc André-Citroën was a combined product from two teams of landscape architects and architects – Alain Provost with architects Jean-Paul Viguier & Jean-François Jodry, and Gilles Clément with architect Patrick Berger. Proposals from the two teams were considered sufficiently similar for them to be invited to produce a joint final design. The central feature of the park – and a common element in both of the winning designs – is a canal-bordered rectangle opening onto the left bank of the Seine. It was intended to be in the monumental tradition of the Champs-de-Mars, the Esplanade des Invalides and the Jardin des Plantes. It is a slightly sloping lawn, 300 metres by 100 metres, with a single diagonal path across one corner. This part of the park, designed by Provost, sets the tone for a place characterized by rectilinear minimalism. Toward the edges of the park, six busier, intensely symbolic, colour-themed gardens and the Jardin en Mouvement (Garden in Movement) were designed by Clément. The park

contains about a hectare of water in a variety of forms. It is punctuated by two conservatories at the head of the central lawn and a set of six light and lofty glasshouses regularly spaced above the theme gardens.[78]

HISTORY

Designation as a Park

Like Bercy, the Javel area was annexed to Paris as part of its reorganization by Baron Haussmann. In the eighteenth century the hamlet of Javel had belonged to the Abbey of St-Geneviève-du-Mont. In 1784 the Count d'Artois established a chemical factory in Javel. The 80 hectares that were annexed to the city had less than 75 inhabitants. Only riverside quays were developed there until the construction, at the end of the nineteenth century, of the Pont Mirabeau to the north of the park site. This was accompanied by construction of three roads radiating from the bridge at 45 degrees. The southward road is the Rue Balard. It runs east of the park. The site was occupied by melon clôches until the establishment of the Citroën works.[79]

Little change was made on the site beyond the construction, commencing in 1915, of sheds for car manufacture. These were used during the First World War for the manufacture of shells. The car assembly lines, the first in France, were established by André Citroën (1878–1935) in 1920. The Citroën works relocated in the early 1970s to Aulnay-sous-Bois outside Paris and 23 hectares were acquired by the city. Following the establishment in 1977 of a directly elected government for the City of Paris, the Zone d'Aménagement

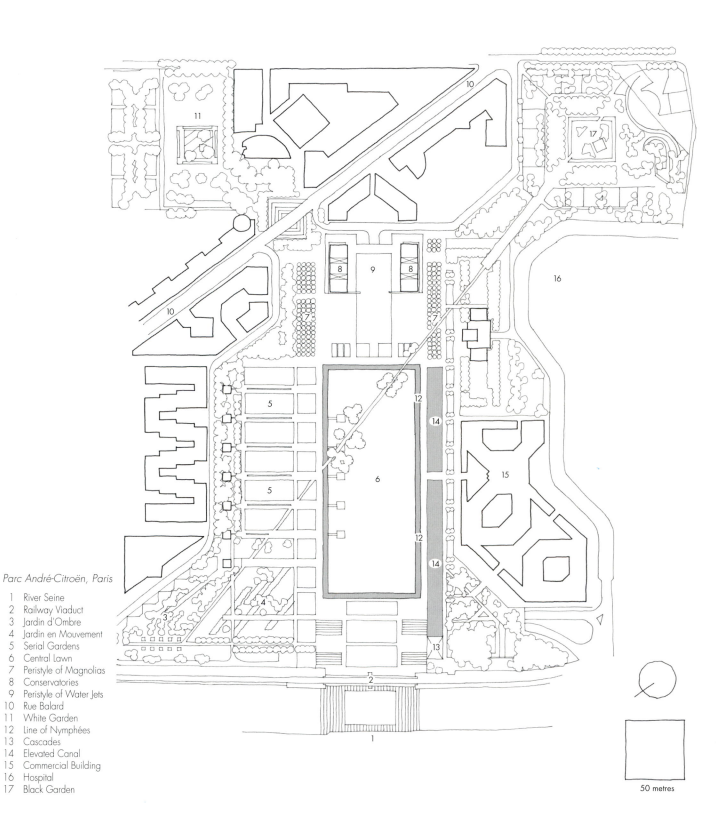

Parc André-Citroën, Paris

1   River Seine
2   Railway Viaduct
3   Jardin d'Ombre
4   Jardin en Mouvement
5   Serial Gardens
6   Central Lawn
7   Peristyle of Magnolias
8   Conservatories
9   Peristyle of Water Jets
10 Rue Balard
11 White Garden
12 Line of Nymphées
13 Cascades
14 Elevated Canal
15 Commercial Building
16 Hospital
17 Black Garden

50 metres

Concerté (ZAC – comprehensive development area) Citroën-Cévennes was set up in 1979. As with the ZAC de Bercy, a public park was proposed as the focus of the development area. In addition to the park, the ZAC Citroën-Cévennes was to include a hospital, offices and 2,500 new apartments.

Condition of the Site at the Time of Designation

Shortly after the site was acquired in 1970 'it was envisaged as the location for part of the World's Fair that France dreamed of holding in 1989' – the bicentennial of the French Revolution. By the time the design competition was held in 1985 the site had been completely cleared of all previous development. A few obsolete municipal warehouses to the north of the site were cleared to make way for the Richard Meier-designed headquarters of television company Canal+. Nathan Starkman, director of the APUR during the 1990s, described the site as having been 'a blank page for the imagination of its creators'. The clearance was so effective that 'not a trace remained of the sixty years of industrial occupation. So the memory of these places was destroyed, with the exception of the negative effect they have had on urban planning, since the size of the automobile plant had blocked the process of urbanization of this quarter'.[80]

Key Figures in the Establishment of the Park

Just as President Mitterand (presided 1981–95) inspired the establishment of Parc de la Villette, so Jacques Chirac (Mayor of Paris 1977–95 and Mitterand's successor as president) inspired the establishment of the Parc André-Citroën. Political rivalry between the two men was manifest in the building projects that they sponsored. Where Mitterand had his programme of state-sponsored *Grands Projets*, Chirac's Paris began a programme of construction and restoration of streets, squares, parks and gardens that it boasted were 'of a scope not seen since the time of Haussmann'. The Parc André-Citroën was a major element in Chirac's response to Mitterand's 35-hectare Parc de la Villette. Where the competition for la Villette had called for a multicultural urban park for the twenty-first century, the competition for Parc André-Citroën called for a park that would form part of the ensemble of green spaces along the river, that would 'reflect the influence of Paris, both in France and abroad, and above all should imprint upon garden history a hallmark truly representative of contemporary trends'. Where the competition for la Villette became a final choice between proposals from two architects, the competition for Parc André-Citroën requested proposals from landscape architects working with architects. This was 'a way of stating clearly that what was needed above all was a specialist in plants'.[81]

In the event, the City – much like the judges for the state at la Villette – narrowed its deliberations to two entries. These were from Alain Provost with architects Jean-Paul Viguier & Jean-François Jodry and from Gilles Clément with architect Patrick Berger. The final design of the park is a reflection of the approach of the two landscape architects. Provost (b. 1938), 'France's most prolific landscape architect', is a minimalist geometrician. His work is typified by the smaller, squared-up Parc Diderot on the northern edge of La Défense for the municipality of Courbevoie. There, parallel hedges and lawns flank a regular, wave-shaped cascade running down a steep hill – a masterclass in landform design. Parc Diderot is a sharply detailed, tightly controlled – but powerful – exercise in reductionism. Provost was the *mandataire commun* (common representative) for the Parc André-Citroën design team. Clément (b. 1943) is a horticulture-oriented landscape architect with an agricultural background and an extensive garden design portfolio. In the original Clément–Berger submission the Jardin en Mouvement was proposed in the central square. The collaboration of Clément and Berger – who eventually designed the northern part of the park – has been compared with that of the mason and gardener. The collaboration between Provost and Clément was 'more of a peaceful existence than a community of ideas'. It has been suggested that the main characteristic shared by Provost and Clément is the romantic passion of their writing.[82]

PLANNING AND DESIGN

Location

Parc André-Citroën was intended to be the focus of the ZAC and 'in all stages of its conception the mutual influence between the park and the surrounding buildings was the subject of reiteration and redefinition'. Regrettably, decisions made by the APUR before the staging of the competition reduced the ability of the park to fulfil its mandate as a focus for the quarter. In particular, designation of land south of the park site for what is now the Hôpital Européen Georges Pompidou, and the definition of the surrounding development sites by 45-degree angles led to the park being 'trapped in the district, as if concealed from the view of the city'. The most imposing of these developments is the lumpen, glass curtain wall complex (currently occupied by Groupe Banque Populaire) directly south of the central lawn. The site was also cut off from the river by rail lines. It was, nevertheless, destined to become 'the only park in Paris to actually touch the river'.[83]

Competition Brief

The same procedure was adopted for the design of both Parc André-Citroën and Parc de Bercy. They were the subject of Europe-wide competitions (as opposed to the global competition for la Villette) organized by the APUR. The competition for Parc André-Citroën was launched in July 1985. Ten teams of landscape architects and architects were short-listed from sixty-three applicants – forty-five from outside France – and invited to 'propose their version of a contemporary urban park'. The fundamental requirement of the competition brief was to 'treat this new park at a double scale but to give it a unified image overall'. It was to operate, on the one hand, as part of the great open spaces of Paris – particularly those bordering the Seine – and, on the other hand, as part of the daily life of the new quarter and the rest of the 15th *arrondissement*. Competitors were called on to enrich their proposals with original spaces, programmes and themes, and to address the treatment of new buildings bordering the park. It was not to be 'a neo-constructivist fairground, nor an

"English-style" or a "French-style" park – the new park could only find its legitimacy through its own poetry'. Nevertheless, the competitors had to draw up designs for what was, essentially, 'a niggardly space'.[84]

Original Design Concept

The similarities in form between the competition submissions from the Provost team and the Clément team were greater than the similarities in content. Both focused on the canal-bordered central rectangle; both had a series of rectangular gardens aligned roughly north–south along its northern edge. But that is more or less where the similarities end. The Provost scheme evoked André Le Nôtre's geometry and reduced the vegetation to regular monochrome blocks set within a thick irregular peripheral screen. This enclosure reinforced the one big idea of a huge central lawn focusing on the Seine. The Clément proposal, by contrast, eschewed 'static visual order . . . in favour of the idea of a dynamic management of spontaneous vegetation'. Clément's Jardin en Mouvement occupied most of the central rectangle. Most of the edges of the site were occupied by a series of individual rectilinear 'theme' gardens.[85]

In the combined scheme responsibilities were divided on the basis of:

- Provost–Viguier & Jodry: southern area of park including central lawn and surrounding canals, *nymphées* (line of towers along the canal); Jardin

des Métamorphoses (Garden of Metamorphosis – in westernmost triangle of park) and Black Garden in the south-eastern corner. Provost was made responsible for overall landform. Viguier & Jodry were responsible for the railway viaduct and, eventually, the riverfront plaza
- Clément–Berger: northern area of park including conservatories at head of central lawn; White Garden and play area east of Rue Balard; Serial Gardens including greenhouses and water channels between the gardens, and Jardin en Mouvement (in northernmost triangle of the park). Clément was responsible for park lighting and Berger was responsible for site furniture (which included a range of finely flexed benches and recliners).

Construction began in 1987. Provost, writing in 1991, noted that the design was influenced by the existing buildings surrounding the site – and that 'it was therefore not necessary to increase the diversity of the site, but rather to carve out an easily identifiable place'. In a thinly veiled reference to la Villette, he commented that 'the choice made was not to present a dense forest of social instruments fitted out with a minimum of natural elements, but to create a Park with a maximum of natural elements, but sufficiently equipped for innovative use'. Provost suggested that 'the design embodied four main principles – nature; movement; architecture and artifice' and that 'the will of the conceivers was to create a Park that . . . merits the name – strong, wise, generous, poetic . . . based on the strong and indispensable presence of water, the controlled dynamism of the earth and the rhythm of vegetation'.[86]

Spatial Structure, Circulation System, Landform, Materials and Planting

The park was formally opened in September 1992. But its spatial structure was not fully formed until the opening in summer 2000 of the final connections between the central lawn and the banks of the Seine. This completed the relationship between the two conservatories flanking a central peristyle of water jets; the steeper slope between them and the lawn; the subtler slope of the lawn itself, and the river. The importance of this relationship to the overall design is reinforced by the orientation of water features towards the river.

The central lawn has a distinct and imposing presence. It has been compared to Notre Dame Cathedral – 'a monumental symbol of the bustling city centre . . . yet at the same time it is a place for tranquillity and contemplation'. The effectiveness of

Serial Gardens (May 2000)

Central Lawn and surrounding
canal from the west
(May 2000)

the lawn is reinforced by the conservatories; by the white arc of the viaduct; by the overall landform of the park; and by its other built elements. The conservatories are each 15 metres high and 45 metres long. They sit on a raised platform and might be expected to dominate the lawn. They are the focal point of the park but they are not overpowering. Their only widely visible structural members are their teak columns. The conservatories close the central vista and relate well to the scale of surrounding buildings. The enclosure and centrality of the lawn are also emphasized by the southward incline of the six Serial Gardens, by the water chutes between them, by the glasshouses above them, by the blocks of pleached trees north of the lawn and by the regular solid verticality of the grey and black marble *nymphées* opposite them. The slashing directness of the 850-metre-long diagonal path through the park – almost paralleling Rue Balard, and the fact that the lawn is – uncharacteristically for Paris – freely accessible, pull it back from the brink of sterility.[87]

Provost stated that 'a garden without water doesn't work'. He believed that at Parc André-Citroën it should be 'legible, reasoned, guided, understandable, domesticated, playful, urbain, programmable – bouncing, falling or sometimes suspended'. And water – including the impressive peristyle (120 vertical jets of variable height)

between the conservatories, the canal around the central lawn, the chutes between the Serial Gardens, the elevated canal above the *nymphées* and the cascades – is a characteristic component of the design. It occupies one hectare of the park. But it is Clément's planting design – particularly the Serial Gardens – that creates the fragmentation that is a necessary antidote to the monolithic geometry of the park.[88]

The Serial Gardens 'express developmental stages in nature according to alchemical theory about the transformation of lead into gold. Each garden is devoted to a metal. Its colour gives the garden its name. Colour and the senses determine the choice of plants; water establishes the ground plan of the garden'. The Serial Gardens are comparable in scale and intensity of content with Ken Smith's 'collection boxes' in Yorkville Park. They demonstrate the growing interest towards the end of the twentieth century in small-scale gardens within parks – subdivisions capable of creating contrast and the illusion of escape, and of providing intense sensory experiences. The Serial Gardens have been derisively compared with the German *Bundesgartenschau* gardens 'where a number of thematic gardens are joined into a kind of horticultural IKEA'. The argument here is that they are 'cyberspace gardens' enabling people to make rapid leaps between different worlds. But that is surely part of

*Detail of water jets
(June 2000)*

*The Purple Garden
(June 1999)*

what urban parks have always aimed to do – and Clément does it very well in the Serial Gardens.[89]

His Jardin en Mouvement is designed to be 'constantly changing, like fallow ground' where 'nature dominates' and 'the gardener only regulates'. The initial seed planting comprised 40 per cent wild herbaceous plants for dry sites, 40 per cent for damp sites and 20 per cent ornamental plants for both types of site. Marc Treib described it as a 'Darwinian approach to park design' where paths are determined by users and plant successions are determined by 'nature' – and the intervention of gardeners. Located close to the northern entrance of the park, it could be a potent statement about the relationship of humankind and nature in urban settings. Regrettably, its unkempt character and frequent muddiness leave it looking like a less managed ornamental area rather than a didactic garden. The adjacent Jardin d'Ombre, with its reinforced grass paths through an intricate and intimate collection of ornamental shrubs and herbaceous perennials, is a more self-assured foil to the surrounding city and the geometry of the park than is the Jardin en Mouvement.[90]

MANAGEMENT, USAGE AND PLANS

As with Parc de Bercy, the design and management of Parc André-Citroën are handled by two separate organizations. Design is handled by the project section of the Direction des Parcs, Jardins et Espaces Verts of the Ville de Paris. Maintenance of parks is divided by *arrondissement* and is undertaken by directly employed staff. Again, as with Parc de Bercy, funding for construction and management comes entirely from the Ville de Paris. Initial construction of the main part of the park is reported to have cost FF388 million.[91]

User studies of the park are not available. Anecdotal evidence suggests, however, that use is relatively weather sensitive, and that, in its early years at least, the park was performing a primarily local role. This begs the question of whether the location of the park and its inward-looking design militate against casual visits.[92]

The principal proposals for the park at the start of the twenty-first century were to complete the direct visual and pedestrian link between the park and the banks of the Seine, and to create a footpath link along the banks of the river between Parc André-Citroën and Parc de Bercy to the east.

Substantial highway works were required between the park and the Port de Javel before the link to the river could be completed in June 2000. The 12-kilometre footpath along the river was due for completion in autumn 2001.[93]

CONCLUSIONS

A combination of industrial decline and rivalry between French President Mitterand and Paris Mayor Jacques Chirac provoked the development of three major new parks in the core of the capital during the last 20 years of the twentieth century. Parc André-Citroën and Parc de la Villette were intended to be models of the urban park 'for the twenty-first century'. Neither of them could have been as indulgent in their design without the counterbalance of the Bois de Boulogne and the Bois de Vincennes – redesigned for mass recreation under Haussmann. Both Parc André-Citroën and Parc de la Villette treated their sites as a *tabulae rasae*.

In the event Parc André-Citroën is a hybrid between competition proposals from landscape architects Alain Provost and Gilles Clément. Provost, a lyrical geometrician, was responsible for the focal feature of the park – its rectangular central lawn – and for the carefully controlled landform that encloses the lawn and tilts it down to the River Seine. Clément, a lyrical plantsman, was responsible for the design of the more significant gardens in the park. His symbolic planting of these individual gardens is one of the more engaging aspects of the design. Together with their architect collaborators they have produced a stylized, self-conscious, slickly detailed, urbane monument to late twentieth-century minimalism. But not to the exclusion of subtlety and delight.

The park was conceived in the tradition of monumental Parisian spaces perpendicular to the Seine. An opening between the park and the river was finally achieved ten years after the completion of the park. Nevertheless it has not entirely dispelled the feeling that the park is an inward-looking place whose role is directed more toward the immediate neighbourhood than toward Paris as a whole. Perhaps the extended footpath links alongside the river will reduce this sense of separation from the city. It is ironic, however, that a park named after a car manufacturer should be characterized less by its Jardin en Mouvement than by a static green rectangle at its centre.

7 Parc des Buttes-Chaumont, Paris

24.7 hectares (61 acres)

INTRODUCTION

Sublime and seductive, the Parc des Buttes-Chaumont is the most acclaimed product of the design team directed by engineer Jean-Charles Adolphe Alphand (see location map on page 32). Supported by horticulturist Jean-Pierre Barillet-Deschamps, architect Gabriel Davioud and, latterly, landscape architect Édouard-François André, Alphand was responsible for the reshaping of the Bois de Boulogne and the Bois de Vincennes, and articulation of the Champs-Elysées. His team also created the Parc Montsouris and the gardens of the Champs-de-Mars and twenty-four other gardens and squares across Paris. These parks were part of dramatic plans for the remodelling of Paris that were called for by Napoléon III (Emperor 1852–70) and executed under the direction of Baron Georges-Eugène Haussmann, Préfet of the Seine (1853–60) and Minister for Paris (1860–69).[94]

Haussmann's remodelling brought about the boulevards, the building lots, the promenades and street planting that remain inimitably characteristic of Paris. He also arranged the development of city-wide systems of water supply and sewerage. Alphand and his team created at Buttes-Chaumont a paisley-shaped park enclosed by new roads and traversed by railway tracks. Layers of flat and falling water, exotic planting and curvaceous paths were superimposed on the reshaped landform of a worked-out gypsum quarry. Punctuated with rustic structures, false wood fencing and metal site furniture, the park reflects synchronous developments in engineering and botany. Picturesque and poetic, sublime and seductive, it sits between late romanticism and proto-modernism in the stylistic lexicon of European urban parks. Completed in 1869, the design remained virtually unchanged for the rest of the nineteenth century and throughout the twentieth. Procedures for restoration of the park were commenced in November 1999.

HISTORY

Designation as a Park

Napoléon III began his programme of improvements in Paris with the donation in 1852 of the Bois de Boulogne to the city, so that it could be redesigned for public use in the style of the Royal Parks in London – particularly Hyde Park. His ideas for the city had therefore begun to take shape before he called on Haussmann in 1853 to direct its remodelling. Indeed, Loyer suggested that the model which Napoléon and Haussmann adopted had been initiated by Louis XVI (reigned 1774–92). Louis XVI, in turn, had sought to introduce to Paris the type of baroque radial plan developed in the city of Rome by architect Domenico Fontana for Sixtus V (Pope 1585–90). The 17.54-metre height limit for the cornice of new buildings was set in 1784. It gave rise to a building typology that remains the norm in central Paris.[95]

Following the French Revolution (1789) and the execution of Louis (1792), a call was made to the artists of the Parisian academies to make proposals for development of the city. This resulted in the *Plan des Artistes*. Conceived in 1796 – it too was based on classical models – but focused on the Seine. Between 1800 and 1859 the population of Paris grew from 547,000 to 1 million. Compulsory purchase legislation was established in 1841 and

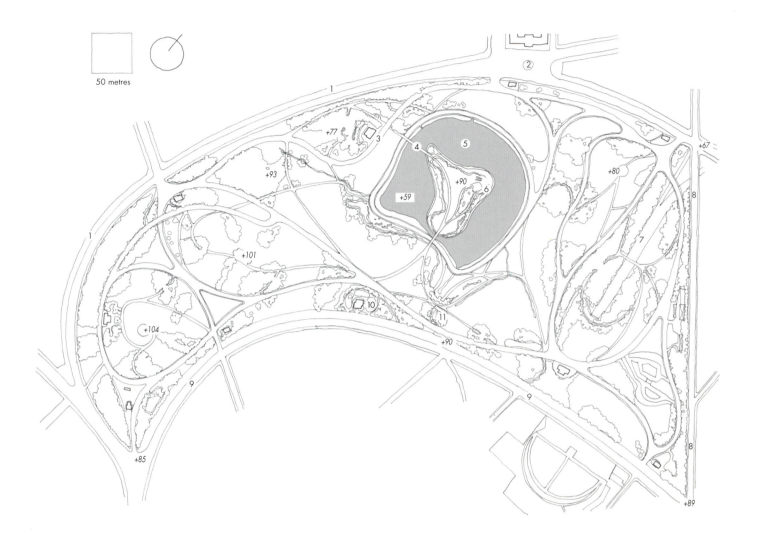

50 metres

*Parc des Buttes-
Chaumont, Paris*

1   Rue Marin
2   Hotel de Ville/Place
     Armand Carrel
3   Restaurant/Café
4   Suspension Bridge
5   Lake
6   Temple of Sibyl
7   Railway cutting
8   Rue de Crimée
9   Rue Botzaris
10   Park Office
11   Cave

+59 = elevation in metres
above sea level

1848. The speed and extent of Napoléon III and Haussmann's changes were extraordinary. Nevertheless it was not until 1860 that the communes of Belleville, Bercy, La Villette and other peripheral settlements were absorbed into Paris. The site of the Buttes-Chaumont was acquired by the city in 1862 with the specific purpose of converting it into a park for the growing population of Paris. Work on the park commenced in 1864. It was opened in 1867 to coincide with the Universal Exhibition that year. Construction works were completed in 1869.[96]

Condition of the Site at the Time of Designation

The name Buttes-Chaumont indicates the nature of the site – *butte* means mound or hillock and *Chaumont* derives from the words *chauve* – bald, and

mont – mountain. When the site was acquired in 1862 it comprised 'old quarries, enormous in size, and surrounded by acres of rubbish . . . it was by cutting away the ground around three sides . . . and leaving the highest and most picturesque side intact that the present results were brought about'. Alphand himself described the *buttes* as having 'the sad privilege' of being the site of the gibbet of Montfaucon and the haunt of gypsies. City authorities note that the site also contained sewage works and knacker's yards. The press release in November 1999 announcing the restoration of the park noted that 'there remain underground three levels of old mining galleries that were filled in. The relief of the cliff and peak were created from a rocky promontory that was left by the miners and re-profiled with millstone cement to create their current form. A bed of clay was spread on the remodelled slopes to protect the underlying gypsum and to assure the growth of vegetation, and 200,000 cubic metres of soil were imported to the site'.[97]

Key Figures in the Establishment of the Park

Napoléon III was the instigator of what is commonly referred to as 'Haussmann's Paris'. Vernes attributed Napoléon's interest in the remodelling of Paris to nostalgia for England – where he lived from 1837 to 1840 and from 1846 to 1848 – and to 'latent Saint-Simonisme'. Haussmann (1809–91) has been described as 'ruthless, canny and obstinate'. It has also been suggested that 'he was one of the most obnoxious of recorded beings'. Born in Paris, his family were French Protestant textile manufacturers from Colmar in Alsace. Haussmann trained as a lawyer. He became a civil servant in 1831 and spent the next twenty-two years in the provinces where he was renowned as a tough negotiator. From 1851 to 1852 he was Préfet of the Gironde – where he was probably impressed by the seventeenth-century

remodelling of Bordeaux – before being summoned by Napoléon to become Préfet of the Seine.[98]

Haussmann's task was to establish Paris 'as a symbol and model of progress'. Between 1853 and his resignation in 1869 he organized wholesale change in the structure and appearance of the city. His work involved improvements in circulation and sanitation, and provision of new public spaces and their unification through the planting of street trees. 'Properties were expropriated, whole areas – formerly "strongholds of insurrection" – demolished, new avenues created, enormous road junctions constructed, bridges and squares built, drains and drinking-water mains excavated'. More than 90 kilometres of new boulevards were created; more than 50 kilometres of existing streets were widened and the city was provided with a dependable supply of water. Chadwick credited Haussmann as 'creator of the first real urban park system – that almost hackneyed, yet too-seldom realised cliché of current town planning'. Loyer noted that 'haussmannisme' was 'more than an episode in the history of Paris' and that, driven by practicality

Montmartre from the Temple of Sibyl (June 2000)

rather than by any theoretical position, Haussmann created 'an urban model' that has 'survived multiple social and economic changes without losing its vitality'.[99]

Haussmann's resignation resulted from obstinacy in the face of increasing opposition to certain of his proposals. Russell noted, however, that unlike the many speculators who benefited from his works, Haussmann was not corrupt. He was also extraordinarily astute in his appointment in 1854 of Jean-Charles Adolphe Alphand (1817–91) as an engineer in the newly formed Service des Promenades et Plantations de la Ville de Paris. Alphand was born in Grenoble and graduated as an engineer in *Ponts et Chausées*. He worked for various provincial *départements* before being assigned in 1840 to the city of Bordeaux where he reached the rank of first-class engineer and was responsible for administration of the seaports of the Gironde region. In 1857 Alphand was appointed Chief Engineer; in 1861 he was appointed Director of the Service and in 1867 he was also given responsibility for *Voies Publiques* ('public ways'). Following Napoléon III's abdication in 1870, Alphand refused the position of Préfet of the Seine of the Third Republic but accepted – by decree of President Adolphe Thiers (presided 1871–73) – the position of Directeur des Travaux de Paris. This role included responsibility for highways, refuse, promenades, planting, architecture and planning – the 'health and beauty of the visible outdoor areas of Paris'. It was extended in 1878 to include water and sewerage services. Alphand remained Director of Works until his death in 1891.[100]

Alphand's initial appointment and establishment of the Service provoked scepticism from Haussmann's critics. But his first task – remodelling the Bois de Boulogne to the west of Paris – and his many subsequent tasks continue to provoke praise. Alphand then took charge of the remodelling of the Bois de Vincennes to the east of Paris; construction of the Parcs des Buttes-Chaumont and Montsouris; the redesign of Parc Monceau, and design between 1854 and 1870 of twenty-four squares created by Haussmann's boulevards. Alphand participated in preparations for the Universal Exhibitions of 1867, 1878 and 1889. He designed areas of the Champs-de-Mars for the Exhibition of 1867 'as an inextricable maze, an unending labyrinth of curves, a profusion of vegetation, sheets of water and paths, bewildering in the complexity of its layout'. Intensely patriotic and assiduously anonymous, 'Alphand was proud to devote his career to the service of the state'. Vernes noted that 'more precisely than the lawyer Haussmann, the engineer was capable of

ennobling the technical necessities of urban management with artistic finishing touches' and that 'Haussmann only imperfectly gave credit to the creative genius of his collaborator, concerned to appear the one and only master of the transformation of Paris'.[101]

Horticulturist Jean-Pierre Barillet-Deschamps (1824–75) was brought to Paris – also from Bordeaux – by Alphand in 1860 as Chief Gardener for the city. 'Under this title he proceeded to revive the genre of landscape architecture. His adaptation to the urban realm of art exercised almost exclusively in the private domain made him as much as Alphand, a precursor of the urban landscape architect'. Architect Gabriel Davioud (1824–81) joined Alphand and Barillet-Deschamps in the Service when they were working on the Bois de Boulogne. While Alphand designed landforms, water bodies and pathways and Barillet-Deschamps laid out 'groves of trees and the undulating lawns dotted with charming island beds', Davioud designed whimsical kiosks, lodges, restaurants, bars, cafés and aviaries in a rustic style referring to Gothic architecture and to Swiss chalets. Landscape architect Édouard-François André (1840–1911) also joined the Service in 1860 as a pupil to Alphand. He went on to win the design competition in 1867 for Sefton Park in Liverpool.[102]

PLANNING AND DESIGN

Location

One of Haussmann's first projects was the creation in 1853 of the Boulevard de Strasbourg. This runs southward from the Gare du Nord and extends across the Seine into the south of the city. It formed a new 'frontier' between the rich to the west and the poor to the east. This was deliberate. Haussmann also 'understood very well that his works would have the effect of wiping out a large part of the private planted areas of the city and therefore promoted the art of roadside planting. Having to choose between the creation of two or three appropriately spaced parks and a large number of smaller gardens spread along the arteries of the city, he preferred the latter system'. Haussmann and Alphand also planned the parks of Buttes-Chaumont in the north of the city and Montsouris in the south as counterparts to the remodelled Bois de Boulogne to the west and Bois de Vincennes to the east. Vernes suggested that 'Alphand's 'avenues of gardens' prefigured the 'parkways' of American cities and that his network of 'promenades' prefigured the 'park system' that ordered their extension in the twentieth century'.[103]

Shape and Natural Landform of the Site

The Parc des Buttes-Chaumont occupies a paisley-shaped site on the northwest-facing slopes of Belleville. The acute angle at the southernmost point of the park has an elevation of 85 metres. Elevations of the park along Rue de Crimée are 89 metres at the south and 67 metres to the north. Quarrying operations and Alphand's reshaping of the site left five peaks – at elevations of 104, 101, 93, 77 and 80 metres respectively – running south to north-east across the park. These are largely grassed and/or planted. The dramatic focal point of the park, however, is the Temple of Sibyl. This is situated at an elevation of 90 metres on a sheer-faced rocky island 30 metres above the 1.5 hectare shield-shaped lake. Another major landform element is the grotto between the high point of Rue Botzaris (elevation of 96 metres) and the lake. This was exaggerated in the creation of the park and has a height of 20 metres; a width of 14 metres and contains 8-metre-long artificial stalactites – introducing a sublime element to the design.

Original Design Concept

In her studies of Alphand's work, Marceca noted that 'creation of the nineteenth century public park' was 'enriched by contributions emerging from different fields of knowledge: botany, agronomy, hydraulics and topography'. She suggested that Alphand saw Buttes-Chaumont as a 'site for the glorification of technology and of the machine' noting that he made 'overwhelming use of metal, demonstrating the extent to which he is aware of the technical possibilities of the new materials'. In her response to Bernard Tschumi's dismissal of the nineteenth-century urban park as 'an undefiled Utopian world-in-miniature, protected from vile reality', Meyer commented that 'Buttes-Chaumont was never conceived or perceived as a *replica of nature*; its transformation from a scarred remnant into a verdant, undulating panorama . . . required massive technological ingenuity. That effort was not concealed . . . rather, it was exaggerated in the precise streamlined engineered topography and road alignment . . .'.[104]

Davioud-designed lodge at one of Rue Botzaris entrances (June 2000)

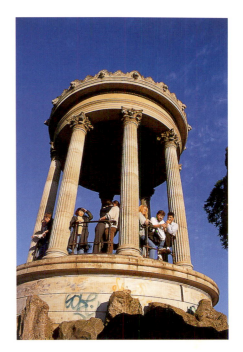

Above: *Temple of Sibyl*
(June 2000)

Left: *'the deep slopes allow*
parts of the site to face the sun
throughout the day'
(June 2000)

Equally Vernes highlighted the engineer Alphand's instinctive affinity for 'the technical concept of networks which . . . was expressed in the vegetated promenades that crossed Paris and created links between his gardens'. Vernes also noted that 'each element of his conception – whether metal, stone or vegetation – became part of the general urban system' and that the Alphadian park is 'at the same time "an indispensable annex to urban ways" and a machine to circulate and to ventilate . . . a "rational" alternative to the historic city'. He suggested that 'Alphand sought to annex visually the garden to the city and the city to the garden'. This all points to Buttes-Chaumont as a park whose function was symbiotic with the city and whose form and fitting-out were inspired both by pre-existing site conditions and by synchronous technological developments. In short, the concept derived from functionalism rather than pastoralism.[105]

Spatial Structure, Circulation System, Landform, Materials and Planting

Alphand's design process involved the sequential composition of landform and water; then vegetation; then paths – which were subordinate to the rest of the composition. Landform is certainly the principal element in the spatial structure of Buttes-Chaumont. The high points in the park provide panoramic views across the city; the lower areas, particularly by the water, provide complete enclosure and a sense of distance from the city; the steep slopes allow parts of the site to face the sun throughout the day. Unlike other major parks in Paris, Buttes-Chaumont contains few flat areas. Its dramatic landform obscures its relative smallness. The main entrance from Place Armand Carrel presents an astonishing Disney-like view of the rocky cliff face with the Temple of Sibyl above it. The rocky crags, the grotto and the alarmingly high bridges to the island provoke a sense of hazard while allowing the park to be experienced from a giddying variety of viewpoints.[106]

The essence of Alphand and Barillet-Deschamps' planting was to use large-leafed trees – like Paulownias, Catalpas and Magnolias – as background and plants with prominent foliage – like Acanthus, Begonias and Cannas – as foreground. Other exotic plants such as bananas and bamboos were also used in groups or isolated clumps. Latterly this style of planting has been reintroduced in the park. Chadwick observed that Olmsted was critical of Barilett-Deschamps' 'profuse use of certain, novel, exotic, and sickly forms of vegetation'. The remarkable feature of the woody planting at Buttes-Chaumont is the 'profuse use' of silver-leafed cedars; yellow-leafed robinias and copper-leafed beech trees. Sickly or not, they certainly combine with the extraordinarily steep lawns to contribute to the theatrical 'other-worldliness' of the park – nineteenth-century virtual reality.[107]

Merivale noted that Alphand's 'rules' for the design of paths – his third layer – produced continuous curves offering constantly changing views. They generally meet at acute angles. They were generally concealed – in much the way that Paxton concealed paths in Birkenhead Park – by recessing them slightly. This conflicts with Robinson's view that French gardens had 'too many walks' and that 'the way these are wound about in symmetrical twirlings is quite ridiculous. In these cases,' Robinson suggested, 'the garden is made for the walks, not the walks for the gardens'. Marceca suggested that the 'curved and serpentine lines act as metaphors for both the technological and the biological cycles'. Meyer noted that at Buttes-Chaumont the vehicular circulation system – originally for horse-drawn carriages – inscribes the base of the mounds whereas the pedestrian circulation system provides access to the high points in the park. At the end of the twentieth century private cars were an unwarranted nuisance on the carriage roads, but the winding paths continued to reveal a superb sequence of unfolding views within the park and out to the city.[108]

Buttes-Chaumont continues to display a number of Alphand's characteristic details including his 'false wood concrete' fences and step edges; his seats and his signs. The latter are part of the enduring vocabulary of municipal engineering artefacts that he designed. The park as a whole continues to reflect its origins at the meeting point of romanticized ruralism and industrialized rationalism. By the end of the twentieth century the design remained vital but the condition of much of the park had deteriorated.

MANAGEMENT AND PLANS

The design and management of City of Paris parks are handled by two separate organizations. Design is undertaken by the project section of the Direction des Parcs, Jardins et Espaces Verts. Maintenance is divided by *arrondissement* and is undertaken by directly employed staff. Management of parks by the City of Paris is highly centralized and does not lend itself to the establishment of 'friends' or other direct consultative groups.[109]

At a press conference on 5 November 1999 the City of Paris announced an ambitious programme for restoration of the park. Salient points from the ensuing *communiqué* were that:

- the park had just celebrated its 132nd birthday. Its pathways, rock formations, water effects and planting all continue to awaken the imagination; active people continue to appreciate its undulating landform; walkers and dreamers are still seduced by its vegetation and picturesque character
- the most important streams are dry; access to some rock areas is prohibited; the rock face of the island – the spectacular centrepiece of the park – needs stabilization
- restoration works are proposed that will reinstate the character of the original composition and respect the spirit of the age of its creation – while employing current technology
- work is required to overcome underground instability; damage to hard surfaces; erosion of path edges; deterioration of the drainage system; leakage from streams and problems of overgrown vegetation around them; deterioration of false rock features; instability of foundations for the three bridges; structural impoverishment of topsoil; invasive vegetation and departures from the spirit of the original planting; profusion of fencing types; deterioration of site furniture – necessitating replacement by pieces from the original moulds; deterioration of buildings – requiring restoration of their polychromatic rural character with a combination of wood, brick and tilework, and deterioration of fittings.

The *communiqué* announced a competition to appoint a team – including a landscape architect and architect – to design and oversee the works for the restoration of the park. The estimated budget was FF447 million including taxes – FF67 million for professional fees and FF380 million for the works. The programme envisaged shortlisting five teams in May 2000; selection of the winning team in January 2001 and commencement of works on site in 2002. It was anticipated that work would be undertaken in six phases and that the rest of the park would remain open during the execution of each phase.

CONCLUSIONS

The Parc des Buttes-Chaumont originated from Haussmann's ruthless pursuit of Napoléon III's will to remodel Paris and provide it with 'English-style' urban parks. In the event, the plan form of the Parc des Buttes-Chaumont is more like an elegy to the French curve. Many commentators become preoccupied with the technological metaphors inherent in the plan form. But the landform is the most remarkable feature of the park. It results from an extraordinarily accomplished act of land restoration that remains an object lesson in the use of earthworks to create spaces and manipulate visitors' perceptions. It provides panoramic views across Paris and allows complete escape from the city in a remarkably limited land area. This sense of escape is heightened by the combination of sublime and picturesque effects, the sweeping lawns, the exotic planting and the rustic detailing. Buttes-Chaumont is a place apart and yet very much part of Napoléon III, Haussmann and Alphands' Paris. Heavily used by doggers and joggers, it is about to undergo a much-needed programme of restoration to atone for more than 130 years of heavy use.

8 Parc de la Villette, Paris

35 hectares (86 acres)

INTRODUCTION

Proclaimed the urban park of the twenty-first century since its conception in the 1970s, Parc de la Villette is a major production by the French national government. (see location map on page 32). It is an event-driven cultural quarter in three main parts on the site of a former abattoir. Thirty-five of the 55 hectares of the site are allocated to public open space – the park proper. The remainder is occupied by La Cité des Sciences et de l'Industrie – a national science museum primarily located in the converted 1960s' abattoir building, and La Cité de la Musique – a purpose-built national centre for the study and performance of music and dance. The 35 hectares of the park include the converted nineteenth-century Grande Halle (Great Hall). It is the largest public park in central Paris. The three parts of la Villette are under the direction of three different organizations – each separately answerable to different ministers of the French national government.

The design of the park was the outcome of an international design competition staged in 1982–83. It attracted 472 entries from thirty-seven different countries, overwhelming the panel of twenty-one judges. The panel called for second submissions from nine short-listed joint winners. The eventual winner was French-Swiss/American, Architectural Association-educated architect Bernard Tschumi. His submission was an essay in the architectural theory of 'deconstruction' or 'disjunction'. The design comprised three layers – a grid of 'points' (bright red metal *folies*) and a series of 'lines' describing a set of (what turned out to be very flat, geometric) 'surfaces'. It derived more from postmodern literary analysis than from landscape or architectural design precedents. And it reflects the emergence of computer technology capable of representing this type of layering.[110]

Tschumi stated that the urban park 'can no longer be conceived as an undefiled Utopian world-in-miniature, protected from vile reality' and that his park 'could be conceived as one of the largest *buildings* ever constructed'. He proclaimed that it flew in the face of the conventions of modern architecture and the emerging tenets of postmodern architecture. His design treated the site as a *tabula rasa* whose only context was urbanity. It kicked sand into many landscape architect's faces and it probably became the most written about and mimicked urban park since Central Park, New York. Anglo-Saxon commentators have described the organization of the competition as 'daft' and the park itself as 'silly'. Geoffrey Jellicoe observed that English landscape architects would have placed Tschumi's design last out of the nine second-stage submissions – 'and indeed wondered why it was placed at all'. English, also AA-educated, architect Piers Gough proclaimed that 'hell will be like this; a place where vicious intellects deny natural pleasures; where time off will be more mechanized than time at work'.[111]

HISTORY

Development of La Villette

La Villette (literally 'small town') is on a plain between the hills of Buttes-Chaumont and Montmartre. There were Roman and then medieval settlements in the area. It was also a resort

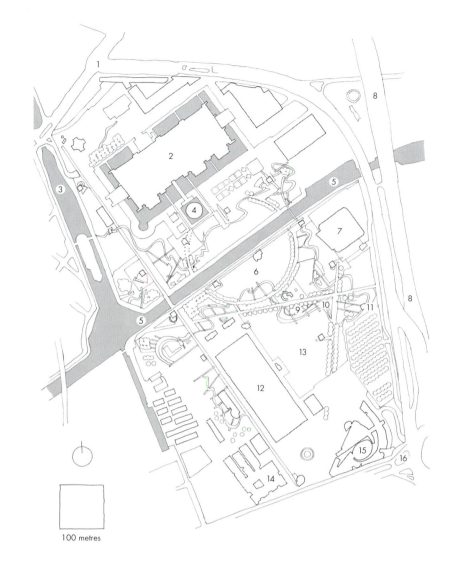

100 metres

destination from the fourteenth century for royal and ecclesiastical dignitaries, and a source of wine, cereals and market produce for the City of Paris. By the sixteenth century the area had 400 inhabitants. La Villette continued to perform resort and agricultural functions during the seventeenth and eighteenth centuries. It was constituted as a municipality in 1790 following the erection in 1785 of the city wall. La Villette remained a separate market town with tax-free status and a thriving entertainment industry. Early in the nineteenth century shortage of water in Paris prompted Napoléon I (Emperor 1802–15) to order the construction of the 25-kilometre-long Canal de l'Ourcq to bring drinking water from the River Ourcq to an 800 metre by 80 metre rectangular reservoir – le Bassin de la Villette. The Canal was opened in 1808. It was improved in 1812 to allow navigation and extended

southward in 1821 (Canal St-Martin) and northward in 1827 (Canal St-Denis) to create a direct link to the looping River Seine. By 1840, 15,000 boats per year were using the canals. The reservoir still provides 60 per cent of Paris's non-potable water.[112]

Between 1800 and 1859 the population of Paris grew from 547,000 to 1 million. In 1853 Napoléon III (Emperor 1852–71) authorized Haussmann to orchestrate the complete reorganization of the City of Paris. In 1860 the city was expanded from twelve to twenty *arrondissements* (districts); eleven whole communes and parts of thirteen others were annexed. La Villette was annexed to the 19th *arrondissement*. This coincided with the construction of new military defences on the line of the current Boulevard Périphérique and the concentration of particular industrial activities into specified zones.

Haussmann's proposal for La Villette combined a slaughterhouse and meat market for the whole city in one location. He oversaw development of a 40-hectare complex that came to employ 3000 people. Haussmann regarded the project as an accomplishment parallel to his road-building operations. The Grande Halle of the cattle market – 250 metres by 85 metres – was completed in 1867, the year the abattoir was opened.[113]

The abattoir complex was served by a rail link from the south. The ramparts were dismantled in 1919 and were replaced by the – much expanded in the 1970s – Boulevard Périphérique. In 1923 the Canal St-Denis and the Canal de l'Ourcq were deepened and their locks lengthened. Despite its accessibility, business at the abattoir began to run into trouble from the early twentieth century. The equipment was modernized in 1930; but a more serious threat arose in the 1950s with the growth of refrigeration and the capacity to kill livestock where they were reared. Nevertheless, a decision was made in 1959 to demolish the dilapidated abattoir and to build a new national meat market – the 270 metre by 110 metre by 40 metre-high Grande Salle – on land north of the Canal de l'Ourcq. High-rise public housing was erected south of the canal in the 1960s and the adjacent Grande Halle lay empty. Technical and financial problems delayed completion of the new abattoir. It eventually opened in 1969 but only operated as a slaughterhouse until 1974.

Designation and Development of the Park

Meanwhile, under a convention made with the national government in August 1970, the City of Paris gave up all rights and obligations over la Villette and ceded the land and its management to the state. The national government announced in October 1973 that the slaughterhouses would cease operation in March 1974; that the land would be allocated for low-income housing; economic activities and a considerable area for social and public facilities. Between 1974 and 1979 – under the presidency of Valéry Giscard d'Estaing (presided 1974–81) – a design competition was staged and abandoned – largely because of disagreement over the allocation of land between park and housing. Investigations were made into the feasibility of converting the slaughterhouse into a Museum of Science and Industry, and into the development of an auditorium. Finally, in October 1978, President d'Estaing announced the decision to establish the Museum of Science, an auditorium and a park.

In July 1979 the Établissement Public du Parc de la Villette (EPPV; Public Authority for the

Parc de la Villette) was created. During 1980 the design competition between twenty-seven French architects for development of the Science Museum was staged and won by Adrien Fainsilber. But little progress was made with the park until after the election in May 1981 of President François Mitterand (President 1981–95). Mitterand visited the site in July that year and reaffirmed the mission of the EPPV. In March 1982 he announced a programme of *Grands Projets* – major development proposals for his (first) seven-year period in office. La Villette formed a major part of that programme. The Museum of Science and the park were augmented by a greatly expanded scope for the auditorium to become a Cité de la Musique including the Conservatoire National Supérieur de la Musique. In May 1982 Minister of Culture Jacques Lang announced the competition for the park; in August French architects Reichen and Robert were appointed for restoration of the Grande Halle; in December the nine winners of the park competition were announced. In March 1983 Bernard Tschumi was declared winner of the second stage of the competition.

A design competition for the Cité de la Musique was launched in January 1984. Christian de Portzamparac was eventually selected as architect for the first phase in January 1985 by the President himself. That same month Mitterand opened the restored Grande Halle and in May 1985 he opened the Géode – the 36-metre diameter stainless steel-faced sphere containing an IMAX cinema directly south of the Science Museum. In November 1985 Philippe Starck won an international competition for the design of street furniture for the park. In March 1986 President Mitterand returned to open the Science Museum itself and in October 1987 he was back again to open the first section of the park. He eventually made his final official visit in January 1995 to open the Cité de la Musique. Meanwhile, in 1993, the EPPV became the Établissement Public du Parc et de la Grande Halle de la Villette (EPPGHV) and the Établissement Public de la Cité de la Musique was created; setting them alongside the Établissement Public de la Cité des Sciences, created in January 1985, as the bodies responsible for running the three principal components at La Villette. Construction of the park was completed in 1995.

Size and Condition of the Site at the Time of Designation

The 55-hectare site is more than 1000 metres from north to south and more than 700 metres at its widest point. Lodewijk Baljon, team-member for one of the nine short-listed park designs, noted that the site had been 'completely built on or paved' and that 'after the demolition of various buildings, a surface layer of asphalt, concrete, sand, rubble and fragments of foundations remained'. He also noted that at greater depths 'there are layers of deposits, chiefly marl, between the hills of Montmartre and Buttes-Chaumont. The uppermost layer consists of clay deposits and is seven metres thick. This layer is scarcely porous . . . and can be dug to a depth of 10 metres without encountering ground water'. Baljon noted the impact of the two existing buildings (but not their microclimatic effects); that the slopes of Buttes-Chaumont were visible to the south and that noise from the Périphérique was 'constant and penetrating'.[114]

Tschumi claimed that his design was 'motivated by the fact that the site is not "virgin land" but is located in a populated semi-industrial quarter, and includes two enormous existing structures'. He also claimed, however, that his design 'rejected context, encouraging intertextuality and the dispersion of meaning. It subverted context. La Villette,' he stated, 'is anti-contextual. It has no relation to its surroundings. Its plan subverts the very notion of borders on which "context" depends.' He went on to state that 'the inadequacy of the civilization vs. nature polarity under modern city conditions has invalidated the time honoured prototype of the park as an image of nature'. This polemic suggests that the actual condition of the site was of little or no significance to Tschumi. His proposals were not site specific. They were 'a diagram looking for a site'.[115]

Key Figures in the Establishment of the Park

Clearly there are two principal figures in the establishment of the park – President François Mitterand (1916–96) and architect Bernard Tschumi (b. 1944). Deyan Sudjic noted that 'nothing . . . was to prepare Paris for the scale of what was to come when Mitterand took over the presidency (in 1981). After a brief pause for reflection, he adopted a few of the projects started by Giscard d'Estaing . . . and added a whole stream of his own ideas . . . and presented them all as a single package, the *Grands Projets*, to be completed in time for the celebrations marking the bicentennial of the French Revolution in 1989'. Sudjic described the projects as 'a highly self-conscious attempt to remodel the fundamental character of Paris, a mixture of hubris and cultural ambition that that could only be French'. Comparisons with the endeavours of Napoléon III and Baron Haussmann are inevitable. The fundamental difference, however, is that while

Haussmann's work can be seen as a 'highly original urban recomposition that wavered between nostalgia and the *tabula rasa*', the *Grands Projets* were individual building projects that treated their sites as passive recipients of vain monuments to 'culture'.[116]

La Villette was, of course, the largest of these sites. And Tschumi was very much the kind of designer whose theory-driven, anti-contextual, neo-constructivist approach suited Mitterand's culturally ambitious programme. Tschumi has a culturally diverse background – studying in Zurich and Paris; teaching in London and the United States. He came to the project with relatively little practical experience and the competition provided him with an excellent vehicle to project his theories of 'disjunction'. These theories revolve around the disaggregation of architecture, architectural programming and the meaning of architecture. Tschumi's specific aim was 'to prove that it was possible to construct a complex architectural organization without resorting to traditional rules of composition, hierarchy and order'. His investigations did not directly address issues in landscape architecture – other than to make some broad generalizations about urban parks. This is a pity. As Christophe Girot pointed out, the realities of landscape architecture are 'far more complex' than those of building architecture since they have 'much more to do with space and time; ten or twenty years is almost nothing in terms of development for a landscape'. Tschumi is clearly a radical thinker who might contribute more to the discipline of landscape architecture if he were to investigate it more fully.[117]

PLANNING AND DESIGN

Location

The park is located at the north-eastern edge of the tightly defined central area of Paris. It is essentially a 'transitional zone between the old city districts, with their dense and ordered fabric, and the neighbouring suburban municipalities, whose development has been more open and less ordered'. This 'transitional zone' has traditionally been a primarily working-class residential area with a significant ethnic component. It sits between the Portes (Gates) de Pantin and de la Villette on the Boulevard Périphérique – the multi-lane inner ring road that now occupies the line of nineteenth-century defences around the French capital. There are Metro stations near each of these gates. The location of the Cité des Sciences to the north of the Canal de l'Ourcq and of the Cité de la Musique at the southern end of the site casts the park in the role of a mall between two major anchors.[118]

Competition Brief

The briefing documents for the design competition were extraordinarily detailed. They were driven by an overwhelming desire that the competition should generate a new model for the urban park – an urban park for the twenty-first century. Excerpts from these documents are given in Baljon's *Designing Parks*. A summary is given here.

Observations on existing urban parks were that:

- in the seventeenth and eighteenth centuries Parisian parks played a part in the social life of the city; they were constantly visited by a miscellaneous, primarily adult population; they were places to exchange ideas, to hear items of news and to look for amorous adventure
- during the eighteenth century Haussmann realised a hierarchical system of squares, parks and woods supplemented by tree-lined avenues; in addition to providing embellishment, green space had to serve as an antidote to the pollution and discomforts of the city – they provided clean spaces in which Parisians, particularly children and families, could stroll and relax
- during the past thirty years urban open space had become green space demonstrating impoverished social function and diminished creative considerations
- the Parc de la Villette offered a unique opportunity to reflect on the functions – which determine the atmosphere and activities of urban

parks – and the forms that were becoming manifest in landscape architecture.

The Objectives noted that:

- Parisian parks had become green areas for the non-working population – life and the city are elsewhere; the Parisian park was dying and, since Haussmann, nothing new had been created
- the district of la Villette had to be re-animated – the park was not so much a lung as a heart
- the park had to combine urban planning and cultural innovation; it was to serve as a new cultural instrument – it was to be part of an urban planning policy that completed the city and opened it up to the suburbs
- the cultural and symbolic reference for the park was pluralism; a meeting point of cultures, a park of reconciliation. Three unifying concepts were to be applied to the design – *urbanism/man* [sic] *and the city; pleasure/body and mind; experimentation/knowledge and action*
- the park was to be a bridge between the Science Museum and the Music Centre – a poetic solution that had neither the dictatorship of a too obvious structure nor a chaotic mosaic of unstructured eclecticism; it was not to be a jumble and collage of countless incoherent elements from a dislocated world; it was to be an open-air cultural facility.

The Programme paid particular attention to the need to address the relationship of the disparate

Canal and water chutes, Cité des Sciences (June 1999)

Philip Starck-designed seats and reflected folie (June 2000)

structures and activities proposed for the site and to integrate the development with its neighbourhood. The Programme identified four 'activities' – major pursuits; reception services and businesses; internal circulation; and logistics and administration – and required the provision of set areas for each of these divided into open air, sheltered, and built facilities. The Programme also contained complex diagrammatic representations of the functional relationship between the activities.[119]

Original Design Concept

Tschumi's design is based on the (extensively documented) structure of three superimposed systems:

- *points* – a grid of twenty-five bright red metal-faced *folies* derived from a 10.8 metre cubic module on a regular 120 metre grid across the site. The *folies* – representing 'disjunctions and dissociations between use, form and social values' – are arranged in a point grid that 'inherently suggests the bars of the asylum or prison'; that 'articulates space and activates it' and that 'plays a political role, rejecting the ideological a priori of the master plans of the past'. They accommodate many of the programmatic requirements of the brief
- *lines* of pedestrian movement comprising two perpendicular galleries parallel with the two canals; the sinuous 'cinematic' circuit of sequential views on a promenade through ten individual theme gardens – each garden representing the cinematic frames, and the walkway representing the sound track; and direct *allées* of trees between the principal activity areas on the site
- *surfaces* – the largely flat, open-air activity areas of the site – surfaced according to the particular activity for which they are programmed and with residual spaces finished in traditional Parisian sealed gravel.

The design should be considered in terms of Tschumi's stated objectives of finding an 'organizing structure that could exist independent of use, a structure without center or hierarchy, a structure that would negate the simplistic assumption of a causal relationship between a programme and the resulting *architecture*' [my italics] and staging a 'series of tensions that enhances the dynamism of the park'.[120]

In the event, Tschumi's grid of *folies* and his perpendicular *galeries* line up very tidily with the orthogonal grid already established by the massive nineteenth and twentieth century abattoir buildings and by the alignment of the canals. Given the substantial presence of these artefacts, subservient geometric manoeuvres were one of the main devices through which the park could engage with the wider site. The grid – so railed against by Olmsted and Cleveland in the nineteenth century – is a favourite form for large-scale spatial organization in the twentieth century. It serves to disperse traffic in North American cities and it can be used to disperse people throughout urban parks – particularly people who are seeking isolation.[121]

Tschumi's first-stage entry – without the *galeries* – was more adventurous than the second-stage entry, which was dominated by a regular, almost classical, axiality. The *galeries* became the dominant element in the layout and reinforced the rigidity of the grid of *folies*. Indeed, a publicity document on the 'architecture' of the park produced by the EPPGHV in 1995 stated that the *folies* 'punctuate the entire surface of the park and confer a homogeneity and a tidy rhythm on it'. Not exactly what Tschumi seemed to be saying. They are, however, its most characteristic feature.

By the early twenty-first century the *folies* were beginning to be obscured by the maturing plane trees lining the *allées*. Initial planting was largely unilateral. This has been balanced by subsequent planting on the other sides of main *allées*. Ironically, the vegetation about which Tschumi wrote so little is helping to create the disjunction about which he wrote so much. There is also a sense that as the trees have grown, so has the collection of seats, signs and showpieces – particularly along the north–south Galerie de la Villette. Jellicoe noted in 1983 that 'Tschumi's design for the spectacle of people in movement is not . . . very convincing'. Treib commented in 1999 that Tschumi's cinematographic circuit differed from precedents like Gordon Cullen's serial vision in *Townscape* in that it dealt with impressions of reality rather than with reality itself.[122]

The components that do most to 'enhance the dynamism of the park' are the one-off, individual features – particularly the ten 'theme' gardens – particularly Alexander Chemetoff's Bamboo Garden – the largest at 3000 square metres, and Bernard Leitner's adjacent Sound Garden. They are set below Tschumi's flat grass surfaces – now justifiably known as the Prairie du Cercle and the Prairie du Triangle. Well conceived but needing high levels of maintenance, the gardens provide a welcome change of level. This provides enclosure and enables them to provide a sense of escape; to play to the senses; to create their own microclimate and then to exploit it. They reveal 'what the park chooses to ignore: climate, earth, cycles of water, and the networks of complexity that characterize the urban landscape'. Starck's revolving aluminium seats are a welcome individual feature; as are the long-lived dragon slide (which preceded Tschumi's involvement) and Claes Oldenburg's gigantic bits of buried bicycle that appear through the otherwise dreary Prairie du Cercle. Elsewhere metal – *Géode, galeries, folies*, litter bins, Starck's seats – predominates.[123]

MANAGEMENT AND USAGE

Managing Organization

The park is managed by the L'Établissement Public du Parc et de la Grande Halle de la Villette (EPPGHV). This is a public body created in January 1993 and attached to the Ministry of Culture and run broadly on the lines of a commercial enterprise. Direction of the EPPGHV is controlled by a Conseil d'Administration. The Conseil has fourteen members: three appointed by the Minister of Culture – including the President of the EPPGHV; eight with proscribed rights – comprising two representatives from each of the Ministries of Culture and Finance; the President of the Conservatory of Music; the President of the Cité de la Musique; the President of the Science Museum, and the Prefect of the Ile-de-France; three members elected from the salaried staff for three-year terms of office. The Conseil d'Administration also has participants acting in a consultative capacity. These include, for instance, the Managing Director of the EPPGHV.

There are two other public bodies directing activities at la Villette – la Cité de la Musique (including the Conservancy) – which falls under the remit of the Ministry of Culture, and la Cité des Science et de l'Industrie (CSI) – which comes under the remit of the Ministry of Industry, Post and Telecommunications. The three bodies are each symbolized by a different-coloured geometrical shape derived from the layout of the park and worked into the 'logo-style' for la Villette. The park is represented by a green triangle; the Cité des Sciences by a red square and the Cité de la Musique by a blue circle. Cooperation between these three public bodies is (intended to be) achieved by the formation, in September 1996, of a Council of Presidents that convenes bimonthly on matters of a 'supra-institutional' nature. The Council deals with issues like promotion as a tourist destination; operation of visitor season ticket initiatives; co-ordination of special events such as millennium celebrations and major festivals. There are also a number of autonomous cultural organizations operating facilities at la Villette. These include the Hot-Brass (latterly Triangle Rouge) jazz café; the Zénith rock venue; the theatre Paris-Villette and the Théatre international de la langue française. Maintenance of the 8 hectares of *prairies* and the 3 hectares of shrub planting and nearly 3000 trees in the park is undertaken by a team of five full-time gardeners under the direction of the EPPGHV.

Funding

Funding for the EPPGHV comes from a combination of government subvention and ticket sales. The running costs for 1998 were FF195.8 million – of which FF122.2 million (62.4 per cent) was state subvention and the remaining FF73.6 million (37.6 per cent) was mainly received from charges to other site operators and from events. The breakdown of operational expenditure for 1998 is summarized in Table 8.1. This shows an exceptional FF65.8 million for major repairs and improvements to buildings and external areas. The FF89.5 million in running costs includes FF63.4 million in staff salary and employment costs.

Place de la Fontaine aux Lions to south of Grande Halle (June 2000)

Table 8.1 Breakdown of operational expenditure for 1998 (FF millions)

	Cultural productions	Operations, maintenance, security	Total
Running costs	106.3	89.5	195.8
Capital costs	11.9	53.9	65.8
Total	*118.2*	*143.4*	*261.6*

Source: EPPGHV Rapport d'Activité 1998

Table 8.2 gives a breakdown of budgets into running and capital costs for the first few years of operation of the EPPGHV. This shows that 1998 was an exceptional year both in terms of rise in expenditure overall and in terms of relative and absolute increase in expenditure on capital items. These included, in addition to work on the buildings, major investment in the irrigation system for the park. The average figure is roughly the same as the annual budget for maintenance of London's (also state-financed) Royal Parks.

Table 8.2 Breakdown of running and capital costs (with percentages) (1994–98)

Year	Running costs (%)	Capital costs (%)	Total
1994	162.7 (83)	34.5 (17)	197.2
1995	151.7 (86)	25.7 (14)	177.4
1996	170.5 (87)	25.0 (13)	195.5
1997	166.6 (87)	25.6 (13)	192.2
1998	195.8 (75)	65.8 (25)	261.6

Source: EPPGHV Centre de Ressources

User Characteristics

It is estimated that the overall site of la Villette receives around 10 million visits per year. Figures for 1992 recorded 8.4 million visitors overall, of which 2.5 million visited the outdoor attractions. Figures for 1996 showed a total of 9 million with 3.6 million and 0.9 million respectively for the use of open spaces and attendance at events. The French/English guide produced by the EPPGHV in 1999 gave a total of 10 million. Publishing the overall figure reflected the emerging policy of trying to market la Villette as a complete cultural ensemble rather than as three separate facilities.[124]

This reflects the recommendations in the December 1996 report by Sophie Tiévant of surveys on the use and image of the site. She found that:

- each of three main organizations occupying the site targeted and serviced its specific users as if it were an individual entity
- users of the park had a clearer idea of the range of facilities available on the site than did the users of the two main facilities, but park users tended to ignore the indoor spaces
- perception of an integrated ensemble of activities was carried better by the park than by the other activities. Comments included observations that the only common thread was the cultural theme of the facilities.

Tiévant concluded that:

- the site operators were not benefiting from the added value of the concentration of diverse facilities. Any such benefits were primarily the result of spontaneity on the part of users
- the site should be promoted as a tourist destination, a family facility and a place to which to make return visits
- the site is located in a predominantly working-class district – but provides cultural facilities particularly for young people from the suburbs.

She recommended that:

- activities should be encouraged outside the buildings
- the level of information and publicity on the site as a whole should be increased
- a permanent exposition be established on the history of the site
- multi-pass tickets be made extensively applicable
- the name la Villette be used for the site as a whole rather than for any individual enterprise.[125]

Extensive user surveys have also been carried out by the EPPGHV itself. These are primarily directed towards market research for the facilities and events in the park. They also provide a clear profile of the people using the park – *les espaces de plein air*. The surveys found that there were about 3 million visitors to the park in 1993. The studies from 1993, 1994 and 1995 showed a very young age profile for park users (Table 8.3).

Table 8.3 Age profile for users

Age	%
< 24	49
24–33	24
34–43	13
44–53	6
54 <	8
Total	*100%*

In terms of origins of visitors, the surveys found that:

- 65 per cent of park users lived in Paris compared with 70 per cent of users of the open-air cinema and 20 per cent of users of the Salon de l'étudiant
- 44 per cent of park users lived in the 19th *arrondissement* compared with 11 per cent of the

users of the open-air cinema and 3 per cent of users of the Expo-langues

- 23 per cent of park users lived in the suburbs compared with 69 per cent of users of the Salon de l'étudiant and 25 per cent of users of the open-air cinema.

Park users therefore were predominantly young, living locally and relatively less educated. Users of the facilities within the park were generally older, lived further away and were relatively more educated. This paints a picture of a place tending to work on two distinct levels – as a set of cultural facilities for a widespread population and as a casual recreation facility for the local population – a neighbourhood park. Requests from the open space users included better signage; more comfortable places to sit and better shelter; more extensive planting; more information on cultural aspects of the site; greater legibility of the activities in the *folies* – more 'standard', park-like facilities.

Bamboo Garden and Sound Garden (June 2000)

CONCLUSIONS

Parc de la Villette was intended to be a model for the urban park of the twenty-first century. The competition for its design attracted a huge number of entries. The winning design by architect Bernard Tschumi has been widely documented – not least by him. His theories were exciting, radical and iconoclastic. The results on the ground do not justify the fanfare that preceded them. They suggest that architectural theory does not translate easily into landscape architectural practice. Meyer drew attention to Tschumi's ignorance of landscape history in the design of Parc de la Villette. She suggested that his systems of points, lines and surfaces might benefit from a fourth system – the landscape. She is probably right – except that the existing landscape, the 'genius of the place' might be seen as the first system. Essential underlay; not *tabula rasa*. This ignorance of landscape architectural history is manifest in Tschumi's suggestion that parks are *hortus conclusus* and 'the replica of Nature'.[126]

Tschumi missed and dismissed the role of the park as interpreter of time and place. This denied him the opportunity to explore the relationship of the (Parisian) urban dweller and nature in the twenty-first century. Instead, he produced an ultimately unsatisfying exploration of non-place-specific architectural theories. He created an open space between government cultural institutions. The park continues to suffer from trying to mediate between two major cultural entities and two major existing structures on a site divided in two by a canal. Baljon noted, however, that Tschumi's design is 'exceptionally suited to involving various designers (artists, architects, garden designers, industrial designers) in realizing the plan . . . and that this is possibly a true characteristic of the park of the twenty-first century'. Certainly the participation of designers like Chemetoff, Leitner, Starck and Oldenburg helps to punctuate the park with brighter moments.

Slowly *allées* and groves of trees are subsuming Tschumi's sea of metal; the lawns flood with people and the gardens complete the contrast with the city. 'Hell' is becoming more relaxed. Overall, however, Parc de la Villette is not so much a new form of urban park as a culturally programmed, architectural theory-driven, state-financed setting for cultural facilities. It has contributed a great deal of debate – but not much more – to the development of park design. Tschumi stated that 'the difference between the theorist and the practitioner . . . is that the theorist's only responsibility is to his [*sic*] theory'. Park designers are responsible for creating places for users rather than for themselves.[127]

9 Parque de María Luisa, Seville

39 hectares (97 acres)

INTRODUCTION

The Parque de María Luisa was converted in the early twentieth century from a private royal park to a public park. Designed in its current form by French landscape architect Jean-Claude-Nicolas Forestier (1861–1930), it was named for Princess María Luisa de Borbón y Borbón (d. 1897), Duchess of Montpensier and sister of Queen Isabella II of Spain (reigned 1843–68). It remains an enchanting product of a skilful mediation converting the pre-existing park into, first, the site of an International Exposition and, then, a public park. Forestier achieved this transition through adherence to two of the principal paradigms of landscape architecture – respect for existing site qualities and respect for nuances of regional design, history and climate. He converted an already well-treed site with a number of historic settings into an essay in Moorish landscape design for a public park. The park has a strong rectilinear layout punctuated with tile-studded *glorietas* (arbours dedicated to local literary figures) and shaded from the intensity of the Andalusian summer by a canopy of deciduous, principally plane, trees. To the south and east the subtle intimacy of Forestier's landscape design gives way to the bombast of architect Aníbal Gonzáléz's designs for the Plaza de España and the Plaza de América. These two exhibition spaces were formed as extensions to the park so that it might host the Ibero-American Exposition in 1929. Forestier's original design, prepared in 1911, was intended for an Exposition to be staged in 1914 but that was postponed because of the outbreak of the First World War.[128]

HISTORY

Designation as a Park

The site was designated as a public park a few years before its selection as the site for an Exposition. The principal reason for its allocation in 1893 for public use was as part of an arrangement to create better commercial transport links between the River Guadalquivir to the west and the railway station to the north-east. The need for healthy urban living conditions and opportunities for public recreation were also seen as secondary justifications for the park. There had, however, already been public parks in Seville since the 1830s when a Jardin de Aclimatación (botanical and zoological garden) and the Jardines de las Delicias (Gardens of Delights) – between the river and the site of the Parque de María Luisa – were established. The Jardines de las Delicias were extended in 1869 to 7.5 hectares according to designs prepared in Paris by horticulturist Jean-Pierre Barillet-Deschamps. In common with other European cities, Seville experienced rapid population growth during the nineteenth century. And in common with other Spanish cities, there was demand for public use of royal land.[129]

The site formed part of the estate of the Palace of San Telmo which had been allocated in 1849 – by virtue of a law passed by Isabella II – for the use of the Duke and Duchess of Montpensier. On 13 March 1893 the municipal government of Seville arranged with María Luisa that she should retain the palace and immediately adjacent gardens but that the city would take over the land that was attached to the palace to the south of the new avenue. The agreement stated that the site should 'offer to the city an extensive and pleasant park to serve the

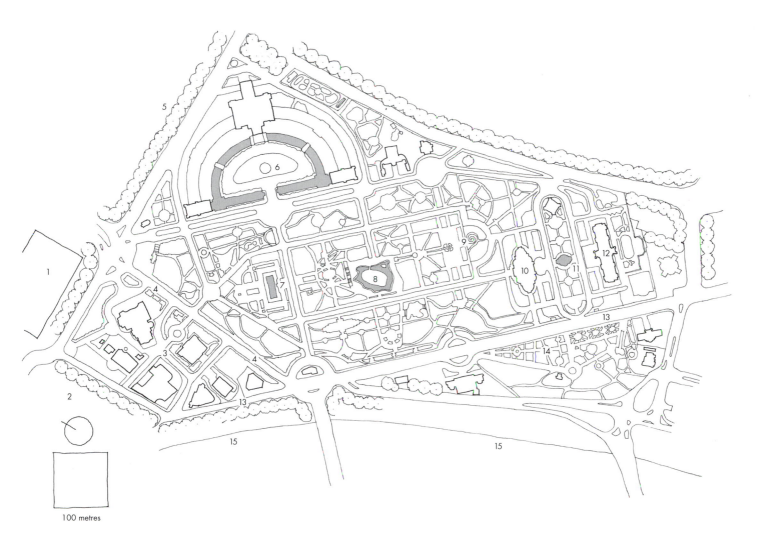

needs of modern life'. Plans from 1894 show the area of the nascent park and new road as 20.7 hectares. The park and Jardines de las Delicias (Garden of Delights)now have a total area of 39 hectares.[130]

History and Condition of the Site

Andalusia, the southernmost region of Spain, was first settled in about 25,000 BC. It was subsequently conquered or inhabited by the Phoenicians, Greeks, Carthaginians and, from about 200 BC to 500 AD, was part of the Roman Empire. Moors – Muslims of mixed Arab and Berber descent – conquered southern Spain in 710 and controlled much of the peninsular until the final fall in 1492 of Granada, also in Andalusia, to the Catholic Monarchs. In 1503 Seville was granted a monopoly on trade with the 'New World' and Spain was charged by papal order with 'converting the Indians'. For nearly two centuries, until the focus of trade moved to Cadiz at

the mouth of the Guadalquivir, Seville was the richest port of the most powerful nation in Europe.[131]

On the south side of the walled city, between the Jerez Gate and the river, the area named San Telmo – for the patron saint of navigators – had been occupied since the Middle Ages by the Bishops of Morocco. This land was transferred to the Holy Office in 1560. It was intended that a college for navigators be built there. Although a college was established on the site in 1628, plans for a substantial marine university occupying arable land in San Telmo were not made until 1681. Construction of the building now known as the Palacio de San Telmo was largely completed by 1724 – although further additions were made until the 1770s. It was designed by architect Leonardo de Figueroa (1650–1730) 'creator of the Sevillian Baroque style' involving the use of 'cut-brick construction in white or yellow walls surrounded with red trim' which became characteristic of the city.

Typical signage (May 1999)

The adjacent tobacco factory – famed as the setting for Bizet's 1875 opera *Carmen*, now part of the University of Seville and still the second largest building in Spain – was also completed in the 1770s.[132]

The palace building served as a marine university until 1847. It was used briefly as railway offices and then as part of the Literary University before its acquisition by the Dukes of Montpensier in 1849. The extensive and fertile *huertas* (orchards or horticultural gardens) of Naranjal and grounds of the convent of San Diego to the south were attached to the building when it became a ducal palace. They comprised about 150 hectares. It has been noted that within this area French landscape architect Lecolant designed 'romantic gardens with abundant picturesque elements . . . which stretched to what is today the Plaza de América'. Negotiations for their transfer to the city of Seville began with the death in 1890 of Duke Antonio of Borbón and were completed in 1893. The palace itself continued to be occupied by María Luisa until her death in 1897. It then became a metropolitan seminary until 1990 and was restored ahead of the Exposition in 1992 to become the seat of the President of the Andalusia region.[133]

A plan of Seville from 1890 shows a relatively regular pattern of planting across the site. Imbert, however, wrote about 'the English-style vegetation of the old San Telmo gardens' noting that Forestier had to deal with 'existing irregular clumps of mature trees'. Forestier himself noted that 'some of the avenues are irregular, because they were already there, and as they were bordered by beautiful, old trees, it would have been a mistake to disturb them'. The park was virtually abandoned from 1893 until approval of the site in 1910 by King Alphonso XIII as the venue for the Hispano-American Exposition. There were reports during the 1900s of plants being sold to private gardens, of trees being sold for carpentry, of the pigeons being stolen by breeders, of offers by a lion tamer for the establishment of a zoological collection, of proposals for the creation of a sports field and of complaints from the municipal engineer about public respect for the vegetation and water bodies in the park. In January 1911 the Executive Committee for the Seville Exposition invited Forestier to redesign the park as the focus of an event then scheduled for 1914.[134]

Key Figures in the Establishment of the Park

María Luisa agreed to release the land for the park in 1893. It was not until 1909 that Seville industrialist Don Rodriguez Caso made a proposal to the City of Seville for the staging of an Hispano-American Exposition. He 'saw the exposition as a

*Seating in deep shade
(May 1999)*

*Main avenue of plane
trees (May 1999)*

way to reaffirm cultural and commercial exchanges with the Americas following the loss of the Spanish colonies in the nineteenth century'. The principal individual figure in the design of the park was Jean-Claude-Nicolas Forestier. Born in 1861 Forestier graduated from École Polytechnique in 1880 and studied forestry in Nancy. In 1887 he began work under Jean-Charles-Adolphe Alphand four years before the latter's death. Alphand was by then Directeur des Travaux de Paris. Forestier was employed by the Parisian authorities for the remaining forty-three years of his life. His earlier projects included work in the Bois de Vincennes; from 1905 he redesigned the Bagatelle in the Bois de Boulogne and from 1908 to 1928 he developed the gardens of the Champs-de-Mars.[135]

Forestier's design for the Parque de María Luisa, when he was 50 years old, was the first of his many landscape design and planning projects outside France. In 1915 he went to Barcelona, at the invitation of painter José Maria Sert, where he designed the Parque Montjuich. The Marquesa de Casa Valdés described that scheme as 'one of the finest parks in Spain' and stated that Forestier 'clearly initiated a new phase of gardening in Spain'. He went on to prepare plans for a number of Moroccan cities (from 1912); to propose a park system for Buenos Aires (1924) and to develop the master plan of Havana, Cuba (from 1925 until his death in 1930).

The latter work was influenced by the City Beautiful Movement but 'contrary to Alphand or Olmsted for whom the design of parks and gardens belong to a global vision of the city, Forestier's projects and realizations appear like particular responses to specific problems, conditioned by the geographic, cultural and urban reality of the site'.[136]

Imbert noted that 'Forestier derived the morphology of his designs from a consideration of climate and its corresponding plant palette rather than from strict adaptation to function' and that he 'was able to bridge the gap between the detail-oriented sensitivity of a jardinier-artiste and the expansive scale of the land engineer and city planner'. Sitting on the verge of modernism but driven more by contextualism than by functionalism, he remains an under-acknowledged figure in twentieth century landscape architecture.[137]

PLANNING AND DESIGN

Location

The Parque de María Luisa is located directly south of the original walled settlement of Seville. Its size and proximity to the densely built-up centre of the city inevitably make it a pedestrian destination for residents and tourists. It is augmented in this respect by the associated gardens and open spaces between

Retained pond of the Glorieta de los Patos (May 1999)

Statue at edge of deep shade (May 1999)

the park and the city centre. These include the gardens of the Palacio de San Telmo, the gardens of the Alcazar – each 6 hectares in area – and the Jardin de Prado de San Sebastian, completed in 1996 on a 3.5 hectare site directly north of the Plaza de España. The latter site was once used for the burnings ordered by the Spanish Inquisition. Although the park also has a strong visual connection with the Garden of Delights and the river beyond, it is surrounded on all sides by heavily used highways and is enclosed by impenetrable ornate fencing.

Shape and Natural Landform of the Site

The central section of the park is a roughly northwest to south-east aligned rectangle of about 600 by 300 metres. The Avenida María Luisa defines an equilateral triangle at the northern end of this rectangle; the Plaza de España defines a 180-metre semicircle to the east and the Plaza de América comprises a 300-metre southward extension of the park. The Garden of Delights forms a skinny triangle separated from the rest of the park by the Avenida de las Delicias and lying between it and the River Guadalquivir. The site is generally flat, rising only gently from the river. There is a higher point to the south that Forestier used as a backdrop to his rose garden. Soils are generally sandy and free-draining and require intensive irrigation.

Original Design Concept

Forestier's design remains an object lesson in sensitivity to context. It explored Moorish garden design traditions at the same time as responding to existing site characteristics, to climatic imperatives and to the emerging functionalist paradigm of recreational utility. First he established a grid of tree-lined avenues across the site. This was skewed to accommodate existing trees and elements like the pond (now the Glorieta de los Patos) and the Monte Gurugu from Lecolant's design. It created the basic structure of the park – into which further individual gardens, water features and more exotic planting could be installed. It also created the deep shade essential to human comfort in the extraordinarily hot, humid and sunny summer conditions in Seville. The *glorietas* are shrine-like gardens that are evenly spread through the park – presaging Tschumi's grid of *folies* at la Villette. They were dedicated in the 1920s to local authors and artists. The intimate scale and subdivision of Forestier's original design were contrasted by the grafting-on to the park of architect Aníbal González's Beaux-Arts designs for the Plaza de España and the Plaza de América, and

of the gardens of the Palace of San Telmo in preparation for the 1929 Exposition.

French garden design critic Georges Gromort stated that 'the Arabic garden was small, enclosed, intimate if not secret: major routes, as well as uncovered spaces were alien concepts since the benefit of the shade would be lost. In a large park where the composition must be enlarged to accommodate crowds, the intimacy that created the charm of Arabic patios could only be reduced . . . when applied to another purpose'. But, as the Marquessa de Casa Valdés noted, 'turning such a vast area of land . . . into Moorish gardens, divided by hedges into compartments, each one different with its fountain, benches and tiles, each imparting a sense of seclusion, was a work of genius'. Helen Morgenthau Fox commented in her introduction to Forestier's *Jardins* that he exploited the qualities of colour, perfumes and privacy in his Spanish designs. He also employed one of his favourite motifs – the pergola – as a means of dividing space and displaying plants.[138]

The overpowering first impression of the park is the deep shade created by the regular rows of close-planted mature plane trees. The avenues that they create are in complete contrast to the hard, harsh, hot and out-of-scale spaces of the Plaza de España and the Plaza de América. The next layer of the park, the *glorietas*, present a further reduction in scale. Here Moorish elements are introduced – particularly tile work and water features – together with symbolic statuary, seating, site-specific signage and luxuriant planting. Functionalism meets poetry.

MANAGEMENT AND USAGE

The park currently contains more than 3500 trees; nearly 1000 palms and more than 1000 Seville orange trees. Overall it contains more than 100 different tree species. Unsurprisingly therefore it is managed largely as it was designed – for heavy public use but with gardens of distinctive regional character and with strong botanical value. Interpretation programmes – particularly of plants, bird life and of the *glorietas* – indicate that current policies are largely conservative measures intended to protect and display the existing resource. This approach is also evident in the many references in the Servicios' guide to the park which refer to maintenance 'according to the original design'.[139]

The park is directly funded by the Ayuntamiento de Sevilla (city council). It is managed by the Servicio de Parques y Jardines of the Delegación de Medio Ambiente (environment division) of the

Glorieta at edge of Monte Gurugu (May 1999)

Glorieta at edge of Monte Gurugu (May 1999)

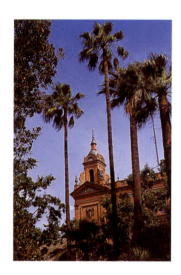

Plaza España (May 1999)

Ayuntamiento. The offices of the Servicio de Parques y Jardines are located in the former Moroccan Pavilion for the Ibero-American Exposition – an ornate mock Arabic structure with a romantic central courtyard. All maintenance work is carried out by direct labour – including largely manual irrigation. The Servicios de Parques y Jardines does not conduct detailed user surveys.

PLANS FOR THE PARK

Landscape planning for the city of Seville is currently based on setting target levels for different open space typologies for each resident on an area by area basis – an hierarchical, supply-based approach. The population of the city in 1995 was roughly 750,000. Studies for the 1997 Plan Verde para la Ciudad were based on the distribution of eight open space typologies between six city districts. These showed variations between 1.02 square metres per resident in the most poorly provided districts and 18.24 square metres in the best provided. Averages for the city overall were roughly 5 square metres of forest space and 4.5 square metres of all other types of open space.

The overall figure for the Distrito Sur – in which the Parque de María Luisa is located – was 5.74 square metres. Planning policies are aimed at reducing these deficiencies. This is demonstrated by completion in 1996 of the Jardin de Prado de San Sebastian directly north of the Plaza de España. The park itself is the main constituent of the typology of Jardines Históricos o de Interés Cultural (Gardens of Historic or Cultural Interest).

CONCLUSIONS

French landscape architecture often seems to be simplistically linked with the rectilinear designs of renaissance landscape architect André Le Nôtre (1613–1700). Chadwick, for instance, suggested that in his Spanish projects it is Forestier's 'earlier liking for the work of Le Nôtre which seems to prevail'. Certainly his design for the Parque de María Luisa is also based on a rectilinear structure – but it is not an export version of a symbolic national stereotype. In strictly formal terms it is an example of early modernism meeting the Moorish garden. But Forestier's approach was highly contextual; comparable in process (if not in product) with the pragmatic approach of Repton – a fresh approach by a mature practitioner from another country who quickly came to terms with existing site conditions and sought to relate them to regional design traditions and new use requirements. Imbert described him as 'an ambassador of knowledge extracted from the French tradition . . . situated at the juncture of the *jardin à la française* and the cubist/modernist garden'. His design for the Parque de María Luisa was a practical response to climatic conditions and is an enduring testimony to creative interpretation of context in landscape design.[140]

10 Birkenhead Park, Merseyside

58 hectares (143 acres)

INTRODUCTION

Birkenhead Park was the first publicly funded urban park in the world. Designated in 1843; designed in 1844 and built during 1845 and 1846, it was officially opened on 5 April 1847. Birkenhead is on the Wirral peninsula to the west of the River Mersey and Liverpool. The park was financed by the sale of adjacent residential building lots. By the beginning of the twenty-first century Birkenhead Park reflected the decline in financial support and deterioration of the physical fabric of many of Britain's older and larger, locally financed public parks. Despite its landmark position in the history of public parks, Birkenhead Park remains very much a local facility used almost exclusively by local residents in what is one of the poorest parts of the European Community. Unlike the provision of most other local authority services in Britain, the provision of public parks is not a statutory, legally mandated service.[141]

The park was designed by horticulturist, engineer, politician and railway enthusiast Joseph Paxton (1803–65) – best known for the design of the Crystal Palace, centrepiece of London's 'Great Exhibition' of 1851. The layout is effectively in three parts – the inner and outer park, and within the inner park, the upper and lower park. The division into inner and outer park was described by a curvaceous carriage road separating the residential plots from the pedestrian-only, pastoral inner parkland. Access was not allowed to the plots from the carriage road. Ashville Road bifurcates around the Boothby Ground and runs across the centre of the park making the carriage route a figure of eight and separating the upper and lower park. The upper and lower park each contain a lake on their north-east side fed by water drained from the grass areas.

Frederick Law Olmsted (1822–1903) visited Birkenhead Park in 1850 and 1853. It is generally accepted that the design of the carriage routes in Central Park was based on Paxton's model, and that Ashville Road was the inspiration for Olmsted and Vaux's sunken cross routes. Equally, Regent's Park was a strong precedent for Birkenhead Park. While Regent's Park was a private development by the Prince Regent, latterly King George IV (reigned 1820–30), it established a basis for significant urban parkland at the heart of commercial residential development. Construction of Regent's Park began in 1811 and the park was eventually opened to the public in 1835. Birkenhead Park was also planned as 'a self-financing venture employing the simple device of surrounding the park with plots for single houses and terraces, and selling them at an enhanced value because of their relationship with the park'.[142]

HISTORY

Designation as a Park

Until 1820 Birkenhead 'was merely a handful of houses and a few scattered farms . . . an agricultural area with a population of just over one hundred'. That year a steam-powered ferry link was established with the burgeoning port and industrial city of Liverpool on the east bank of the Mersey. Commuting commenced. The first shipyard was installed in 1825 and a street system was laid out by 1826. By 1831 Birkenhead had a population of 2569

100 metres

people. In 1833 Parliament passed an Act establishing the Birkenhead Improvement Commission to run the town. Many of the Commissioners were local merchants with businesses in Liverpool. The Select Committee on Public Walks also published its report in 1833. That Committee had been charged with recommending 'the best means of securing open spaces in the vicinity of populous towns'. The population of Birkenhead was recorded as 8529 in the 1841 census. Following a suggestion that year by Isaac Holmes, a Liverpool Councillor and Birkenhead Improvement Commissioner, Birkenhead became the first town to react to the new mood for the provision of public open space. In April 1843 the Second Birkenhead Improvement Act was passed. This provided for the Commissioners to purchase land and set aside not less than 28 hectares for a park, 'the first occasion upon which land for a freely accessible public park was obtained by Act of Parliament'.[143]

Size and Condition of the Site at the Time of Designation

The Commissioners purchased 91 hectares of 'swampy, low-lying land which fell 20 metres in a fairly uniform slope'. Of this land, 51 hectares was to be for public use. The land was part of the Birkenhead Estate owned by a Mr F. R. Price. It 'contained a small farmhouse which was known as a beer den where illegal gambling and dog fighting took place. The land was purchased cheaply because of its poor quality'. Parklands Consortium noted that on maps from 1824 there are references to 'Seven Acres Marsh' and from 1842 to 'Low Fields Lane'. Numerous sources quote Paxton's letter to his wife in 1843. 'I think I must have lost a pound of propriation for I walked at least 30 miles about to make myself master of the locality and it is not a very good situation for a park as the land is generally poor but of course it will redound more to my credit and honour to make something handsome and good out of bad materials'. Parklands Consortium noted that the site is underlain with boulder clay and that 'the drainage problems facing Paxton at the very beginning of this venture were never completely vanquished'.[144]

Key Figures in the Establishment of the Park

The key figures in the establishment of Birkenhead Park were Sir William Jackson (1805–76) – Chair of the Improvement Committee set up following the 1843 Improvement Act, designer Joseph Paxton and Park Superintendent Edward Kemp (1818–91). Jackson was the son of a Warrington doctor who died in 1810. The family moved to Liverpool. He was eventually apprenticed as an ironmonger and opened his own store. This was successful domestically and overseas. But by his mid-thirties Jackson's health was suffering from overwork and the unhealthy air of Liverpool. He sold his businesses; retired to Italy; spent a winter there and then returned to live in Birkenhead. He was soon elected to the Board of Commissioners and eventually became its Chair. In 1846 he moved to the new Manor House in Claughton – with grounds designed by Paxton – near the park. He resigned his position as Commissioner to avoid mixing his public duties with his personal dealings. That same year he became Member of Parliament for Newcastle-under-Lyme – a position he held for the next nineteen years – and, from 1865, for North Derbyshire.[145]

Paxton's life ran parallel to Jackson's. He was born into a Bedfordshire farming family; he shared Jackson's interests in new technologies – like railway construction; he went on to become a Member of Parliament – for Coventry from 1854 until shortly before his death in 1865, and was knighted. Paxton's most noted skills, however, were as a horticulturist and building designer. Parklands Consortium described him as 'one of the most exciting landscape designers of his day'. George Chadwick, however, described him as 'singularly successful in applying new techniques in the fields of horticulture and engineering . . . including not only his increasingly ingenious essays in wood and glass and iron, but also his waterworks . . . but he may not have been a very original artist in other spheres. In his gardens and parks he seems quite content to work in an accepted stylistic system . . . rather than to try to create a new aesthetic'. Chadwick also noted that Paxton had a genius for organization and was 'something of a showman'. These traits were clearly displayed by the design of the Crystal Palace – the 550-metre-long structure was 'designed in such a way that all its parts could be factory-made and assembled on site . . . the first ever example of . . . large-scale industrialised building'. Paxton's experimental, investigative and entrepreneurial character was also demonstrated in 1849 when he became the first person to get the giant water lily, *Victoria amazonica*, to flower in Britain.[146]

Paxton 'had no professional education of any kind and everything he did was outside the formal structure of a professional institute'. He was an apprentice gardener with the Royal Horticultural Society from 1823 to 1826 when he was invited by the Duke of Devonshire to become head gardener at Chatsworth – a palimpsest of parkland landscapes contributed to by George London and Henry Wise between 1687 and 1706; by Grillet, a student of André Le Nôtre (1613–1700), and by Lancelot 'Capability' Brown (1716–83). Paxton was tutored there by architect Sir Jeffry Wyatville (1766–1840) 'who had been employed by the Duke for twenty years from 1817'; he also went on the Grand Tour to Switzerland, Italy, Greece, Asia Minor and Spain with the Duke. He contributed to and edited the magazines *Horticultural Register* (1831–34), *Paxton's Magazine of Botany* (1834–49) and *Paxton's Flower Garden* (1850–53). The first issue of *Paxton's Magazine of Botany* included an article on the design of ornamental cottages for 'Gentlemen's Estates' – an interest which was reflected in his work on cottages for the Chatsworth estate and the lodges at Birkenhead Park.[147]

Paxton's direct involvement with the park ran from 1842 to his final payment in 1846. In 1845 he recommended the appointment of Edward Kemp to supervise initial construction of the park. Kemp was born in south London; he trained as a horticulturist under Paxton at Chatsworth and moved to Birkenhead in 1843 to supervise initial construction of the park. He eventually became Park Superintendent and held that post and lived beside the park until his death in 1891. Kemp clearly had a major role in the detailed design of the park – particularly the lake edges and the planting. Olmsted noted that 'the public credited Kemp with the design of the park'. He did become a park designer in his own right. His *How to Lay Out a Garden* and *The Parks and Gardens of London* were published in 1850 and 1851 respectively. In 1857 he was considered by New York's Central Park Commissioners for the post of Superintendent and was consulted in connection with the proposed design competition for that park. Kemp undertook a number of design projects outside Birkenhead Park including cemeteries in Birkenhead and Liverpool; Hesketh Park, Southport; Stanley Park, Liverpool and Saltwell

Lewis Hornblower's
Grand Lodge (July 1999)

Park, Gateshead. Much of the building work in Birkenhead Park – including the boathouse, bridges, railings, gates and the grandiose Grand Entrance – was designed by architect Lewis Hornblower (1823–79). Hornblower had been appointed on Paxton's recommendation to supervise the building of the park lodges, fencing and mechanical works.[148]

Development of the Park

Construction of the park was largely completed by mid-1845 and most of the detailed work was completed by the end of 1846 – well ahead of the official opening in April 1847. Recurrent themes in the subsequent development of the park were the prolonged difficulty in selling the surrounding residential plots and the gradual increase in the number of sporting activities that were allowed. The area of the park was increased in 1903 through the purchase of the 7.6 hectare Boothby Ground – the land described by the bifurcation of the northern end of Ashville Road – which had failed to sell for residential development. Although the park has remained relatively unchanged from the original design drawn up by Paxton and implemented by Kemp, various minor additions have left residual marks on the park. It has also become far more rundown. Its decline in the second half of the twentieth century can be attributed to:

- use of large parts of the park for allotments and removal of railings during the Second World War
- significant reductions in numbers of maintenance staff in the 1940s and 1950s
- decline in floral content and apparently random tree planting in the 1960s followed by the ravages of Dutch Elm disease during the 1970s
- restrictions on local government spending under the rightist governments of Prime Ministers Thatcher (governed 1979–90) and Major (governed 1990–97).[149]

PLANNING AND DESIGN

Location

The development of Birkenhead Park was based on the ideals of the 1833 Parliamentary Select Committee on Public Walks that 'the working classes . . . be able to walk out in decent comfort with their families'. The park was the focal point of a 'model' urban development on the west shore of the Mersey. It was described in 1989 as 'an inner city park surrounded by a population . . . suffering

high unemployment, drug abuse and general levels of deprivation'. In 1993 the statistical area in which the park is located had an unemployment rate of 34 per cent overall and of 51 per cent for males. In 1999 Birkenhead was still widely regarded by Liverpudlians as being 'removed' and the Wirral was still seen more as a resort area than the site of a significant urban park. Olmsted visited the park by ferry and on foot in the 1850s. He would now be able to take a train to within a few hundred feet of Ashville Road. Nevertheless, the condition of the park validates Jane Jacobs' observation that a park is 'the creature of its surroundings'.[150]

Shape and Natural Landform of the Site

The park is broadly rectangular in shape with its longer side oriented roughly north-west to southeast. The area of the park within the carriage road is roughly 1000 metres long by up to 400 metres wide. It is shaped like an hourglass with the carriage road squeezing together where it meets Ashville Road. The smaller part of the park – the upper park – terminates in a point at the western end with an elevation of 23 metres. This is the highest location in the park. The lower park has a squarer shape than the upper park. Its elevation also falls from 23 metres at the west to 6 metres at the eastern corner. The upper lake has an area of 1.07 hectares and a water level of 10.57 metres. The lower lake has an area of 1.47 hectares and a water level of 6.55 metres. The lakes were designed as collection points for the drainage of the respective parts of the park. Earth derived from excavation of the lakes was used to create berms around them.

Original Design Concept

Chadwick noted that 'consciously or not' Paxton was 'imitating Regent's Park in some degree' except that at Birkenhead 'single villas were intended alongside the terraces instead of in the interior of the park'. Chadwick also noted that 'at this time, the general form of recreation was "promenading"' and that 'Birkenhead Park is an exceedingly competent essay in a style in which Repton and Nash had already pioneered: an informal, gently picturesque landscape . . . its greatness lying in its utility, in its combination of suburb and public recreation area, ahead of anything else anywhere at its time'. Another difference from Regent's Park is that Paxton arranged for access to the houses to be from the public roads outside the park and not from the carriage road inside the park. He 'was determined that the park should not be, nor appear to be, the property of the houses which surrounded it'. It was conceived very much as a People's Park. Parklands Consortium noted in this respect that 'Paxton was clearly aware that he was designing for a new kind of client, demanding a new kind of use'. There was no central focus; no areas were allocated to any individual interest group and the visibility of the properties reflected 'a deliberate mixing of classes'. Parklands Consortium also suggested that 'a rustic, sturdy and northern European' narrative underlay the design and 'signified the confidence of a people shaping itself into a proud and powerful nation'. They concluded that the park is a 'dramatised and condensed compendium of ideal English landscapes and waterscapes – with more exotic highlights' and that 'the park and its surrounding houses . . . were to represent a proud monument to an ideal version of Englishness, as it was developed for an ideal urban community'.[151]

Spatial Structure, Circulation System, Landform, Structures and Planting

Newton described the design as 'fairly typical of its times, with the over curvaceous quality bequeathed by the landscape gardening school'. He felt that the relationship between the park and the buildings was ambiguous and left 'an uncertain feeling as to where the park's limits actually lie; it is almost as though the town and its housing were ruthlessly invading it'. Newton also suggested that the lakes are 'so narrowed and twisted to almost river-like proportions that they lose something in outdoor scale'. A similar observation had been made by Olmsted. He described one of the lakes as 'the pond, or lake as they call it'. Chadwick, by contrast, described them as 'most successful' and suggested that they show 'Paxton's landscape style at its best'. They do not, however, have anything like the presence or defining quality of the Reptonian lake in St James's Park. They are simply too small to be effective focal points. Perhaps Paxton sought to make them an intimate contrast to the open water of the Mersey. This then begs the question of whether he actually saw the enclosed meadows, designed as a pastoral setting for large crowds of visitors, as the more significant component of the spatial structure.[152]

The original circulation system for the park was radical in the extent to which it separated carriages and pedestrians. It reflected the democratic principles behind the park. Although the grandiose Grand Lodge was intended to define the main set-piece entrance, the park is accessible from many different points. All the entrances are broad and straight in contrast to the serpentine carriage road. This has now changed from a horse route to a bicycle route. The original pedestrian paths across the

View from the boathouse (July 1999)

Planting in berms and path at edge of the upper lake (July 1999)

The 'Swiss' Bridge over the lower lake (July 1999)

centre of the park were slightly recessed below the level of adjacent lawns – in much the way that Alphand accommodated the paths at Buttes-Chaumont – and remain relatively unobtrusive. The path system was lightly curved but direct and logical. Along with the contrastingly straight additions – like the north–south path through the lower park and Coronation Walk – the original path system defines the areas of the park that are now allocated to different sporting activities. But the paths are now finished in tired blacktop rather than Paxton's original 'Red Jersey Gravel'.

The natural slope of the land facilitated the creation of rolling meadow-like parkland. This was changed around the lakes where the irregular berms and mounds were created. These landforms served three purposes. First, they avoided the need to remove excavate from site. Second, they created enclosure around the lakes. The level of enclosure now feels unduly confining particularly in association with the deeply indented shoreline of the lakes. Third, they increased the early impact of the trees that were planted on them.[153]

Paxton was responsible for the design of many of the lodges – including the Italian, Gothic, Castellated, Central and the two Norman Lodges – and of railings in the park. This display of controlled eclecticism – particularly where it has been restored in recent years – makes a major contribution to the character of the park. Hornblower's elephantine Grand Lodge – which Paxton insisted be scaled down and which the normally enthusiastic Olmsted called 'heavy and awkward' – remains outrageously out of scale. This is re-emphasized by the diminutive obelisk at the end of the straight, wide entrance road from the Lodge. Other remaining structures include the boathouse and the residue of the 'Swiss' bridge. The boathouse was completed before the opening of the park in 1847. It was restored with funds from Mobil Oil in 1989 – and now has a pebble mosaic floor by Margaret Howarth that demonstrates a delightful attention to detail that is sadly lacking elsewhere in the park. The 'Swiss' bridge was one of five bridges that were originally completed – two to the island in the upper lake; three to the island in the lower lake.[154]

The essence of Paxton's design was to create picturesque pastoral meadows fringed by clumps of exotic trees. Both he and Kemp were consummate gardeners. They had a wide range of newly imported plant species at their disposal and were clearly keen to use them. Parklands Consortium noted that, in 1999, variegated holly, purple-leafed beech, pale green swamp cypress, lime green weeping willow and silver pear were still growing in the park. Colour and experimentation were an integral part of the design. It has been suggested that Paxton and Kemp's aim 'would probably have been to create an arboretum rather than a native woodland . . . but that from the 1950s onwards, substantial new planting was put in with little regard to the original Paxton design'.[155]

MANAGEMENT AND USAGE

Management and Funding

More than 150 years after its establishment as the first publicly funded urban park in the world, Birkenhead Park remains the responsibility of the local authority – currently Wirral Metropolitan Borough Council. The provision and management of urban parks in Britain are non-statutory local government functions. For the last half of the twentieth century 'like many other parks' in Britain, Birkenhead Park was 'maintained to a minimum level rather than managed'. A 'Friends' group was established in 1976 and Birkenhead Park was designated a Conservation Area in 1977. But, to all intents and purposes, it was treated as 'just another local park' until preparation of a Management Plan was commenced in 1986. This marked the start of efforts to address the historic significance of the park and led to the establishment of a Management Committee comprising managers, user groups and other interested parties. Nevertheless, the park continued to languish during the 1990s – particularly as a consequence of mandatory requirements for all local authorities to call tenders for all landscape maintenance operations. This had the effect of 'sucking out up to 50 per cent of the landscape maintenance budget' for the Borough and redistributing it to other council departments. This inevitably led to further reductions in maintenance levels in all of the seventy-five park properties in the Borough.[156]

The Urban Parks Programme of Britain's Heritage Lottery Fund is likely to be a major source of funds for refurbishment of the park. This programme was launched in January 1996 as a vehicle for the distribution of funds from the National Lottery for the restoration of historic parks. The Fund provides up to 75 per cent of the cost of refurbishment works. The other 25 per cent has to come from other sources and the local authority must guarantee that it will allocate sufficient funds for maintenance of the park. This poses a challenge to still revenue-poor local authorities. It invites discussion of alternative ownership and management structures for the maintenance of restored parks. It would be ironic if Birkenhead Park – proudly proclaimed to be the first locally funded public park in the world – were restored with national funds, and more ironic if this led to it moving away from the control of the local council.

User Characteristics

Birkenhead Park remains – as it was intended to be – very much a local park. A detailed survey of visitors carried out in 1992 concluded that:

- the annual grand total number of visitors was 450,023
- 82.6 per cent of visitors lived within 3 kilometres of the park
- 55.8 per cent of visitors to the park on weekdays were alone (39.9 per cent at weekends)
- 98.3 per cent of visitors had visited the park before
- two-thirds of visitors came on foot
- the principal reason given for visiting the park (by 32 per cent of respondents) was 'to pass time'.[157]

PLANS FOR THE PARK

The *Birkenhead Park Management Plan* was produced in May 1991. This established the Management Committee and was the principal policy document for the park until the completion in July 1999 of the *Birkenhead People's Park Restoration and Management Plan*. The latter document was prepared as a vehicle for applying for money from the Urban Parks Programme. Whereas the *Management Plan* took a pragmatic view of the park as a local facility with a significant place in the history of urban parks, the *Restoration and Management Plan* adopted 'the prime aim of restoring the park as a major work of art, representing the best of British landscape design in the nineteenth century'. This aim was tempered by acknowledgement that 'some practical compromises . . . have to be made to accommodate current use' and that the park is located in an area of social and economic deprivation.[158]

The *Restoration and Management Plan* comprised three sections:

- Governing Principles and Practical Strategies for the Repair, Restoration and Development of Birkenhead Park
- Capital Works relating to the Whole Site
- Capital Works and Maintenance Requirements relating to Individual Character Areas.

It carried a capital cost of about £10 million. It did not include a marketing strategy for the restored park. The *Plan* consistently reflected an interpretation of the park as a 'work of art' and sought to impose this interpretation on its refurbishment and on-going management. The implicit statement in the *Restoration and Management Plan* is that faithful physical restoration of Birkenhead Park to its mid-nineteenth-century form is socially, functionally and financially justifiable.[159]

CONCLUSIONS

Newton's view of Birkenhead Park was that 'when all is said and done, the technical quality of the design is obviously of far less importance than the simple fact of the park's having come into being'. Chadwick commented that 'it is most desirable that this park, perhaps above all others in this country, should be maintained in sympathy with its designer's original aims – one does not wish to imitate Paxton's style, but rather to ensure that all his buildings are kept up and that additions to his landscape are in harmony with it'. In the event, it seems that, as far as urban parks are concerned, the restoration ticket is the only one that wins on the British National Lottery. This is regrettable. It will, however, be instructive to observe whether such exercises in nostalgia can foster long-term social and economic change in the hinterland of parks in severely deprived areas. In the meantime, Birkenhead Park retains its pivotal position in the history of urban parks but remains a badly rundown, albeit locally valued, facility.[160]

11　Regent's Park, London

107 hectares (265 acres)

INTRODUCTION

Regent's Park came into existence as a result of a property venture. The venture was initiated in 1811 by the government of the Prince Regent, the title from 1811 to 1820 of King George IV (reigned 1820–30), for whom the park is named. The Prince Regent was a prolific developer, particularly of his own palaces and estates. He was also the 'patron and protector' of architect John Nash (1752–1835). Nash's landscape designs were strongly influenced by Humphry Repton (1752–1818). The public part of the current Regent's Park was originally designed to promote the sale of adjacent residential properties. It has an area of 107 hectares. Together with the 29 hectares of Crown Estate surrounding and enclosed by the public part of the park, 'The Regent's Park' as a whole is the largest Royal Park in central London. Nash had envisaged the park as 'the final, splendid termination of a processional route from Carlton House northwards, although the building of Regent Street and the improvements to St James's Park were still yet to come'. Regent's Park was not initially conceived as a public park and was not opened to the public until 1835. The full impact of Nash's scheme for linking the park to the commercial heart of London can be most clearly understood from the top of Primrose Hill, the area of Royal Park directly north of Regent's Park.[161]

The unity and character of Regent's Park derive as much from its unique setting at the centre of Nash's 'Regency' terraces as from the design of the park itself. Indeed, the layout of the park still reflects its ambivalent origins. Three of the principal physical elements of the layout – the Broad Walk, the Boating Lake and the Inner Circle – are somewhat tenuously related, and the Inner Circle encloses an almost separate second park within the park. Whereas the park was originally conceived as 'borrowed landscape' to be viewed from the surrounding terraces, the buildings now provide a stunning backdrop for users of the park. The assembly of gardens, buildings, ornaments and planting within the park make it an enchanting place and a fascinating historical spectacle. The Regent's Park accommodates a wide range of activities and land uses in addition to the Regency terraces. These include London Zoo, the Regent's Canal, the London Central Mosque, an open-air theatre, Regent's College, Winfield House – the residence of the United States Ambassador, two other residences – The Holme and St John's Lodge, and numerous cafés, kiosks, gardens and play areas. The range of activities that it provides and the sheer size of Regent's Park are reflected in the fact that visitors generally stay longer than in any of the six Royal Parks in central London.[162]

HISTORY

Designation as a park

The Regent's Park occupies an area that had been enclosed as a hunting park by King Henry VIII (reigned 1509–47) under the name Marylebone (or Marybone) Park. The roughly circular shape of the park suggests that Henry's surveyors were not restricted in the land that they chose to enclose. It remained as a royal hunting park stocked with deer until Charles I mortgaged the Crown Estate to pay for arms during the Civil War (1642–49). The site was sequestered during the Commonwealth

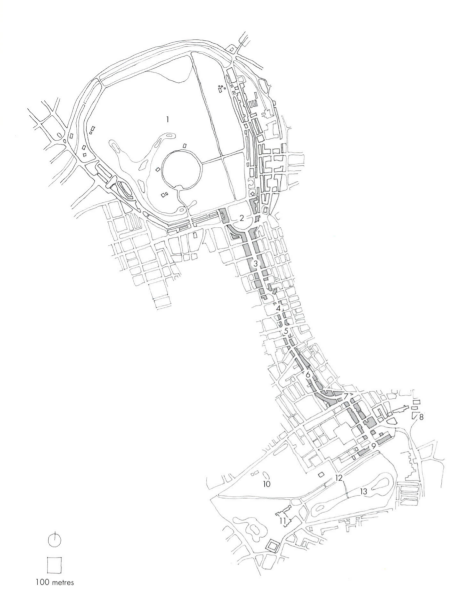

100 metres

A statutory commission had been established by Parliament in 1786 to review the control and profitability of Crown land throughout the country. Marylebone Park was reviewed in the commission's first report. Rents were low relative to the value of the land and so were raised. The final report of the commission, in 1793, recommended that all Crown land should be retained by the Crown and controlled by a board of three commissioners. This was accepted – but not implemented until 1810. Instead, Scot John Fordyce, one of the three members of the commission established in 1786, was appointed Surveyor General of Land Revenues. The Duke of Portland immediately began negotiations to try and extend his interest in the park. Fordyce, however, recommended to the Treasury that before any part of the park was disposed of, 'a general plan should be formed for the Improvement of the whole of it'. He also sought approval to appoint a surveyor to prepare an up-to-date plan of the park so that a competition with a 'considerable reward' could be staged for its design.[164]

In the event only three plans were submitted to Fordyce. And they were all from John White, the Duke of Portland's surveyor. White made it quite clear that he was not seeking the 'considerable reward' but was simply demonstrating the Duke's continuing interest in the land. Fordyce's final report in 1809 made little mention of the park itself but did recommend the 'cutting of a great thoroughfare between the park and Charing Cross', in order to improve access to the Law Courts and Houses of Parliament. Summerson commented that 'underlying the whole document is a wonderfully clear perception of the park as a social and architectural . . . totality'. Meanwhile, in 1806, Nash, who was already working for the Prince Regent in a private capacity, had accepted an appointment as architect to the Office of Woods and Forests and brought in James Morgan as his partner. Fordyce died in August 1809. In 1810, in line with the recommendation made in 1793, the Office of Woods and Forests was merged with the Office of Land Revenues.[165]

One of the first issues confronting the new commission was that the Duke of Portland's lease on part of Marylebone Park was due to expire in January 1811. Instructions were issued to a pair of surveyors and to a pair of architects to prepare designs for the park and for the new street connecting it to Westminster. The surveyors were the Thomases Leverton and Chawner, who had been appointed to the Office of Land Revenues in 1809. The architects were Nash and Morgan. Whereas Morgan had done most of their work for the Office of Woods and Forests, Nash, ever alert to opportunities for self-advancement, treated this commission

(1649–60) when it was sold in lots to the highest bidders. The deer were moved to St James's Park; most of the trees on the site were felled for timber and the land was then let as tenanted pasture and returned to the Crown when the monarchy was restored in 1660. It then passed via two of Charles II's favoured noblemen to a group of speculators and was divided into two leaseholds, one of which reverted to the Crown in 1803. The other leasehold had been extended to 1811 by which time it was owned by the fourth Duke of Portland. His father, the third Duke, had developed Portland Place. The Portlands also owned land to the northwest of the park and the fourth Duke regarded control of the park as the key to consolidating his estates.[163]

Regent's Park, London

1   Primrose Hill
2   Regent's Canal
3   Outer Circle
4   London Zoo
5   The Broad Walk
6   Readymoney Fountain
7   Winfield House
8   Cumberland Terrace
9   Cumberland Green
10   London Central Mosque
11   Hanover Terrace
12   Boating Lake
13   The Holme
14   Open Air Theatre
15   Queen Mary's Garden
16   Inner Circle
17   St John's College
18   Chester Terrace
19   Sussex Place
20   Regent's College
21   Avenue Gardens
22   Clarence Gate
23   Cornwall Terrace
24   York Gate
25   Park Square
26   Park Crescent

100 metres

as his own. Leverton and Chawner's proposals called for an unadventurous extension northwards of the rectilinear pattern of the Portland estate. They made no allowance for the road link to Westminster and their estimates of return on the investment were not encouraging. Nash's report, by contrast, was 'thorough, shrewdly analytical and written with a sort of *bravura* which renders it immediately convincing'. His estimates of returns on investment were equally optimistic.[166]

Nash's original plan, drawn up in March 1811, proposed a much higher density of development than was eventually accepted. The graphic style that he adopted, using dots to represent buildings, was highly deceptive. He showed terraces around three sides of the park; a major double circus in the centre of a more or less square road system, and a series of smaller circuses, squares and crescents all fringed with terraces. It appears to be inspired more by the work of the Woods in Bath or by the New Town in Edinburgh than by the Portland estate or other squares that had become the norm for residential development in London following Inigo Jones's layout for Covent Garden in 1630. Nash's proposals envisaged the introduction of the canal to the site; Leverton and Chawner's did not. He also proposed a sinuous, riverine network of lakes in the lower parts of the site to the south and west of the major circus. This was loosely based on the line of the River Tyburn which flowed through the site on its way southward to the Thames. Nash also allocated a site for a *guingette* (a pleasure resort) for his patron, the Prince Regent.[167]

Nash drew attention to 'the fact that wealthy landowners infinitely prefer living near an open space . . . a park where there were opportunities for riding, driving and walking was, he believed, an irresistible magnet'. His proposals finally reached Prime Minister Spencer Perceval in August 1811. Nash was called for interview by the suburban-dwelling Perceval and instructed to reduce the density of the development and to increase the amount of open space near the residences. He rapidly produced a revised plan. The double circus enveloped by the sinuous lake, the southern circus and the site for the Prince Regent's pavilion remained, albeit in revised forms. A scattering of villas within the open spaces was still proposed, but the lines of terraces were pushed to the edges of the park, and the canal was realigned to skirt rather than run through the site. In the event the double circus was not built and only half the smaller southern circus, Park Crescent, was built. Nevertheless, by 1816 the roads, fences and excavation of the lake were completed and the canal was opened in 1820 – but only three of the villa sites had been let before Regent Street was opened

in 1819. The building of the Regency terraces that remain the finest feature of the park did not begin until the 1820s.[168]

While completing his two designs for the park in 1811, John Nash had also been instructed to draw up proposals for the new road from Portland Place to Charing Cross. The proposals were published the following year and demonstrated that Nash had greater originality as a developer-architect, planner and urban designer than he did as a landscape architect. The proposed alignment followed a natural cleavage between the tangled streets of Soho to the east and the ordered estates of the nobility to the west. Portland Place was made to revolve around the landmark of All Saints Church and into Langham Place running southward to Oxford Circus. From there the modishly broad Regent Street, nearly twice as wide as the buildings enclosing it, ran south-eastward into a smooth curve terminating at Piccadilly Circus. The Circus enabled Nash to redirect the new road to align with Carlton House. In 1825 the then King George IV decided to demolish Carlton House, which had been his London home since reaching the age of majority in 1783, and to rebuild Buckingham House as a royal palace. Carlton House had been the focal point at the southern end of Nash's scheme linking St James's Park via Regent's Street and Portland Place to Regent's Park. Its axis had even determined the position of Piccadilly Circus. Nash was instructed to draw up proposals for a building to replace Carlton House. Construction of the current Carlton House Terrace began in 1827.

Key Figures in the Planning and Design of the Park

John Nash is recognized as the author of the designs for Regent's Park and St James's Park. However, the influence of Humphry Repton on Nash's landscape design work cannot be understated. Repton, who decided one sleepless night in 1788 to take up landscape design as a means of overcoming his financial problems, had, by the mid-1790s, developed a successful practice based on the design of grounds for country houses. He also became involved in designing the houses themselves – and began to feel the need for architectural assistance. This was probably why, when he met Nash in about 1795, Repton felt that there would be benefits from collaboration. The highly mercantile Nash was drawn by the chance to meet 'Repton's wide circle of influential friends and clients'. They agreed that Repton would recommend Nash for any architectural work required as part of his commissions in return for a fee of 2.5 per cent of the cost that work. The deal was strengthened by the fact that Nash employed Repton's eldest son, John Adey, who was completely deaf since infancy and already an accomplished drafter, from 1796 to 1800.[169]

Repton's second son, George Stanley, also joined Nash's staff as a pupil in 1802. This was despite the fact that his father and Nash had fallen out shortly before that date. George Stanley continued to work with Nash until 1820. There were two catalysts for the argument between Repton and Nash. First, Nash had passed off a number of John Adey Repton's designs as his own. Second, and of far greater impact, was the fact that, following Repton's introduction of him in 1797 to the then Prince of Wales, Nash began a thirty-year period of royal patronage from which he appears to have deliberately excluded Repton. The breakdown of their partnership is not altogether surprising. Nash was 'one of those architects whose reputation for original genius induced an excess of self-confidence' whereas Repton was 'tidy-minded, punctual and conscientious'. Chadwick suggested that 'although the partnership between Repton and Nash lasted only a relatively short time its effects were far-reaching, quite beyond the large number of works carried out and their own value as compositions of building and landscape'. Clearly, Repton's theories of landscape design had a strong influence both on Nash and on his own son, George Stanley.[170]

The influence of Repton on urban park design has to be understood in the context of the influence of aesthetics and economics on the development of 'landscape gardening' in the second half of the eighteenth century – the age of the 'Industrial Revolution'. One of the more immediate results of the Industrial Revolution in England (as opposed to later consequences such as the development of industrial cities) was the emergence of a wave of entrepreneurial, mainly Whig, landowners with an interest in improving their recently acquired rural estates. Publications like Edmund Burke's *Inquiry into the Origin of our Ideas of the Sublime and Beautiful* (1756) testify to emerging interest in the field of aesthetics and, in particular, the debate about these two qualities. The nature of the 'Sublime' is illustrated by Burke's proclamation that 'whatever is fitted in any sort to excite the ideas of pain and danger; that is to say, whatever is in any sort terrible, is a source of the sublime'.[171]

'Capability' Brown, whose career began to take off in the 1750s, drew inspiration from literary allusions and produced landscapes of 'Beauty' characterized by smoothness and gentle serenity. The eventual reaction against Brown's almost formulaic flowing landscapes was the creation of 'Sublime' and 'Picturesque' landscapes. The work of William Chambers, particularly his 'Chinoiserie' at Kew Gardens, is often cited as an example of the 'Sublime'. Picturesque landscapes, whose basis was in variety and intricacy, can be characterized as being appropriate subjects for a painting. Repton's landscapes are generally regarded as falling between Brown's work and the 'Picturesque'. Repton wrote that he was 'aware of the common objection to all efforts that may be deemed deceptions; but it is the business of taste, in all the polite arts, to avail itself of stratagems by which the imagination may be deceived'.[172]

Repton's stratagem with respect to landform was that 'the ground looks, when finished, as if art had never interfered'. With respect to water, it was that it 'should rather imitate one large river than several small lakes; especially as it is much easier to produce the appearance of continuity than of such vast expanse that a lake requires'. Repton's sixteen *Sources of Pleasure in Landscape Gardening* reflect a practical approach that 'embraced at once the Beautiful, the Sublime, and the Picturesque'. His approach to landscape design is demonstrated as much in Regent's and St James's Parks as in his own work. Hunt described Repton's work as being 'Pope's "consult the genius of the place" rescued and brought up to date'. Chadwick described Nash's design for St James's Park as being 'laid out and planted just as Repton might have had it'. So much so that even Geoffrey Jellicoe attributed the design of St James's and Regent's Parks to Repton. Users of these parks are fortunate that the Prince Regent was patron to an architect schooled in landscape design by such a master as Humphry Repton.[173]

Development of the Park

Park Crescent at the northern end of Portland Place was built in 1819–21. The first terrace to be built around the Outer Circle of the park was Cornwall Terrace in 1821, designed by Decimus Burton. This was followed in 1822 by the wildly exotic Sussex Place, designed by Nash himself and in 1823 by the more sober Hanover Terrace, also by Nash. The long blocks of York Terrace, either side of the York Gate, were also built in 1822 and 1823 to designs by Nash. The relentlessly horizontal, 280-metre-long Chester Terrace was completed in 1825 and the crowning glory of the east side of the park, Nash's palatial Cumberland Terrace was built in 1826. He intended that it should complement his patron's *guingette* on the other side of the Outer Circle. The Office of Woods, Forests and Land Revenues, however, had other ideas. They terminated the development programme for the park in 1826. The Gardens of the Zoological Society of London ('London Zoo') at the northern end of the

Broad Walk were laid out by Burton in 1827 and the Inner Circle was taken over as the Royal Botanic Garden in 1840. Designed by Robert Marnock and with a conservatory also by Burton, the Inner Circle began its life as a park within the park.

The Regent's Park had a jumpy gestation as a property development and its emergence as a public park was comparably protracted. In the early 1830s public access was restricted to roadways. Only residents were allowed to use the park itself. In 1832 Nash was asked to facilitate greater public use and arranged for extension of (what became known as) the Broad Walk northward from Chester Road to the Zoo. This runs along a gentle ridge running south-east from the Zoo and offered views into the heart of the park. Nash also designed a serpentine path through Cumberland Green to the east of the Broad Walk, offering views to the terraces that he had designed a decade earlier. By 1835 therefore reasonably large areas in the south and east of the park were opened to the public. In 1841 the northern park area was opened to the public and from then until 1883 very little additional land was released for public use.

By the 1860s the park had started to take on many of the Victorian trappings that were to be thrust into Nash's Regency jewel box. The lower Broad Walk was redesigned in 1863 by William Andrew Nesfield in the 'French-Italian' style. It was named 'Avenue Gardens'. Between 1865 and 1874 Nesfield's son, Markham, designed the informal 'English Gardens' to the east, between his father's gardens and the park boundary. By 1870 the Broad Walk had, by all accounts, become a veritable Victorian promenade littered with lodges, bandstands, shelters, drinking fountains and seats. The boating (and skating) lake and northern parkland were used less intensively. The grassland continued to be grazed and these areas retained a sense of rurality. By the end of the nineteenth century further land had been released for public use and a new gate, Clarence Gate, had been created.

In the early twentieth century grazing ceased and much of the ground was laid out for sport – a reflection of the synchronous 'Reform Park' in the United States and the emergence of the Volkspark in Germany. Institutions replaced private lessees. The scale of building was radically disrupted when Bedford (now Regent's) College was built on the grounds of South Villa; Queen Mary's Garden took over the remains of the Royal Botanic Society Garden in the 1930s; the park was requisitioned during the World Wars; surrounding terraces damaged by war-time bombs were restored from 1957 onwards and the open-air theatre, established in 1932, was made into an amphitheatre in the 1970s

and refurbished in 2000. Another change caused by war was the removal of most of the railings around the Inner and Outer Circles and their replacement by hawthorn hedges reinforced with chain link fencing. These remain a distinctly rural early nineteenth-century enclosure motif in a distinctly urban early nineteenth-century setting. During the 1980s the Zoo, as zoos seemed to do at that time, talked both of leaving the park altogether and of expanding; and the Avenue Gardens were reconstructed in 1993. The 'kept' – but apparently not controlled – waterfowl collection in the park is the largest publicly owned collection in the United Kingdom.[174]

Natural Condition of the Site

The development of Regent's Park has been strongly influenced by its underlying geology. It sits on deep deposits of London clay which give way, more or less on the east–west line of Marylebone Road, to gravel terraces between there and the River Thames. The gravel terraces were relatively easy to clear and build on; the London clays less so. Primrose Hill, to the north of the park, rises relatively steeply to an elevation of 65 metres, giving long views southward across Regent's Park and the gentle slope from there to the Thames. The park itself is relatively flat. Its northern edge has an elevation of around 38 metres; the low point is the boating lake at 29 metres. The lake, with an area of about 9 hectares, occupies part of the original line of the River Tyburn, a minor tributary of the Thames formed by two brooks flowing southward from Primrose Hill and Barrow Hill. It is fed from the park's land drainage system but, since it does not have an outlet, it is mechanically aerated. The high point of the park, 41 metres, is beside Readymoney Fountain at the south-east point of the Zoo. The general slope of the park from north to south is therefore about 10 metres with a noticeable westward slope in the area of the Inner Circle and away from the ridge along which the Broad Walk is aligned. The subtle roll of the land to the west and north-west from the top end of the Broad Walk creates the only strongly enclosed space in the park.

Throughout the last 350 years, since tree cover on the site was stripped during the Interregnum (1649–60), the park has suffered from its shallow gradients and its poorly drained clay soils. Much of Nash's early planting was difficult to establish and slow to develop. These problems were exacerbated by the dumping of building rubble from the Second World War on parkland areas, including the former line of the Tyburn to the north of the lake, and then

Regent's Canal at London Zoo (July 1996)

Central London from
Primrose Hill (July 1993)

Central London from Primrose Hill (July 1993)

covering it with inadequate topsoil. Large sums have had to be spent over the past 150 years on invisible investment in subsoil drainage throughout the park.

PLANNING AND DESIGN

Location

John Fordyce and John Nash, in turn, went to extraordinary lengths to achieve the creation of the new processional route between the park and Westminster. 'Nobody, it seems . . . believed that the new street would ever be built. Things like that did not happen in London.' This is a reflection of the sense that existed of the distance between the heart of London and the park. Now, of course, the park appears ridiculously central in any map of London. It is, however, on the north side a major east–west road, the Marylebone Road, which is designated an Inner Ring Road. It therefore remains, to some extent, on the 'wrong side of the tracks' and is used as much by local residents as by visitors from outside Greater London. Just as the park sits on the outside of the highway system, it also lies outside the Circle Line of the underground rail system – the line outside of which business London tends to give way to residential London. Beyond Nash's Terraces to the north-east and east of the park are lower-lying relatively poorer residential areas. These include Camden Town and the predominantly public housing estates towards Euston, St Pancras and King's Cross railway stations and yards. To the north-west and west are inner suburbs of predominantly private,

high-priced housing, particularly St John's Wood. So, just as Nash located Regent Street and Langham Place along a line of social cleavage, Regent's Park and Primrose Hill still continue that line northward. As far as the park itself is concerned, Nash stated that as it 'increases in beauty it will increase in value, and the occupiers will stamp the character of the neighbourhood'. In this he was prescient of Jane Jacobs' observation in 1961 that 'far from uplifting their neighbourhoods, parks themselves are directly and drastically affected by the way the neighbourhood acts upon them'.[175]

Original Design

The principal physical elements of the park are the vehicular circulation system comprising the Outer Circle and, subtended by the Chester and York Roads, the Inner Circle; the Broad Walk; the Boating Lake; the isolated gardens within the Inner Circle; the northern parkland and the Zoo. Despite the various changes and embellishments that these elements have undergone, they remain much as Nash designed them. The only problem is that he never designed them as elements in a unified public park. They are the remnant framework of an abandoned exercise in property development. The park does, however, reflect the fact that Nash developed a great deal of understanding of the relationship between buildings and their settings from his work with Repton. Chadwick suggested that Nash acquired from Repton the idea of 'appropriation' – whereby each villa had a 'pleasant prospect' without being visible from other villas – and management of the lake – with its ends concealed by bridges and planting. The lake has a long shoreline relative to its surface area; the curve of the shoreline and the careful placing of the six islands create serially revealed views and obscure the full extent of the water.[176]

The Nash terraces remain more or less continuous from Hanover Terrace in the west to Gloucester Gate in the north-east. The only breaks are where the Colosseum was replaced by the chateau-style terrace of Cambridge Gate in the 1870s and the scalpel-sharp Royal College of Physicians – designed in the 1960s by Denis Lasdun, architect for London's National Theatre. St John's Lodge and The Holme are leased as private residences. The only footpath other than the Broad Walk that remains as Nash designed it, is the one through Cumberland Green installed in 1832.

Nash originally intended the Broad Walk as the continuation northward of Portland Place into The Regent's Park. It takes full advantage of the natural landform of the site and offers an uplifting, if firmly directed, walk with a sequence of views between blocks of trees – westward into the major space in the park and eastward to the later Nash terraces. It is difficult to tell from surviving drawings whether Nash was simply following an already established line of former field boundaries and the extension of Portland Place, or whether works were undertaken to create these effects. The re-creation in the 1990s of Nesfield's design for Avenue Gardens at the southern end of the Broad Walk and the restoration of the Readymoney Fountain at its northern end have created some uncomfortable contrasts of scale. Avenue Gardens feels far too wide and distinctly short of benches. The Mall in Central Park, New York, also restored in the 1990s, demonstrates a more appropriate density of seating. The Fountain is too 'stumpy' to act as an effective focal point on such a major axis.[177]

Trees now obscure views between the lake, the park west of the Broad Walk and the terraces. Nash's framed views from the buildings have largely been obscured – albeit temporarily. Constant review of the growth of the trees in the park is necessary for the full impact of the surrounding buildings to be effective. The pattern of tree planting in the park is generally independent of the park circulation except for the Broad Walk and the cherry avenue along Chester Road. Trees are generally located in a continuous but relatively narrow fringe around the perimeter of the park. An often broader band of trees wraps around the lake and adjacent residences. These fringes and bands are comprised of deciduous forest trees infilled with smaller ornamental species. Constant attention is also needed to ensure the consistency and condition of footpath surfaces and of the extensive hawthorn hedges. The visible evidence suggests that maintenance leans towards horticultural apoplexy at the centre and anaemia at the edges.

It is also regrettable that such a large park so near the centre of a metropolis prohibits wheeled recreation. Over the past twenty years, however, the park has become a major venue for casual (and not so casual) summer evening softball games. One effect that Nash certainly would not have sought to create is the (now) ironic symbolism of the plan form. The similarity of the shape of the lake, Inner Circle and Broad Walk to a baseball bat, a ball and a catching glove is uncanny.

MANAGEMENT AND USAGE

Managing Organization

Since 1993 London's Royal Parks have been managed by the Royal Parks Agency, an executive agency of British national government – first under the Department of National Heritage and latterly under the Department of Culture, Media and Sport. The Royal Parks Agency took over responsibility for the parks from another ministry of central government, the Department of Environment. Under that ministry, the parks had remained somewhat secretively run by civil servants with relatively little interference from their political bosses. The post of Bailiff of the Royal Parks – formerly a royal gift, offered perhaps to a suitable military figure (now superseded by the post of Chief Executive of the Royal Parks Agency) and the majority of the superintendent posts were held by horticulturists. Other professional services were either provided from other agencies of the Department of Environment or bought in by them on an as-needed basis.[178]

Direct labour teams under the direction of the superintendents of the respective parks undertook horticultural maintenance and minor new works. Before Prime Minister Major's realignment of responsibilities in 1993, the status quo had been radically disrupted in 1985 by proposals from the government of then Prime Minister Margaret Thatcher. She introduced proposals to 'privatize' a wide range of government services, including maintenance of the Royal Parks. Until that time there had been little or no public consultation over the running of the parks and no formal mechanism for local residents or other park users to communicate with the parks' managers.

Privatization was widely perceived as a means of reducing the cost of maintaining the Royal Parks with little concern for any effect on their quality. This perceived threat spawned 'Friends' groups for

Performance of Bad Penny *by the boating lake (June 1993)*

Triton Fountain, Queen Mary's Garden, Inner Circle (October 1993)

each individual park. It now appears to be accepted that procuring maintenance services by competitive tender from outside contractors was less detrimental than originally feared. It has, however, led to loss of familiarity with the parks and loss of the training ethos that could be generated with an in-house workforce. The 'Friends' groups – which are generally dominated by vociferous and articulate local residents – remained in existence and continue to act as unofficial consultative bodies for the park managers. Prime Minister Blair's government (elected in 1997) also required that reviews be made to try and achieve cost-efficient delivery of public services. Establishment of the Royal Parks Agency was intended to distance the running of the parks from central government functions. As part of that move an independent 'Royal Parks Review Group' was appointed in July 1991 to provide recommendations on the future direction of the parks.

The Royal Parks Agency currently manages the parts of The Regent's Park that are public park. The Agency shares responsibility for the Outer Circle with another agency of central government, the Crown Estate Paving Commission. The Commission is responsible for cleaning roads and maintaining sidewalks and terrace gardens. Crown Estate areas that are leased to other occupiers are the responsibility of those occupiers.[179]

Funding

The majority of the funds for the running of the Royal Parks comes direct from central government. In the financial year 1997–98 central government covered 82 per cent of the cost of running them. The remaining 18 per cent was earned from direct events (e.g. leasing of sites) and services (e.g. franchises and car parking charges). About 200 events take place in Regent's Park each year and the park is often used for commercial film, television and still photography – with a proviso that a true representation of the park is given. The budget for works and maintenance for the park in 1998–99 was £2.2 million. The 1999–2000 budget for the Royal Parks as a whole was raised – on a one-off basis – by £5.4 million to £26.4 million. This was the first increase in four years. It was to allow for commemorative capital works and repair work in the wake of the death in August 1997 of Princess Diana.[180]

Usage

The Royal Parks Agency undertakes annual surveys of the usage of all the Royal Parks. Sizes of the Royal Parks in central London and estimated numbers of visitors in 1995 are given in Table 11.1.

Royal Horse Artillery on Cumberland Green in front of Cumberland Terrace (May 1993)

Table 11.1 Size and estimated numbers of visits to Royal Parks in Central London (1995)

Park	Area (hectares)	Visitors (000s)
St James's Park	35	5,500
Green Park	20	3,400
Hyde Park	145	4,700
Kensington Gardens	110	2,500
Primrose Hill	26	1,100
Regent's Park	107	3,900
Total	440	21,100

Source: Royal Parks Agency Annual Report for 1995

Table 11.2 shows the origin of visitors to the central Royal Parks from user surveys in 1997. It demonstrates that Regent's Park is used primarily by local residents and by residents of Greater London. Regent's Park is effectively a city park where Primrose Hill is a local park and St James's and Green Parks are more national and international parks.

More than 70 per cent of the visits to the central Royal Parks are for 'peace and quiet' or for 'fresh air' – what has been described as 'a peaceful walk in pleasant surroundings'. This is a reflection of the respective locations of each of the parks; of the attractions and activities surrounding them and of the facilities that they offer.

Table 11.2 Origins of visitors to Central London Royal Parks

Park	Local resident	Greater London	Elsewhere in the UK	Over-seas
Regent's Park	32	35	10	22
Green Park	7	25	21	45
Hyde Park	13	27	18	39
Kensington Gardens	25	21	13	39
Primrose Hill	64	23	4	8
St James's Park	9	29	23	37

Source: Royal Parks Visitor Survey for 1997

PLANS FOR THE PARK

Before the establishment of the Royal Parks Agency and before the Review Group report on Regent's Park (both in April 1993), management of the park had tended to concentrate on recurrent maintenance;

alleviation of land drainage problems and, when resources allowed, refurbishment of run-down areas – particularly key gardens like Queen Mary's Garden and Avenue Gardens. The Royal Parks Agency stated in its *Framework Document*, also produced in April 1993, that its key aims in managing the parks was for them to:

- offer peaceful enjoyment, recreation, entertainment and delight to those who use them
- be enhanced, preserved and protected for the benefit of present and future generations
- be managed efficiently and effectively and in accordance with principles of public service.

In April 1998 landscape consultants Colvin and Moggridge presented a *Management Plan* for the park. The plan reflected the incremental way that the park was designed. It is a set of tactics based on prioritization, programming and prudence. This has been the approach in Regent's Park since 1811 and, short of a radical redesign, is one of the few approaches that can be taken. Its effectiveness is dependent on a long period of consistent management and a continuity of design control so that, over time, the assemblage of tactics ensures the integrity of the works that are undertaken. The Management Plan called for reinforcement of the identity of the park; protection of the historic integrity of the circulation system; treatment of boundaries to reflect the principles intended by Nash; appropriate density of tree cover in the park fringe; emphasizing the natural 'picturesque' [*sic*] character of the boating lake; integrating the sports fields with the wider park; managing Avenue Gardens so that they develop towards planned maturity; rebuilding a conservatory in the Inner Circle; restricting new monuments; standardizing seats, lights, bins and barriers; continued soil improvement; softening edges of the boating lake; restoration of area around Readymoney Fountain; ensuring healthy continuity of trees; creating significant new areas of wildlife habitat and wildlife corridors; maintaining a healthy stock of kept birds; controlling the Canada Goose population, and reducing the dominance of the Zoo. All in all it is a pragmatic approach that reflects the conservative taste of the 1990s for a high level of preservation and a nod towards ecology and sustainability. It should give the park far greater consistency and integrity of appearance and one or two localized highlights. But it will not do much more than nudge the status quo. And that, maybe, is just the way the British like it.

CONCLUSIONS

Regent's Park was created as the centrepiece of a real estate venture. In this respect it was the model for Victoria Park in the east end of London, for Birkenhead Park and for many North American parks. It is tempting to suggest that the current layout and form of Regent's Park arose as much by accident as from conscious design decisions. There are, nevertheless, many set-piece elements of great individual value in the park. The form of the lake, for instance, is redolent of Repton's writing about bridges that 'to preserve the idea of a river, nothing is so effectual as a bridge; instead of dividing the water on each side, it always tends to lengthen its continuity by shewing the impossibility of crossing it by any other means, provided the ends are well concealed'. But it is difficult to overcome the feeling that the finest qualities of the park are a by-product of Nash's architectural design rather than the direct result of his landscape design. These qualities are, of course, the views of the crescents and latterly other, taller buildings, from the park. These views are most powerful in winter when the mature trees create less of a screen. Such powerful views challenge any notion that parks should exist in antithesis to their urban settings. They compare with the dramatic contrast between Grant Park, Chicago and adjacent commercial buildings or between Central Park, New York and adjacent residential buildings. Park and building reinforce each other's character and reaffirm each other's role in the city.[181]

The stuttering start to the development of the park left it with a bitty layout and further bits have been added over time. Two interesting issues are the saga of the Zoo and the emergence of ecologically managed habitats for native wildlife. The Zoo, like Central Park's, went through a period of uncertainty in the 1980s that nearly resulted in its closure. Financial difficulties and debates about political correctness combined to threaten their continued existence. In the event, unlike Stanley Park Zoo in Vancouver, they were not removed. The parallel, more politically acceptable practice of promoting 'natural' areas has also continued in Regent's Park. This is a significant change in direction for an otherwise horticulture-driven management that appeared more attuned to hosting the Zoo and nurturing exceptional rose displays than to accommodating uncontrolled wildlife. The on-going challenge for the management is to develop a strategy for the park that is as robust and unified (not uniform) as the terraces outside it.[182]

12 Grant Park, Chicago

320 acres (130 hectares)

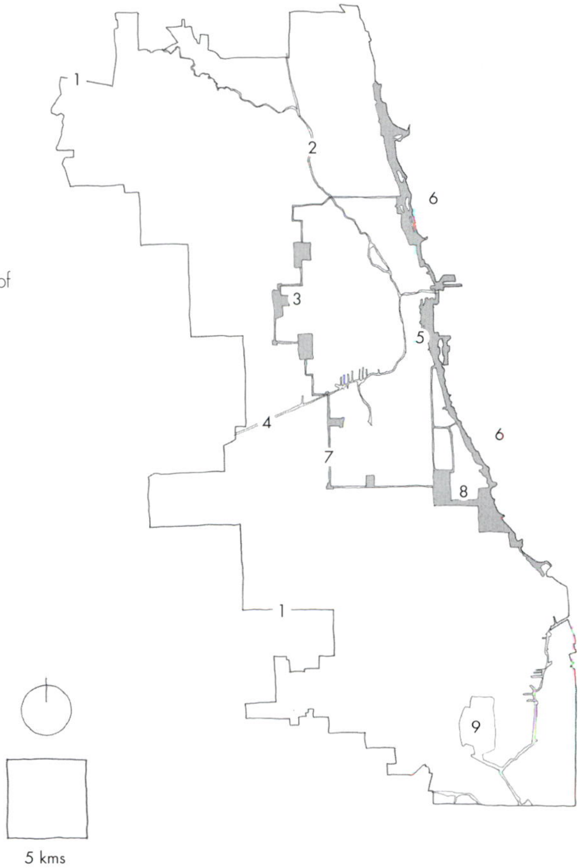

Location of Grant Park, Chicago

1 Administrative boundary of Chicago
2 North Chicago River
3 Humboldt, Garfield and Douglas Parks
4 Chicago Canal
5 Grant Park
6 Lake Michigan
7 Boulevard System
8 Washington and Jackson Parks
9 Lake Calumet

5 kms

INTRODUCTION

Grant Park is the Beaux-Arts centrepiece of Daniel H. Burnham and Edward H. Bennett's Haussmann-like 1909 Plan of Chicago. It sits on reclaimed land at the pivotal point where the third largest city in the United States meets the western shore of Lake Michigan and at the heart of a line of lakefront parks. Part of the site was originally designated as a park – under the name Lake Park – in 1847. It was extended as a result of railroad construction and through refuse disposal – particularly after the 'Great Fire' of 1871. Most of the construction of the current park did not occur until the last half of the 1920s. Grant Park is now regarded as the 'Front Yard' of Chicago. It is where Queen Elizabeth II landed on an official visit to the city in 1959; where Pope John Paul II held a Mass in 1979 and where the Chicago Bulls celebrated their NBA championships in the 1990s.[183]

A grid of railroads and heavily used highways dissects Grant Park and divides it up like compartments in a giant toolbox. The sides of that box are defined by the solid walls of high-rise buildings along its northern and western sides. This abrupt break results from a decision made in 1836 that the land between Michigan Avenue and the lake should be 'Public Ground – A Common to Remain Forever Open, Clear and Free of any Buildings, or other Obstruction Whatever'. That decision was upheld in three lawsuits brought by businessman Aaron Montgomery Ward between 1890 and 1911. The park has been run since 1934 by the Chicago Park District – a municipal corporation that owns and manages 7300 acres (3000 hectares) of park properties. It is a relatively autonomous body with its

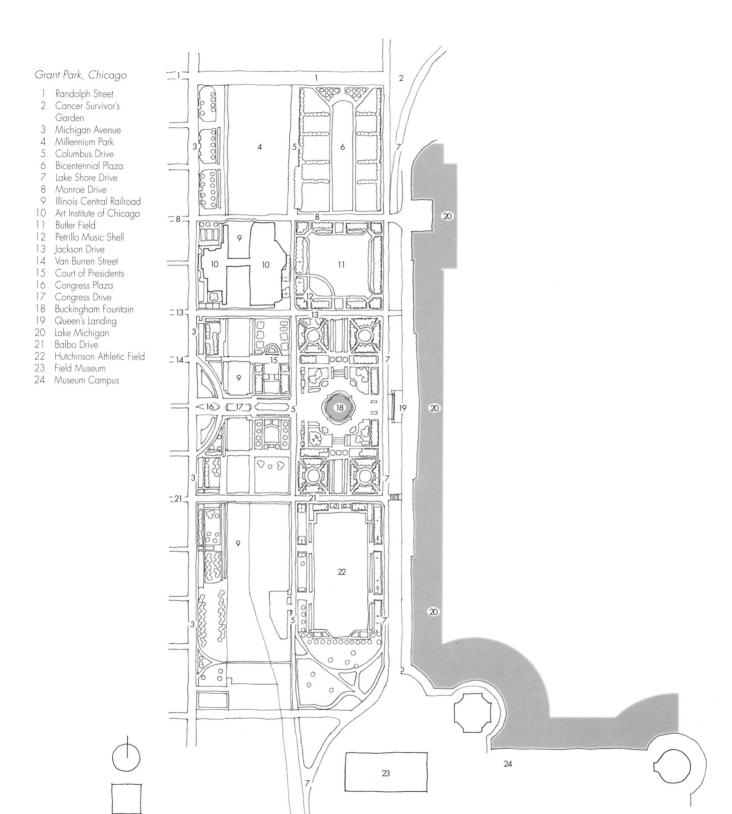

Grant Park, Chicago

1   Randolph Street
2   Cancer Survivor's
    Garden
3   Michigan Avenue
4   Millennium Park
5   Columbus Drive
6   Bicentennial Plaza
7   Lake Shore Drive
8   Monroe Drive
9   Illinois Central Railroad
10 Art Institute of Chicago
11 Butler Field
12 Petrillo Music Shell
13 Jackson Drive
14 Van Burren Street
15 Court of Presidents
16 Congress Plaza
17 Congress Drive
18 Buckingham Fountain
19 Queen's Landing
20 Lake Michigan
21 Balbo Drive
22 Hutchinson Athletic Field
23 Field Museum
24 Museum Campus

100 metres

own tax-raising powers. The park remains a work in progress with major construction operations and planning exercises on-going at the start of the twenty-first century.[184]

HISTORY

Date and Designation

Chicago is located where the Chicago River flows into the south-western corner of Lake Michigan. The river was linked by a shallow lake – Mud Lake – to the south-westward flowing Des Plaines River, a tributary of the Mississippi. American Indians already operated a *portage* between these two river systems when a French colonial settlement was established on the site of Chicago in the 1770s. The American government obtained six miles square (nearly 10 kilometres square) of land at the mouth of the Chicago River in 1795. The Federal Reserve of Fort Dearborn was established in 1803 to provide protection for traders and settlers from Indians – who had been armed by the British – rather than from the British themselves. In 1816 the government acquired a 20-mile-wide (32 kilometres) strip of land extending 100 miles (160 kilometres) from the mouth of the Chicago River to the Illinois River – another tributary of the Mississippi – for the construction of a canal. In 1823 the military abandoned Fort Dearborn; in 1830 the government decided to build a harbour – completed

in 1833 – at Chicago; also in 1833, the federal and state governments agreed a formula to develop the Illinois and Michigan Canal. By that year the population had grown to more than 150 – the figure required by the State for incorporation as a village – and in August 1833 Chicago became incorporated.[185]

By 1835 – the year when funding to construct the canal was actually procured – the population of Chicago was 3265. In November 1835 'concerned citizens' discussed the future of the Fort Dearborn land. They resolved that a square block of 20 acres (8 hectares) with one side fronting the lake should be reserved as a public square. Although that piece of land was eventually developed, the citizens' resolution prompted the State Commissioners in charge of canal construction to make their inscription in 1836 on the land sales map reserving the (then small amount of) land east of Michigan Avenue as 'Public Ground'. Ownership of the lakefront land was transferred to the City of Chicago in 1844. It was formally dedicated as Lake Park in 1847 but no improvements were made and the city could not afford to construct seawalls to prevent erosion of the shoreline. The canal was eventually completed in 1848 – shortly before Chicago began to develop as a railroad centre. The population of Chicago reached 20,000 in 1848; 30,000 in 1850; 38,700 in 1852; 60,000 in 1854 and nearly 120,000 by 1857. In 1850 one rail line entered the city; by 1856 there were ten rail lines with 3000 miles (4800

Park from the Museum Campus (April 2000)

kilometres) of track. In six years the city 'had become the world's largest railroad center'. The establishment of one of those rail lines – the Illinois Central (IC) – was instrumental in the development of Grant Park.[186]

The City agreed in 1852 that the IC could build a train trestle in the bed of the lake providing they also built a stone breakwater to protect the shoreline. The IC also bought land to the north of the park and filled the area between the Chicago River and Randolph Street – the north side of the park. The State began drafting legislation to allocate the whole lakefront to the IC. Citizens objected. Legislation was passed in 1861 reconfirming the dedication of the land east of Michigan Avenue as open space and in 1863 granting title to the 'submerged lands east of the IC right-of-way to the city of Chicago in trust for the public'. These Acts required that development east of Michigan Avenue could only proceed with the approval of all adjacent landowners.[187]

In 1869 the State Legislature established the first three independent Park Districts – the South, West and North Park Districts – each with their own tax-raising powers. It also passed legislation that year granting the IC title to the lake bed for one mile (1.6 kilometres) into the lake from the Chicago River to 11th Street. Also in 1869, the federal government decided to develop Lake Calumet 20 kilometres south of downtown Chicago as a port and industrial base with access both to Lake Michigan and to the Mississippi. This diverted demand for development of the downtown lakefront.[188]

By 1871 Chicago had a population of nearly 300,000 living in densely developed, primarily wooden buildings. The 'Great Fire' that occurred in October 1871 killed more than 300 people; left 90,000 homeless and destroyed more than 17,000 buildings. The fire led to rapid, lower-density redevelopment of the city including extensive parks and boulevards. It also led to the area between the shoreline and the IC trestle being filled with rubble from the fire. The site continued to be used as a dumping ground during the 1870s and 1880s. The IC began to fill areas east of the trestle in 1881. The City made minor improvements to the area between Michigan Avenue and the IC line. But by 1890 relatively little had been done to turn Lake Park into a public amenity.[189]

Key Figures in the Establishment of the Park

For nearly fifty years Lake Park was protected from development – largely because of citizen pressure. Between 1890 and 1913, that pressure was personi-fied by mail order entrepreneur Aaron Montgomery Ward (1844–1913). Ward's business was on Michigan Avenue. This gave him direct rights, under the Acts of 1861 and 1863, to prevent building on the lakefront. Two armouries had, however, been built in the park by the federal government in 1881. In 1890, following the agreement that Chicago would host the World's Columbian Exposition – originally scheduled for 1892 – consent was given for the construction of the World's Congress Building – which subsequently became the Art Institute of Chicago. Ward's first lawsuit, filed in October 1890, was simply to 'clear the lakefront . . . of unsightly wooden shanties, structures, garbage . . . and other refuse'.[190]

The city responded in two ways. First, by removing all the buildings in the park other than the two armouries; second, by proposing to build a city hall, police station, post office, stables and power plant in the park. Ward eventually won his first lawsuit in 1897. An injunction was issued requiring the removal of all buildings except the Art Institute. In 1893, the City and the Illinois National Guard announced plans to build new armouries on the newly formed land east of the IC line. Ward filed suit again. An injunction was issued. The authorities appealed to the State Supreme Court. The decision for Ward was upheld on the basis of the provision in the Act of 1863 that the submerged lands were also held in trust for the public. In 1896 responsibility for Lake Park was transferred from the City to the South Park District. The Commissioners embarked on a major landfill programme to increase the area of the park. In 1901, following a petition from the Grand Army of the Republic, the commissioners agreed to rename the park for President Ulysses S. Grant (1822–85).[191]

Ward's legal battles to protect the park from buildings continued until shortly before his death. The longest and most bitter dispute was over the proposal to build the Field Museum on the Congress Drive axis. Ward filed his third lawsuit. The museum was to be a gift to the city from Marshall Field to contain collections that had been displayed at the Exposition. Field died in 1906. He left $8 million for construction of the museum – on condition that the city provide a site free of cost within six years of his death. Ward resisted immense public pressure – particularly in the *Chicago Tribune* – to withdraw his case. He did not. His case was upheld in 1909. He was pilloried in the press. He responded by commenting that he 'fought for the poor people of Chicago, not the millionaires' and that city officials would crowd the lakefront with buildings 'transforming the breathing spot for the poor into a showground for the educated rich'. A site for the museum – on land then owned by the IC and now the anchor of the Museum Campus – was agreed a month before Field's deadline expired.[192]

While Ward had been fighting to prevent buildings in the park, Daniel Hudson Burnham (1846–1912) had been actively seeking to promote them. Burnham was chief architect and, with landscape architect Frederick Law Olmsted (1822–1903), co-designer of the 1893 Exposition in Jackson Park. Burnham's family moved to Chicago from Massachusetts in 1854. After 'several false starts' he went into partnership with John Welborn Root (1850–91) in 1873. Root died – of pneumonia – before the opening of the Exposition. The firm was renamed D. H. Burnham and Company. Shortly after the end of the Exposition, Burnham started exploring ways to link Jackson Park to the downtown and to redesign the downtown lakefront. His plans for Lake Park showed 'a neo-classical museum in the center . . . flanked by formal plazas, with long rectangular buildings at each extreme end'.[193]

In 1896 Burnham was invited to discuss his proposals at a meeting of the Commercial Club – 'an elite organization of the city's sixty top businessmen'. He also presented his proposals to audiences like the Woman's Club, the Art Institute, the South Park District Commissioners and the Merchants Club – a similar club to the Commercial Club. In 1903 Burnham was appointed as architect for the Field Museum – then proposed to be in the centre of Grant Park – and the Olmsted Brothers were appointed to design the park. They prepared a number of schemes, all with the Field Museum at the centre. In 1904, D. H. Burnham and Company and the Olmsteds were appointed by the South Park District to design a system of neighbourhood parks. Burnham hired Edward H. Bennett (1874–1954), an École des Beaux-Arts-trained, English architect, to work on them. In 1906 the Merchants Club commissioned D. H. Burnham and Company to prepare a complete city plan. Later that year the Merchants Club merged with the Commercial Club, in whose name the *Plan of Chicago* was published in 1909.[194]

The *Plan of Chicago* reflected Burnham's call to 'Make no Little Plans; They have no magic to stir men's blood and probably themselves will not be realized. Make big plans: aim high in hope and work.' The plan proposed extensive parks, parkways and forest reserves including 23 miles (37 kilometres) of continuous open space along the lakefront; a regional highway system; a consolidated railroad system; a gigantic civic centre with a dome of Speer-like proportions, and a cluster of institutional buildings in Grant Park – the focal point of a massive Beaux-Arts blueprint for the city. The precedent of Haussmann's plans for Paris is self-evident. The *Plan of Chicago* contained 'routine solutions, cutting boulevards through dilapidated housing and enforcing sanitation measures . . . it symbolized the maturation of the City Beautiful' while containing 'elements looking forward to contemporary planning'. The plan 'was essentially an architect's conception: an ordering of the city to visual ends; but in it for the first time regional items were seen as an essential basis.' The critical point is that 'Grant Park and the entire park system on the lakefront are essentially what Burnham proposed'.[195]

The *Plan of Chicago* was adopted by the City in 1910. Meanwhile, pending the outcome of Ward's third lawsuit, the Olmsted Brothers continued to develop a series of symmetrical layouts for Grant Park that incorporated the Field Museum. After Ward's victory and once an alternative site for the museum had been agreed in 1912, filling of the southern area of the park was commenced. Also in 1912, the IC agreed to depress its railroad through the park below grade. Construction of the museum eventually began in 1915 – to Burnham's design, three years after his death. Also in 1915, the South Park Commissioners retained Bennett (rather than the Olmsteds) to prepare new plans for Grant Park. He performed this role until 1930 when the city administration became bankrupt. Minor park construction to Bennett's designs began in 1915. But it was not until 1922 that a presentation drawing showing his firm's full intentions for the park was produced. That plan was adopted in 1924.[196]

In 1925 the South Park Commission accepted from Kate Sturges Buckingham, daughter of a grain elevator mogul, the donation of a fountain in memory of her late brother, Clarence. No ordinary fountain, the Buckingham Fountain was based on the Latona Fountain at Versailles. It has a 280-foot-diameter (85 metres) bottom pool with three concentric pools above it and a central fountain spouting to 137 feet (42 metres). Planned by Bennett and designed by French sculptors and engineers, the Buckingham Fountain sits at the pivotal point of the park and the city – the place where Burnham would have placed the Field Museum. The intricate Beaux-Arts central section of the park – between Michigan Avenue, Jackson, Balbo and Lake Shore Drives – is the only part to be fully developed to Bennett's design. It included the Court of Presidents and the arcing Congress Plaza – a gateway to the city. Bennett ensured that the central section of the park was densely decorated with neoclassical architectural ornaments and noble sculptures – including the seated Lincoln by

Buckingham Fountain
(September 1990)

Augustus Saint-Gaudens (erected in 1926) and the Art Deco 'Equestrian Indians' by Ivan Metrovic that flank Congress Plaza (erected in 1928).[197]

Development of the Park after 1930

In 1926 a State Bill was introduced for the bridging of the Chicago River to the north of the park. This eventually led to the massive expansion of traffic on Lake Shore Drive. The 1930s, however, was a period of economic crisis; the city went bankrupt; another World's Fair – celebrating the centenary of the city – was held in 1933 in Burnham Park, directly south of Grant Park. Its main impact on Grant Park was the installation of Art Deco features like the bandshell in Hutchinson Field modelled on the Hollywood Bowl. In 1934 the twenty-two separate Park Districts were amalgamated into the Chicago Park District. The Park District received substantial funding from the Works Progress Administration (WPA). This led to creation of the lakefront terrace and installation of significant amounts of planting – strengthening Bennett's *allées* of American elms and reinforcing them with ornamental understorey trees and formal hedges.[198]

Grant Park, like many other urban parks in the United States, had a troubled time in the 1950s, the 1960s and much of the 1970s. Vehicular traffic mushroomed; urban highways were widened; new freeways were cut through inner urban areas and huge car parks were created as the mobile classes decamped to the suburbs. Parks became underfunded 'no-go' areas. Surface car parks had been created north of Monroe Drive as early as 1921. In 1953 an underground garage was constructed between Monroe Drive, Randolph Drive and the IC lines. This led to reconstruction as a roof garden of the Bennett design for the area. In 1955 Congress Drive was extended to the lake. Additional underground garages were built between Jackson Drive and Van Buren Street in 1961, and below the Richard J. Daley Bicentennial Plaza in 1976.

The park became infamous as the site of 'a major confrontation between anti-Vietnam War protesters and an overzealous police force' during the 1968 Democratic Party Convention. The one recorded rape-murder in the park occurred in the late 1960s. Further demonstrations were staged in the park in 1972. The bandshell became a focus for the demonstrations and 'it became impossible to draw the large crowds necessary to support major concerts to the southern end of the park'. The bandshell was removed in 1978 and replaced by the Petrillo Music Shell at the south-west corner of the Butler Field.[199]

The renaissance of Grant Park since the 1980s can be attributed in large part to the relocation of its major concert venue and establishment during the mayoralty of Jane Byrne (1979–83) of a series of annual music festivals. During the 1990s the recovery of the park has been reflected in two major physical developments. First, removal of the branch of Lake Shore Drive east of the Field Museum to create the Museum Campus – planned since the 1960s and completed in 1998, it provided a wide pedestrian underpass between the museums and the park. Second, construction of the Frank Gehry-designed music pavilion in the 16.5-acre (7 hectares) northwest corner of the park – Lakefront Millennium Park. That project included car parks on either side of and above the IC tracks; a below ground auditorium; the pavilion and Great Lawn – capable of seating 14,000 people, and rehabilitation of the gardens fronting Michigan Avenue. The Cancer Survivor's Garden was created in 1994 following re-alignment of Lake Shore Drive at the north-east corner of the park. The Buckingham Fountain and the Congress Plaza and flanking gardens were restored in the 1990s and many of the American elms in the park were replaced with disease-resistant cultivars.[200]

PLANNING AND DESIGN

Location

Conceived as the pivotal point of the *Plan of Chicago*, Grant Park remains at the physical heart of the city.

Lincoln Memorial, Court of Presidents (April 2000)

The commercial centre has gradually moved northward along Michigan Avenue to what 'the astute real estate developer Arthur Rubloff dubbed the Magnificent Mile in 1947'. Congress Drive is still the axis of the park and the park is still the axis of the city, but the declining height of buildings southward along Michigan Avenue is a visible reflection of relative real estate values and of the changing social ecology along the western edge of the park. Nevertheless, 'on any business day, over a half-million people occupy an area less than three square miles, creating the extraordinarily dense Downtown District'.[201]

Shape and Natural Landform of the Site

Grant Park is a north–south aligned rectangle lying parallel to the shoreline of Lake Michigan. It is about 5750 feet (1750 metres) long by 2800 feet (850 metres) wide. The site was reclaimed from the lake and the resulting terrain is relatively flat. There are gentle falls towards the lake between a series of horizontal planes. In section therefore Columbus Drive is 'several feet' higher than Lake Shore Drive – and the lakefront walk is significantly lower than Lake Shore Drive. One other noticeable change of level is the relative elevation of the Richard J. Daley Bicentennial Plaza.[202]

Original Design Concept

The *Plan of Chicago* saw Grant Park representing the city to the world 'just as Louis XIV intended Versailles to symbolically represent France to the world. In both cases, the wall – the edge of the city – faces the park directly, and the center of the city is in line with the center of the park'. Bennett's 1922 plan for Grant Park saw it as 'a formal landscape inspired by the French Renaissance . . . a system of lawn panels, formal flower beds, *allées* of elm trees, classical details, and a monumental fountain at the center of the park'. His layout was subdivided into a series of *salles* (rooms) and smaller spaces (*cabinets*) – each furnished with a 'sculpture, fountain or other set piece or activity'. The older, smaller spaces along Michigan Avenue are more garden-like in scale and design; the newer, larger spaces to the east of the IC are designed for more communal use and for sporting activities.[203]

Spatial Structure, Circulation System, Landform, Materials and Planting

The French Renaissance principles adopted by Bennett are still clearly evident. Congress Drive remains a dominant east–west axis and the

Buckingham Fountain remains the focal point – particularly when the central jet is at full height. The Park District's *Grant Park Design Guidelines* (1992) identified a series of symmetrical spaces aligned north–south across the Congress axis: Michigan Avenue; Congress Plaza; Court of Presidents; Butler and Hutchinson Fields, and the Lake itself. The Park District term for this is the *Historic Template*. The central north–south axis through the fountain and through the less elevated Butler and Hutchinson Fields is stronger on plan than on the ground. The Fields feel secondary. They are lower and the re-establishment of the elm groves around the fountain plaza makes the linkage more tenuous. Equally, the development of areas like the Millennium Park and the Bicentennial Plaza as distinct *salles* with individual characters and purposes, further subdivides the park. This is re-emphasized by the asymmetry of the Bicentennial Plaza on the north–south axis of the fountain and the fact that there is no direct pedestrian link from that plaza to the fountain.[204]

But it is the dissection of Grant Park by highways that really shatters its unity. The layout looks beautifully balanced on plan and stunningly sharp from surrounding skyscrapers. It works well through a vehicle windscreen – particularly set pieces like the view south from the boulevard of Lake Shore Drive to the Field Museum. But for pedestrians it is an ordeal. Apart from the few festival days when highways like Columbus Drive are temporarily closed to traffic, it is impossible to walk between any of the *salles* or *cabinets* without having to wait for traffic lights. Most days of the year Columbus Drive and Lake Shore Drive are like freeways. This discomfort is compounded by the fact that the park has relatively few benches.[205]

MANAGEMENT AND USAGE

Managing Organization

The Chicago Park District is a municipal corporation established in 1934. It is governed by a seven-person Board of Commissioners. The Commissioners are directly appointed on staggered five-year terms by the Mayor of Chicago 'with the advice and consent' of the City Council. In practice, the Mayor has a relatively free hand over who s/he appoints. By all accounts, there have been periods when political affiliations were more critical than abilities or interest in parks. Day-to-day operations are the responsibility of the General Superintendent – who is appointed, in principle, by the Commissioners. In practice this position is also a mayoral appointment, as are a number of the other senior positions in the Park District. The separation of the Park District

*Column at Congress
Drive (April 2000)*

from the rest of city government is emphasized by the fact that it collects dedicated taxes – the Park Assessment. As a consequence, operational budgets for Chicago's parks are higher per unit area than for most other US cities. In 1986, however, the Park District was placed under Federal supervision 'because of racially discriminatory policies and poor management'. This led to the establishment of local Advisory Councils – citizen's boards reporting to the Park District, and Friends of the Parks – a watchdog group that 'speaks for the parks'.[206]

Use

The Chicago Park District does not conduct regular user surveys. Estimates were made in the early 1990s, as part of the Lincoln Park Framework Plan, that the lakefront had 61 million visitors per year – primarily to Grant, Jackson and Lincoln Parks. The Park District is also aware that there was a steady increase in the use of Grant Park through the 1980s and 1990s: 'Grant Park was hardly used in the 1970s – before the annual music festivals were started.' They are also aware that the park has a pattern of extraordinarily heavy use for festivals and holidays – 'half a million people each 4th July' – and that 'a big factor is how we generate more use of the park the whole year round'.[207]

PLANS FOR THE PARK

Current thinking about the future of Grant Park began with the 1972 *Lakefront Plan*. That aimed to 'maintain and improve the formal character and open water vista of Grant Park and prohibit any new above-ground structures'. Little further action was taken until the early 1990s – following Richard M. Daley's first election victory in 1989. While Mayor Daley is no less concerned with short-term results than most politicians, his strong support for parks manifested itself in the Park Board's creation in 1989 of an Office of Research and Planning. Two significant documents were produced in July 1992 – the nomination for the *National Register of Historic Places* and the *Grant Park Design Guidelines*.

The *Guidelines* made a clear distinction between historic rehabilitation and restoration – and established the principle of the Historic Template as the basis for plan-making for Grant Park. This approach aimed to 'preserve the park's historic character while accommodating the need for change'. The *Guidelines* talked about:

- parkland consolidation – the need for a unified scheme for the park and improvement of the roadways 'so that they unite the pieces of the park rather than separating them'
- land use and activation – expanding the variety and duration of uses
- accessibility – development of signage and connections
- structures and infrastructure – provision of facilities to cater to recreational, cultural and leisure time users
- reforestation – 'more tree, shrubbery and flowers'

all within the context of maintaining the 'envelope' of the park as a lakefront site that remains 'forever open, clear and free'.[208]

The *Guidelines* were intended as the first stage in a four-stage process. They were to be followed by a *Physical Plan*, a *Management Plan* and a *Capital Improvements Plan*. The second stage, named the *Grant Park Framework Plan*, was issued in March 2000 for proposals from pre-qualified consultancy teams. The *Request for Proposal* noted that the plan was intended to 'establish a consensus-based vision for both the short-term (five years) and long-term (twenty years) future of the park'. Goals for the *Framework Plan* included:

- expand the role of the park as a regional, citywide and local resource
- activate the park as a whole on a year-round basis

- protect and enhance its unique landscape qualities
- preserve and interpret its historical character
- integrate the park with the lakefront open space system.

The *Framework Plan* was set in the context of *Cityspace: An Open Space Plan for Chicago* produced in January 1998. That was a quantitative exercise aimed at achieving, first, a minimum standard of 2 acres (0.8 hectares) of open space per 1000 residents for all neighbourhoods by 2010 and, eventually, a standard of 5 acres (2 hectares) per 1000 residents for the city overall. Within this plan, Grant Park was categorized – with Burnham, Jackson and Lincoln parks – as a 'Magnet Park'; an area of more than 50 acres (20 hectares) attracting large numbers of visitors from the entire metropolitan area and having a 'service area' of one mile (1.6 kilometres).

CONCLUSIONS

Grant Park, saved for 'the poor people' of Chicago by Montgomery Ward, was shaped by Burnham and Bennett. The land for the park was created through incremental reclamation of the Lake Michigan shoreline and protected through bitter legal disputes. The park was conceived as the pivotal point of one of the earliest and most radical adventures in urban planning. It was developed through piecemeal additions around its Beaux-Arts heart. It is still dissected by railways and highways. But, without Ward and without Burnham, the lakefront opposite Grant Park might now be completely inaccessible. It is 'the landfill centrepiece' of an 'extraordinary linear park'.[209]

Bandshells have been barometers of the health of Grant Park. The Lakefront Millennium Park inserted in the north-west corner of the park – as near as possible to the downtown – is a remarkable reassertion of confidence in the future of festivals in the park. But the bridge between there and the Bicentennial Plaza is, in some ways, more significant. Along with the tunnels between the Buckingham Fountain and the lake edge and between the park and the Museum Campus, the bridge symbolizes a concerted attempt to unite the disparate parts of the park. Without such linkages Grant Park will remain magnificent in concept and perfect in plan – but a painful ordeal for pedestrians. The challenge is to develop a circulation strategy that energizes the Historic Template.

13 Stadtpark, Hamburg

151 hectares (375 acres)

INTRODUCTION

The Hamburg Stadtpark (town park) was the prototypical *Volkspark* (people's park). Conceived and constructed between 1900 and 1914, it represented a new model of public park for the rapidly growing urban population of a recently formed and increasingly industrialized nation at the beginning of a new century. The utilitarian name of the Stadtpark is apposite. The *Volkspark* was intended for active public recreation and as an expression of the spiritual unity and cultural identity of the German nation. It represented a significant break from the precedent of the pseudo-rural, scenic urban park that had become the norm in Europe and North America during the second half of the nineteenth century. The essence of the *Volksparks* was that 'they must provide large spaces for games of all sorts, which must be available to all. Only then will they become part of the life of the German people . . . tree-lined avenues should enclose these sports grounds and lead to large areas of water. There people of every social class will be able to gather to enjoy the delights of a place designed to compensate for the tracts of countryside eaten away by housing and industry, and to provide an oasis of peace in which to escape the pressures of the working week'.[210]

The final design of the Stadtpark was prepared by architect Fritz Schumacher (1869–1947) and engineer Fritz Sperber. It was completed in 1910 as the synthesis of the two favoured entries to a design competition. The strong axial design is unsurprisingly pragmatic and yet extraordinarily dramatic. As well as being a significant landmark in the development of park design, the Stadtpark remains, at

151 hectares, the largest and most heavily used purpose-built public park in Hamburg, the second largest city in Germany. The layout of the park is characterized by an axis of more than 1500 metres running between the 38-metre-high water tower (*Wasserturm*) and the main entrance at the south-east corner of the park. This axis incorporates 12 hectares of open lawns (*Festwiese*) and an 8-hectare oval lake (*Stadtparksee*) subtending a rectangle that is now divided off for swimming. The lake originally formed the focus for a major 'people's café' located between this rectangle and the main entrance to the park. It is often suggested that this type of baroque-derived layout expresses 'a world view whose religious, philosophical and political content is outdated'. This is hardly true of the Hamburg Stadtpark where the water tower 'simply replaced the castle' and was 'above suspicion because it had a common function'. The axis developed by Schumacher and Sperber 'arises from essentially practical, rather than purely visual considerations'. It remains in place – although its dominance has been eroded over time – and it continues to define the structure of the park.[211]

HISTORY

Designation as a Park

By 1867 Hamburg had a population of 265,500 but only 45 hectares of open space for public recreation. From the end of that decade suburbs were developed to the north of the city along the banks of the Aussenalser. New parks were created in these suburbs – including the 10.5-hectare Sternschauzen Park in Rotherbaum (1867–69) and a 13-hectare

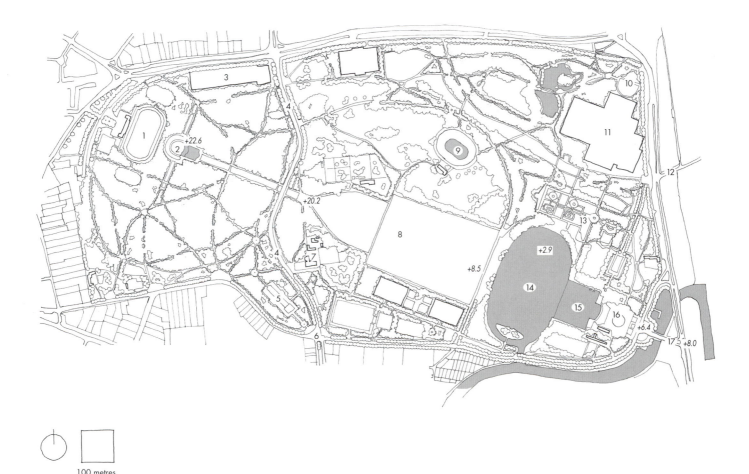

+8.5 = elevation in metres
above sea level

park on the banks of the Aussenalser (1873–1908). Some other, smaller parks were also created between 1870 and 1890, under the direction of district engineers and generally in a scenic style.[212]

The Chief Engineer for Hamburg in the 1890s, F. A. Meyer, was clearly aware of the need for additional open space for recreation and as a means of improving the health of citizens. Maass noted that 'in their early phase of growth, the cities were hit every year by epidemics of cholera and towards the end of the century high levels of TB and infantile mortality'. In 1896 Meyer drew up an expansion plan for the city – confined as it then was to a wedge of land pointing northward up the valley of the River Alser. His plan recognized that most of the existing open space was on the west bank of the Alser, an area inhabited by wealthier citizens. It called for a large park to the east of the river and to the north of the suburb of Winterhude, about 5 kilometres from the centre of the city. Meyer's plan was approved by the City Council in 1896 – but it was not until 1902 that funds were available for pur-

chase of land. The initial purchase in 1903 included a small wood (*Sierichsches Gehöltz* – the name still given to the woodland area surrounding the water tower) and some adjacent agricultural land. The site fell by about 12 metres from the north/north-west to the south and east. The *Goldbekkanal*, part of a network of natural and human-made links to the Alster, already extended from the Aussenalster to the south-east corner of the site.[213]

Preliminary designs for the park were prepared in 1903 but it was not until 1904 that a firm decision was made to develop a large *Volkspark* at Winterhude. In February 1904 a nine-person commission was appointed by the Hamburg Senate to oversee design and construction of the park. This commission included vociferous public figures like Alfred Lichtwark (1852–1914), Director of Hamburg Kunstehalle (Art Centre) and a strong proponent of the park; Justus Brinckmann (1843–1915), Director of the Museum of Art and Trade, and Wilhelm Cordes (1840–1917), Director of the huge Ohlsdorf Cemetery to the north-east of the park site, and city officials. Lichtwark had written an essay, *Makartbukett und Blumenstrauss*, in 1892 that directed 'attention to the peasant's gardens at Hamburg which he preferred to the English landscape parks'. Chadwick also noted that Lichtwark was 'very much against the general "landscape" style'.[214]

Initially the commission itself sought to draw up proposals for the park. One much publicized example was a sketch by Lichtwark that showed an axial arrangement of trees, buildings and water bodies running directly east–west through the length of the park. The only firm decisions that were reached during this period were the location of the water tower in the north-west of the site (determined by another commission of the Senate and eventually designed by architect Otto Menzel) and to call for designs by open competition. The call for entries was issued in 1908 and generated widespread discussion about the appropriate style of a major city park for the twentieth century. Sixty-six entries were submitted. Three commendations, three third prizes and three second prizes were awarded; but no first prize. The variation between the entries is characterized by the submissions from landscape architect Röthe with architect Bungarten, awarded a second prize, and the commended entry from architect Laeuger. The former included an *allée* focused on the water tower and an oval lake and restaurant at the south-east corner – but was otherwise redolent of Alphand's smoothly curved design for Buttes-Chaumont from the 1860s. The latter looked like an elaborate version of Lichtwark's axial sketch. Oberingenieur (City Engineer) Sperber was asked in January 1909 to produce workable versions of these two schemes. His proposals also failed to satisfy the commission.[215]

In November 1909 Fritz Schumacher was appointed Oberbaudirektor (City Architect). Schumacher had been an active member since 1902 of the Bund Deutscher Heimatschutz – an alliance for German values and the protection of its natural and historical heritage. The alliance was also involved with the Denkmalpflegetagungen (Congress for the Protection of National Monuments). A monument in this context was 'not necessarily simply a building of architectural merit but may also be a wood, a lake, a traditional costume or building technique'. Commission member Justus Brinkmann was responsible for crafts on behalf of the Bund Deutscher Heimatschutz. Vernier noted that Brinkmann went 'with Schumacher into the countryside around Hamburg to grasp the "essence" of the peasant tradition'.[216]

In December 1909 Schumacher was asked by the commission to work with Sperber to produce a common design. The architect preferred a more geometric layout; the engineer preferred something more traditional. In his 1928 book *Ein Volkspark*, Schumacher described the design as a geometric skeleton embedded in a free form body – and there is little question that he was the principal proponent of the axis. This design was unanimously approved in April 1910. It carried a cost estimate of 7.7 million marks and a proposed construction programme of seven years. Vernier suggested that 'it is possible to interpret the significance as national symbol of Schumacher's regular layout, in which the reservoir, technological object and equilibrator of the city and its internal circulation of water becomes monument, in which the small waterfall runs down a barrier made of bricks and in which the basin takes on the shape of a perfect ellipse'. Vernier also suggested that the (now demolished) dairy, the meadow, the lake, the cascade (also now demolished) and the brick that Schumacher used throughout the park are all symbols of the region, land, national character and origin – underpinning the essence of the Stadtpark (and other *Volksparks*) as an expression of social equality and national identity.[217]

Development of the Park

Construction of the park began in July 1910 with work on the ponds, canals, roads and paths. The first completed areas were opened to the public in July 1914 – the same year that Otto Linne was appointed as Hamburg's first Gärtendirektor (Director of Parks), a post that he held until he retired in 1933. Schumacher retained control of all the buildings and structures in the park – including a strong influence on Menzel's design of the water tower which, along with the dairy building, drinking hall, Landhaus 'Walter' and the café, was completed by 1916. The second construction phase began after the First World War. The stadium was completed in 1919; the paddling pool in 1921; the open-air theatre in 1924 and the special gardens by 1925. A planetarium was installed in the water tower in 1929 – the year that the park was deemed complete. Like Linne, Schumacher was elected an Honorary Member of the Royal Institute of British Architects (RIBA) in 1928. He retired from his position with the city in 1933. Schumacher's work exemplified the principle of *soziale Stadtbaukunst* (social urban art) – an art that he applied equally in Christian Democratic Cologne and Social Democratic Hamburg.[218]

The Stadtpark was used as a military base during the Second World War. Proposals were drawn up in 1941 for a massive axial extension of the park to the north-east, roughly doubling its area, to create a new stadium and associated sports facilities. The extension did not proceed. But the War did leave its mark on the park in the form of Allied bombing raids. These destroyed the main restaurant – the focal point of the park – as well as the dairy building, the café and the cascade – some of Schumacher's strongest brick structures. The park was used from 1945 until 1953 for the emergency accommodation of 2000–3000 people. Reconstruction began in 1948 and was completed, as far as it went, by 1953. The main entrance, the rose garden, roads, paths and the banks of the lake were rebuilt. But the main restaurant, the counterpoint to the undamaged water tower, has never been reconstructed. Its absence leaves a sadly depleted composition. Furthermore, management following the reconstruction tended to a 'liberal' philosophy that allowed gradual erosion of the original design without proposing any discernible programme in its place. This approach continued after the passing of responsibility for maintenance to the newly created district of Hamburg-Nord in 1962.

The social purpose behind the design diminished and its clear form was diluted. Schumacher's brick cascade on the west side of the lake was removed in the 1960s; avenues of trees were allowed to be broken; the edges of the lake were allowed to crumble; woodland was allowed to become overgrown and to block vistas; rhododendron was allowed to invade woodland and suppress regeneration; sports facilities were privatized and effectively cut off from the park. The drift away from the principles on which the park was built continued until the mid-1990s. In 1995 the Hamburg government established, with Hamburg-Nord, a programme of woodland management with advice from the University of Guttingen and commissioned a *Parkpflegewerk* (Park Management Plan).

PLANNING AND DESIGN

Location

The park is about 5 kilometres north-east of Hamburg city centre. When developed the park was abutted to the south and east by the dense inner suburbs of Barmbeck and Winterhude. It is now completely surrounded by development. The wealthier parts of Winterhude occupy the higher land on the west side of the park and the immediate fringe of housing on the south side. The denser and less wealthy area of Barmbek-Nord lies on the lower land to the east of the park. The area north of the park, Hamburg-Nord, was developed largely after 1945. It has a high business component. The park is easily accessible by public transport. There are U-bahn (subway) and S-bahn (surface rail) stations on all sides. They are all within 400 metres of an entrance to the park. The more heavily used areas within the park are located towards the more heavily populated south and east edges. This was 'logically the best position for the main entrance and the administration building'.[219]

Shape and Natural Landform of the Site

The overall site is roughly rectangular. It is aligned east–west. It is roughly 1.8 kilometres long and 650–1000 metres wide. The platform at the base of the water tower is 22.6 metres above sea level. Levels fall relatively steadily from here to the south and east. The normal water level of the lake is 2.9 metres. The elevation at the main entrance is 8 metres. There are no steep natural changes of level on the site. The steepest and most abrupt human-made slope is between the *Festwiese* and the lake. Equally, there is a vertical drop from the terrace at the east side of the lake. Otherwise the visual effects of the design are achieved with gentle changes of level over long distances.

Original Design Concept

The original intention for the park is expressed in Schumacher's statement that people should use it 'not in the sense of a passive enjoyment of the scenery, but in an active participation to be practiced [*sic*] in the open air: playing, taking part in sports, lying on the grass, paddling in the water, riding on horseback, dancing; going far beyond the appreciation of music, of art, of flowers and of physical pleasure'. Its development also coincided with recognition of the healthier aspects of sun-bathing. This was all a radical departure from nineteenth-century concepts and coincides with the ideologies of the 'Reform Park'. The axial form of the park had distinct precedents: precedents that are often associated with notions of the dominance of rulers over their subjects and of humankind over (the rest of) nature. 'In the people's park . . . the architectonic form was linked to the world of mechanized production. The park became a production machine. Instead of nature, the programme became the source of unity'. Perhaps Schumacher was deliberately appropriating an icon from an outdated value system as an expression of confidence in a new value system. The impact of the already long axis is strengthened by the deliberate narrowing of the clearing between the trees. The axis is the anchor for the rest of the park. All other spaces are secondary to, but not dominated by it – and all paths

Penguin Fountain (July 1987)

seem to relate to it. 'Straight and curved lines have been placed close to each other. As a result, a simple direct connection between the elements of the park is created . . . there are no residual spaces or left over corners'.[220]

The gently falling landform and the layout of the planting reinforce the pre-eminence of the main axis. The surface of Hindenburgstrasse where it crosses the axis is easily concealed by the landform; the abrupt slope between the lake and the *Festwiese* is also well concealed. Pohl commented that 'the layout is certainly not playful. It is well tested and suitable for mass use. It is functional'. There is no vagueness; there is a predominance of horizontal elements contrasting with the water tower; there are no statues 'of whatever hero, but only some contemplative statues'. There is a restricted palette of simple, dark planting that creates a distinct contrast with the broad open spaces. It would be easy to dismiss the layout as an aspirational statement from an emergent nation. But the *Festwiese* connotes freedom rather than domination; the axis creates a legible structure and provides orientation without suppression. 'The axis is not forced upon the observer by the use of planting in avenue form; aside from this central spine there is no attempt to impose an axial organisation'. Current activities within the park – family and ethnic group gatherings; casual games; swimming; barbecuing; rowing; partying; sunbathing; hanging-out – seem to locate themselves without conflict as a result of the original design. 'Across this broad expanse . . . only the contrast between the large number of people and their conspicuously low density allow one to grasp the true proportions' of the *Festwiese*. The park is intended to be 'a simple utility and consequently the arrangement is unpretentious'. The unchallenging legibility is liberating rather than limiting.[221]

MANAGEMENT AND USAGE

Managing Organization

Hamburg, like Berlin and Bremen, is a city state. It is one of sixteen *Länder* making up the Federal Republic of Germany. The park was designed and constructed by the City of Hamburg. The city's area was relatively limited at that time but the *Land* was extended in 1938 to include former Prussian cities like Altona (which already had its own *Volkspark*) and Harburg. The *Land* was subdivided into seven subsidiary administrative districts in 1962. The Stadtpark is in the district of Hamburg-Nord. The district has been the executive agency responsible for maintenance of the park since that date. The

city retains responsibility for strategic management and for funding, via the districts, of all parks in Hamburg. No breakdown was made during the 1990s of the funds spent exclusively on the Stadtpark. Although Hamburg is a rich city, its leaders have a trading disposition and are not eager to spend money on institutions that aren't seen to make money. The relatively limited land area of the city state has meant that a lot of development since the 1960s has occurred outside its administrative (and tax collecting) boundaries. There is no 'Friends of the Stadtpark' group – although there was one in the 1930s and consideration was being given in 1999 to the establishment of a new group specifically for the Stadtpark. Apart from being a formal vehicle for the expression of concerns about the park, this is seen as a potential generator of funds for its conservation – much along the lines (or aspirations) of North American models.[222]

User Characteristics

Few figures exist for use of the Stadtpark. It was estimated in 1999, however, that the park received:

- 3–4 million visits per year (use levels remain high year round)
- 100,000 visits over a summer weekend
- significantly more visits than during the 1980s.

PLANS FOR THE PARK

The official attitude to the Stadtpark is that it is 'an old park and an historically important park . . . but it is not a museum'. The buildings, the natural habitat and the park itself are protected by federal laws. The current management philosophy, however, is to 'provide an old park for the future'. The *Parkpflegewerk* (Management Plan) adopted in November 1997 was based on that attitude. The plan comprised:

- a chronology of the development of the park and an assessment of the meaning of Schumacher's design
- a review of how the Stadtpark can be the '*Volkspark*' of the future'
- a listing of management objectives to achieve this end
- an assessment of the action necessary to achieve these objectives
- a schedule of priorities and an estimate of costs for their achievement
- an examination of external factors – like traffic levels and accessibility – that will affect the future of the park.[223]

The review of the Stadtpark as the 'Volkspark of the future' examined how the park might continue to operate as an after-work recreation area and as a substitute for vacations. It cited a federal survey from 1995 which recorded that quality of life was reflected for 74 per cent of citizens by 'scenic' surroundings and for 70 per cent by 'city parks and green spaces'. Objectives set for management of the park were to:

- give first priority in the planning of facilities and in the programming of activities to recreation and to experiencing nature
- continue to cater for people of all social classes and of all ages
- restrict the exclusive use of facilities and areas of the park by specific user groups
- adopt a long-term policy of free public access to all parts of the park
- provide facilities that will encourage use of the park in winter and in bad weather
- increase the attractiveness of the flower gardens – which were a fundamental component of the Stadtpark in the 1920s – and develop new planting themes for them
- improve signage and visitor information
- increase the attractiveness of park entrance areas;
- increase the range and improve the condition of play equipment
- develop a collaborative approach to park management which creates, as well as attractiveness and utility, a culture of music and the arts.

The plan called for:

- a design competition to re-evaluate the use, form and circulation of the main entrance area so as to create a new focus at the end of the main axis (while retaining the lido)
- proposals to make the north-east, Toronto

Bridge at southern end of Stadtparksee (July 1999)

*Paddling/Playpool
(July 1999)*

Bridge, Borgweg/Hindburgstrasse and Linnering entrance areas more legible and better connected with the overall circulation system of the park
- a new use and programme for the *Neue Welt* (New World) play area,

and in the inner areas of the park:

- re-establishment of the strength and clarity of the *Festwiese*
- restoration of the lake edge footpath and giving of clear form to the island in the lake
- a new planting theme for the herb garden.

The priorities for immediate action were seen as:

- redevelopment of the play pool
- repair of water supply and irrigation system
- renewal of lake edges; provision of stable walkway restoration of northern bank; provision of a café
- clearing undergrowth around back of stadium and to sides of water tower to restore vistas

- woodland management measures including heavy cutting back of rhododendrons.

The estimated cost of all the proposed works was DM9.55 million – DM9.08 million for works and DM0.47 million for fees.

The summary of the plan concluded that:

- the Stadtpark remains a very popular facility that merits a special place in the history of park design
- management of the park must retain unity of purpose and form in its planning, restoration and maintenance
- high priority must be given to the main entrance and lido and to the north-east entrance areas
- importance must also be attached to measures for improvement of the lake edges; for maintaining diversity and removing vegetation that suppresses competition in the woodland areas
- the Stadtpark needs a friends group to develop an ethos of collaboration between its managers and the citizens who use it.

*Water tower/planetarium
(July 1987)*

CONCLUSIONS

The Stadtpark was one of the first modernist parks in the world. The idea behind its creation was that active recreation should be given priority over the passive enjoyment of romantic, generally pastoral, scenery. This was a radical departure from precedents in Europe and North America. Despite its radical concept, the form of the Stadtpark is, ironically, distinctly neo-baroque. The axis around which the park is organized has immense visual power. But it did not represent, as had originally been the case with such forms, the domination of one class of humankind over another so much as the emergence of the park in Europe as an urban utility. The *Volkspark* 'was intended to be the place for activities and feelings that would lead man [*sic*] back to his [*sic*] natural roots. Instead of exotic and precious plants, preference was shown for the traditional forms of the German landscape and its sacred plants, oaks and conifers; instead of picturesque flower-studded avenues great unrestricted grassy surfaces . . . the identification of physical and sporting activities with the spiritual rebirth of the German *Volk* led to a heightening of the cathartic function of park amenities'.[224]

The *Volkspark* also acted as a precedent for another uniquely German model for the public park – the *Jugendpark* (Youth Park) promoted by Leberecht Migge and others during the period of the Weimar Republic (1918–33). Migge's work was an approach where 'function now began to create form, instead of being accommodated within a form that was preconceived'. The Stadtpark remains an immensely popular and heavily used facility. Maass noted that 'although the name and its origin have been forgotten by now, these parks are widely used by the population, and usually form the greater part of public green space inherited' by many German cities. She also noted that 'the people's parks possessed two features that are still valid today – a broad conception of culture in the open air and functional open spaces'.[225]

The clean horizontal lines of the park and the unambiguous spaces that they define remain remarkably reassuring; the axis is the backbone of a smooth-flowing circulation system that unfussily unites the various activities within the park. The Management Plan approved in 1997 was based on the principle of the Stadtpark being the '*Volkspark* of the future'. That plan recognized the historic significance of the park but, rather than retaining the original form for its own sake, it sought to continue the philosophy that function should be the principal determinant of the character of the park. It remains an exemplary demonstration of the application of a modernist approach to park design.

14 Landschaftspark Duisburg-Nord

200 hectares (495 acres)

INTRODUCTION

If Parc de la Villette is the French prototype for the urban park of the twenty-first century, then the Landschaftspark Duisburg-Nord (Duisburg North Landscape Park) is the German prototype. Duisburg is one of seventeen separate cities along the River Emscher in the Ruhr District of north-west Germany – once the largest industrial region in the world. The principal industries were coal mining and steel making. The mines started to close in the late 1950s. By the end of the 1970s many of the steelworks had also closed as the focus of heavy industry moved from early industrial countries to 'newly industrialized countries'. The site of the Landschaftspark included a coal mine and coking plant – which ceased production in 1977 – and a steelworks which ceased production in 1985. Development of the park was one of a number of high-profile projects undertaken as part of the Internationale Bauausstellung Emscher Park (International Building Exhibition – IBA) that ran from 1989 to 1999.

The name Emscher Park was given to the 70-kilometre-long 'green backbone with six pairs of ribs leading off to the sides' extending from Duisburg on the Rhine in the west to Bergkamen in Westphalia to the east. The Emscher Park covered 800 square kilometres of which only 320 square kilometres were not built up. The title 'Park' reflected the intention that the IBA should be a demonstration of 'social, cultural and ecological measures as the basis for economic change in an old industrial region'.[226]

Rather than demolishing the steelworks, its largest blast furnace and most of the associated infrastructure have been retained as central, publicly accessible features of the Landschaftspark. And rather than removing volunteer vegetation, it has been retained as an evolving reflection of the history of the site. The idea of retaining much of the steelworks plant was probably influenced by the precedent of Gasworks Park on the shore of Union Lake in Seattle. There landscape architect Richard Haag's design kept much of the industrial plant in situ – but set it in newly sculpted grassy landforms.

At Duisburg landscape architects Latz + Partner (husband and wife team Peter and Anneliese) took this approach to an altogether more radical and dramatic level. Their design adapts and reinterprets the industrial features and natural processes already occurring on the site. Massive concrete-walled storage bunkers, a network of rail beds, an immense gasometer, cadaverous blast furnaces and a cavernous power station building have been retained and adapted to be safe for public access. Bridges and walkways have been built to enable visitors to experience the site; gathering spaces – like the Piazza Metallica – have been worked into the scheme; gardens composed of found materials have been created in the bunkers; naturalized vegetation has been encouraged, and a lighting scheme that brings the rusting hulks glowing back to life has been added. Physically and ideologically, it is a multilayered post-industrial project. Where the design of Parc de la Villette was based on principles of deconstructivism, the design of the Landschaftspark Duisburg-Nord is based on decomposition.[227]

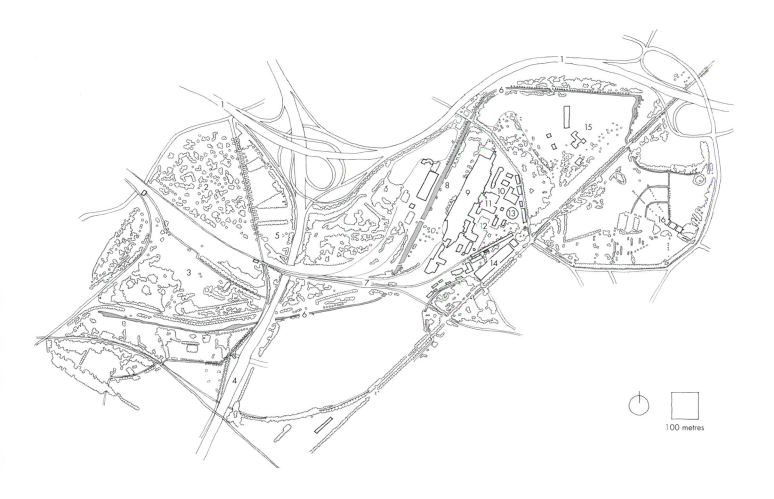

HISTORY

Designation as a Park

Coal mining and iron production began in the Ruhr valley in the Middle Ages. The availability of the river as a transport route was instrumental in the development in the late seventeenth century of coal mining on an industrial scale. By the mid-eighteenth century the population had reached 230,000; by 1871 it was 700,000; by 1895 it was 1.5 million and by 1905 it was 2.6 million. Development involved the rapid expansion of many small villages into relatively large cities. It was uncoordinated and lacking in infrastructure – particularly water, sewerage and transport. In 1905 a plan to unify the cities of the Ruhr valley was discussed; newspapers carried stories about plans for the industrial area and for establishment of a *Zweckerband* (special purpose district). The strongest force for integrated planning beyond administrative borders came from the International Planning Exhibition in Dusseldorf in 1910. The exhibition focused on the establishment

of a 'Green Spaces Commission' and of a system of 'green ribbons' to counteract the degradation of the area between the Ruhr and Emscher rivers. In the event no such organization was established until the end of the First World War.[228]

Reparation conditions after that War required intensification of coal mining. The perceived need for an overall planning agency also increased and establishment of the Siedlungsverband Ruhrkohlenbezirk (SVR; Ruhr Coal Mining District Housing Association) was approved by the Prussian Assembly in 1920. It covered an area containing 3.6 million inhabitants living in 346 settlements, including the seventeen autonomous municipalities that still exist in this polycentric region. Robert Schmidt, the first Director of the SVR, focused attention on open space planning, lines of regional communication and direction of development northward within the area. The SVR was subverted for the centralized purposes of the Third Reich but resumed its environmental planning role in the 1950s. Plans made at that time acknowledged the

*Walkways inserted into
the bunkers by the
Sinterplatz (June 1999)*

*Cycleway on line of
former rail track
(June 1999)*

to encourage and coordinate projects sponsored by municipal authorities and other agencies. More than one hundred projects were undertaken by the IBA; sixteen commercial projects were developed on 500 hectares of derelict industrial land; sewage treatment works, housing and highways were built; DM5 billion was invested in the region – two-thirds from public funds, the rest from private investment.[230]

Condition of the Site at the Time of Designation

The first development on the site of the Landschaftspark was the sinking in 1899 of the first shaft of the Friedrich Thyssen 4/8 mine. The first coking plant was started in 1905. The mine shafts were closed in 1959 – the first to close in the Ruhr area. The coking plant was closed in 1977 and demolished in 1980. The smelting works had produced 37 million tonnes of pig iron by the time it ceased production in 1985. The cost of demolishing the works would have been prohibitive. Furthermore, conservationists began to regard the hulk as an industrial monument; climbing clubs started to practise on the iron ore bunkers, and diving clubs started to practise in the water-filled gasometers. Thyssen surrendered the site to the City of Duisburg in 1989 for DM1 only. Politicians and citizens argued that the company had made money from the site for more than eighty years and that it should be responsible for restoration of the land. The company responded to the effect that 'if you don't take the site, we will close it up and leave it exactly as it is'.[231]

According to Peter Latz, 'the industrial remains were not the biggest problem in setting up the park'. There were soils that contained arsenic or cyanide which had to be completely removed from site. Other toxic soils were buried in the sintering pools and covered with new earth. Extensive areas of the site comprised barren slag tips that were beginning to support volunteer plant associations. But the biggest problem was the condition of the River Emscher which was effectively a canalized open sewer flowing through the site. The sewage disposal strategy adopted around the end of the nineteenth century produced about '400 kilometres of open sewers' and 'only one central water treatment works located where the Emscher flows into the Rhine'. The river now runs through an underground pipe and clean water flows through the Landschaftspark on the original line, directly above the pipe.[232]

The IBA Emscher Park was established in December 1988. It had five main landscape planning objectives:

decline of coal mining – 200,000 miners lost their jobs in the 1960s – but did not recognize the beginnings of structural decline of heavy industry in the area. Plans drawn up in 1966 continued to protect the network of seven green wedges developed by Schmidt. This became the backbone of the IBA Emscher Park established in 1989.[229]

The Emscher Park was established 'as a ten year programme to identify new perspectives for the future of an economically and socially weakened region . . . there was no hope to replace big scale old industries by big scale new industries'. Politicians and planners for the IBA concluded that 'widespread ecological renewal must precede any lasting economic revival'. Great importance was attached to the quality of landscape and watercourses (the Emscher in particular had become an open sewer); to industrial monuments as cultural artefacts; to provision of new dwellings, and to offering new forms of work. Following the fall of the Berlin Wall and the reunification of Germany in 1989, the former East Germany became the focus of federal economic investment. The IBA, by contrast, was an institution owned by the Land of North Rhine-Westphalia. It had private sector status. It had few direct employees. It was designed

- preserving the remaining leftover landscape
- linking up the isolated, separate areas in the agglomeration
- re-zoning separate areas as parkland
- coming to agreements both regionally and locally on individual projects with a long-term perspective
- maintaining and managing the new open spaces in a permanent regional park association.[233]

The establishment of the IBA and its call in May 1989 for proposals for the exhibition coincided with the emergence of the recreational potential of the site in Duisburg-Nord. The Landschaftspark was envisaged as a 'stepping stone' within the Emscher Park system. Its establishment required the concerted action of four organizations. First, the Landesentwicklungsgesellschaft Nordrhein-Westfalen (Land Development Association of the *Land* of North Rhine-Westphalia) purchased large parts of the site from Thyssen and the railway company. They were supported in this by the Grundstücksfonds Ruhr (Ruhr Real Estate Fund). The third body was the City of Duisburg which re-zoned the land as open space. Finally, funds for the design and construction of the park became available from economic restructuring aid for Reinhausen miners. This money was directed by the IBA towards major projects like the Landschaftspark.[234]

In 1990 expert opinions were sought on the value of the smelting works as an example of industrial archaeology, and on the extent of ground and water pollution. Existing vegetation was mapped and evaluated. A design competition involving five preselected landscape architect-led teams was established. The teams were Cass Associates from Liverpool, England; Bernard Lassus et Associés from Paris; and three German teams, including Latz + Partner. Their proposals were presented in March 1991 after a six-month study period. The competition has been characterized as highlighting the contrast between Lassus's 'sophisticated French symbolic garden . . . with three minutely designed garden zones to reflect the landscapes of specific eras' and Latz's 'pragmatic approach' which 'wanted to turn as little as possible inside out and leave as much as possible of what had been formed, first by industry and then by decay and pioneering plants'. The Lassus team's entry was called 'the day before yesterday, yesterday, today and tomorrow'. It proposed the wilful use of dense rows of trees to subdivide the site into eras that represented its pre-industrial condition, its industrial and its post-industrial uses. The Latz entry, by contrast, explored 'the value of everyday nature, claiming it has much to offer our day-to-day life'. Their entry

addressed the question of 'whether the remains of the industrial mass production plant – vast buildings and sheds, gigantic ore dumps, chimneys, blast furnaces, railway tracks, bridges, cranes and so on – could really serve as the basis for a park'. Latz + Partner were appointed to the project in 1991. The park was officially opened on 17 June 1994.[235]

Key Figures in Establishment of the Park

Landscape architect Peter Latz (b. 1939), working with Anneliese Latz and their team at Latz + Partner, is clearly the key figure in the design of the Landschaftspark. His upbringing reveals the influences both of 'landscape' and of 'architecture'. He grew up in post-Second World War Germany and financed his schooling by growing fruit and vegetables. His father was an architect. He portrays an approach to design that is 'dependent on the unique nature of the place in question'. Latz described his work as 'continuously scanning the entire repertoire of our landscape and garden culture and being able to draw on its resources at any time to find the optimum solution'. His approach has been described as appearing 'to challenge every notion' and he has been described, somewhat harshly, as subscribing 'to every theory, every concept, preferably a different one every single day'. Certainly his work is pragmatic and eclectic rather than formularized. As he put it, 'a definitive design rarely exists to begin with'. Latz described his work at Duisburg-Nord as having begun by writing 'stories about a falcon circling a mountain. And it gradually became clear to me what I would do with the blast furnaces'. But it wasn't the meaning of the furnaces themselves that interested him as much as the layers that they represented; 'the syntax of the levels, the degree of regularity with which one or a number of things are repeated'. He likened Duisburg to the Duke of Bomarzo's decaying Italian Renaissance gardens at the Villa Orsini. He also commented that he is not 'of the opinion that Classicism, Romanticism and other cultural movements are alternative functions'. He believes that 'they can exist synchronously'. As he put it 'we must try to step back from the clichés, and from this distance we should consider what kinds of potential are really available to us'.[236]

PLANNING AND DESIGN

Location

The Landschaftspark is between the Duisburg districts of Meiderich to the south and Hamborn to the north. The Thyssen works used to be a barrier between these two parts of the city. It is beginning

*Cowperplatz
(June 1999)*

to create an effective link between them. The park benefits from the fact that it is located on all the cultural/recreational routes that were established by IBA Emscher Park – the Landmark Art Route; the Industrialized Nature Route; the Industrial Culture Route, and the Architecture Route. The park is also located on cycleways that connect it to the larger neighbouring cities of Dusseldorf and Dortmund.

Shape and Natural Landform of the Site

The site of the Landschaftspark is a roughly 3-kilo-metre-long strip aligned east–west along the valley of the Emscher. It varies in width between 500 and 1000 metres. It is dissected by highways and former rail lines. The north–south Autobahn 59 divides the site into segments of roughly one-third to its west (the Schachtgëlande – coal mine area, and Kokergelände – coking plant area) and two-thirds to the east (the smelting works and associated structures and storage areas). The Kokergelände is officially closed to the public under federal law because the ground is contaminated. The recently constructed Autobahn 42 runs east–west along the northern edge of the park. The drone of traffic on the A42 does nothing to diminish the industrial aura of the site. The former rail line to the on-site power station runs north-east to south-west across the eastern end of the park. It separates an area of farmland and allotment gardens from the former industrial area. The farm used to produce food for the Thyssen canteens; it is now run as a demonstration farm for local schools. The allotment gardens were formerly used by immigrant Polish workers for vegetable growing. They are now used by immigrant Turkish workers for vegetable growing. The natural landform of the site was relatively undramatic. The long period of mineral extraction and importation to the site, its reshaping for industrial activity and the ongoing disturbance by transport infrastructure have, however, created significant level changes and physical barriers along its length. The works themselves are also significant vertical elements protruding above the adapted landform and naturalized vegetation of the site.

Original Design Concept

Conversion of derelict land into parks in the IBA Emscher Park 'often led to destruction of that mysterious atmosphere between decay and revitalization that had made the sites so attractive'. There is, however, abundant evidence of a 'traditional almost middle-class aesthetic approach, in which the landscape, the architecture and the landmarks are seen from a vague, distant vantage point

in appreciation – if not awe – of their beauty'. 'This approach represents a rejection of old cultural values and is a sign of a new consciousness in which labour . . . is regarded as an important aspect of the Ruhr's past'. 'Instead of clinging to nostalgic memories of a bucolic landscape, one that never existed at the Ruhr even in its pre-industrial days, efforts have been concentrated on the remnants of the industrial past. As a consequence, the open space type of the traditional urban park has been subtly integrated into the new landscape'. The Landschaftspark fits into this context well and has been likened to 'a kind of prototype of a new generation of park for industrial conurbations elsewhere'.[237]

Latz's pragmatic approach to his work generally and his decompositional, syntactic approach to the Landschaftspark have already been mentioned. He described the working method for Duisburg-Nord as being 'one of adaptation and new interpretation, a metamorphosis of industrial structures without destroying them; the blast furnace is not only an old furnace – it is a menacing dragon ahead of daunted men, and it is also a mountain top climbed by alpinists and rising above its surroundings'. He described the function of the urban park at the end of the twentieth century as being quite different from the function of the *Volkspark* in the early twentieth century. Like John Brinkerhoff Jackson, Latz has stated that whereas the *Volkspark* had a programme derived

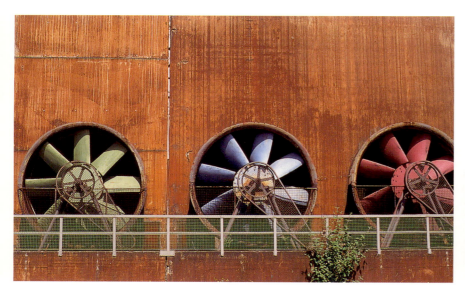

Repainted turbines (June 1999)

Sunbathers on purpose-built decks along the new canal (June 1999)

from social relations in the 1920s, 'when park users were a collective . . . nowadays everyone goes alone; the dog owner, the diver, the cyclist. There is no such thing as a park for all'. This is seen as another justification for treating the many layers in the park as being independent of each other and realizable non-sequentially.[238]

Spatial Structure, Circulation System, Landform, Materials and Planting

It has been suggested that 'a map of the site is meaningless unless it is in three dimensions'. In the original competition entry Latz + Partner sought to avoid showing the whole site and to present different parts of the park as five discrete entities. Their design made very few changes to the spatial structure of the works or the spatial structure of the site overall. They encouraged multilevel access wherever it was safe for humans to go – and they concentrated on redefinition, redirection and reinterpretation of what they found on site.[239]

Various descriptions of the design by Latz and by others talk about different numbers of outer parks and subdivisions within the park. The point here is that while the park has major features that act as imageable focal points – like the Piazza Metallica, the Cowperplatz or the gardens in the Sinterplatz (cinder place) – it does not have a prescribed circulation system. It does, however, have a carefully inserted, brightly coloured (to signify safety) catwalk that gives 'visual access' to the slowly rusting remains. Latz stressed the importance to the park of the 'harp of railway tracks' – the Bahnpark. This is a multilevel splay of rail tracks whose beds have been retained or restored as

closely as possible to their original layout and levels (and re-surfaced in an uncomfortably angular grey gravel) so that their geometry can be re-experienced and reinterpreted.[240]

Latz + Partner also determined that the line of the clean-water, surface-level Emscher Canal – the Wasserpark (water park) – should exactly follow the direct line of the former open sewer. No artifice; no pseudo-naturalness. Pedestals for aquatic plants and platforms for that most German of activities – sunbathing – were constructed along the new watercourse. The steelworks is the dominant vertical element on the site, but two horizontal elements – the canal and the perpetually present pipeline – are the principal source of unity from one end of the park to the other. The vegetation in the park is largely comprised of the ruderal species that preceded designation of the park. Birch and willow have been allowed to continue their colonization of large parts of the site – particularly the coking areas and the rail banks – and species introduced with the iron ore have been encouraged to continue to grow

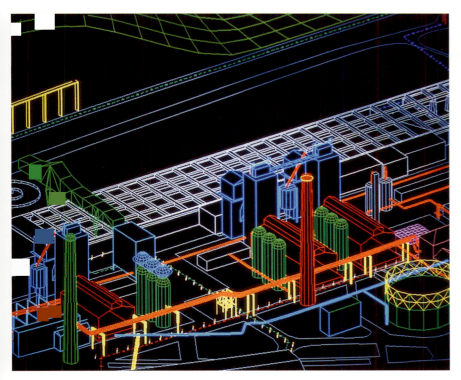

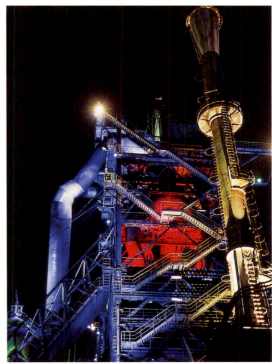

Computer illustration of Studio Park's scheme for lighting the former steelworks (October 1996)

Right: *Lighting scheme in operation (October 1996)*

on areas close to the works. The vegetation of the site overall is dominated by the emerging pattern of colonization by a blend of native and exotic pioneer species. Specified planting close to the works comprises no more (or less) than tight grids of standard trees that stand in stark counterpoint to the rusting hulks that they confront.

MANAGEMENT AND USAGE

Managing Organization

The Kommunalverband Ruhrgebiet (KVR) took charge of the Emscher Park following the end of the IBA 'on a contract basis with the Land of North Rhine-Westphalia' for an initial five years. Management of the Landschaftspark is undertaken by Landschaftspark Duisburg-Nord GmbH – a form of private limited company established in 1995 and wholly owned by the City of Duisburg. Directors of the company include representatives of the City; representatives of the Land and representatives of the IBA/KVR. Landschaftspark Duisburg-Nord GmbH is constituted with the objective of making money from the park. It is charged with maintaining the park; managing events; renting-out of facilities; running the open-air cinema and attracting citizens of Duisburg to the park. By 1999 the company employed six full-time staff. Horticultural mainte-

nance of the park was originally carried out by the City of Duisburg using unemployed direct labour on training programmes. The internal organization of the City changed in the latter part of the 1990s and much of its maintenance work – including horticultural maintenance – was privatized and let by competitive tender. Most of the early contracts were won by 'sister' (i.e. spin-off) companies. Maintenance of facilities which are leased out – like the gasometer used by the diving club – is undertaken by the lessee. At the end of the 1990s there were between 250 and 300 people working on the site on regular maintenance or on new minor works projects.[241]

Funding

The site was purchased by the City of Duisburg from the Thyssen company for DM1 in 1989. The cost up to 1999 of constructing the park, excluding demolition and decontamination work, was DM30 million. This came from a combination of federal and regional government funding programmes – partly to counteract unemployment in mining regions and partly as a result of the IBA. Installation of the underground sewage main cost 'more than all the other equipment in total'. Maintenance costs for the entire park in 1999 were DM3.5 million. Until the end of 1999 this was largely derived from the Land of North Rhine-Westphalia (DM2.9

million) with the City of Duisburg providing the remaining DM0.6 million. The objective at that time was that funds for running the park should be derived one-third each from the Land, from the City and from the staging of events. Events – particularly the leasing of space for outside organizers – were only beginning to generate a profit by 1999. There are, however, reflections of Bryant Park Restoration Corporation in the way that the management company is set up.[242]

User Characteristics

The management company reckoned that about 300,000 visits were made to the park in 1998 and that numbers would increase year after year from then on. Visitor numbers to two events during June 1999 – both one-off and one day only – attracted 50,000 and 20,000 visitors respectively. Repeat visitors include numerous cyclists and dog walkers. User numbers are also increased by:

- the energetic marketing policy for the park including the development of a range of facilities for extreme sports
- the availability in the park of a range of indoor and outdoor event spaces
- high level of freedom by German standards for access to a decommissioned industrial site.

PLANS FOR THE PARK

Development and management of the park were driven throughout the 1990s by Latz + Partner's original proposals. These can be characterized as minimal intervention in the processes that were already occurring on the site. This philosophy called for naturalized vegetation – whether indigenous to the region or imported, say, with iron ore from South Africa – to be allowed to continue the process of succession. It also called for the steelworks to be allowed to continue to deteriorate – providing they presented no threat to human safety. In the latter part of the 1990s Latz + Partner still had staff permanently based on site overseeing the implementation of their designs. They were working alongside a growing team from the management company who were directing greater energy towards the marketing of the park. The management team's endeavours included:

- rental of venues (like the 'Delta Music City'); management and promotion of events and marketing the park as a venue for activities like film-making and for product launches

- sponsoring the development of works like the refurbishment of the gasometer by a diving club (completed in January 1999) and the construction of a 140-bed youth hostel
- generating publicity for the park among local citizens
- running and publicizing the increasingly well-known, extraordinarily elaborate lighting programme for the steelworks. In 1999 this was extended to use on Friday, Saturday and Sunday nights throughout the year
- provision of facilities for disabled access and organizing programmes for retraining of unemployed people in on-going construction activities.[243]

CONCLUSIONS

The Landschaftspark Duisburg-Nord is an essay in change over time. It presents developing volunteer vegetation against the spectacular backdrop of a defunct and slowly decaying steelworks. It can be described as a post-industrial park – a symbol of the grip of nature being re-established after the grip of industry has been relaxed. It combines a process-based, decomposition-driven theoretical approach to landscape architecture with place-directed pragmatism. It can be compared with – and contrasted to – Parc de la Villette as a late twentieth-century approach to designing the urban park for the twenty-first century. Where Tschumi regarded 'nature' as having little or no role in the city, the Landschaftspark put 'nature', its processes, and humankind's interventions in them, at the heart of the park. It contains a potent metaphor that 'nature' is more powerful than humankind. The intended moral message might read as a confession of humankind's wilful destruction of natural resources; or a self-righteous statement of our willingness to engage in a healing process. Certainly, in Treib's terms, the park is a site where 'meaning condenses at the intersection of people and place'.[244]

Whatever conclusions may result from those reflections, the Landschaftspark has to be respected as probably the largest new urban park to be created in Western Europe – if not the world – since the Bos Park in Amsterdam was commenced in the 1930s. It is most significant as the embodiment of post-industrial sublimity. It pitches the awe-inspiring presence of the redundant steel works against the poetry – and power – of natural processes. But, at the start of the twenty-first century, it is still the immense power and the associations of the machine that make the stronger impression.

15 Prospect Park, Brooklyn, New York

526 acres (213 hectares)

INTRODUCTION

Prospect Park is the less well-known but more highly praised younger sibling of Central Park (see location map on page 4). Both were designed by landscape architects Frederick Law Olmsted (1822–1903) and Calvert Bowyer Vaux (1824–95) – pioneers of the profession in the United States. Prospect Park was designed shortly after the American Civil War (1861–65) as a place that would give 'a sense of enlarged freedom'. It is composed of roughly even proportions of meadow, forest and lake enclosed by landform and unified by a sophisticated circulation system.[245]

Prospect Park is one of the simplest but most subtle landscape compositions in North America. The Long Meadow in particular is the apotheosis of Olmsted and Vaux's 'American Pastoral' style. Like Central Park, it reflects the smooth-flowing lines of Lancelot 'Capability' Brown's 'Beautiful' style and Humphry Repton's 'Picturesque' style. Also like Central Park it reflects the segregated circulation system that Paxton designed for Birkenhead Park. Nevertheless, both Central Park and Prospect Park were a distinctly American response to the vast scale and rapid rectilinear growth of its largest settlement.

The gestation of Prospect Park was remarkably straightforward. The site that was originally selected was dissected by Flatbush Avenue. The Brooklyn Park Commissioners agreed to reallocate land so the park could occupy one undivided tract of varied, but largely fertile, terrain. The first President of the Commission, James Samuel Thomas Stranahan (1808–98), retained that position for twenty-two years without interruption. He remained avidly enthusiastic about the park and apparently incorruptible. A paragon. Olmsted and Vaux were appointed to the project in May 1866 and remained in complete control of design and construction until 1873 – a year of economic depression. The park continued to be developed and managed for a further twenty years in accordance with their design.

Between 1890 and 1915, the park began to reflect the Beaux-Arts neo-classicism promoted by the 1893 World's Columbian Exposition in Chicago. The entrances were redesigned in the emerging style and substantial neo-classical buildings were erected in the park. Management and maintenance went into decline after 1915. After the Second World War sports facilities were added; budgets were reduced, and the park fabric deteriorated. Facilities that were out of character with the Olmsted–Vaux concept, like the ice rink, were added in the 1960s. The original design remained relatively undisturbed for over a century but investment in the park continued to decline. A Friends group was established in 1966. But it was only in 1980 that a Park Administrator was appointed and charged with leading the recovery of the park. The Prospect Park Alliance – a not-for-profit fundraising organization was formed in 1987. Slowly but slowly rehabilitation based on the Olmsted–Vaux plans got underway in the 1990s. And in much the way that the original designers sought to accommodate large numbers of visitors in a vulnerable pastoral landscape, so the Prospect Park Administrator has 'to mediate between demands for historic preservation; for increased active and passive recreation, and for ecological integrity'.[246]

Prospect Park, Brooklyn,
New York

1   Grand Army Plaza
2   Prospect Park West
3   Meadowcroft Arch
4   Endale Arch
5   The Long Meadow
6   Flatbush Avenue
7   Litchfield Villa
8   Picnic House
9   Brooklyn Zoo
10   Bandshell
11   Tennis House
12   The Pools
13   Ambergill
14   Ravine
15   Willink Entrance
16   Prospect Park
      South West
17   Nethermead
18   Boathouse
19   Lookout Hill
20   Breeze Hill
21   Concert Grove
22   Ocean Avenue
23   Carriage Concourse
24   Prospect Lake
25   Parkside Avenue
26   Parade Ground

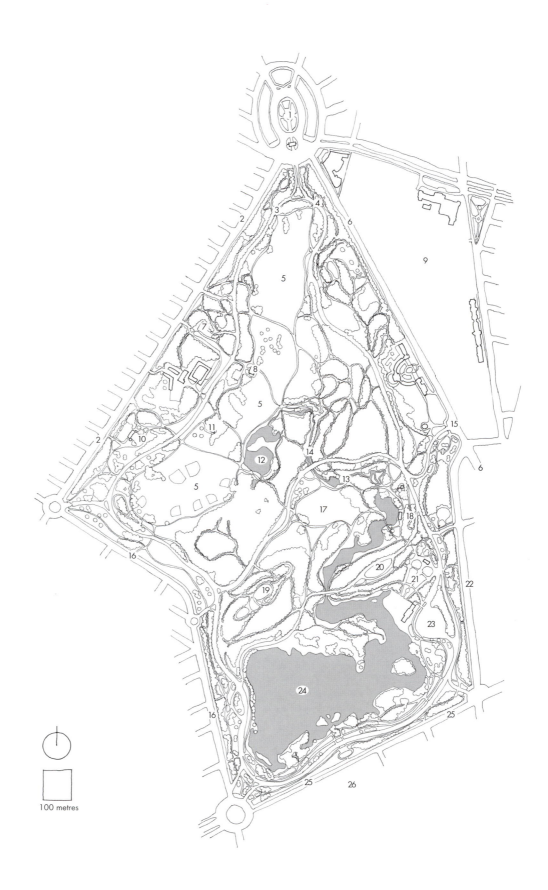

100 metres

HISTORY

Designation as a Park

Brooklyn developed as a physically and administratively separate city from New York. It received its charter in 1834. The two cities were not physically linked until completion of the Brooklyn Bridge in 1883. They were merged administratively in 1898. The population of Brooklyn was 24,310 in 1835, 48,000 in 1840 and 266,661 in 1860 – at which time it was the third largest city in the United States. Even without the bridge, Brooklyn was becoming a major suburb of Manhattan. Whereas Manhattan is a long, thin fortress with moat-like water surrounding it, Brooklyn, on the far larger Long Island, had space to expand – albeit in the same gridiron pattern that had been established for New York by the 'Commissioner's Plan' of 1811.[247]

Just as concerned citizens and journalists like William Cullen Bryant had lobbied for the creation of Central Park, lobbyists for a comparable park in Brooklyn included Walt Whitman – Editor of the *Brooklyn Times* from 1857 to 1859 – and Edwin Spooner – Editor of the *Brooklyn Star*. There were three main motives behind the call for a park – concern for the health and well-being of Brooklynites; concern to maintain the attractiveness of Brooklyn as a suburb of Manhattan, and concern to emulate the already widely discussed Central Park. In April 1859 the New York State Legislature appointed fifteen commissioners to select sites for public parks in Brooklyn. In February 1860 the Commissioners recommended seven sites. 'The largest and by far the most important' was 'Mount Prospect Park' on Prospect Heights. In April 1860, the legislature approved the creation of Prospect Park and authorized the issue of bonds for land acquisition and for construction of the park. Stranahan was appointed President of the Park Commission later that year and Egbert Viele, Chief Engineer for Central Park, was appointed to draw up plans.[248]

Size and Condition of the Site at the Time of Designation

The originally designated site comprised around 170 acres (69 hectares) at the northern end of the eventual park plus the 'East Side Lands' – around 125 acres (50 hectares) to the east of Flatbush Avenue, already a major highway. The East Side Lands were included because they covered Mount Prospect, at an elevation of 198 feet (60 metres) the second highest point in Brooklyn, and the Mount Prospect Reservoir. The terrain was formed by the Wisconsin Glacier. The Harbor Hill Moraine, a terminal moraine from that glacier, runs the length of Long Island. It covered all the originally designated park area and deposited 'boulder-strewn stony loam' across it. The outwash plain of the glacier to the south was largely covered by 'remnant sandy and silty loams'. Bedrock is about 350 feet (105 metres) below ground level and 'the rich soil . . . produced large vigorous trees and a general luxuriance of vegetation that had not been possible in the thin rocky covering of Central Park'.[249]

The easternmost encounter of the Battle of Long Island in 1776 during the War of American Independence occurred within the (proposed and final) site area. The occupying British forces cleared much of the area for firewood and encouraged settlers to grow vegetables on the cleared land. Viele noted, however, that by 1861 'nearly one half the area is wooded with trees of large growth, many of them specimens of oak, maple, hickory, dogwood, chestnut . . .'. Much of the outwash plain to the south was being used as farmland. Viele's plan allowed for underpasses either end of Flatbush Avenue and for one bridge over it. Viele, formerly an infantry colonel, left New York to join the Union Army later in 1861. He had been paid for his work.[250]

No further work was undertaken during the Civil War. Stranahan, who had developed a 'more comprehensive understanding of the role of parks in creating a new urban landscape' did, however, approach Vaux towards the end of 1864 to advise on the design of the park. They visited the site together in January 1865. Vaux recommended acquisition of more land to the west (now the western end of the Long Meadow) and south (now Prospect Lake) and disposal of the East Side Lands, excluding Flatbush Avenue from the park. The relatively short, depressed transverse routes that were critical to the success of Central Park would not have worked here. Also, being aware of the popularity of skating in Central Park, Vaux wanted a suitable area for a larger lake. Stranahan accepted Vaux's recommendation and took it to the State Legislature. They approved it in May 1865. Olmsted, Vaux and Company Landscape Architects were appointed later that month.[251]

Key Figures in the Establishment of the Park

Vaux developed the design for Prospect Park on his own until Olmsted's return from California towards the end of 1865. Once again Vaux had to cajole Olmsted into joining him in a major New York park project. And while 'the question of the precise role of each man is the subject of endless partisan argument', it is widely recognized that Vaux made the principal strategic recommendations for the design of Prospect Park – their 'masterpiece'. It is also reckoned that while 'Olmsted had the important administrative ability to surround himself with talented people and to employ them well' and that 'his brilliance as an administrator . . . guaranteed the quality of his [sic] completed parks', he was 'hardly the creative artist that Vaux was'. It is Olmsted's name, however, that has become the generic term for their work and describes design principles that are 'so completely characteristic of the nation' that it is difficult to distinguish them 'from the look of the country itself'.[252]

Calvert Bowyer Vaux (1824–95) was born in Pudding Lane, London. His father, a doctor, died in 1833. He and his younger brother obtained places at the 'well-endowed' Merchant Taylor's School. Vaux left school at the age of fifteen and was articled to London architect Lewis Nockalls Cottingham (1787–1847), an exponent of Victorian Gothic architecture. Vaux supplemented his income by moonlighting. He lettered railway maps and used the additional money to make sketching trips to France and Germany. His nascent architectural career changed radically when he was recommended in 1850 by the Secretary of the Architectural Association of London to Andrew Jackson Downing (1815–52). Downing – 'America's Repton or Loudon' – was a leading advocate for a major park in New York. He was seeking an architect to work with him in the United States. Downing drowned, tragically, two years later. By then, however, Vaux had assimilated many of his mentor's 'Picturesque' approaches to landscape design and went on to adapt and apply them, with Olmsted, in their own 'American Pastoral' style.[253]

Frederick Law Olmsted (1822–1903) was born and brought up by strict churchmen in New England. In 1840 he was sent to New York to work as a clerk after a severe case of sumac poisoning in 1836 had prevented him from entering college. Olmsted returned to New England and, in 1843, sailed to Canton, China as a ship's boy. He then spent time as a special student at Yale studying 'scientific farming' before running the farms that his father bought for him – first in Connecticut during 1847 and then, from 1848 to 1855, on Staten Island. During this period Olmsted made his first trip to Europe, visiting Birkenhead Park and numerous country estates. He followed that trip by working as a peripatetic writer and in 1855 moved to New York, where he began his forty-year career as a landscape architect and where he lived and worked for most of the following twenty-five years. He spent the first two years of the Civil War as Executive Director of the United States Sanitary Commission, a forerunner of the Red Cross. He was praised for his organizational skills and energy but eventually resigned, as was his wont, because he could not get his way. He spent 1863 to 1865 running a goldmine at the Mariposa Estate in California before Vaux persuaded him to return to New York to work on Prospect Park.[254]

The opportunity for Vaux and Olmsted to turn Prospect Park into the 'perfect' expression of their 'American Pastoral' style owed a great deal to the patronage of James Samuel Thomas Stranahan, millionaire and President of the Brooklyn Board of Park Commissioners from 1860 to 1882. Stranahan was raised on a farm and trained as a civil engineer and land surveyor. He earned his fortune in building construction and had served as a State Congressman. Stranahan has to be admired for the fact that he recognized the need and dealt equitably with the replacement of Viele by Vaux and Olmsted; that he supported Vaux's proposal to alter

Beaux-Arts serpent vase at Grand Army Plaza entrance (April 2000)

radically the location and extent of land for the park, and that he stood between the designers and the sometimes corrupt Brooklyn city government. Imaginative landscape architecture can only be achieved with imaginative clients. Without Stranahan, Prospect Park might have proved as vexing to Olmsted and Vaux as did Central Park.[255]

PLANNING AND DESIGN

Location

Vaux recommended acquisition of what were termed the 'Rather Expensive Lots' to the west of the originally designated site in order to facilitate a unified design for the park. These lots were already owned by wealthy Brooklyn families – but had not yet been developed. Graff speculated that the Brooklyn city fathers saw a parallel between this area and the enhanced value of lots facing Central Park. Sure enough, developers built single family homes in Flatbush (south of the park); row houses in Park Slope (north and west of the park), and apartment houses along Ocean and Eastern Parkways (south and east of the park). 'By the 1890s Park Slope had supplanted Brooklyn Heights as the location of choice for many of the city's wealthiest residents'. And 'by the 1920s, its surroundings had become so popular that developers tore down some of the houses facing the park and built the handful of apartment towers that are now visible from the Long Meadow'. Much of this development was inspired by the parkways, modelled on Alphand's work in Paris, that Olmsted and Vaux proposed for Brooklyn in 1868 and subsequently advanced as a means of insinuating public open space into cities throughout America.[256]

Shape and Natural Landform of the Site

Vaux's proposed revision of the park area was approved by the State Legislature in 1868. It created a compact, six-sided site containing three distinct types of terrain – rolling, steeply sloped and flat – that were ideally suited to the pastoral landscape of meadows, forests and lakes that Olmsted and Vaux sought to create. They supplemented the natural landform with a densely planted 15- to 20-foot-high (4.5 to 6 metres) berm around the edge of the park. This is redolent of the woodland shelter belts with which Lancelot 'Capability' Brown encircled country estates. It might also have been a precedent for the berms around Disney theme parks, precluding views to or from their enclosed 'kingdoms'.

The moraine that formed the site left a

remarkably diverse topography. Directly south of Prospect Park West and on Lookout Hill are high points with elevations of over 180 feet (55 metres). The Long Meadow falls gently from 150 feet (46 metres) at the Endale Arch end to 120 feet (36 metres) at its southern edge adjacent to The Pools. The Pools themselves fall from 135 feet (41 metres) at the Grotto Pool through the Ambergill and the Ravine to the Nethermead and Prospect Lake, both with elevations of 62 feet (19 metres) – a horizontal distance about 2000 feet (600 metres). Olmsted and Vaux arranged for this water system to be fed from a deep well below Lookout Hill. It has been fed by city water since about 1900.

Original Design Concept

Olmsted and Vaux's concept for the park was clearly articulated in their *Report to the Commissioners of Prospect Park* in 1866. They described it as being intended to provide 'a feeling of relief' for people escaping from the 'cramped, confined and controlling circumstances of the streets of the town . . . *a sense of enlarged freedom*'. They also stated that 'supposing the more hilly land to be covered by plantations, and a greensward to be formed upon the open ground . . . and the low plain to be mainly occupied by a lake, we have the three grand elements of pastoral landscape that we were seeking'. These three 'grand elements' were the 75-acre (30 hectares) Long Meadow; the 200-acre (80 hectares) Forest – including the Ravine, and the 60-acre (24 hectares) Prospect Lake. Each of these is larger than its equivalent in Central Park – the Sheep Meadow (or the 1930s Great Lawn); the Ramble and the Lake. The 40-acre (2 hectares) Parade Ground to the south of the park was designated in 1868 following a recommendation in the 1866 Report.[257]

Spatial Structure, Circulation System, Landform, Materials and Planting

The entry sequence through Endale Arch into the Long Meadow is one the most highly praised visual experiences in the world. Hiss described this sequence as 'probably the best sort of introduction to our [sic] country's experiential heritage' and talked about being 'overtaken by a sense that in the midst of a crowded city you can be present in and a part of a serene and endless world'. Garvin likened it to 'Dorothy opening the door of her black-and-white house to wander into Technicolor Oz, enters into a gorgeous landscape devoid of any trace of the city'. Simpson described the 'darkening mystery of the path culminating in the tunnel of Endale Arch, and then, in as dramatic a flash of light as the nineteenth

Overleaf: The Long Meadow from 35 Prospect Park West (October 1999)

century – lacking electricity – ever saw, the golden white sun of the meadow. One has arrived in the countryside'. Endale Arch, completed in 1867, was paired with Meadowcroft Arch, completed in 1870, west of the entrance from Grand Army Plaza, to create set-piece pedestrian portals to the park.[258]

The Long Meadow itself is probably the single most iconic element in all of Olmsted and Vaux's work. Newton noted that 'the Long Meadow illustrates with compelling force the psychological effect of curving space. As one enters from the north, first eyes and then feet are pulled irresistibly toward the hazy distance of the south where the meadow curves to the right and out of sight. Moving along under the impulse, one feels the pull continue and senses the start of an outstanding characteristic of Prospect Park . . . sequence'. Beveridge described the Long Meadow as 'the special triumph of Olmsted and Vaux's plan . . . there are few places where one can recapture more of the sense of place that Olmsted [sic] intended'. Simple materials are skilfully combined to create a seemingly endless space.[259]

Where the Long Meadow was an exercise in Olmsted and Vaux's American Pastoral style, the Ravine was a more picturesque contrivance punctuated with rustic wooden bridges and shelters. The water course was artificial and more characteristic of the Adirondack or Catskill Mountains than it was of Brooklyn – which probably accounts for its rapid deterioration when maintenance levels declined in the twentieth century. An isolated stand of remnant forest was 'enhanced to create a larger and more continuous expanse of woodland core . . . and a woodland buffer at the Park's edges'. New planting in the park was a mix of native and exotic species. Many of the exotic species have disappeared altogether, while others – like the sycamore and Norway maple – have regenerated at the expense of native species. Olmsted and Vaux left a poor legacy in this respect.[260]

The Prospect Lake was sealed with puddled blue clay from a peat bog within the site. The Lake displays the same subtle complexity as the Long Meadow – it is never fully visible from any single viewpoint. It is the sump for the water system and it served as a skating venue in winter. The one formal part of the park – the Concert Grove – was located adjacent to the Carriage Concourse at the east end of the Lake. Like The Mall in Central Park, this was intended as a major gathering space that would reduce pressure on less robust parts of the park. Like The Greeting in Franklin Park (and unlike The Mall) it was located on the periphery – and was the only place where buildings, statues and similar items were intended to be put.

The circulation system in Central Park is generally reckoned to be derived from the precedent of Birkenhead Park. It is acknowledged for its masterly separation of transverse roads, carriage drives and pathways. The circulation system in Prospect Park demonstrates further development of that approach. First, Vaux ensured the exclusion of extraneous traffic from the park by proposing the revised site allocation. Then, Vaux and Olmsted developed a figure of eight circuit of carriage drives on the enclosing berm and through the centre of the park, allowing access to Breeze Hill and Lookout Hill. All but one of the entrances to the carriage circuit were located at the junctions of the six roads surrounding the park. A separate system of bridle paths runs largely alongside the carriage circuit. The berm was pierced by a series of pedestrian arches – like the Endale and Meadowport Arches – allowing pedestrian access to the interior of the park. The footpaths within the park were designed as a seemingly endless series of rambles. Rybczynski, visiting the partly restored Ravine in 1997, noted that 'so skillfully did Olmsted and Vaux lay out the path, engage the senses, mask distances, and direct attention from one event to another, that I have entirely forgotten that just over the brow of the hill lies Long Meadow and beyond it Flatbush Avenue'.[261]

Development of the Park after Olmsted and Vaux

Construction of the park was substantially complete by January 1871. The one area that remained to be finished was the (already designed) additional land to the west. Vaux and Olmsted dissolved their partnership in 1872. Olmsted was appointed Commissioner of the New York Department of Public Parks and Vaux was appointed Consulting Landscape Architect. They were both retained as consultants to Prospect Park. In 1874 Vaux went into partnership with the multi-talented Jacob Wrey Mould (1825–86) designer, with Vaux, of the Concert Grove and of Bethesda Terrace in Central Park. Development of Prospect Park continued for the next twenty years or so to follow the direction established by Vaux, Olmsted and Stranahan.[262]

In the 1890s the wave of neo-classicism promoted by the World's Columbian Exposition hit the park. This had already begun with the proposal in 1885 to erect a neo-classical arch in Grand Army Plaza to commemorate the Civil War. The arch was completed in 1892. It was followed by monumental designs from McKim, Mead and White for the rest of the Plaza and the other entrances to the park. Their standard treatment was to turn them into circles and to add a selection of columns, colonnades or oversized statues. This was antithetical to

Olmsted and Vaux's proposals. But they were less significant than the three neo-classical buildings added between 1905 and 1915 – the Boathouse; the Tennis House and the Willink Entrance Comfort Station. These were followed by the Picnic House in 1927 – in the elbow of the Long Meadow – and the Zoo, under the Works Progress Administration, in 1934. The Bandshell adjacent to Prospect Park West was built in 1939 in the kind of peripheral location that Olmsted and Vaux might have found more acceptable. In 1959 baseball diamonds were introduced to the south end of the Long Meadow. In 1960 the skating rink was clumsily implanted at the edge of the Lake on the axis of the Concert Grove.

The insertion of new entrances, structures and sports facilities in and around the park ran parallel with the reduction of administration and resources for the park. The Brooklyn Parks Department was relocated in 1892 to Litchfield Villa, completed in 1857, on Prospect Park West. The Boroughs of Brooklyn, Staten Island and Queens were amalgamated with New York in 1898. Parks in Brooklyn and Queens continued to be administered from Litchfield Villa until 1934 when Mayor Fiorello La Guardia appointed Robert Moses sole commissioner of a unified Department of Parks for New York City – a position he held, for better and worse, until 1960. The park celebrated its centenary in 1966 and 'despite superficial sprucing up . . . looked much the worst for wear'. The occasion did, however, create the impetus for establishment of the Friends of Prospect Park, the first step towards the start of its renaissance in the 1980s.[263]

MANAGEMENT AND USAGE

Managing Organization

In 1981 New York Mayor Edward Koch issued his 'first ten-year capital plan'. It included $750 million for rebuilding the city's parks. The permanent workforce at the parks department – which had fallen from over 5200 in 1965 to less than 2500 in 1980 – also began to be rebuilt. The first immediate change at Prospect Park was the appointment in 1980 of a Prospect Park Administrator to act as manager and principal advocate for the park. Improvements in the condition of the park took a major step forward at the end of that decade – following the establishment in May 1987 of the Prospect Park Alliance. This is a non-profit public/private partnership with the City of New York. The Alliance provides 'a formal structure for raising private funds and establishing a set of guidelines for their expenditure, and serving as an advocate by working with the community'. It also acts as an agency for the organization of volunteer labour in the park. The number of volunteers rose from 600 in 1987 to 5000 – donating over 24,000 hours – in 1997. By contrast, the full-time staff for all management and maintenance operations in the park fell from eighty-eight to forty-eight over the same period. In 2000, there were twenty-eight full-time staff plus 'workfare' labourers equivalent to forty full-time labourers.[264]

Funding

Funding for Prospect Park in 1999 came roughly 40:60 from the Prospect Park Alliance and public sources – principally the City of New York. Contributions for capital works are also made on a discretionary basis by the Borough of Brooklyn. By comparison, funding for the Central Park Conservancy came roughly 80:20 from private and public sources. The Alliance generated an income of $392,557 in its first eighteen months; $3,028,573 in 1997 and $4,129,754 in 1999. Rehabilitation and maintenance of the park to current standards are therefore highly dependent on private contributions. Tax deductions are allowable to donors.

Usage

In the same way that the Bryant Park Restoration Corporation set out in the early 1980s to increase visitor numbers – on the principle that 'use drives out abuse' – the newly appointed Administrator set out to promote use of Prospect Park. Regular user surveys have been undertaken since that time. The estimated number of visits in 1980 was 1.7 million. By 1988, the figure had risen to over 4 million visits – of which 70 per cent were by people living within ten minutes of the park. By 2000, it was in excess of 6 million – although the origin of visitors and their racial composition had changed little over the preceding twenty years. In other words, the park is continuing to serve its core constituency of local residents – but its managers appear to have learned how to serve them better.[265]

PLANS FOR THE PARK

A series of historic landscape reports was commissioned in the early 1980s. These were intended to 'explain, inventory and assess the park's historical and natural resources and to act as a guide for its restoration'. The first of these reports, completed in 1984, focussed on the Ravine – the picturesque but erosion-prone 'heart of the park'. These reports prompted two particular outcomes. First, recognition of the fact that the Olmsted–Vaux plan from 1874 was the ideal template for physical rehabilitation of the park – but with major woodland management measures designed to improve its ecological health; second, the establishment in 1987 of a Landscape Management Office to implement these measures. A further step towards rehabilitation of the park was the establishment, in 1991, of an on-site Design and Construction Office to supervise physical restoration work.[266]

The *Landscape Management Plan for the Natural Areas of Prospect Park* was completed in 1994. Its aim was to 'sustain the natural, cultural, recreational and aesthetic resources of the park over time while providing for a high level of public access and participation'. The plan identified six proposed land cover types. Management intentions for each of them were:

- Forest Core (essentially the area between the Long Meadow and the Lake) – closed canopy, multilayered native forest
- Perimeter Woodland (mainly outside the carriage route) – transition zone from the city, featuring closed canopy native woodland; more intensively used and more fragmented than the Forest Core; not expected to achieve a high level of ecological integrity
- Specimen Trees (Long Meadow, Nethermead and Lake shores) – trees in mown grass
- Tall Grass Meadow (small pockets like edges of Long Meadow) – maintained by periodic mowing
- Horticultural Zones (entrances and areas adjacent to buildings) – high use areas requiring intensive maintenance
- Water Features (Lake, Ravine and Lullwater) – increase habitat diversity of natural areas, including measures like removal of rampant *Phragmites* from The Pools.[267]

Woodland rehabilitation began in 1994 and was followed in 1996 by commencement of the first of three phases of physical restoration of the Ravine. These works were largely designed and implemented on the basis of historical photographs. By 2000 most construction works and management operations were being supported by increasingly sophisticated GIS records. Ongoing management plans were being prepared on a five-year cycle. A programme for restoration of buildings and other structures began in the mid-1990s – including eventual removal of the skating rink from the Concert Grove. The Alliance agreed in 1998 to adopt the Parade Ground as part of its responsibilities. In March 2000 the Borough of Brooklyn allocated

*Fresh mulch around trees
at the edge of the Long
Meadow (April 2000)*

*Entrance to the Long
Meadow through the
Endale Arch
(October 1999)*

$10.3 million to a four-year refurbishment programme for the sports facilities there. Such measures help the park management to mediate between the demands for historic preservation, increased active and passive recreation, and ecological integrity. Such conflicts are reflected by the continued presence of baseball diamonds on the Long Meadow.

CONCLUSIONS

Beveridge noted that Olmsted and Vaux 'set the pattern for the urban park in America, provided a concept and rationale for the urban park system, designed and named the parkway, and created the country's first significant examples of Greenways'. Prospect Park is widely regarded as their finest park design. The entry sequence though Endale Arch is a masterpiece of sensory manipulation. The Long Meadow to which it leads has achieved iconic status among human-made landscapes. But the qualities of Prospect Park could not have been achieved without the lessons that they learned from Central Park, without the quality of site that they persuaded the park commissioners to provide, or without the protection of someone as sensible and sensitive to the project as James Stranahan. Even though Prospect Park has been described as a 'masterpiece'; a 'perpetually contemporary' classic and a 'great American work of art', it has also been perpetually vulnerable. Over time, the integrity of its concept has been threatened by new structures; the stability of its landform has been threatened by overuse; visitors' safety has been threatened by under-use; its ecological stability has been threatened by invasive plant species, and its survival has been threatened by under-funding. In short, the durability of good park design depends on good management – which, thankfully, it is currently enjoying.[268]

16 Tiergarten, Berlin

220 hectares (545 acres)

INTRODUCTION

The Tiergarten – literally 'animal garden' or 'garden of beasts' – sits at the edge of the physical and political centre of Berlin. It is generally acknowledged to be the oldest, largest and most important park in the city; often referred to as the 'Central Park' of Berlin and comparable to London's central Royal Parks. Originally a private park owned by monarchy, the Tiergarten was enclosed for hunting and subsequently made accessible to the public before being redesigned expressly for free public use.[269]

The Tiergarten has a 500-year history whereas 'very few of the city's older buildings predate 1850'.

The history of Berlin, the history of Prussia and the history of Germany have unfolded around it. The park was the scene of public protests during the political unrest of 1848; the site for the Prussian Siegessäule (Victory Column) placed in 1870 and relocated in 1938; the setting for the Reichstag (Federal Assembly building) completed in 1894, destroyed by fire in 1933 and completely resurrected for the return of the federal government of the reunited Germany in 1999. The neo-classical Brandenburg Gate, at the eastern edge of the Tiergarten, was completed in 1791. It was designed as a gate in the customs wall on the west side of the city but attained the status of a triumphal arch after Prussia's defeat of Napoléon in 1814. It was retained when that wall was removed in the 1860s and remained a military setting for the unification of Germany in 1871, and during the two World Wars. The Gate is a German monument and the enduring symbol of the city of Berlin. From 1961 to 1989 it sat on the line of the Berlin Wall that divided the occupied city. During that period the Tiergarten was no more (or less) than a major recreation area at the eastern edge of West Berlin.[270]

Berlin has been characterized by periods of rapid growth and sudden change. It has often been occupied by the troops of other countries – by Austria in 1757; by Russia in 1760; by France in 1806–08 and 1812, and by the United States, Soviet Union, the United Kingdom and France from 1945 to 1994. It has a long history of hosting immigrants including Protestant Huguenots from France and Jews expelled from Vienna in the 1670s and 1680s; skilled labour, largely from Saxony in northern Germany, during the 1730s, and *Gastarbeiter* (literally 'guest workers'), largely from

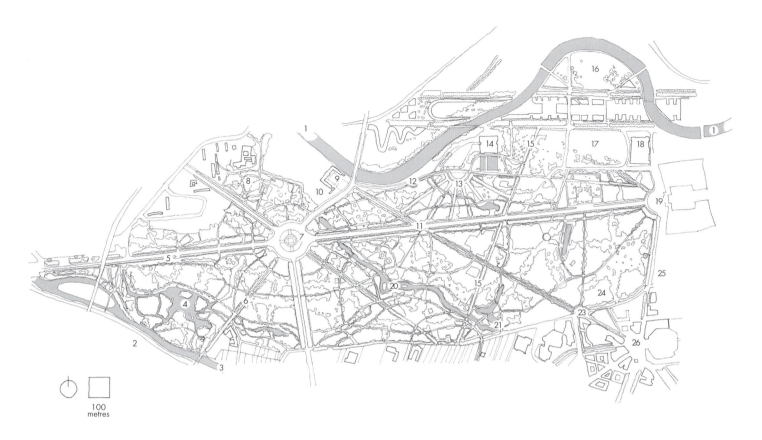

Turkey, since the 1950s. Similarly, the Tiergarten has been continuously redefined by the events that have occurred in and around it. It displays the geometry of King Friedrich I (1688–1713); masterly hydraulic design and scenography of landscape architect Lenné in the 1830s; the bombast of Hitler and his architect Speer in the 1930s; the reparatory garden and meadow-making of Alverdes in the 1950s, and a burst of late twentieth-century preservation.[271]

The Tiergarten is a palimpsest. Its physical elements reflect its function first as a hunting ground, then as public pleasure gardens; as a site for national monuments; as the setting for the democratic functions of the Prussian and then German nation; as part of Hitler's plans for *Germania*; as a major recreation area for an entrapped oasis of Western democracy, and, once again, as the setting for national government functions. The Tiergarten now has a heavily wooded appearance – which is remarkable given that it was virtually clear-felled for firewood in the latter part of the 1940s. And, aside from the obvious east–west slash of the Strasse des 17 Juni, the park has a relatively mysterious character that only slowly reveals its full complexity and intricacy. At the start of the twenty-first century the park was being prepared for its multiple roles as

heritage site, urban recreation area, ecological refuge, and setting for national government functions.[272]

HISTORY

Development of Berlin and of the Tiergarten

Berlin grew from the two cities of Cölln, on the left bank of the River Spree and, on the right bank, Berlin. In 1359 Berlin–Cölln joined the Hanseatic League – a group of free-trading and mutually defending European cities that included London and (the then larger) Hamburg. In 1411 the region came under the control of Friedrich of Hohenzollern. He was a 'noble' from South Germany sent by the Holy Roman Emperor to quell a dispute for control of the cities between the Dukes of Pomerania and the brutal Quitzow Brothers. He conquered and took the title *Kurfürst* (Elector) – of Brandenburg – ruling until 1440. His successor, Elector Friedrich II (ruled 1440–70) laid the foundations for Berlin Castle in 1442 on land in Cölln and established a royal court. The population of the cities in 1450 was 6000.[273]

In 1527 Prince Joachim – later Elector Joachim II (ruled 1535–1571) – acquired, for use as a game reserve, the land that now includes the Tiergarten. It remained woodland crossed only by footpaths until the rule of Elector Friedrich Willhelm (ruled 1640–88). Major works did not begin in the park until 1695. By the beginning of the seventeenth century the population of Berlin–Cölln had doubled to 12,000. That century saw aggressive, absolutist rulers in much of Germany seeking to extend their territories and was characterized by the Thirty Years' War (1618–48). By the end of that war the population had reduced back to 6000. Nevertheless, Friedrich Willhelm, subsequently termed the 'Great Elector', increased his territory and sponsored the expansion of Berlin including the axis of Unter den Linden running between the castle and the eastern edge of the Tiergarten. The Great Elector also had the entire park re-fenced and stocked with deer and grouse, and had new oak trees planted. Elector Friedrich III (ruled 1688–1713 – also known as Friedrich I after having himself crowned King of Prussia in 1701) founded Friedrichstadt on land south of Unter den Linden. It included Friedrichstrasse – the north–south axis that was completely re-established in the 1990s following the reunification of Berlin.[274]

Construction commenced in 1695 of a new palace to the west of the Tiergarten. This was subsequently named the Charlottenburg Palace, for Friedrich's wife Sophie Charlotte. Unter den Linden was extended westward through the park to the new palace. The Grosser Stern (literally 'Big Star'), the Kurfürstenplatz (literally 'Elector's Place' – later named Zeltenplatz, literally 'Tent Place', after the refreshment tents that were located there from 1745) and the six, now restored, avenues that radiate from it were constructed. These developments marked the end of the use of the park for hunting. In 1709 Friedrich officially created the single city of Berlin. The population had grown from 20,000 in 1688 to 60,000 at the end of his reign in 1713. He was succeeded by King Friedrich Willhelm I (reigned 1713–40) – who, by all accounts, was an aggressive, boorish, parsimonious bully obsessed with military expansion. Berlin became a garrison city; the economy expanded; skilled immigrants arrived, particularly from Saxony, and the population grew to 90,000 by 1740. Friedrich Willhelm's only contribution to the Tiergarten was to have a section removed from it for the westward extension of Dorotheenstadt and Friedrichstadt. He also had a new wall constructed around the extended city and created adjacent to it the *Quarré* – Pariser Platz, the now-restored square directly east of the Brandenburg Gate.[275]

Friedrich Willhelm's son, King Friedrich II (reigned 1740–86) was a completely different char-

acter from his father. He saw himself as an Enlightenment figure; he befriended French author–philosopher Voltaire and had him move to Potsdam as court librarian. While Friedrich pursued legal and administrative reforms – such as granting religious freedom and abolishing torture – he did also use his father's full treasury and large army to wage wars against Austria (1740–42, 1744–45) and against Russia (1756–63). This led to Austrian troops occupying the city in 1757 and Russian troops occupying it in 1760. His eventual victory over Russia earned him the sobriquet 'Friedrich the Great'.

When he was not fighting, Friedrich devoted himself to major construction projects – including construction of the Forum Fredericianum (comprising the world's first free-standing opera house – now Humboldt University, and the state library) towards the eastern end of Unter den Linden; converting Unter den Linden itself into an even grander boulevard, and transformation of the Tiergarten into a pleasure park. Most of these projects were designed for him by architect Georg Wenzeslaus von Knobelsdorff (1699–1753). Implementation of Knobelsdorff's design for the Tiergarten began shortly after Friedrich's accession in 1740. He called for removal of the fence around the park; creation of a double avenue around Grosser Stern, adorning it with baroque statues; strengthening and lengthening of the avenues radiating from Grosser Stern and from Zeltenplatz; creation of the avenue from Potsdamer Platz north-west to create the Kleiner Stern (literally 'Small Star') where it met the Charlottenburger Chaussee, and the formation of a series of other, smaller avenues and circular clearings in the woodland. The park had been formally opened to the public in 1740 and, 'by the time of his death' (in 1753) Knobelsdorff 'had almost completed laying out sections of the park.'[276]

When Friedrich the Great died in 1786 Berlin had a population of 150,000 and Prussia was emerging as a European power. His successor, Friedrich Wilhelm II (reigned 1783–92), was an extravagant ruler who left his son, Friedrich Wilhelm III (reigned 1797–1840), with huge debts and left Berlin with its most enduring monument – the Brandenburg Gate. This neo-classical structure was designed by Carl Gotthard Langhans (1732–1808) and built between 1788 and 1791. The statue of a goddess in a chariot drawn by four horses (*quadriga*) faces into the original city and away from the Tiergarten. Changes in the park during the reign of Friedrich Wilhelm II included building of the Bellevue Palace between 1785 and 1790 (and extension of Knobelsdorff's avenue from Potsdamer Platz to the Kleiner Stern) and largely romantic works by Ehenreich Sello ('the Younger', Head Gardener to the court from 1768–95). These works included creation of the *Neue Partie* (New Part) of the park with the Rousseau Insel in 1792. Bellevue Palace was damaged in the Second World War. It was restored to become the federal President's second residence in 1955, and was declared the President's official residence in 1993.[277]

In October 1806 Napoléon and his army marched through the Brandenburg Gate and occupied Berlin until 1808. They removed the *quadriga* and shipped it to Paris. The French re-occupied the city briefly on the way back from their ill-fated Russian campaign. They were subsequently defeated by Prussia and the *quadriga* was returned to Berlin in 1814. Between 1810 and 1840 Berlin's population doubled making it, at 400,000, the fourth most populous city in Europe. During this period both Karl Friedrich Schinkel (1781–1841) – 'the greatest German architect of the nineteenth century' – and Peter Joseph Lenné (1789–1866) – 'the greatest German landscape architect' – became involved with proposals for the extension of the city and redesign of the Tiergarten. Schinkel began work as a painter of panoramas and dioramas then as a stage set designer before obtaining a post in the Administration of Prussian Buildings in 1810. This was followed by a senior post in the newly formed Public Works Department in 1815. Lenné shared patrons in the Prussian royal family and aristocracy with Schinkel. From 1816 Lenné was employed by Friedrich Wilhelm III at Sanssouci in Potsdam – founded in 993 – the older neighbouring town of

Luiseninsel garden (July 1999)

Berlin, capital of the state of Brandenburg and which had been adopted as a garrison town and royal residence between 1713 and 1786 by Friedrich Wilhelm I and his son Friedrich II.[278]

In 1814 Schinkel prepared a plan for 'embellishment of the Tiergarten that he had drawn up with the court gardener, Steiner'. Lenné drew up his first plan for the Tiergarten in 1816. It was based on a combination of 'the straight avenues of Knobelsdorff's previous layout' for horse-riders and curving paths that revealed unfolding views for pedestrians. Those proposals were not acted upon and in 1818 Lenné was commissioned to redesign the Tiergarten in order to improve its drainage and to enable it to function effectively as a public park. The proposals that he presented to the King in 1819 were 'for a public park in part of it to commemorate the war against Napoléon'. Public or 'popular' parks had been discussed by Christian Cay Lorenz Hirschfeld (1742–92), Danish-born Professor of Philosophy and Aesthetics at Kiel University, in the fifth and final volume of his *Theorie der Gärtenkunst* ('Theory of the Art of Gardens') in 1785. He wrote about parks as 'places of recreation and moral improvement for all social classes' and suggested, in an idea taken from Jean Jacques Rousseau and acted upon by Sello ('the Younger') on the Rousseau Insel as early as 1792, the use of 'statues of national heroes rather than mythological deities, fauns etc'. The redesign of the Tiergarten as a 'popular park' was not discussed again until after the social unrest and political protest of 1830. In the meantime, under the

direction of Karl Friedrich Simon Fintelmann (1775–1837; Head Forester from 1819 to 1837), no new works or alterations to the layout were effected and the woodland grew a great deal denser.[279]

Lenné's revised proposals, presented in 1832, called for the thinning out of substantial areas of forest and the creation of a major network of water bodies to drain the site. Most of Knobelsdorff's avenues were retained and supplemented with winding paths through new clearings in the forest. Work began in spring 1833 on the south-west sector and advanced year-by-year through the seven sectors until the final sector, north of the Charlottenburg Chaussee, was completed in 1840. Lenné did not hold an official position in the Tiergarten. His designs were executed under the direction of Gottfried Klengel, eventually appointed Inspector of the Tiergarten in 1838, a pupil of Lenné at the Gardening School he had established in 1824. Klengel was succeeded in 1842 by Gerhard Koeber who, as Assistant Head Gardener, had produced the much-published plan of the park in 1840 – the year in which the Tiergarten was officially opened as a public park.

Both Lenné, in 1834, and Schinkel, in 1835 – inspired, perhaps, by the example of Regent's Park, proposed residential development in the Tiergarten. But Friedrich Wilhelm III – clearly not inspired by the Prince Regent's example – was opposed to any development in the park, and was not prepared to give up the area allocated since 1742 to the breeding of pheasants. His successor, King Friedrich Wilhelm IV (reigned 1840–61), who was also interested in building and landscape architecture, commissioned Lenné in 1841 to design a Zoo on part of the royal pheasantry to the south-west of the Tiergarten. Lenné created the *Neue See* (New Lake), opened in December 1846, in this area. The Zoo, opened in 1844, now boasts a larger number of animal species than any other in the world.

Most of Lenné's work was retained until the Second World War and changes in the late nineteenth and early twentieth centuries were largely limited to the erection of monuments. Königsplatz (King's Place), renamed Platz der Republik (Place of the Republic) during the Weimar Republic (1918–33), was laid out in the 1870s and the Siegessäule celebrating Prussian victories over Denmark (1864), Austria (1866) and France (1870–71) in the 'wars of unification' was unveiled there as 'the first national monument of the newly formed second German empire'. The ornate Italianate Reichstag designed by Frankfurt architect Paul Wallot (1841–1912) was eventually constructed between 1884 and 1894 on the north side of the Platz der Republik.[280]

The population of Berlin had grown from 170,000 in 1800, to 500,000 by the early 1850s, to 820,000 at the unification of Germany in 1871, and to two million by 1900. In 1920 its population reached four million and it was the third largest city in the world after New York and London. By 1910 it had the highest number of residents per building of any city in the Western world. The park witnessed events like the dispatch of troops to the First World War and the declaration in 1918 of the establishment of the Weimar Republic from the windows of the Reichstag. But it experienced relatively little further change in its layout until the commencement of Hitler and Speer's plans for the conversion of Berlin into the new city of *Germania*. Speer was authorized to drive a north–south axis through the city and to create a massive domed hall directly north of its point of intersection with the east–west axis of Charlottenburg Chaussee and Unter den Linden. The hall was to be north of and at right angles to the Reichstag at the tip of the arc in the Spree (*Spreebogen*). The space enclosed by the hall, and by the Reichstag and other proposed buildings on the west side of the Platz der Republik was to become a massive parade ground. Speer's axis would

Siegessäule [Victory Column] (July 1999)

have ripped through the south-east corner of the Tiergarten.[281]

The only part of Speer's proposals in the area of the Tiergarten actually to be implemented were the widening of the (now) Strasse des 17 Juni, the redesign of Platz der Republik and the relocation of the Victory Column from there to the Grosser Stern. This space was enlarged from 90 metres in diameter to an even grosser 200 metres and the column was heightened by the addition of another tubular section. Enlargement of the Grosser Stern meant the felling of the oak trees planted some 300 years earlier by the Great Elector. The Victory Column was re-opened in April 1939 to mark Hitler's 50th birthday. The Strasse des 17 Juni was also widened – from 27 to 53 metres – so that it could serve as a military parade ground and as an auxiliary landing strip. The road remains disproportionately wide but is being reduced in scale by the lines of lime trees planted on each side during the 1990s.[282]

The park suffered badly in the Second World War and in the unusually cold winter of 1945/46 nearly all its remaining mature trees were cut down for firewood. It is estimated that only 700 of the original 200,000 trees remained. Cleared areas were used for growing vegetables until 1949 when restoration of the park began under Tiergartendirektor Willy Alverdes (1896–1980). The restored park was intended to be peaceful, spacious and natural. The designs prepared by Fritz Witte and Hans Migge in 1950 and by Willy Alverdes in 1952 both show schemes that ignored Knobelsdorff and Lenné's avenues – apart from the Charlottenburg Chaussee and the three other highways radiating from Grosser Stern. Lenné's water bodies – with their function of draining the site – were retained. Von Krosigk suggested that 'abandoning the concept of avenues and plazas meant losing the characteristic variety of structure, appearance and orientation, the grandiose synthesis of baroque and natural landscape elements which had characterized the Tiergarten for centuries'.[283]

Alverdes and his team made rapid progress with the redevelopment of the park. New garden areas like the Englischer Gärten – named for the number of plants donated from Britain (the park was located in the British occupied part of Berlin) and opened by then Foreign Secretary Anthony Eden in May 1952 – typified the new approach to the design of the Tiergarten. Following severe bomb-damage in the Second World War the remains of the 'tents' at Zeltenplatz were removed in 1954 to make way for the Congress Hall, an independent contribution from the United States to the 1957 International Building Exhibition (IBA). The site was chosen to

be in direct line with the Reichstag and, with its yellow double-pointed roof, to be in direct line of view of Soviet Union-occupied East Berlin.[284]

The Tiergarten had grown up facing the Mitte area – the centre of Berlin. Suddenly, when the Wall went up in August 1961, it found itself at the very edge of West Berlin – and the eastern end of the park in particular, adjacent to the cordoned-off Brandenburg Gate and the shored-up Reichstag, took on an eerie air of abandonment – visited mainly by sightseers, graffitists wanting to leave their messages on the Wall and Western politicians wanting to use the Gate as a backdrop for their messages. A preservation report for the park was commissioned in 1984 ahead of the celebration of the 750th anniversary in 1987 of the establishment of Cölln-Berlin. It made detailed proposals for varying the age structure and composition of the even-aged post-war woodlands; for naturalizing the banks of Lenné's water bodies and for improvement of water quality. The report suggested that intensive garden restoration should be restricted to particular historic gardens. It also initiated re-establishment of Knobelsdorff's avenues, calling, in particular, for strengthening of the Bellevueallée from Bellevue Palace to Potsdamer Platz; Fasanerieallée, southwest from Grosser Stern, and the six avenues radiating from Zeltenplatz. The Luiseninsel, Grossfürstenplatz with Triton Fountain, Rousseau Insel and monument, and the Lessing monument were all restored for the 750th anniversary.

The Berlin Wall came down on 9 November 1989 presaging the reunification of Berlin and of Germany. On 2 May 1991 the Tiergarten and its constituent elements were afforded legal protection as historic monuments. On 20 June 1991 the Bundestag voted to relocate the federal capital from Bonn to Berlin. For more than ten years from that date the Tiergarten, and particularly its eastern end, became embroiled in a public and private building bonanza in preparation for the transfer of government in 1999. Developments adjacent to the park included restoration of the Brandenburg Gate, Pariser Platz and the Reichstag; construction of the 2.4-kilometre-long highway tunnel from south of Potsdamer Platz (where major private developments have been undertaken) beneath the east end of the park to the north of the new Lehrter railway station; construction of the government quarter at Spreebogen, running east–west directly north of Platz der Republik and spanning the river twice; redesign of Platz der Republik and of the remains of the arc. Construction of the tunnel allowed removal from the park of Entlastungs Strasse (literally 'Relief Street') the north–south highway constructed as a substitute for routes through East Berlin after the

Quadriga on Brandenburg Gate (July 1999)

Wall was built. New offices for the Federal President, adjacent to Bellevue Palace, were completed in 1998.

'In rebuilding the Reichstag, Potsdamer Platz, and its old urban grid, Berlin has chosen to embrace an early phase of modernity that concluded in 1918, and to distance itself from more recent and disquieting assaults on tradition.' Lenné's Baumsaal (literally 'Tree Hall'), lines of lime trees on the eastern edge of the park directly south of the Brandenburg Gate, were replanted in 1991. In directing the design and management of the Tiergarten, Berlin appears to have decided to embrace Lenné's design as it stood in 1840.[285]

Original Condition of Site

Berlin is located in a broad, sandy glacial valley. The name 'Berlin' is believed to derive from the Slav word *Birl*, meaning swamp. The site of the park was 'originally a fenced-in woodland, dotted with meadows, small water-pools and patches of marshland' and in the nineteenth century much of it was inaccessible and 'extensive drainage of the swampy Tiergarten woodland became necessary'. Lenné exploited the natural fall of the land northward towards the Spree to de-water the site while creating its abundant sinuous water bodies. The extraordinary system of groundwater control for the Tiergarten tunnel also illustrates the natural conditions of the site. Ground water levels throughout Berlin are relatively high. The normal way of controlling this around buildings is to construct a waterproof cut-off trench. It was feared with the tunnel, however, that this would endanger trees and buildings in the park area. For this reason a groundwater monitoring system was established for building sites at Potsdamer Platz and Spreebogen – 'a step unprecedented in the Federal Republic' – that would allow water to be pumped back into the ground if depressed levels became a threat to trees.[286]

Key Figures in the Establishment of the Park

A host of rulers and their designers have been involved in the design and development of the Tiergarten. The most prominent is Peter Josef Lenné – 'the greatest German landscape architect'. He was a forerunner to Joseph Paxton, Calvert Vaux and Frederick Law Olmsted. Lenné was also a remarkable urban planner and municipal engineer. His work on the Tiergarten was the embodiment of the principles that Hirschfeld proposed for the design of public parks. Lenné was the son and grandson of head gardeners at Bonn and trained

there and in Paris. He travelled extensively in Germany in 1809 and then worked in Paris before spending a short time working with his father at Koblenz. Lenné then worked in Munich and Vienna before working as 'Garden Engineer' in Laxenburg and spending further time in Koblenz before starting work in Berlin in 1816 on designs for Sanssouci, the Neuer Gärten at Potsdam and the Tiergarten. The first of Lenné's public parks to be constructed was at Magdeburg where, in 1824, 50 hectares adjacent to redundant fortifications were designed for public use. Lenné described this project as the first example that he had encountered in all his 'life as an artist' of work of this scale being undertaken by town authorities rather than by royal patrons. 'Prior to Lenné's work, the leanings of the German gardens to the English landscape style had lacked conviction: the great gardens of the eighteenth century were either unashamedly formal and vast in scale, or else plunged equally heartily into an ostentatious blend of the Rococo and the sublime . . . under Lenné's guidance a more English style was to be seen: English that is in developing rather more towards the Gardenesque in general, although perhaps maintaining a sidelong glance at the Picturesque . . ..'[287]

In addition to his substantial work at Potsdam, particularly on Sanssouci and Charlottenhof Park, Lenné became increasingly involved, after the accession of King Friedrich Wilhelm IV in 1840, with urban planning and canal construction for Berlin. He regarded the redesign of the Tiergarten as an initial stage in giving 'a comprehensive shape to the entire urban structure, making use of landscape and of gardens'. He proposed a second public park in the north of the city – eventually designed by Lenné's most distinguished pupil and effective successor, Gustav Meyer (1816–77) – and named Friedrichshain. Lenné planned, also in the 1840s, the building in the Köpiniker Feld of the later-named Luisenstadt and proposed the construction of a wide ring road around the city. He designed Humboldt Harbour (1842–48) north of the arc in the Spree; the Landwehr Canal (1844–50) to the south-west of the Tiergarten, and the (eventually refilled) Luisenstadt Canal (1848–52) to the south-east of the Mitte section of the city.[288]

After Schinkel's death in 1841, Lenné became the closest collaborator with King Friedrich Wilhelm IV (reigned 1840–61, but went quite literally mad and was succeeded by his brother, Kaiser Wilhelm I, in 1857). Friedrich Wilhelm had initially been relatively reform-minded and can be credited with the redesign for public use of the Tiergarten. Nevertheless, he became more and more bitterly opposed to constitutional reform and the combination of crop failures in

1844 and increasing urban poverty led to riots in 1848, a year of revolt across Europe, including running battles in the Tiergarten and in Unter den Linden. Friedrich Wilhelm became increasingly conservative, increasingly resistant to constitutional change, and increasingly senile. By the time he was removed from power 'the period of romantic planning in Berlin whose inspiration bore the stamp of Lenné, drew to a close'.[289]

PLANNING AND DESIGN

Location

The Tiergarten lies at the heart of Berlin. It is 'approximately in the geometric centre forming an urban oasis' and part of the 'excellent provision with areas of recreation landscape and small parks distributed throughout the city'. Similar to the state functions of St James's Park in London, the 'Hohenzollerns' funeral processions, marriage corteges and military parades approached the city from the Tiergarten, entering through the Brandenburg Gate'. In the reunified city 'its central location and its size, as well as its design elements – for instance the avenues and plazas, especially along its edges – create manifold links with its urban environment'.[290]

Shape and Natural Landform of the Site

The site is the shape of an acorn squash lying with its tapering top to the west and with the Strasse des 17 Juni running 3.2 kilometres virtually through the axis of the park. The width of the park, apart from the western end, is between 800 and 1200 metres. The natural landform is relatively flat and mostly drains northwards to the Spree, which runs along most of the northern edge of the park. The southwestern part of the park drains via Lenné's Landwehr Canal into the Spree.

Original Design Concept

The original purpose of the Tiergarten was as a royal hunting ground. Knobelsdorff's geometric design from the 1750s reflected this purpose. Lenné's first designs for the park in 1816 and 1819 envisaged it as a monument to the defeat of Napoléon. By the time his design for the Tiergarten was completed in 1840 Lenné noted that 'the more progress a people makes in the fields of culture and of economic well-being, the more varied and articulate its material and spiritual needs become. These include public walks, whose creation and variety cannot be too strongly recommended in a big city,

not just for the amusement of the population, but also with a view to its health'. Von Krosigk described Lenné's basic concept as 'setting off valuable old trees . . . and clearing grove-like areas which in some places had become so overgrown with underwood as to become impassable. The sweeping curves of the paths were laid as close to water as possible, so that a visitor strolling through could enjoy constantly changing vistas. . . . There were separate paths for pedestrians, riders and carriages'. But the park was principally 'a stage for the bourgeois performance, and it gave . . . the well-to-do classes yet another chance to show off their social status'.[291]

Spatial Structure, Circulation System, Landform, Materials and Planting

First impressions of the Tiergarten are that it is solid deciduous woodland from edge to edge and that the woodland is subdivided only by the slashes of major highways radiating from the Grosser Stern. There are few apparent clearings in the woodland and the size and density of the trees are remarkable given that they were planted almost entirely in the second half of the twentieth century. This same impression is obtained at ground level and from the top of the Siegessäule. When you start to move along these highways you notice first the lines of more recently planted lime (basswood) trees along the edges of most of them, and the low metal trip rails between the limes and the rest of the park. You are also aware that, however high these trees grow, Strasse des 17 Juni will remain an out-of-scale hyper-highway unless and until it is re-narrowed and/or avenues of trees are also planted down its central reservation.

The trip rails are the first clue that the park is in fact a carefully conceived composition. As you walk along the highways it becomes clear that the woodland conceals extensive open areas and a network of sinuous water bodies – both of which lead the eye into and through the park. The water bodies and openings are much more noticeable than the long and relatively thin allées being re-established through the woodland. It also becomes apparent that the land is relatively flat – or gently sloping towards the water bodies – and that this flatness contributes to the apparent solidity of the woodland. The restored 'Gardenesque' statuary that punctuates the park sometimes seems surreal. Equally, without a strong focal point, the restored Zeltenplatz seems like a somewhat arbitrary piece of residual geometry.

Certain parts of the park – particularly the southern and eastern edges – spent a long time

*Northeast segment of the park
and Strasse des 17 Juni from
the Siëgessäule (July 1999)*

making the transition from being the back of a park at the edge of West Berlin to being at the heart of the renascent capital. The division of the city encouraged the outer edges of the park to become anaemic. Alverdes and his successors encouraged the adjacent inner parts of the park to develop as low-maintenance meadows. Once the Wall was removed the Berlin government moved quickly to re-establish Lenné's Baumsaal along the edge of the park south of the Brandenburg Gate. This made the statement that this land is part of the park, that it is cared for and that development must not cross it. The land inside the park should receive the same degree of conspicuous care once the tunnel has fully replaced the north–south Entlastungs Strasse. Lenné Strasse and Tiergarten Strasse, along the south side of the park, should also be redesigned to express the distinction between the park and the commercial and diplomatic quarter to the south. Indeed, there is a strong argument for establishing these edges and then projecting the park outward into the surrounding neighbourhood.[292]

Restoration of the Reichstag, another redesign of Platz der Republik, development of the Spreebogen and other new government and diplomatic buildings have had a massive impact on the north-east end of the park. But, as with its recovery after the devastations of the 1940s, this is another example of the resilience of this park and its robustness in the face of dramatic changes. The current policy of the government of Berlin is to steer it back as far as practicable to the form that Lenné had achieved in 1840.

MANAGEMENT AND USAGE

Managing Organization

Along with Hamburg and Bremen, Berlin is a city state and is one of the sixteen *Länder* making up the Federal Republic of Germany. A referendum was held in spring 1996 in Berlin and in the surrounding *Land* of Brandenburg on a proposal to merge the two and locate their centre of government in Potsdam. The proposal was rejected by both sides and Berlin continues to operate as a city state with twenty-three subsidiary boroughs. The boroughs are responsible, among other things, for the maintenance of all public parks in their administrative areas. Strategic planning and management for historic parks are the responsibility of the Landesdenkmalamt (Office for the Preservation of Historical Buildings, Gardens and Landscapes) of the Senatsverwaltung für Stadtentwicklung, Umweltschutz und Technologie (Department of

City Planning, Environmental Protection and Technology). Following the 'demise' of the parks department in spring 1999, Berlin, like Hamburg, now has a separation of policy-making and executive functions for the city's major public park. There is, however, relatively strong cooperation between them – even if the strategists can be characterized as being restoration-driven and the operators as being more recreation-driven.[293]

Usage

It was noted in 1985 that, along with regional recreation areas on the fringes of West Berlin, the Tiergarten was 'completely overrun by all Berliners, weekend for weekend [*sic*]'. It remains remarkably popular as a recreation place for less mobile residents of the still dense inner city – particularly Turkish *Gastarbeiter* whose practices of barbecuing and playing casual games of soccer in the park's larger open spaces are sometimes frowned on by other users.[294]

PLANS FOR THE PARK

The Landesdenkmalamt states that 'the objective of garden preservation measures in the Tiergarten is to restore a form that enhances and sets off the park's historic and artistic development. The Tiergarten is to be preserved for future generations in its characteristic and unique variety – the result of centuries of growth – as a recreation area and a major element of Berlin's history'. Rose and Gustav Wörner, the landscape architects appointed to draw up proposals for the Tiergarten in 1984 ahead of the 750th anniversary of the city, were subsequently appointed to prepare a full Management Plan. That plan was approved by the Department of City Planning and Environmental Protection in February 1992 and came into effect in 1993. The principles on which it was based included that the Tiergarten is the central park for the whole city and has a significant role as a recreation space for all citizens; has a centuries-long cultural history and significance in the development of garden design – reflected particularly in its scenic composition; has developed significant ecological importance – despite the importance of form-giving elements in its design, and was traditionally closely integrated with its surrounding areas by its avenues and its carefully located entrance plazas. It was also noted that return to a single previous historical state would not be practicable.[295]

Overriding objectives for the management of the park were that:

- the whole park was accorded historic monument status on 2 May 1991 and must therefore be protected as much as possible from development and disturbance
- development proposals for surrounding areas must take into account the protection of the historic value of the Tiergarten. This was particularly directed at the development of the government quarter in Spreebogen, the Reichstag and surroundings, the extension of Bellevue Palace and the Tiergarten tunnel.

Next on the agenda were park planning priorities, including:

- preservation and partial restoration of the historic structure of the park
- removal of Entlangungs Strasse and, after completion of the tunnel, reunification of the areas of the park that have been separated since 1961
- better integration of Strasse des 17 Juni into the structure of the park and completion of tree planting along its entire length
- opening up of the banks of the Spree including a new footbridge from Brandenburg Gate via Zeltenplatz to Moabit on the other side of the river
- restoration of the principal avenues through the park and, in particular, the historic Grosser Querallée (Great Diagonal Avenue) between Spreebogen and the restored diplomatic quarter south of Tiergarten Strasse
- respecting and protecting the southern edge of the park and, in the long term, creating a tree-lined promenade along it
- restoration of the Kemperplatz entrance plaza and re-creation of the avenue between Bellevue Palace and Potsdamer Platz that runs through the plaza
- consideration of new planting on both sides of Ebert Strasse, north and south of the Brandenburg Gate.

With respect to landscape design and maintenance within the park, policies included:

- managing the woodland areas, which were nearly all planted in the 1950s, to develop a more varied structure with shrub and herb layers
- preserving the Lenné-designed water bodies, developing a more natural approach to the management of their banks and taking measures to improve their water quality
- limitation of Gardenesque elements to the traditional decorative garden areas like the Luiseninsel,

the Rose Garden and the Englischer Gärten
- developing a programme for the overhaul of the historic statues and monuments and their surroundings
- continuation of the approaches that were developed in 1984 to those areas that only became available after the fall of the Wall in 1989.

The Landesdenkmalamt has 'only initiated management plans for the purposes of preserving areas of importance to garden history'. Its deputy director, von Krosigk, does state, however, that 'only if ecology, garden arts and land use are regarded as equals, and only if the differentiated models for maintenance are under a common management, will there be any accountable future for the listed monuments in a way which is fitting both to the profession and to the nation's culture'. The continued demands imposed on the Tiergarten for heavy use by residents and the new demands imposed by users of the government-related buildings should ensure that any predisposition on the part of the Landesdenkmalamt towards historic preservation is tempered by growing recreational demand.[296]

CONCLUSIONS

The decision in June 1991 to relocate the German federal government to Berlin intensified the massive building boom that followed the fall of the Wall in November 1989. That boom generated a flurry of publications that focused on architectural design and (to a certain extent) landscape design as expressions of Berlin's search for an appropriate post-Cold War identity – an identity developed with no small amount of angst. 'Berliners want all good things for Berlin: they want to settle its account with history, they want to transform history, transcend history, locate a piece of history that every Berliner can agree is neutral and possibly even agreeable, and at the same time is incontestably German'. The Tiergarten has not been spared a process in which 'preservation has become professionalized and bureaucratized, giving preservationists a distinct identity and point of view'. Whereas Alverdes sought to give the post-Second World War Tiergarten a more casual, relaxed and democratic character, the post-Cold War approach tends towards an eclectic historicism that takes Lenné's finished design in 1840 as its basic model. With the reunification of Germany and the return of capital functions to Berlin, the Tiergarten will resume its role as the park at the heart of the nation.[297]

17 Central Park, New York

843 acres (341 hectares)

INTRODUCTION

Central Park is a skinny streak of surrogate nature set into the rectilinear grid of Manhattan (see location map on page 4). Commenced in 1856, it was the first purpose-built public park in North America. It remains a paradigm.

Central Park gave birth to the concept of public land; to the 'American Pastoral' landscape style and to the profession of landscape architecture in North America. It was inspired by socially conscious advocates like William Cullen Bryant (1794–1878) and Andrew Jackson Downing (1815–52) and designed by rookie landscape architects Calvert Bowyer Vaux (1824–95) and Frederick Law Olmsted

(1822–1903). Completed through the stringent management of Andrew Haswell Green (1820–1903) and good husbandry of Samuel Browne Parsons (1844–1923), Central Park was redefined between 1934 and 1960 by Robert Moses (1888–1981) as one many recreation facilities. Popularized, starved of funds and brought to the edge of destruction in the 1960s and 1970s, it has inflamed the idea that parks are dangerous places. It has been undergoing rehabilitation as 'a work of landscape art' since the early 1980s in a programme directed initially by Elizabeth Barlow Rogers (b. 1936) and largely funded by private money.

The site that was eventually designated for the park is centrally located – hence the name – in the

Reservoir joggers (October 1999)

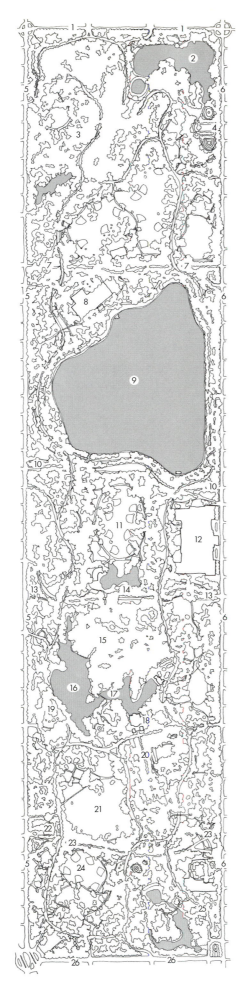

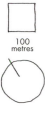

100
metres

capsule-shaped island of Manhattan. The park stretches two and a half miles (4.1 kilometres) between 59th and 110th Streets but covers only half a mile (840 metres) between Fifth Avenue and Central Park West – Eighth Avenue. By contrast with, say, the virtually circular Regent's Park, it has a high ratio of edge to overall area. This has been a boon to real estate agents – and, latterly, to the funding of the park – but it presented a massive challenge to the Olmsted–Vaux concept of the park as a pastoral escape from the city. Furthermore, its largest single feature is the (Jacqueline Kennedy Onassis) Reservoir occupying 107 acres (43 hectares) and almost filling the site between 86th and 96th Streets. This effectively cuts the park into two distinct parts. The length and subdivision of the park were addressed better by 'Greensward' – the Olmsted–Vaux entry to the 1857–58 design competition – than by the other thirty-two entries. They proposed – still in the days of horse-drawn transport – to direct all cross-town traffic onto four below-grade transverse roads that were completely separate from the park and developed an internal circulation system that segregated carriage drives, bridle paths and footways. This defined a sequence of vistas through a pastoral composition of meadows, lakes and woodland. Chadwick described the circulation system as an example of 'farsightedness' that 'was nothing short of astounding'.[298]

HISTORY

Designation as a Park

The call for a major public park in New York probably originated from Robert Brown Minturn (1805–66), a merchant who had travelled widely in Europe. It was taken up and forcefully articulated by William Cullen Bryant and Andrew Jackson Downing. Bryant, a relatively unsuccessful poet, was Editor of the New York *Evening Post*. The son and grandson of doctors, he was a proponent of fresh air and exercise. In July 1844 he wrote his first editorial urging the city to create a park. He suggested Jones' Woods – a 160-acre (65 hectares) parcel of land on the East River between 68th and 77th Streets and Third Avenue. Downing, a nurseryman and landscape designer living in the Hudson Valley, north of New York, published his first book, *A Treatise on the Theory and Practice of Landscape Gardening, Adapted to North America*, in 1841. In 1846 he was appointed editor of *The Horticulturist and Journal of Rural Art and Rural Taste* and began to be recognized as a leading figure in the development of landscape design in the United States. Despite their age difference, Bryant and Downing were close friends and both used their Editorships as opportunities to advance their views about parks; views strengthened by their respective visits to London in 1844 and 1850.[299]

By 1850 New York had a population of 654,000 and living conditions were 'truly oppressive . . . coal smoke polluted the air, there was no means of sewerage disposal, the streets were unpaved and filled not only with people and carriages, but also with geese, chickens, pigs, and sheep which were driven down the thoroughfares'. Both mayoral candidates in 1850 pledged that they would create a large city park. The electee, Ambrose C. Kingsland, recommended to the Common Council of New York in April 1851 that they purchase and lay out a park 'on a scale which will be worthy of the city . . .', but did not name a specific site. A committee of the Council considered alternative sites. Those for the park expressed their views in Bryant's *Evening Post*; those against it, in the *Journal of Commerce*. The Council agreed, still in 1851, to apply to the State Legislature for enabling legislation to purchase the Jones' Woods site. Downing immediately published a piece welcoming the decision but decrying the site as too small. Influenced by the need for the new park to accommodate a new reservoir, and by the fact that the Jones' Woods site would remove valuable shoreline from the real estate market, Kingsland appointed a further committee to consider further sites.[300]

In January 1852, that committee recommended a central site between 59th and 106th Streets and between Fifth and Eighth Avenues. They preferred the new site to Jones' Woods on the basis of 'size, convenience of locality, availability and probable cost'. The Council dithered. The factions for and against continued to argue. The faction in favour of a park argued which was the better site. In April 1853 the State authorized the acquisition of Jones' Woods; in May 1853 the Council reaffirmed its support for the principle of a large park; in June it requested the State Legislature for authority to acquire the central site. After further debate and public discussion, the Council stood by its decision and in November 1853 started to acquire the land. By July 1856 the purchase was complete. The population of New York had more than doubled since 1845, but at that time the built-up portion of Manhattan had only reached 38th Street.[301]

Size and Condition of the Site at the Time of Designation

The originally designated site extended from 59th to 106th Street – an area of 773 acres (313 hectares). It was extended northward to 110th Street in 1863 – an addition of 70 acres (28 hectares). The site included the rectangular 37-acre (15 hectares) Croton Reservoir, built in 1842 – now the site of the Great Lawn. Allowance also had to be made for construction of the 107-acre (43 hectares) reservoir. The site comprised 'two large swamps, a portion of salt marsh, an upland bog and uneven, thin-soiled, boulder-strewn tableland' with outcrops of Manhattan mica schist, ribboned with granite intrusions from a second epoch of geological unrest. The northern end of the site contained a steep, wooded stream valley and a brook flowing through a break in a series of low bluffs. Overall, the site 'consisted of five major drainage watersheds – part of a natural drainage system that flowed to the East River'. The mica schists close to the surface precluded building without major site formation works and the lack of soil precluded agriculture. 'While there was a section of gently rolling meadow above 98th Street, there was no such area in the lower park.' The site was already occupied when it was designated. 'Before construction could begin . . . the site had to be cleared of hundreds of squatter's shacks, pig farms and other structures, as well as swamps and open sewers'. Clearly, the site was far more difficult than the one that Olmsted and Vaux addressed later at Prospect Park.[302]

Key Figures in the Design of the Park

Bryant and Downing are widely acknowledged as the principal advocates of the park. Bryant's role was recognized in the naming for him in 1900 of the park behind the New York Public Library. It has been widely suggested that, had Downing not drowned in July 1852 – trying to save the victims of a steamboat disaster, he would have been chosen to design Central Park. He had already been 'commissioned in 1851 to design the grounds of the Capitol, White House, and Smithsonian Institution'. Downing 'provided the basis for the style in which . . . parks . . . were to be designed' and 'saw the necessity, appreciated by devotees of the "Picturesque", and clearly enunciated by Repton, of mastering the natural character or prevailing expression of the place'. Although Downing died before his designs for public works were implemented, he did convey many of his views to Vaux, the architect he had recruited in London in 1850 to work with him in Newburgh, New York on the building elements of his commissions. Vaux continued to work in Newburgh after Downing's death – initially completing their joint commissions and then in partnership with a former employee, Frederick Clark Withers. Contacts he had made on residential projects led to commissions for commercial projects in New York. In May 1856 Vaux dissolved the partnership with Withers and moved to New York.[303]

Egbert Ludovicus Viele (1825–1902) had been appointed Chief Engineer for Central Park by the Democrat-led City Council's commissioners – the Mayor and his Street Commissioner. In early 1857 a layout plan prepared by Viele was adopted. The plan was widely criticized in the press for its lack of imagination. Vaux campaigned against it, declaring it 'a disgrace to the city and to the memory of Mr. Downing'. The Republican-led State Legislature stepped in that summer and appointed its own nine-person commission. Vaux petitioned them to stage a design competition for the park. They retained Viele as Engineer; began an immediate search for a Superintendent and announced a design competition in August 1857. Meanwhile, Olmsted had moved to New York in 1855, migrating from 'scientific farming' on Staten Island to become part-owner of a publishing firm. The following year he made his second trip to England – this time as a literary agent – and returned to find the firm on the verge of bankruptcy. By summer 1857 he was looking for another job. In short, Olmsted's 'political connections and a bit of résumé padding won him the post of Superintendent'. He was appointed, under Viele, in September 1857.[304]

Vaux and Olmsted had first met in 1851 at Downing's nursery in Newburgh. Vaux encouraged Olmsted to join him in the competition for the park because he knew that Olmsted was in favour with the commissioners and because his post made him familiar with the large and varied site. Olmsted was reticent about entering the competition because it might strain already difficult relations with Viele. Viele was indifferent. Still in debt from his publishing venture and believing that victory would bring not only the prize money, but also more control of the project – and thus, a higher salary – he agreed to join Vaux. They spent winter evenings and weekends working on the awkward-shaped drawings for the awkward-shaped site. In April 1858 'Greensward' was awarded first prize by a jury comprised solely of the commissioners. Their choice 'reflected the preference of the board's Yankee Republican majority for the English naturalistic design tradition'.[305]

Olmsted was appointed 'Architect-in-Chief' and Vaux was named his 'Assistant'. This 'laid the foundation for the persistent but erroneous belief that Olmsted was principally, if not solely, responsible for the design of Central Park'. This is ironic given that 'a precedent was established in the assembling of a team of specialists to deal with the technical questions raised'. Those specialists included Austrian-born horticulturist Ignatz Pilat (1820–70) who worked on the park from 1858 until his death from tuberculosis, caused by overwork; drainage engineer George Waring (1833–98); and, also English-born, architect Jacob Wrey Mould (1825–86). Mould has been acknowledged as an innovative designer, song writer and opera translator – and described as 'ugly and uncouth' and having 'an unfortunate propensity for shady business dealings'. He also had the virtue of being able to work equally well in metal, brick and stone – which accounts for the exotic carved stonework at the Bethesda Terrace and many of the bridges that he designed with Vaux. Mould, by all accounts also helped with the competition drawings – a skill which Olmsted had not acquired at that stage in his career. In fact, Vaux and this team of co-designers were 'Architect-in-Chief' Olmsted's first instructors in landscape architecture and Central Park was his very first project.[306]

PLANNING AND DESIGN

Original Design Concept

Central Park was built largely in accordance with the principles and layout established in the Olmsted–Vaux plan. That plan represented a continuation of the social attitudes expressed by Downing, that users of whatever social class, 'would enjoy together the same music; breathe the same atmosphere of art, enjoy the same scenery, and grow into social freedom by the very influences of easy intercourse, space and beauty that surround them'. One of Olmsted's fullest statements about the design of Central Park, and the purpose of parks generally, was his 1870 address 'Public Parks and the Enlargement of Towns' to the Lowell Institute. He mocked the *Herald* newspaper for an editorial in 1858 that questioned the social programming and made the observation, even in 1870, that 'the Park is not planned for such use as is now made of it, but with regard to future use, when it will be in the centre of a population of two millions hemmed in by water at a short distance on all sides'. Olmsted's vision of the future of American cities – before the motor car had even been invented – was exceptional. His social views were more paternalistic.[307]

Franklin Park, Boston became Olmsted's ultimate vehicle for expressing his views on the purpose and appropriate nature of urban parks in nineteenth-century North America. In his account of the plan for that park he noted that the 'various evils of town life' had been 'so well contended with' that 'much less time is now lost to productive industry; the average length of life much advanced, and the value

Opposite: *Allée through centre of Conservatory Garden (April 2000)*

Cast iron bridge near the Reservoir (October 1999)

of life augmented'. Olmsted therefore suggested another reason for establishing large urban parks. As he put it – 'a man's [*sic*] eyes cannot be as much occupied as they are in large cities by artificial things, or by natural things seen under obviously artificial conditions, without a harmful effect, first on his [*sic*] mental and nervous system and ultimately on his [*sic*] entire constitutional organization'. In short 'the beauty of rural scenery' is a restorative antidote to the artificiality and oppression of urban conditions – and this view was 'too well established to need argument'. Such statements support the view that Olmsted never abandoned his anti-urban sentiment.[308]

Olmsted's paternalism was already apparent in his description in 1858 of the purpose of Central Park being 'to supply to the hundreds of thousands of tired workers, who have no opportunity to spend their summers in the country, a specimen of God's handiwork'. Accordingly, the Greensward Plan made minimal provision for active recreation or for buildings that did not contribute directly to the primary purpose of the park. Beveridge noted, however, that 'Olmsted always wished to satisfy the need of users of his large parks for refreshments, and felt that by serving beer and wine he could forestall the proliferation of bars nearby'.[309]

The Olmsted–Vaux plan 'conceived of the park as a place where the city dweller could find refreshment from the sights and sounds of urban life and enjoy scenery that would seem both limitless and natural. To this end, the park boundaries were thickly planted . . . the southern part of the park was pastoral; the northern part . . . was more heavily wooded. But there were constant scenic effects in both halves. The only formal element in the park was the Mall, planned for fashionable "promenading" . . .'. The boundary planting and the Mall were two elements that other competitors did not propose. But it was the circulation system that was the real 'standout' feature of the Olmsted–Vaux plan. First their transverse routes would keep extraneous cross-town traffic out of the park. Then, internally, their segregation of routes for different modes of movement through the park allowed adoption of 'the Reptonian principle of appropriation . . . by freeing the user of a particular system from the necessity of conflict with other users'.[310]

Vast amounts of rock were blasted and moved or removed from site; an extensive drainage system was installed and huge volumes of topsoil were brought in from New Jersey. The design, nevertheless, retained a strong reflection of the natural conditions of the site. Water bodies like the Lake and the Reservoir (and later, the Harlem Meer) occupied the five natural drainage basins; rockier

Untermyer Fountain in the North Garden of the Conservatory (October 1999)

Plan; the Bethesda Terrace, originally called the Water Terrace, and the Belvedere Castle on Vista Rock. The Promenade was aligned inward to direct views towards the centre of the park. At the end of the quarter-mile-long (400 metres) tree-lined *allée* Vaux and Mould placed a combination of steps down to a tiled arcade under the 72nd Street Transverse; broad stairways decorated with Mould's stone carvings and sweeping carriage ramps down to the Terrace and boat landing on the edge of the lake. The view to the Belvedere has been obscured by the trees in the Ramble. The original centre-piece of the Terrace was a simple water jet. This was replaced in 1873 by the *Angel of the Waters*, a 'life-size' sculpture by Emma Stebbins that has become a focal point of the park. Although the longer view to the Belvedere has been obscured by vegetation in the Ramble, the Angel is clearly visible at the end of the Mall, precisely positioned to float above the parapet of the 72nd Street Transverse.[312]

Vaux considered the original Water Terrace 'the best thing he had ever done'. The sequence of views in the other direction is also highly rated – 'the walk from the Belvedere through the Ramble across Bow Bridge to the Bethesda Fountain is perhaps the most elaborate, intricate and fascinating of any Olmsted park experience'. This, of course, is a reference to Olmsted in a generic sense. The Bow Bridge, for instance, is an outstanding example of Vaux's siting and design and of Mould's detailing. But the reference is to Olmsted himself in the comment that 'Central Park still suffers from his ignorance of the nature and habits of plant material. His most devastating blunder was precipitated by a train trip across the Isthmus of Panama in September 1863 which caused him to take off on a tropical extravaganza. In an ecstatic letter to Pilat, Olmsted gave directions on how to transform a North American woodland, the Ramble, into a Panamanian jungle'. Put more kindly, 'he designed parks at a time when it had become fashionable to collect exotic flora'. However, 'due to poor choice of materials and environmental stresses Central Park has lost nearly all its original plants'. Olmsted's tropical reverie probably led to the introduction to the park of the highly invasive wisteria. He is not generally held responsible for the *Fallopia japonica* (Japanese Knotweed) that remains rampant in the Ramble.[313]

and higher ground was adapted to create areas like the Ramble and landmarks like the Belvedere on the Vista Rock. Intermediate areas were filled to create meadows. 'The "Greensward" design . . . was an essay in Downing's "Beautiful" style suitably adjusted to meet the site conditions and the problems posed by the largest park then to be designed *de nouveau*.' Indeed, 'Olmsted perceived the park as a work of art, injecting culture with the salutary influence of nature. Vaux, on the other hand, saw the park as a designed space that would find its character through democratic use.' In the event, 'Central Park is a series of interlocking landscapes whose specific characters depend on the neighborhoods they abut: the residential East Side population differs from that of the West Side; South is Midtown business and hotels; North is Harlem.' Central Park was the first translation into the public realm in America of the 'western pastoral tradition' – a tradition that 'has been compatible with the idea of nature as a resource to be manipulated by human enterprise'.[311]

Spatial Structure, Circulation System, Landform, Materials and Planting

The Olmsted–Vaux plan proposed thick boundary planting to block views of the buildings that would eventually surround it. Within this screen they used the different component parts of the circulation system to present views into the park. At the heart of the southern section they created one of their most famous and most formal compositions – the Mall, called the Promenade in the 'Greensward'

Key Figures in the Development of the Park

Olmsted and Vaux worked on Central Park from May 1858 until the outbreak of the Civil War in April 1861. The Yankee Republican Olmsted was granted leave and became Executive Director of the

United States Sanitary Commission. Vaux, who was under five feet tall, was too short to enlist. He remained in New York. In April 1862 he and Olmsted were jointly appointed landscape architects to the Board of Central Park Commissioners but relatively little work was undertaken on the park during the war. In May 1863, Vaux resigned on behalf of the two of them – mainly because of disputes with Andrew Green. In September 1863 Olmsted left for California and only returned to New York in November 1865 at the urging of Vaux following their appointment on Prospect Park. In February 1866 they were also re-appointed landscape architects to the Board of Central Park. They were fired in November 1870 after the 'Tweed Ring' gained control of the City Council and replaced the Board with a Department of Public Parks. They were re-hired in November 1871 following exposure of the Tweed Ring. They remained involved with the park until 1873 – by when construction work was virtually complete and the economy was in depression. Olmsted became briefly re-involved with the park between spring 1875 and his final dismissal in December 1877. Vaux served as landscape architect of the City of New York between November 1881 and January 1883 and between January 1888 and his death, by drowning, in November 1895.[314]

Andrew Haswell Green, an industrious, New England-raised, Milton-loving, Protestant, Yankee Democrat, bachelor and lawyer was Treasurer of the Board of Park Commissioners when Olmsted was appointed Superintendent in September 1857. They were friends. Green was appointed to the full-time salaried position of Comptroller of Central Park in fall 1859 – effectively its first CEO – while Olmsted was on recuperative study leave in England. Olmsted's levels of expenditure had been far higher than originally estimated. Green's role was to rein him in. The friendship ended as they vied for control of the park. Both had the interests of the park at heart. Olmsted, as ever, wanted to do everything 'properly' – that is, his way; Green feared that completion of the park would be jeopardized if expenditure was not controlled. Green generally won their clashes; Olmsted often raged against him. He offered his resignation in January 1861. It was not accepted.

After Olmsted left for Washington in April 1861, Vaux had easier dealings with Green and managed to get the Bethesda Terrace built largely as he and Mould had designed it. Green was also responsible for the acquisition in 1863 of the land between 106th and 110th Streets. He was appointed head of the Central Park Commission in the late 1860s and, in 1870–71, stood up to the corrupt 'Democratic' rule of William Tweed and his

Park Commissioner, Peter Sweeny. From that time, the position of Commissioner of Parks became a political appointment. After Tweed's fall from power, Green was eventually appointed City Comptroller. His principal impact on the park in that position was to sanction in 1880 construction of the Metropolitan Museum between Fifth Avenue and the (then Croton) Reservoir. This issue and the question of whether there should be a zoo in the park were two of the earliest examples of proposals generated in the 'belief that the park should educate the public through didacticism rather than through the unconscious influence of natural scenery'. Although Green endorsed the 'vision of a pastoral park, he also believed the park should be a center of educational, scientific and cultural activity'. Olmsted's position as Superintendent was abolished in 1877. He took another trip to Europe and settled in Boston on his return.[315]

'During the last three decades of the nineteenth century, control of Central Park bounced from one political faction to the next.' In 1880 Vaux, who had maintained a cordial relationship with Green, went into partnership with Samuel Browne Parsons Jr, the son and grandson of Long Island nurserymen. In 1881, at Vaux's request, Parsons was appointed unpaid Superintendent of Planting in the park. He was appointed Superintendent of Parks in 1885 and Parks Landscape Architect in 1898. Parsons 'retired' in 1911 after a dispute with the new recreation-minded Commissioner Charles Stover. Parsons was the last remaining link with the founders of the park and their pastoral ideals. His period of involvement witnessed the emergence of demand first, for the park to perform a more didactic role, and then, for it provide more recreation facilities. He also saw, from 1883, the emergence of high-rise residential buildings overlooking the park.[316]

'In a city legendary for rapid change, Central Park was, and is, remarkably resistant to visual alteration. And in no period, perhaps, did it change less than the three decades after the death of its creators.' Nevertheless, in 1912 the gravel carriage drives were asphalted to make them more suitable for automobiles, and in 1926 the Heckscher Playground opened – the first equipped playground in the park. In 1927 a report by landscape architect Hermann W. Merkel 'documented a general decline in the condition of the park'. Only in the late 1920s did spending on Manhattan parks return to the levels of the early 1900s. In 1929 Vaux's Ladies Refreshment Pavilion was re-opened as a casino. By 1930, 70 per cent of Manhattan residents lived in upper Manhattan and about a million people lived within one mile (1.6 kilometres) of the park.

Additional funding ensured that the park 'looked better than it had in many years'. In April 1930 Parks Commissioner Walter Herrick adopted a proposal from the American Society of Landscape Architects (ASLA) for converting the site of the by then redundant Croton Reservoir into a 'Great Lawn'. The area was occupied by homeless squatters who had been put out of work by the depression. The ASLA proposals were not implemented until 1934. Mayor Fiorello La Guardia took office in January 1934 and immediately appointed Robert Moses as sole Commissioner of a unified Department of Parks for all of New York City – a post Moses held until 1960.[317]

Moses was a 'progressive who believed that a healthful environment could influence social behavior'. He had 'faith in the rule of experts' but 'little interest in the natural qualities of urban parks' viewing them all as 'places for active, wholesome play'. Put more bluntly, he was a 'genius urban impresario and civic fascist' who wanted the park to be 'neither English nor French, neither Romantic nor classical, but efficient, purposeful, and unapologetically American'. Primarily using federal money from President Franklin D. Roosevelt's 'New Deal', Moses 'took the style of the moment and converted the details of the romantic landscape into a heavily engineered hard edge International Style . . . the skeleton of topography, lakes, and major architectural elements remained, but the rest changed'. In 1934 alone the Tavern on the Green (west of the Sheep Meadow) was built; handball courts, roller-skating areas, sandboxes and baseball diamonds were added; the Conservatory at 104th Street and Fifth Avenue was razed; a new entrance was completed at 61st Street and Fifth Avenue, and the new Central Park Zoo was opened; 2600 labourers and mechanics planted trees and shrubs, reseeded and weeded lawns and repaired pathways.[318]

By 1960 park area in New York City had increased from 5660 to 14,000 hectares. Maintenance budgets had not increased correspondingly. 'Whereas in the middle and late nineteenth century, genteel reformers like Olmsted had sought to create a public in their own image, in the early and mid-twentieth century progressive reformers like Moses claimed a new kind of authority as professionally trained experts who would manage the public according to abstract principles of efficiency and rationality'. Thereafter, 'the politics of the park would remain . . . tightly embedded in the politics of the city'. In the late 1960s and 1970s the character of the park was affected by three main factors – demographic changes; liberal policies and financial crises. Between 1940 and 1970 the total population of New York increased by

Bow Bridge from the north (October 1999)

Left: 65th Street Transverse (April 2000)

only 6 per cent whereas its black population tripled and its Puerto Rican population increased by ten times. More than a million white residents left the city in the 1950s and 1960s. By 1979 family income levels in New York were 16 per cent below national averages.[319]

Park Commissioner Thomas Hoving, appointed in 1966, and his successor August Heckscher, appointed in 1967, set out to popularize the park. Hoving excluded cars at weekends and promoted rallies, cultural events and 'happenings'. Heckscher continued that trend, allowing free rock concerts, anti-Vietnam War rallies and festivals in the park. But the economy had been in recession from a post-war peak in 1969 and did not recover until 1977. By 1975 the City of New York was broke. First the capital budget for parks was slashed, then the maintenance budget. By the late 1970s the Sheep Meadow was a dust bowl; vandalism had closed the Belvedere; beer cans filled the Lake and graffiti covered the Bethesda Terrace.[320]

In 1978 Mayor Edward Koch appointed Gordon Davis as Park Commissioner. Davis began a programme of 'load-shedding'. In 1979 he appointed Elizabeth Barlow Rogers as Central Park Administrator and in 1980 Mayor Edward Koch announced the formation of the Central Park Conservancy – a board of trustees for the park. Rogers had graduated in City Planning in 1964 and

then moved to New York. She developed an interest first in parks and then in Olmsted, publishing books and articles about both of them. Outraged by the demise of Central Park she began in the mid-1970s to raise private funds and organize volunteer labour. Twenty years after her appointment, former Commissioner Davis commented that when he appointed her as administrator 'she had no money and no power'. By the time Rogers stood down in 1996, the Conservancy had raised more than $150 million – and spent most of it on rehabilitation of the park. Rogers ranks with Olmsted, Vaux and Moses for her impact on the park. She combined quite extraordinary fund-raising abilities with strong organizational skills and a firm vision of what the park should be. Rogers introduced an approach to rehabilitation that sought a balance between restoration of the Olmsted–Vaux design as an unprogrammed pastoral antidote to the city on the one hand, but acknowledged contemporary demands on the other.[321]

With a small team of landscape architects and restoration planners Rogers codified her views in 1985 in *Rebuilding Central Park: A Management and Restoration Plan*. Clearly written and clearly illustrated, it was a practical and persuasive manifesto for preservation of the 'unprogrammed' pastoral park. Like the approach in Prospect Park, it re-established Olmsted and Vaux as the principal planners and designers of Central Park. It was a masterful piece of fund-raising propaganda to promote the park to the corporations and residents whose premises looked out over it.

MANAGEMENT, FUNDING AND USAGE

Managing Organization

Central Park was created by the State Legislature in 1853 but funded by the Common Council of New York. After 1857 it was managed by a Board of Commissioners appointed by the State Legislature – but still funded by the city. The Board was replaced in 1870 by city's own Department of Public Parks. In less than twenty years the park had moved from control by state-appointed professionals to control by Democratic city politicians. In 1898 Staten Island, Brooklyn and Queens were incorporated with the City of New York to form Greater New York. Whereas Samuel Parsons Jr retired as Parks Department landscape architect in 1911 in protest that active recreation was being given priority in the park, Robert Moses paid little heed to the preservation lobby. By the mid-1970s the wheel had come full circle. Senator Daniel Moynihan and others proposed that Central Park be turned over to the National Park Service. But the first major change since 1934 came with the establishment in 1980 of the Central Park Conservancy.[322]

The Conservancy is a private, not-for-profit organization incorporated under the laws of New York State. It manages Central Park under a contract with the City of New York and the Department of Parks and Recreation. The Administrator is appointed by the Mayor and reports to the Park Commissioner but is paid by the Conservancy. This was the first time that a single individual had been made responsible for organizing capital works and day-to-day management and maintenance of the park since Green's appointment in 1859. In 1992 the Conservancy described its partnership with the Department of Parks and Recreation as 'the most successful coordination of public and private resources to date on behalf of an urban park'. In February 1998 the Conservancy signed an eight-year management agreement with Mayor Rudolph Giuliani and Parks Commissioner Henry Stern that made the Conservancy the 'Keeper of the Park'.[323]

Funding

In 1988 the City provided $10.2 million (61 per cent) and the Conservancy provided $6.6 million (39 per cent) of the annual budget for the park. In 1999 the Conservancy provided 85 per cent of the budget. By spring 2000 the Central Park Conservancy had raised over $200 million. The largest single gift was a grant of $10 million in 1998. The largest financial challenge to the Conservancy in the 1990s was a grant of $17 million for major restoration projects – contingent on matching funds being raised from the City and from private donors. That challenge was met in 1996. The majority of projects covered by that campaign were completed in Fiscal Year 1999 and brought the restored proportion of the park to 75 per cent.[324]

Operational costs for the park doubled between 1995 and 1999 to nearly $7 million – largely as a result of the increased maintenance requirements for restored areas. An endowment fund valued at $65 million in 1999 generates income to cover maintenance costs. The Conservancy operates a system of 'zone gardeners'. Twenty-two of the forty-nine zones were supported by endowments in 1999. Paid labour was augmented in 1999 by more than 2000 volunteers contributing more than 40,000 hours of work. As in Prospect Park, the value of this input is not purely financial. It builds positive use and educates users. The Conservancy had about 230 employees in 1999 – more than twice as many as in 1991.[325]

The 1998 Agreement established that the City would provide $1 million per year towards operational costs if the Conservancy raised $5 million. If the Conservancy raises more, the City has to match half of the additional sum up to a maximum City contribution of $2 million per year. Providing the Conservancy achieved the $5 million target, it had a guarantee not made for any other New York City park – an understandable source of resentment with the managers of other parks and the non-profit Park Council. Other park organizations now feel obliged to copy the Conservancy's fund-raising methods. Effectively, the private sector – not the citizenry – now holds the City responsible to it for the funding of Central Park.[326]

User Characteristics

Central Park was largely used in the 1860s 'as a parade ground for the wealthy, although many of the areas surrounding the Park were occupied by shanty settlements or farmland'. In 1862, two million visitors arrived by foot and 700,000 by carriage. The bridle paths drew upper-class horseback riders. The so-called carriage parade became fashionable. The rich had their own coaches (and sleighs for winter); the middle class could rent a hack for one or two dollars an hour'. Olmsted recorded that in 1863, 6000 'pleasure carriages' had been driven in the park in a single day and that in 1865 that had risen to 16,000 in a day. The total number of visits in each of those years was recorded as four million and seven-and-a-half million respectively.[327]

The figure of seven-and-a-half million remained steady until 1870. By that year, Olmsted recorded, every Sunday in summer there were 30 to 40,000 visitors and 10,000 horses kept for pleasure driving. After 1870 the paraders and carriage riders had to share the park, particularly on Sundays, with larger and less genteel crowds. Newspapers that had praised its orderliness in the 1860s lamented its 'relapse into barbarism'. In 1871 and for each of the following three years there were nearly eleven million visits and only about 20 per cent of the two million new visitors arrived by carriage. The rest were pedestrians. By 1884, on a summer Sunday at least, the park was dominated by the working classes while on weekdays the fashionable carriage parade continued in full force. In the 1880s Coney Island had four-and-a-half million visitors – many less than Central Park; but in the 1890s, crowds at Coney Island on summer Sundays were double those in Central Park.[328]

In the early twentieth century, active recreation became more popular. Records show that 20,000 tennis permits were issued in 1915. Visitor numbers remained high until the 1970s. In 1981 the park was 'used very much the same way that Olmsted visualized – as the scene of fundamentally passive, non-competitive activities: strolling, lying on the grass, picnicking in the shade. But most of all, it is used for *the simple act of watching other people do much the same thing*'. A 1982 user survey recorded three million users – of whom 500,000 were not from New York – making fourteen million visits. Visitors came mainly alone on weekdays and just less than half came alone at weekends. A further user survey was conducted in 1995. This found the proportion of male users was 57 per cent (in 1982 this was higher); 57 per cent of visitors were members of a minority (a significant increase from 23 per cent in 1989); 64 per cent of visitors used the park for 'relaxation' (up from 51 per cent in 1989) and 55 per cent of visits were made alone (up from 50 per cent in 1989 and 47 per cent in 1982). By 2000, the number of visits had reached twenty million per year.[329]

Crime

As Superintendent, Olmsted 'organized a force of twenty-four park keepers – one of the first uniformed and well-disciplined police forces in the nation'. Although the first murder in the park was committed in October 1872, Olmsted's force was largely concerned with protecting quality of life rather than life itself. Ironically, by the end of the Moses era the Park, 'no longer a piece of nature but a piece of property, a venue for recreation, not conservation was dangerous'. And, for the last half of the twentieth century many white New Yorkers associated the park with young black and Puerto Rican men, and with crime and fear. In fact, there were no murders in the park between 1955 and 1964 but felonies increased dramatically in actual and in relative terms between 1960 and 1970, when they peaked. In the 1970s and 1980s there were three times as many murders in the lower Fifth Avenue district bordering the park than in the park, and eighteen times more in the police precinct directly north of the park. In 1973 the *New York Times* – a paper not normally known for crime reporting – covered three of the four murders in the park but only about 20 per cent of the 1676 murders in the rest of New York. Equally, the 'wilding' incident in 1989, in which a young investment banker was beaten and sexually assaulted by a group of rampaging youngsters, was given massive international publicity – re-fanning racial fears. Similarly, known gay 'cruising' areas like the Ramble have been characterized as hangouts for 'dangerous perverts'. Overall, it seems that the problems of crime in the park are as much about perception and fear as they are about statistically proven threats. On the other hand, 'every Park official, city administrator and police officer tells us (correctly) that the Park is safe during the day, they all agree on this: only a fool goes there at night'. Nevertheless, in June 2000, seven female European tourists were assaulted between 6:15 and 6:55 p.m. on a Sunday evening after the National Puerto Rican Day Parade.[330]

PLANS FOR THE PARK

The design and management of Central Park since 1980 have been driven by the mantra that 'it was designed as a single unified park and still functions as one'. *Rebuilding Central Park* – the fifteen-year *Management and Restoration Plan* prepared by the Conservancy in 1985 – noted that its condition 'at the time of formation of the Conservancy was truly shocking'. The plan was based on six guiding principles:

- Protection and preservation – it is imperative that its custodians do not accept invasion by other interests and that no further portions of it be dedicated to single interest groups
- Historic character – it does not require a period restoration correct to the last detail but rather the use of the Greensward Plan, wherever possible, as a reference and guide

- Public safety and enjoyment – it is not enough that a park be safe; it must *appear* to be safe as well. Vandalized structures and park furniture create an atmosphere of lawlessness and gloom
- Maintaining cleanliness and structural soundness – good routine maintenance and consistent public education build respect for the park
- Horticultural beauty and ecological health – good forestry and horticultural practices are essential to ensure a park's continued beauty and health, and are made more urgent because of the heavy volume of use of Central Park
- Functional and structural integrity – to overcome fragmented administration of design maintenance and operations.[331]

Wollman Rink, south-east corner of park (October 1999)

Surveys showed the full extent of the damage caused by the years of abuse. Restoration works were undertaken throughout the park during the 1980s and 1990s. Focal built-elements like the Mall and Bethesda Terrace and virtually every other building, bridge, pathway, lake edge and piece of furniture in the park needed attention. Works to restore vegetation ranged from short-term, high cost elements like the reconstruction of the Great Lawn between 1995 and 1997 to longer-term volunteer-based projects like the management back to ecological health of the exotic species-infested woodland areas. The legacy of heavy use and low investment meant that the works really were an exercise in rebuilding rather than simply rehabilitating the park. The principles established in 1985 remained operative in 2000. 'As the Central Park Conservancy focuses on new areas of restoration, implementing innovative park management strategies, and fostering opportunities for enjoyment for the modern park user, a vision shaped more than 150 years ago remains our guiding light'.[332]

CONCLUSIONS

Central Park remains one of the single most powerful precedents in the entire history of landscape architecture. It was 'one of the most innovative and enduring responses to urbanization undertaken in nineteenth century America' and 'the beginning of a whole movement can be traced directly to one example and to two designers working almost as one'. Paradoxically, the work of Olmsted and Vaux is claimed to have been at the root of the City Beautiful Movement and to be 'strikingly modern'. Their design for Central Park was described in 1904 as an 'amalgam of a Herefordshire sheepwalk and the location for a movie version of Hiawatha'. In fact it can be reasonably construed as a precedent for Disneyland – with Main Street USA equating to the Mall and Sleeping Beauty's Castle representing the Belvedere.[333]

Latterly the park has 'reinvented itself as an elite cultural charity'. Garvin noted that this revival of the park results from an 'extraordinary match' between 'market, location and design'. But the question of 'how much New Yorkers have lost in the bargain that restored Central Park for them remains unclear – and debatable'. One thing, however, is apparent. Central Park has changed since its inception from being a complete escape from this amazing city to being an amazing complement to it.[334]

18 Stanley Park, Vancouver

405 hectares (1000 acres)

INTRODUCTION

'Vancouver is Stanley Park and Stanley Park is Vancouver.' Stanley Park is a substantial piece of 'trapped wilderness' occupying a peninsula about a kilometre west of downtown Vancouver. Its designation as a public park was the first resolution made by the first meeting of the newly formed Vancouver City Council in May 1886. This was a remarkable decision given that the population of Vancouver at that time was less than 3000 people. It is believed, however, that its designation had as much to do with real estate speculation as with any direct concern for the creation of a major public park.[335]

The character of Stanley Park derives more from its protection from development than from any conscious act of design. Although much of the southern part of the peninsula was logged in the 1850s and 1860s, the park remains, primarily, mature coniferous coastal forest. The principal human incursions are the encircling Seawall, the Stanley Park Causeway and Lions Gate Bridge – linking downtown Vancouver to North and West Vancouver across Burrard Inlet. The 8.8 kilometre Seawall was built between 1917 and 1975. The Bridge and Causeway were completed in 1938. Other facilities have been added in a piecemeal fashion over time and are largely located around

Location of Stanley Park, Vancouver

1   Stanley Park
2   First Narrows/Lions Gate Bridge
3   North Vancouver
4   Burrard Inlet
5   Coal Harbour
6   West End
7   Downtown Vancouver
8   False Creek
9   Kitsilano
10 English Bay
11 University of British Columbia

1 km

Stanley Park, Vancouver

1   Lions Gate Bridge
2   Prospect Point
3   Mature Forest
4   Stanley Park Causeway
5   Highest elevation in park
    (+70 metres above sea
    level)
6   Siswash Rock
7   Third Beach
8   Beaver Lake
9   Ferguson Point
10 Second Beach
11 Lost Lagoon
12 Georgia Street
    Causeway
13 Stanley Monument
14 Brockton Oval
15 Brockton Point
16 Hallelujah Point

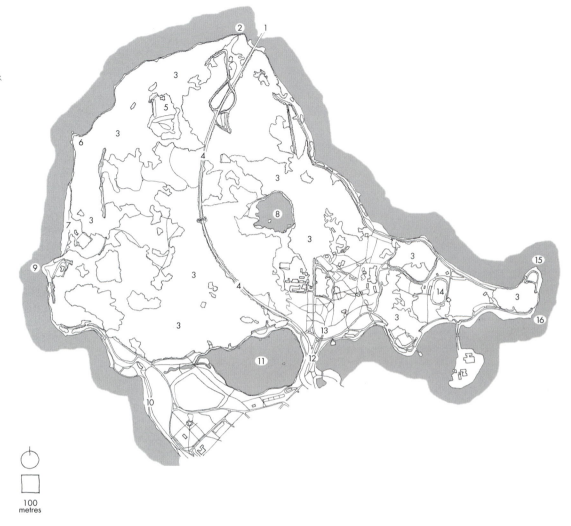

100
metres

the edges of the park, particularly on the southern side. These additions have left the wilderness qualities of the park relatively undisturbed. Most of the trails through the forest follow the line of nineteenth-century logging paths.

There has never been an overall design for the park. This has resulted in its management being characterized by a series of apparently unrelated decisions. Furthermore, the fact that the park is essentially a large, heavily forested and locally steep-sloping, volcanic hill has meant that visitors are attracted in large numbers to the Seawall and to the roads through the park but in far smaller numbers to its remoter parts. The history of the park is a story first of building the Seawall then of resolving conflicts over its use; of debates over how to manage the forest, and of trying to resolve transport issues. The managers of the park – the directly

elected Vancouver Park and Recreation Board – are obliged to wrestle with these recurrent issues.

HISTORY

Designation as a Park

The 'opening up' of the Pacific coast of Canada by European settlers was dependent on railways. The Canadian Pacific Railway (CPR) decided in 1884 to locate its transcontinental terminus at Coal Harbour, directly south-east of the future park. This decision led to rapid growth of the surrounding settlement. The CPR gave the name Vancouver to the settlement after Captain George Vancouver, who was, in 1792, the first Briton to visit the area. Land speculation was an inevitable part of this process of 'opening up' and it seems that land speculation gave rise, however indirectly, to the designation of Stanley Park as a public park.

The proposal at the meeting of the City Council on 12 May 1886 to petition the federal government to lease the peninsula for use as a park was put forward by Lachlan A. Hamilton – an alderman and a surveyor with the CPR. It seems that three separate groups of landowners had a common interest in preventing the land from being released for development. First there was a group of three pioneers who had established land claims in 1862 for the land now covered by the West End of Vancouver. It appeared, however, that the value of their land would be reduced by the CPR's plans to locate its Pacific railhead at Port Moody, 20 kilometres to the east. The pioneers therefore sought support from businessman (and eventual three-term Mayor) David Oppenheimer to lobby the CPR to extend the rail line to Vancouver. The price of Oppenheimer's support was a share in the land. The CPR may already have decided to extend the line. Nevertheless, they became the third party to have an interest in the land adjacent to the Government Reserve on the peninsula.[336]

The idea of designating the reserve as a park is credited to the highly persuasive Arthur Wellington Ross of real estate developers Ross and Ceperly. Ross is reported to have taken William Van Horne, a Vice President of the CPR, around the reserve by boat and to have sold Van Horne on the idea of designating the park. Van Horne agreed to talk to the 'right' people in Ottawa and he and Ross approached Hamilton to raise the matter at the inaugural Council meeting. It is apparent therefore that the decision to petition for designation of the park was the byproduct of profit motives rather than the result of social or environmental motives. In that respect it sits with Regent's and other parks playing a supporting role to property development. The federal government granted approval in June 1887 to the land being leased to the city as a park. In October 1887 a plebiscite agreed to spend C$20,000 on basic works including roads into the park. It was opened in September 1888 and officially dedicated in September 1889 by Lord Stanley, Governor General of Canada, as being for 'the use and enjoyment of people of all colours, creeds and customs for all time'. The park took its name from Lord Stanley.[337]

Condition at the Time of Designation

The peninsula has steep sandstone cliffs above the Seawall between Ferguson Point and Prospect Point. A volcanic dyke crosses the north-west corner of the site from Siswash Point to the basalt columns of Prospect Point creating, at 70 metres,

the highest point of the park. At the end of the eighteenth century, when the site was first seen by Europeans, it would have been almost entirely covered by coniferous coastal forest. The site is known to have been a visiting ground for several thousand Coast Salish Indians before any Europeans visited the region. The first European visitors were Spanish. Don José Maria Narvaez made a cursory investigation of Burrard Inlet in 1791; Dionisio Alcala Galiano modified Narvaez's charts and met with Vancouver in 1792. Vancouver was apparently greeted by Indians. His charts showed the peninsula to be an island – a condition that might have occurred at high tide before the building of the Georgia Street causeway in 1888 and enclosure of the Lost Lagoon in 1916. In the early 1860s a Squamish village of four homes and a lodge – called Whoi-Whoi ('masks village') – stood on the shore of Brockton Point. Excavations in 1888 for road construction uncovered large dumps of broken shells including 500-year-old tree stumps. This suggests that the site had been significant to Indians for many years – whether actually settled or not. The totem poles near Hallelujah Point are a recent memento of the pre-European history of the site.[338]

By the 1840s European squatters also occupied cabins near Brockton Point and Coal Harbour. In 1858 a temporary camp was made at Second Beach for miners from California en route to the Fraser River Gold Rush. In 1859 the park was designated a Government Reserve because of its strategic coastal location in the event of an anticipated war between Britain and the United States. Records show that five small logging companies were active in the peninsula between the 1860s and the 1880s – and that the (not insubstantial) area between Beaver Lake and Lost Lagoon was clear-cut and burned during this period. The rest of the park was selectively logged ('high-graded') for the best Douglas fir, Red cedar and Sitka spruce. The majority of the current trails through the park follow the line of 'skid roads' created during this period for the removal of felled trees. When the park was designated therefore it included a substantial amount of immature forest – covering about 15 per cent of the current forest area together with most of the now cleared areas of the park. By the late 1980s forest covered about 260 hectares (65 per cent of the park).[339]

Development of the Park

The development of the park since its designation has been a story of disjointed decision-making. Apart from the gradual inclusion of various recreational facilities at the edges, the largest single addition for its use as a park was the construction of the Seawall.

Overleaf: Third Beach and North Vancouver across First Narrows (June 1998)

And the single biggest cause of conflict has been the introduction of vehicular traffic to the park – a conflict that began with the first proposal in 1909 to bridge the First Narrows and has continued since completion of the Stanley Park Causeway and Lions Gate Bridge in 1938. Recreational facilities have been added and removed over time. These include: 1890 – sports pitches at Brockton Oval; 1906 – Zoo; 1911 – rowing club building and Tatlow Walk (to give view of giant forest trees); 1916 – filling completed to create Lost Lagoon; 1920 – Rose Garden; 1932 – golf course; 1934 – Malkin Bowl (replacing the 1911 bandstand); 1936 – Shakespeare Garden; 1938 – walkway around Lost Lagoon; 1947 – miniature railway; 1956 – Aquarium; 1962 – Third Beach created by pumping sand from Siswash Rock; 1968 – rebuilding of the swimming pool at Second Beach; 1977–81 – widening of Seawall promenade; 1993 – Zoo closed; and 1997–99 – further widening of Seawall and commencement of shuttle bus. This list reflects a tendency to add, bit by bit, facilities not particularly compatible with the forest character of the park. More major issues have, however, been determined by plebiscite. Such issues have included the original funding for the park – approved in 1887; the Lions Gate Bridge – rejected in 1927 but accepted on account of high unemployment during the depression in the 1930s, and closure of the Zoo in 1993.

Key Figures in the Establishment of the Park

The early advocates of the park had largely commercial motivations. They hardly rate as exemplary advocates. Equally, the disjointed approach that has been adopted in the planning and design of the park has meant that no particular individuals or teams have left a strong mark on its development. The neo-classical British landscape architect Thomas Mawson (1861–1933) was engaged in 1912 to design the Zoo, Prospect Point, Brockton Point Lighthouse and the main entrance. He also prepared proposals for a sports stadium on the north side of the Lost Lagoon – 'a showpiece entrance to a wilderness park' – which caused immense controversy and was eventually rejected on cost grounds. Mawson's proposal to study the whole of the park was also turned down by the Parks Board. The only person who can truly be said to have had a long-running and visible involvement with the shaping of the park is the master stonemason James Cunningham who was involved with the construction of the Seawall from 1931 until his death in 1963. Cunningham, by all accounts, continued to direct the work long after his official retirement – 'even visiting the site in pyjamas and topcoat'.[340]

PLANNING AND DESIGN

Location and Accessibility

The proximity of Stanley Park to downtown Vancouver has obviously been instrumental in its importance. It has been described as 'the sacred point that all parts of the city turn around. Green during the day, contrasting with adjacent high-rise buildings. Dark at night, contrasting with the lights of the downtown'. The two factors that have had the most influence on the relationship between the park and the city have been the construction of the Stanley Park Causeway and Lions Gate Bridge in the 1930s, and the rapid growth of the resident population of the West End – the area between the park and the downtown – during the 1980s and 1990s.[341]

Transport surveys in the early and mid-1990s showed peak daily traffic flows into the park in summer of between 8000 cars on a Monday and up to 14,000 cars on holidays and weekends. These figures include cars that stopped in the park and those being driven straight through it. Table 18.1 shows that roughly half of all park users in the early 1990s arrived by car. Surveys of the origin of parked cars showed less than 30 per cent coming from the city. This suggests – unsurprisingly – that the location and accessibility of the park make it an attractive destination for visitors by car from a wider catchment area and by foot from the West End.[342]

Table 18.1 Means of travel to Stanley Park in 1991

Means of travel	%
Car	48
Bus	10
Bicycle	8
Foot	33

Source: Stanley Park Technical Report January 1992

The resident population of the Downtown – between Main Street and Burrard Street – was 17,000 in 1996. The population of the West End – west of Burrard Street – was 41,000 in 1996. The additional residential capacity of the downtown peninsula as a whole is estimated to be about 37,000. This means that, in addition to its already significant citywide and regional role, the park is having to meet increasing demand to act as a neighbourhood park for local residents. It is also anticipated that the population of the Vancouver region will continue to rise (from 1.6 million in 1991 to 2.9 million in 2021); that levels of tourism in Vancouver will continue to rise, and that levels of car ownership in Vancouver will continue to rise (from 0.57 cars per person in 1991 to 0.6 in 2021). The location, accessibility and increasing catchment area population of the park suggest that it will be subject to increasing usage. The park has changed, in little over a century, from being disproportionately large relative to the population of the city to being threatened by overuse.[343]

Shape and Natural Landform of the Site

The site was a conical island with an almost circular base rising skewly to an elevation of over 70 metres toward Prospect Point. The circle is distended by the lower-lying Brockton Point peninsula jutting eastward into Burrard Inlet. The demands imposed by the increasing levels of park usage are felt primarily on the areas immediately adjacent to the West End – around Lost Lagoon and Brockton Point; along the traffic routes through and within the park, and on the Seawall. The steeper, forested interior of the park continues to display the dramatic and mysterious wilderness characteristics for which the park is cherished. This inherited backdrop of forested hillsides; the extensive views westward to the ocean, northward to the hills above North and West Vancouver and eastward to the downtown are part of Stanley Park's unique character. Creation of the Seawall, of Third Beach and of the limited number of additional recreational trails through the forest are the few human interventions that have added to the experience of the inherent qualities of the park.

Design Concept

The original planning concept for the park was to withhold the land from a highly speculative real estate market. The plebiscite in 1887 agreed an expenditure of C$20,000 on roads, particularly towards Brockton Point, and on basic landscape works. But there appears never to have been a consistent design concept for the whole of the park – either when it was established or at any time since. Mawson's offer in 1912 was turned down; a Draft Master Plan was commissioned in 1985 but was never adopted, and a ten-year Forest Management Plan that was approved in 1989 was scaled back and replanting is now done only in smaller parcels.

Following the apparent failure of landscape architects and foresters for over a century to

*Lions Gate Bridge
(June 1987)*

develop a plan that was deemed acceptable, the Park Board took a more pragmatic approach to defining a concept for the park. In 1991 they established the Stanley Park Task Force to 'determine the community's values and goals' for the park. The Task Force was chaired by a retired judge and its members included an environmental lawyer and community planner, a community activist, an elementary school teacher, a professor of physical education and recreation, a professor of planning and urban historian, and a criminal lawyer and environmental preservationist. Notable for their absence were ecologists, foresters, landscape managers and any kind of artists or designers. The *Final Report of the Task Force* was 'received by the Board' but many of its proposals – like the proposal of a Stanley Park Charter and removal of the swimming pool at Second Beach – were not followed. Indeed, the pool was refurbished and re-opened in May 1995.[344]

The Report quoted at length from a submission by landscape architect Douglas Paterson. He came close to proposing a concept that could guide the planning and design of Stanley Park. He described the park as 'a sentinel at the harbour entrance' and characterized it as an 'urban wilderness for Vancouver residents' adjacent to the downtown. Paterson recognized it as a 'classic Canadian park symbolizing a nation living at the edge of wilderness'; he referred to the 'cathedral-like quality of the forest canopy' and suggested that 'anyplace activities' should not be located in the park. This might sound somewhat vague but what it does do is to acknowledge the intrinsic qualities of the site and to promote these qualities as the basis for planning and design of the park. Paterson also recognized that Stanley Park can no longer continue to absorb all the demands placed on it without its intrinsic qualities being threatened. There has therefore never been a firm planning and design concept for the park and the natural resources of the site have had to adapt to the random pressures imposed on them.[345]

The Seawall is, nevertheless, one of the finest urban park experiences in the world. It provides a continually evolving sequence of views. These views present the park, the city, the ocean and the surrounding mountains in relative context; each heightening the understanding and appreciation of the other. And yet the Seawall is the type of intervention that would probably not be made today – cutting across the ecotone between the shoreline and the forest. Equally, the act of cutting a swath through the forest for the Causeway has had the effect of opening the centre of the park to daily public view. And rapid immersion in the sublime

stands of coniferous coastal forest is only made possible by the pedestrian trails along old skid roads. Clearly, incremental decisions have had more currency than have strategic plans.

MANAGEMENT AND USAGE

Managing Organization

Shortly after the newly formed Vancouver City Council had petitioned the federal government for the peninsula to be allocated as a public park, it appointed a Park Committee to 'manage the park by building trails and gardens'. By 1890, two years after the opening of the park, the Board had become a directly elected body with three commissioners. This was increased to seven plus a City Councillor in an advisory role in 1928. The Councillor position was discontinued in 1966. The Board is proud of the fact that it remains the only organization of its kind in Canada. It is comparable in this respect with the Minneapolis Park and Recreation Board. It is dissimilar in that it does not have its own tax base.[346]

Park Board members are all elected at the same time in elections held every three years as part of the elections for Vancouver City Council. The Board oversees a system that now includes more than 180 parks and associated recreation facilities covering 850 hectares in addition to Stanley Park. The consultative approach of the Board is expressed in the Mission Statement of the Stanley Park Task Force 'to

Stanley Park from downtown Vancouver (November 1999)

discover, through a public consultation process, the community's values concerning the park for present and future generations'. This is reflected in the continued use of plebiscites to resolve controversial matters. Indeed, consultation seems to be as deeply ingrained in the management philosophy for Stanley Park as is the eschewal of plans for it. The former is probably a root cause of the latter. This attitude may change as a result of an internal reorganization of the Board that was effected in January 1999. Under that arrangement the city has been divided into three park regions. Stanley Park and the adjacent West End/Downtown areas including Coal Harbour and False Creek, form one of these regions. Subdivision might lead to a more plan-driven approach to management of the park.

Funding

The annual cost of managing Stanley Park in 1998 was about C$2 million. The Board of Parks and Recreation continues to maintain and stock its parks with plants through the employment of direct labour. It had a permanent staff of 650 rising to 1800 in summer. All plant material used in the parks was grown in the Board's own nurseries. The funds for management and provision of services in the park come from a combination of subvention by Vancouver City Council (50 per cent in 1998); direct charges for car parking, franchises, facilities and events (45 per cent), and sponsorship (5 per cent). Car parking charges were introduced in 1994 and, by 1998, were generating an income of

over C$1 million per year. The free shuttle bus around the park, instituted in 1998, is entirely funded by sponsorship. It is suggested by park managers that the real cost of managing the park did not change significantly during the 1980s and 1990s – only that the introduction of parking charges radically altered the source of funds for meeting those costs. The annual budget for the Vancouver Park Board is established as part of a triennial capital plan.[347]

Usage

In the mid-1980s it was estimated that the park attracted 'two million visitors a year – mostly between May and August'. Figures for 1996 based on traffic and visitor counts indicated seven-and-a-half million visits per year. Extensive user surveys were conducted on site and by telephone from August to October 1991 as an input to the Task Force process. The findings of these surveys are summarized in Tables 18.2–4. The surveys also showed that once visitors had arrived in the park 74 per cent moved around on foot and that less than 8 per cent used their cars to get around. Table 18.2 indicates increasingly regular use of the park. This pattern is probably accounted for in part by the rising numbers of residents in the West End using it as a neighbourhood park.

The figures for place of residence in Tables 18.3 and 18.4 contain some glaring inconsistencies. They reinforce the suggestion that the park is performing a significant and growing role as a

*Woodland trail
(June 1998)*

*Pedestrian/Equestrian
bridge over the
causeway (June 1998)*

neighbourhood park – a role that might be performed by increasing the provision of local park facilities elsewhere in the Stanley Park District.

Table 18.2 Change in level of use of Stanley Park (1986–91)

Level of use	%
More than 5 years ago	58
Same as 5 years ago	29
Less than 5 years ago	10

Source: Stanley Park Technical Report January 1992

Table 18.3 Place of residence of visitors to Stanley Park (1981)

Place of residence	%
Vancouver area	38
Lower mainland	25
Rest of British Columbia	5
Rest of Canada	15
Rest of world	17

Source: Stanley Park Natural and Cultural Heritage Project 1992

Table 18.4 Place of residence of visitors to Stanley Park (1991)

Place of Residence	%
West End of Vancouver	28
City of Vancouver	27
Greater Vancouver	34
Outside Vancouver	11

Source: Stanley Park Technical Report January 1992

Other significant, but not altogether surprising, findings from the 1991 surveys were that:

- the three most important aspects of the park to telephone survey respondents were wildlife, the Seawall and the forest, in that order
- the three most important aspects of the park to visitor survey respondents were the Seawall, forests and trails and beaches, in that order
- the three most popular places in the park were the Seawall, the beaches and Lost Lagoon, in that order, and ahead of the forest and trails
- the three most popular activities in the park were hiking/walking, the Seawall and sightseeing, in that order.[348]

It is interesting to reflect that wildlife was valued more highly by people who were not actually using the park. It is also interesting to note that while the forests and trails are relatively highly valued, they are relatively less used. This suggests that the forest is more highly valued as a backdrop and perhaps for its visual and psychological presence. It also reflects the fact that it is generally difficult to attract people to the top of parks on conical-shaped sites. As Newton put it, 'one of the surest ways of killing or negating a space is to put something high in the middle'. No further user surveys were conducted between 1991 and 2000.[349]

PLANS FOR THE PARK

The Park and Recreation Board has been reticent about comprehensive strategies for Stanley Park. It has preferred to adopt a reactive approach to the planning and management of the park. This has meant that the Board has had to deal over time with a series of recurrent issues. These have been dominated by:

- conflicts between foot and wheeled users of the Seawall
- vehicular traffic and car parking in the park
- composition of the forest areas, and heritage and wildlife interpretation
- integration of the park with adjacent areas of Vancouver.

The Seawall

Construction of the Seawall took from 1917 to 1975. The promenade was widened between 1977 and 1981 and restrictions were imposed on skate-boarding in 1978 and on roller-skating in 1979. The user surveys in 1991 reflected the ongoing disputes between different types of user. The ensuing *Final Report of the Task Force* called for phased elimination of all wheeled traffic (other than wheelchairs and strollers) from the Seawall. The commendable *Transportation and Recreation Report* (1996) began by recognizing that 'many forms of movement in the park are recreation rather than transportation'. The report noted that cycling and skating are 'appropriate recreational activities on the Seawall' and called for better separation for pedestrians from cyclists and in-line skaters. Localized works to effect this recommendation were carried out between 1997 and 1999 at areas of greatest conflict. Continually increasing levels of use of the Seawall will undoubtedly lead to further conflicts. It is encouraging that the Board is now seeking inclusive solutions to such

conflicts. It is also important that measures are taken outside the park to cater for foot and wheeled users of the Seawall.[350]

Vehicular Traffic and Car Parking

The park has been subject to continually increasing levels of vehicular traffic since the opening in 1938 of Lions Gate Bridge and the Causeway. This introduced an alien element to the park – even if it does have the benefit of making large parts of the park visible to road users. The Bridge and the Causeway are owned and run by the provincial Ministry of Transport and Highways and are therefore beyond the control of the Park and Recreation Board. Recent transport planning reviews of how and where to link downtown Vancouver and the growing suburbs of North and West Vancouver across Burrard Inlet have examined widening the Causeway and duplicating the Bridge. The attitude to this from the perspective of the park is reflected in the Task Force recommendation to place the Causeway within the park in a tunnel. This is clearly a wider issue that will run and run.

Transportation issues internal to the park were addressed most recently in the *Transportation and Recreation Report* (1996). That report was adopted by the Board. It proposed that:

- recreation uses in the park should have priority over transportation uses – hence the sharing approach to use of the Seawall
- private car traffic should be discouraged in the park. Parking charges were introduced in 1994. The 1996 Report recommended reducing the number of parking spaces; reducing road capacity for private cars in summer, and instituting car-free days (a measure adopted in Central Park in the 1960s)
- buses were to be given priority over cars and a shuttle bus be introduced. The shuttle was introduced in 1998 with funding from commercial sponsors.

Composition of the Forest

Forest clearance in the 1860s and 1870s, felling of dangerous trees in the 1950s and Hurricane Freida in 1962 all contributed to the loss of old-growth coniferous forest. Shorter-lived deciduous trees and dense shrubs have replaced many of the cleared areas over time. A ten-year Forest Management Plan was approved and commenced in 1989. This programme was designed to increase the native coniferous component of the forest 'to a percentage more representative of when the park was established'. A planting programme had been commenced in the 1940s and a forest maintenance programme was developed in 1980; but the 1989 plan was the only comprehensive plan to date for managing the forest. That plan called for treatments that would affect 42 per cent of the forest area and included the planting of 28,000 trees, principally Western Red cedar. Natural historians and wilderness activists protested that a wider range of plant species and ages would provide habitats for a wider range of wildlife species. The Task Force Report in 1991 called for a new forest management plan designed to 'allow the forest to evolve as naturally as possible'. Current policy remains to replant small parcels on the principles – but not the scale – of the 1989 plan. Even so, some clearance areas have been left unplanted and have been invaded by vines.[351]

Integration with Adjacent Areas

The Vancouver Greenways Plan adopted by the City Council in 1995 treats the Stanley Park Seawall as part of the 'Seaside Route and Seawall Greenway' – one of fourteen Greenways. The city defined Greenways as 'green paths' for pedestrians and cyclists. They can follow rivers, streets, beaches, railways, ridges and ravines. They are intended to 'expand opportunities for urban recreation and to enhance the experience of nature and city life'. The Greenways Plan is based on City and Neighbourhood Greenways. The Seaside Route and Seawall Greenway extends from Coal Harbour (where it joins up with the Harbour Route to the east) around the park, along the West End, around False Creek to Kitsilano and Jericho Beaches. During the latter 1990s works have been undertaken to provide better foot and cycle routes to and from the park along Coal Harbour and English Bay. This pattern of extending the Seawall along the coastlines either side of the West End toward Kitsilano and the downtown is a commendable way of providing foot access at the same time as dispersing recreational pressure over a wider area.[352]

CONCLUSIONS

Stanley Park has two great natural assets – its location and its forest cover. It is the physical and symbolic meeting point of mainland Canada and the Pacific. It is appropriate that this and the next nearest peninsula to downtown Vancouver, the site of the University of British Columbia, should have

been allocated respectively for recreation and education – places for reflection at the meeting of Canada and the world's largest ocean. The park provides views to the downtown, to coastal mountains and to the sea. Its location also makes it highly accessible from the downtown and to the rapidly increasing population of the West End. The forest cover represents an idea of nature on the doorstep of the downtown. It creates a backdrop for most activities within the park – particularly use of the Seawall – and its trails provide an opportunity for sublime escape from the city.[353]

Galen Cranz described three levels of sophistication in attitudes towards the origin of public parks. The first, and most naive, regards them as plots of land preserved in their original state. The second, she suggested, is that they are aesthetic objects that can be understood in terms of an evolution of artistic styles. The third is that they are part of planners' strategies for moral and social reform. Stanley Park, while clearly displaying aspects of the second and third levels, is a rare example of an urban park that *is* largely preserved in its original state. This is partly by conscious decision and partly a consequence of the somewhat naive 'let nature take its course' attitude expressed by the Task Force in 1991.[354]

The Vancouver Park Board has continually adopted a reactive, project-driven approach rather than a strategic, plan-driven approach to the management of Stanley Park. The level of consultation – although not designed to lead to consensus – is commendable. But the project-driven approach is likely to become less appropriate as the recurrent issues facing the park intensify. These issues include growth of population in the region generally and the adjacent West End in particular; increasing levels of car ownership – contributing to increased demand to cross Burrard Inlet, and conflicts between the increasing numbers of different users of the Seawall. Such issues have to be tackled outside the park – with measures like the Greenways – as well as inside it. Since its inception, Vancouver has had the benefit of Stanley Park. And the park has had the benefit of the Park and Recreation Board to protect it. The Board's new Stanley Park District now has to address the challenge of protecting the natural assets of the park at the same time as meeting Lord Stanley's call to make it available for 'the use and enjoyment of people of all colours, creeds and customs for all time'. Lack of strategic decisions will only lead to continued erosion of the park's intrinsic value.[355]

19 Amsterdamse Bos, Amsterdam

935 hectares (2310 acres)

INTRODUCTION

Conceived as an instrument of urban planning, the Bos Park is probably the largest urban park created during the twentieth century anywhere in the world. Like much of the landscape of The Netherlands, it is a completely human-made artifice composed of natural elements. Construction commenced during the Depression in the 1930s under a work creation programme and was executed through manual labour assisted only by horses. This has left 'an emotional bond between the people of Amsterdam and "their" wood . . . many Amsterdammers remember how their father or grandfather – or even they themselves – dug with their own hands the regatta course'.[356]

The Netherlands is the most densely populated country in Europe and one of the most densely populated countries in the world. Planning strategies in the late nineteenth century and throughout the twentieth century sought to address the issue of how to accommodate a growing population with rising aspirations on a limited land area, much of which is below sea level. At the core of these strategies has been identification of *Randstad Holland* – a ring of cities, including Amsterdam, Rotterdam, The Hague and Utrecht – and the principle of maintaining a 'green heart' at the centre of that ring. These cities, which are distinct administrative entities, accommodate around six million inhabitants – 40 per cent of the country's population. The Bos Park was conceived as a 'green wedge' of recreational open space for the people of Amsterdam, directly linked to the 'green heart' of the *Randstad*.[357]

The main entrance to the park is about 6 kilometres from Amsterdam Central Station. Its area is roughly the same as that enclosed by the ring of canals around the centre of the city. The park was designed to meet functional criteria as much as aesthetic dictates. And rather than being comprehensively designed by a single individual, the design was 'the outcome of a balanced team of professors, botanists, biologists, engineers, architects, sociologists and town planners'. The design that they produced – the *Boschplan* – was intended to achieve 'rapid development of a forest for recreation'. It was based on the principle of the land cover being divided in equal parts between forest, open space and water. The plan called for substantial earthworks and drainage operations to de-water the site and for substantial planting operations to create a native forest landscape. The forest was to contain substantial clearings to accommodate water bodies and recreational activities. The current 935 hectares of the park are divided between 420 hectares of forest (45 per cent), 215 hectares of meadows (23 per cent), 135 hectares of water (14 per cent), 70 hectares of wet hay land (8 per cent), 65 hectares of road, paths and car parks (7 per cent), and 30 hectares in other uses (3 per cent).[358]

HISTORY

Designation as a Park

Chadwick's account of the designation of the Bos Park began in the 1850s. He noted that whereas Amsterdam had developed in 'an orderly manner' since the establishment of the 'plan of three canals' in the seventeenth century, by the mid-eighteenth century building land inside the fortifications was in short supply. In 1866 City Engineer Van Niftrik

Amsterdamse Bos,
Amsterdam

1 Nieuwe Meer
2 Tennis Centre
3 Bosbaan
4 Ringvaart
5 Grote Vijver
6 Grote Speelweide
7 Speelvijver
8 Central Hill
9 Sport Park
10 Kleine Vijver
11 Burgmeester-Colijnweg
12 Meadow
13 Schinkelbos
14 De Poel

100
metres

prepared an expansion plan that 'showed for the first time a definite pattern of city parks'. It was probably inspired by Haussmann's designs for Paris in the preceding decade. The plan called for 'parks at either extremity of the town, formally laid out suburbs to the south, and two other parks projecting to the south-west'. One of these became the Vondel Park. A subsequent plan, prepared in 1875 by Director of Works Kalff, suggested only two, smaller, parks within concentric rings of dense development. The Ooster Park resulted from this plan. Chadwick noted the stylistic influences of Alphand in the planting and paths in both the Vondel Park and the Ooster Park.[359]

The first decade of the twentieth century saw increased levels of concern about urban growth and environmental health in The Netherlands. 'Discussions at Woningwet in 1901' prefigured controls on urban growth and 'led to fundamental changes in the laws on house-building and land usage'. There had been much debate in Germany in the 1890s about quality of life issues. The Dutch had similar concerns. Activist Jacob P. Thijsse called in that decade for 'rural recreation parks for city-dwellers' and in 1908 for 'a properly organised system of walks and public gardens to be laid out in Amsterdam'. One of Thijsse's proposals – for 'a landscape area of parkland around Nieuwe Meer, the long, meandering stretch of water to the south of the city – anticipated both the site and the character of the future Bos Park'. Figures like Thijsse and architect/planner Hendrik Petrus Berlage (1856–1934) continued to address the issue of parks and open-air recreation in Amsterdam during the 1910s but 'it was not until 1921 that two events essential to the control of urban growth occurred'. First, a series of changes to the Woningwet Law allowed city planners to specify land uses rather than simply designing street layouts. Second, the size of the city of Amsterdam was quadrupled by the annexation of the neighbouring councils of Watergraafsmeer and Sloten. This meant that Berlage's 1914–15 plan for the southern extension of the city 'which incorporated areas, such as the park, that had until then laid outside the city – was now viable in its entirety'.[360]

Fritz Schumacher, Oberbaudirektor of the City of Hamburg and principal designer of its Stadtpark, addressed an international planning congress on urban development in Amsterdam in July 1924. He advocated landscapes designed to 'penetrate the body of the town as a net of open spaces and . . . establish a connection with outlying points'. From then until 1928 various plans were prepared for the city and for the park, including the *Schemaplan Groot Amsterdam* drawn up between 1924 and 1926 by

director of Public Works A. W. Bos. That plan was largely derived from Berlage's proposals but was also never approved. Bos's proposals for a major park south of the Nieuwe Meer did, however, prefigure the eventual *Boschplan*. On 28 November 1928 Amsterdam City Council finally approved the proposal and agreed the extent of the park. In January 1929, the year of the Great Depression, the Boschcommissie was established to prepare proposals for the park.[361]

Size and Condition of the Site at the Time of Designation

The designated area comprised 895 hectares of polders – reclaimed land lying below sea level and protected from flooding by human-made dykes. The polders were 'reclaimed from the sea of Buitendijk, Buitenveld, Rietwijk, Schinkel and Kleine Noord, including all the old peat lands and catchment areas beside the Nieuwe Meer and the Poel'. Summer water levels of the polders were 4.6 to 4.7 metres below the level of Amsterdam and 4 metres below sea level. Differences in level of up to 4.5 metres already existed between dykes, the Burgemeester Colijnweg (running east–west between Schipol Airport and Amstelveen across the southern part of the site) and the polder.[362]

The site was subdivided into hundreds of long, thin polders about 50 metres wide. The polders in the north-east of the site were aligned north–south; those between the Nieuwe Meer and the Burgemeester Colijnweg were aligned west-north-west to east-south-east, and those to the south of the Burgemeester Colijnweg were largely aligned north-east to south-west. This fine-grained arrangement of polders was 'formed and "de-peated" at different times between 1858 and 1925'. The peat was dried as a major source of fuel. Its removal left uneven ridges and piles of peat at the edges of fields. There was a rich variety of soils in the polders including marine clay, sand, peat and sandy clay. The water table in the polders was relatively constant – which meant that the same water level could be maintained across most of the park. The height of the water table, however, meant that it had to be lowered to between 1 and 1.5 metres below the surface to facilitate tree growth.[363]

Key Figures in the Establishment of the Park

The Boschcommissie presented the report of its studies in May 1931. Around that time changes in the Woningwet Law facilitated the expropriation of the land for the park. Work on the design of the park was taken over by the Town Planning section of the Amsterdam Public Works Department where detailed plans were prepared under the direction of architect Cornelis Van Eesteren (1897–1988). The Utility Works section was responsible for implementation of the scheme. They and the Town Planning section were advised, in turn, by the Horticulture section. It was 'a municipal scheme in all respects'.[364]

Van Eesteren and landscape architect Jacopa Mulder were key figures behind the design strategy. Berrizbeita noted that they travelled to England and to Germany 'to study examples . . . of two precedents . . . the picturesque park and the *Volksparks*' and developed a 'conception of the design and construction of the park as a process rather than as an aestheticized composition' . . . an approach that 'demanded that a critic understand its value less in terms of "how it looks" and more in terms of "how it works"'. The *RIBA Journal* also noted that Van Eesteren was 'chiefly responsible' for the 'landscape planning'; that he was 'President of the last International Congress of Modern Architecture (CIAM), and this design can be taken in part as the modernists' challenge in this difficult corner of design'.[365]

PLANNING AND DESIGN

Location

The *Boschplan* was ratified in its entirety in 1935 and became the first officially accepted initiative in the General Expansion Plan for Amsterdam. The Bos Park became one of five green fingers protected from development. It remains a significant, and probably the most popular, outdoor recreation area and place to experience 'nature' in the Amsterdam region. Its success led to the creation of two further similar such parks in the 1970s – Spaarnwoude and The Twiske. Spaarnwoude was designed as a recreation area and as a buffer between residential areas and the western docks; The Twiske, in the peat landscape of Waterland to the north of Amsterdam, is designed and managed more as an area for the enjoyment of 'nature'.[366]

In the same way that Spaarnwoude acts as a buffer for the docks, the Bos Park has become increasingly significant as a buffer between the rapidly expanding Schipol airport and, in particular, Amstelveen to the east. The continued presence of the airport is used as an argument for protection of the park from demands for development. The continued presence of the park bolsters above-average property prices in Amstelveen. During the 1990s land in the north-eastern corner of the park was released for (private) expansion of the Tennis Centre. This was counterbalanced by expansion of the park to the south-west into the Schinkelpolder. This 40-hectare expansion, the Schinkelbos, was the first stage in a proposed 70-hectare extension of the park as an 'ecological corridor' into the green heart of *Randstad Holland*.

Development of the Park

Work on the park began in 1934. The first operation involved the levelling of the site into a single polder and installation of land drains to lower the subsoil water level in preparation for tree planting. A total length of 300 kilometres of 6-centimetre diameter porous pipe was laid at 15 to 25 metre centres across the entire land area of the park. The land drainage system was designed to discharge into the water courses excavated throughout the park. These are all connected to a pumping station that discharges into the Ringvaart from the west side of the park. The extent to which levels had to be manipulated to make the drainage system operate is reflected in the rapid change of water level at the sluices between the north side of the Bosbaan (rowing course) at 4.5 metres below sea level and the Nieuwe Meer at 0.6 metres below – a rise of 3.9 metres. The other water courses through the park are 1 metre lower than the Bosbaan at 5.5 metres below sea level.[367]

Excavation for the Bosbaan also began in 1934 – at the same time as the building of the covered grandstand, the sluices up to the Nieuwe Meer and the boat houses. The 2200-metre-long course was completed to its originally designed width of 72 metres in 1937 and officially opened by Queen Wilhelmina. In 1964 the course was widened to 92 metres and, in 1996, it was agreed that it should be widened to 118 metres. Excavate arising from the formation of the course and from other water bodies in the park was moved, largely by manual labour, to create a 15-metre-high central hill. Planting of the park was based on the principle of establishing substantial areas of woodland composed of native species. It began in 1937 and was completed in 1967 – with the planting of trees around the hill.

Spatial Structure, Circulation System, Landform, Materials and Planting

The slim, iconic rectangle of the Bosbaan dominates and dissects the northern part of the park. The preferred east–west alignment of the course cuts across the natural line of drainage to the Nieuwe Meer and across lines of communication. Other active recreation areas, like the Sport Park

The Bosbaan (June 1999)

and the Tennis Centre, are also in the north and east of the park – where they can be easily accessed and where they can act as a filter for the quieter and less active recreational areas. The other major feature affecting the layout of the park is the Burgemeester Colijnweg. This runs east–west across the park two-thirds of the way down its length. It has been supplemented since the construction of the park by the elevated Burgmeester Van Sonweg Autoweg. The roads run side-by-side along the line of the pre-existing dyke between the Rietwijk polder and the Schinkelpolder and, in the same way that the rowing course defines a bird sanctuary to its north, the highways define a less active area including sanctuaries and nature reserves to their south.

The configuration of woodland and meadow in the area between the Bosbaan and the Autoweg focuses on a central, wavy-edged clearing running in an arc from the north-east corner of the park via the artificial hill to the *Kleine Vijver* (small pond). Two intervisible clearings radiate to the west and to the south of this pond. A subsidiary clearing runs north-west from the hill to the *Grote Vijver* (large pond). The circular *Speelweide* (grassed play space) and kidney-shaped *Speelvijvert* (play pond) are axially aligned to the south-west of the *Grote Vijver*. An open-air theatre is to its west. South of the Autoweg, apart from the former emergency landing strip for the airport (now a meadow), there are only minor clearings in the forest – other than the water bodies. The marshy areas bordering the Nieuwe Meer, and the Poel and the Kleine Poel in the south-east of the park are managed as nature reserves. Of the 360 species of birds known in The Netherlands, 290 have been seen in the park.[368]

The circulation system is designed primarily for pedestrians, cyclists and horse riders – in that order. This is reflected in the facilities that are provided for each of them. The system comprises 137 kilometres of footpaths; 51 kilometres of cyclepaths; 23 kilometres of bridlepaths – and only 14 kilometres of roadway. The main entrances for all users arriving by whatever mode of transport are, quite logically, on the north and east sides of the park. The roadways and car parks are largely confined to the edges of the park. The footpaths, cyclepaths and bridleways are subliminally threaded through the fabric of the woodlands and 'clearings' in such a subtle way that, travelling at the appropriate speed, the contrasts between them – between enclosure and openness; between dark and light – can be quite sublime.

Native forest was always intended to be the characteristic element of the Bos Park – hence the devotion of resources to lower the water table. Planting was done in the clay-rich indigenous soils mixed with peat. Initial planting comprised 95 per cent broadleaf species and 5 per cent coniferous species. The natural climax vegetation on these soils would be ash–elm forest but the planting of elm was restricted by the risk of Dutch elm disease. In the northern part of the park planting was based on the species mix of the north-west European forest. It comprised 35 per cent oak, 20 per cent beech, 15 per cent ash, 10 per cent maple and 20 per cent other species, including birch, hornbeam, lime and poplar. In the southern part some exotic species were also included. Most of the coniferous species, which were primarily Norway spruce, were planted on the hill – where they might create 'the character of an alpine meadow'.[369]

In the establishment stages of the forest, trees were planted at 1 metre centres and included fast-growing species such as alder and poplar to act as a

Cycle route in the north of the park (June 1999)

windbreak (or nurse) to protect the eventually dominant climax species. After five years the nurse crop was pruned and then it was cleared after fifteen years. Subsequently four annual thinnings were carried out on the other trees and after forty to fifty years long-term specimens were selected leaving a density of 80 to 100 trees per hectare.

Original Design Concept

The Bos Park was created as a result of 'new ideas about the importance of nature and recreation'. The *RIBA Journal* noted in 1938 that 'this was not a problem to be solved merely by the adoption of any of the historical forms of park design . . . the student of landscape architecture will perhaps be pleased to find so few traces of many of the most firmly established features of park design'. Chadwick commented in 1965 that 'the functional basis of the Bos is quite evident, and is the starting point for any consideration of its aesthetic, as well as its social values'. Polano, writing in 1991, however, saw the park as 'a picturesque landscape in an urban context' adapted 'ingeniously to the sporting and recreational needs of the people'. Berrizbeita argued in 1999 that the design lacked 'concern for the "genius of the place" which derives from a visual and experiential interpretation of the site'. She also suggested that 'conceiving landscape as program, or ascribing functional value to parkland is the first radical break from a pictorial conceptualization of landscape' and that 'like the subway system or the stock exchange, the park is a piece of a system that contributes to and strives for maximum productive efficiency'.[370]

So, is it appropriate to regard the Bos Park as the product of a brave new functionalism that turns its back on the picturesque and 'strives for maximum productive efficiency'? Or is it a characteristically Dutch response to an extraordinarily difficult site? First it is worth noting John Dixon Hunt's comment that 'Repton was too attentive to the current needs and sites of his patrons to perpetuate aesthetics irrelevant to their situations' and that his work was 'Pope's "consult the genius of the place" rescued and brought up to date for Repton's clients'. Equally, the unnamed critic for the *RIBA Journal* went on to state that 'the scale of the meadows and the beautiful use made of variations in level' is reminiscent of the work of Repton.[371]

This debate provokes a number of thoughts:

- it is extremely challenging for designers to 'consult the genius of the place' in an almost flat, completely human-made site below sea level. The establishment of 'typically Dutch' (or north-west European) plant associations is, however, a strongly place-related, albeit long-term, strategy
- Lootsma stated that 'we [the Dutch] have learned to see the landscape not as a *fait accompli*, but as the result of countless forces and initiatives'. Equally, Rem Koolhaas/OMA's entry for the Parc de la Villette competition concluded that 'we have confined ourselves to devising a framework capable of absorbing an endless series of further meanings, extensions, or intentions, without entailing compromises, redundancies, or contradictions. Our strategy is to confer on the simple the dimensions of adventure'. Was the design of the Bos Park a forerunner to such flexible and accommodating Dutch approaches to design of the landscape?
- Remco Daalder suggested that 'the influence of the German parks is to be seen in the concentration of activities along an axis; the open-air theatre, playing fields, paddling pools and the canoeing lake. The influence of English country landscaping [*sic*] can be seen in the rounded woodland boundaries, the extensive watercourses and the rolling meadows'. Is the design of the park distinctly Dutch or an eclectic reflection of the European *zeitgeist*?
- the pragmatism reflected in the design of the park can be understood through Lootsma's comment that 'the synthetic regionalization of the Dutch landscape involves not only designers' complete immersion in the real world of market democracy and global forces but also their critical and creative capacity to realign those conditions toward more socially enriching ends'.[372]

MANAGEMENT AND USAGE

Managing Organization

The Bos Park is entirely owned and managed by the Amsterdam City Council – even though only 20 per cent of the land area lies within the city limits. Overall responsibility for the park belongs to the Public Space and Green Committee of the Council. Recreation is the responsibility of another committee – the Openbare Ruimte. The management are all employed by the City and the majority of the maintenance work in the park is undertaken by directly employed personnel. The original site nursery to the north-west of de Poel is now closed and all plant material is outsourced.

Funding

The budget for recurrent maintenance in 1999 was Hfl11 million. This was derived from:

- City Council – Hfl8.5 million
- Sports Commission – Hfl1.1 million (for running Bosbaan and the Sport Park)
- Camp site – Hfl800,000
- Sports facilities – Hfl400,000
- Restaurants, etc. – Hfl200,000

The budget remained relatively steady in real terms during the 1990s. A one-off budget cut of around Hfl1 million was made in 1995 and was absorbed by cutting the number of directly employed staff. Outside contractors were subsequently used as a buffer against similar cuts in the future. In 1999 outside contractors accounted for an expenditure of Hfl3 million compared with Hfl4 million for directly employed staff. Opportunities for increasing the proportion of revenues from recreational facilities have been actively debated. There is also a recurrent debate with neighbouring councils over the fact that 65 per cent of park users live in Amsterdam whereas the City pays the entire cost of its management and maintenance. This discrepancy is used by the city in negotiations over joint funding of regional recreation facilities.[373]

Banks of the Nieuwe Meer (June 1999)

Usage

Detailed calculations of numbers using the park were prepared as part of the *Boschplan*. The estimated capacity of the park was 74,000; estimated maximum visitors in a day was 90,000 to 100,000 with maximum usage by 70,000 people at any one time. The calculations also suggested that as many as 50,000 bicycles might be ridden to the park in a day. By 1985 average weekday and weekend usage ranged from 5000 to 10,000 and from 10,000 to 20,000 respectively, depending on the season. The maximum number of visits per day was estimated to be between 45,000 and 50,000. In 1997 four-and-a-half million visits were made to the park – excluding the Bosbaan and Sport Park. This was an increase of 500,000 since 1985. Sixty-five per cent of visitors lived in Amsterdam and 30 per cent in the neighbouring suburbs of Amstelveen and Aalsmeer. Nearly all visitors lived within 10 kilometres of the park. Sixty per cent of residents of Amsterdam claim to use the park an average of seven times per year. Most visits to the park are relatively short – 70 per cent of visits are between one and three hours. Most visits are for walking,

biking and sunbathing, and for most visitors 'nature' is an important reason to go to the Bos Park.[374]

PLANS FOR THE PARK

City Planning

Demand for new development in Amsterdam continued throughout the twentieth century. The General Extension Plan of 1935 adopted open space as a structuring principle for the city. Expansion and compaction of Amsterdam during the last two decades of the century were largely achieved through construction on sports fields. The Draft Structure Plan for Amsterdam completed in 1993 acknowledged the importance of arriving at a 'balance between the value of open space on the one hand and the need to enlarge the city and increase the density of building on the other'. That plan proposed a 'Main Green Structure' for the city based on principles of safeguarding areas of established spatial and ecological quality and ensuring efficient use of open space. The Main Green Structure incorporated the Nieuwe Meer, the Bos Park and its extension to the south-west into the Schinkelpolder and towards the Green Heart of the Randstad. The future of Schipol Airport is another strategic planning issue that might affect the Bos Park. Consideration was being given in the late 1990s to construction of an island in the North Sea to which the airport might be relocated entirely, or which might become a principal airport while Schipol continued to operate as a secondary airport. Complete removal of the airport would reduce the park's ability to justify itself as a buffer between Schipol and the wealthy suburb of Amstelveen.[375]

Park Management

In 1994 the City Council published a *Management Plan* for the Bos Park over the period 1995 to 2005. This maintained the overall philosophy of 'ecological management' of the park for recreation and nature conservation purposes but sought to create more differentiation within and between different vegetation areas. It identified four types of character zone in the park and proposed management regimes specific to each zone:

- Recreation Zone – in the centre and to the north

Cycle route in th north of the park (June 1999)

and eastern sides of the park– where recreation and other human activities are given highest priority

- Nature Recreation Zone – on the western side of the park – where management is primarily for 'nature leisure seekers'
- Nature Zone – beside the Nieuwe Meer, de Poel and the Schinkelbos – where 'nature' is favoured over leisure seekers
- Urban Fringe Zone – on the eastern edge of the park – where human use, again, is important and woodland is managed to create a dense and dramatic contrast with surrounding built-up areas.[376]

Until 1994 management of all the forest in the park had been based on selecting 'future trees' and carrying out a regular programme of clearing other trees. Wood arising from the thinning was removed and sold – but only generated revenues of one-third the cost of its extraction. In line with the 1994 Management Plan, three measures were introduced to increase the value of the park for nature:

- *transformation management* of the forest – intended to achieve a wider age distribution of trees
- *adaptation of water edges* by removing hardwoods from canal banks to create more diverse habitat
- *grazing* of meadow areas by Highland cattle in about 100 hectares of the meadows to create 'roughland' that can be invaded by a range of non-woody plant species.

CONCLUSIONS

The Bos Park reflects the fact that in the lower lying areas of The Netherlands, distinctions between 'urban environment' and 'natural environment' are artificial. Entire landscapes are human-made. They are engineered with great technical efficiency and then adapted for human use and for the establishment of vegetation and wildlife. More than sixty years after its commencement and more than thirty years after its 'completion' the Bos Park remains – more than most parks – a work in progress. It is an evolving product of design by management. As it

has evolved it has become an integral part of the recreation and open space system of the constantly expanding city of Amsterdam. It continues to be a strategic element in plans for further expansion and densification of the city.

The initial planning and design did, however, create a strong basis from which the park could evolve. Landform, water levels and water movement across the site were manipulated with great subtlety. The hill, which by all accounts was a focal point in the early days of the park, has become less significant as the forest has developed and the conifers are beginning to look increasingly quaint – or 'cute' or just plain out of place. Latterly, greater impact has been created by the contrasts between the maturing forest and the large 'clearings' that appear to have been carved out of it.

The circulation system successfully confines vehicles to the edges of the park – the equally large Bois de Boulogne in Paris might do well to follow this example – and gives the impression that the park really was designed for 50,000 cyclists in a day. The layout and engineering of the cycle routes are perfectly matched by the scale of the spaces that dynamically unfold as you cycle through the park. The few 'formalized' avenues of trees stand in strong contrast to the increasingly naturalized stands of forest. They are a reminder of the fact that the park is an entirely human product. Strangely, perhaps, there are no sculptures or other artworks in the park – unless you count the long slit of the Bosbaan and the 105 bridges that are needed to carry people over the water bodies. As the forest is managed to take on a more diverse and naturalized appearance it might be appropriate, as in the Hoge Veluwe National Park, to install sculptures in the Bos Park.

The Bos Park reflects Dutch prowess in reclamation and hydraulic engineering. It is a major recreation facility in a naturalized forest setting created on entirely human-made land close to a major urban centre. It was largely created by manual labour and is completely funded by public money. It is the definitive democratic major city park of the twentieth century. As a cycling venue and in its approaches to vegetation management at least, it will be a model for the twenty-first century.

20 The Minneapolis Park System

6500 acres (2630 hectares)

INTRODUCTION

The Minneapolis Park System has been justifiably described as 'the best-located, best-financed, best-designed, best-maintained public open space in America'. Yet the Minneapolis system receives far less publicity than the most closely comparable park system, Boston's 'Emerald Necklace'. Equally, its initial designer H. W. S. (Horace William Shaler) Cleveland (1814–1900), receives less attention than he merits. The current Minneapolis Park System divides into two principal parts – the regional park system or 'Grand Rounds' and the extensive neighbourhood park system. The neighbourhood park system provides roughly one park within every six blocks of the city.[377]

The Grand Rounds, like the Emerald Necklace, comprises a network of open spaces thoroughly integrated with their physical and social settings. Both are water-based systems that take advantage of the scenic and recreational value of water as well as working with the natural landform to facilitate surface drainage. Both the Grand Rounds and the Emerald Necklace have predominantly linear layouts through primarily residential areas. This type of layout affords easy access and a strong sense of attachment from neighbouring residents. Unlike the Emerald Necklace, however, the Grand Rounds has the administrative advantage of being run by a directly elected body that is almost independent of the rest of the city's government – the Minneapolis Park and Recreation Board. The Board has the financial advantage of being able to issue bonds, levy taxes and acquire land. The Grand Rounds has the physical advantage of being a virtually continuous circuit that is still growing. The most recent extensions have been into downtown Minneapolis and along the banks of the Mississippi River.

The entire Minneapolis Park System now covers over 6400 acres (2600 hectares) comprising about 4800 acres (1940 hectares) of land and 1600 acres (650 hectares) of water. In 1998 it comprised 170 park properties including the 55-mile (88 kilometres) Grand Rounds, 38 miles (61 kilometres) of walking paths and 36 miles (58 kilometres) of biking/skating paths, forty-seven neighbourhood recreation centres (an essential component of the system in a city with a long, cold continental winter), seven golf courses, eleven supervised beaches, thirty-nine outdoor ice rinks, 396 baseball and softball diamonds and 167 tennis courts. It also included, adjacent to the Walker Art Center, the 11-acre (4.4 hectares) Minneapolis Sculpture Garden, the largest urban sculpture garden in the country. In 1906 the system comprised fifty-seven properties covering 1810 acres (730 hectares); in 1936 it comprised 144 properties covering 5241 acres (2120 hectares).[378]

HISTORY

Wirth noted that there was 'no commercial development of any importance' in the area of Minneapolis on the arrival of Colonel Leavenworth of the United States Army in 1819 or when Fort Snelling was established in 1820. When Minneapolis – a combination of the Indian name *minne* (waters) and the Greek *polis* (city) – was incorporated in 1856 it had a population of 1555. By 1872 the population was 21,014. The growth of the city's population during the 1880s is shown in Table 20.1.

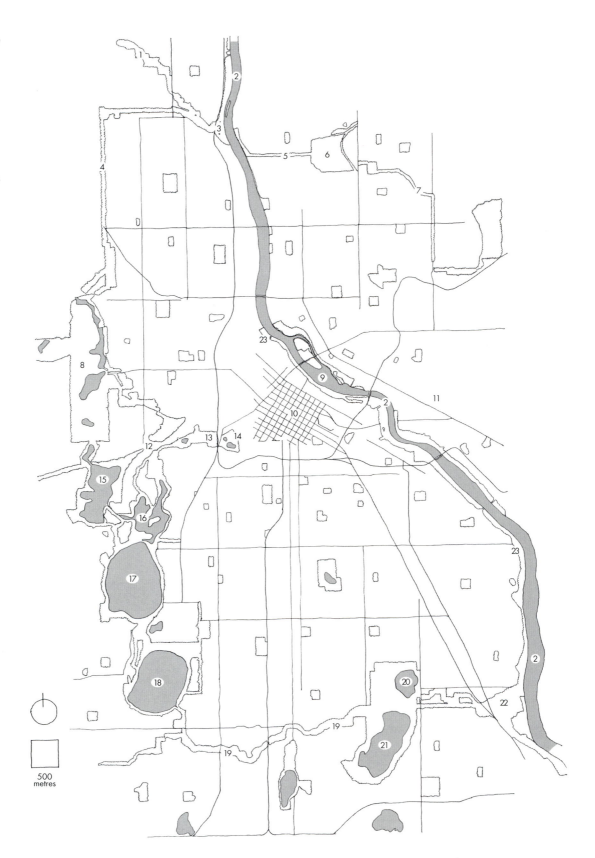

Minneapolis Park System

1   Shingle Creek
2   Mississippi River
3   Webber Park
4   Victory Memorial
    Parkway
5   St Anthony Parkway
6   Columbia Park
7   Stinson Boulevard
8   Wirth Park
9   St Anthony Falls
10 Downtown Minneapolis
11 St Paul
12 Cedar Lake Trail
13 Walker Art Centre/
    Sculpture Garden
14 Loring Park
15 Cedar Lake
16 Lake of the Isles
17 Lake Calhoun
18 Lake Harriet
19 Minnehaha Creek
20 Lake Hiawatha
21 Lake Nokomis
22 Minnehaha Park
23 Great River Road

500
metres

Table 20.1 Population of Minneapolis (1880s)[379]

Year	Population
1880	46,887
1881	63,342
1883	96,272
1885	129,201
1887	143,423

With this increase in population came a demand, orchestrated by local newspapers, for public parks. The Minneapolis Board of Park Commissioners was founded by the City Council in April 1883. This followed a resolution that January by the Minneapolis Board of Trade – but not directly following it. While the Board of Trade was unanimous in its resolution, the City Council sought to retain all its powers over taxation and expenditure. It was only after the Minnesota State Legislature overruled the city and authorized a referendum – which supported the idea by 5327 to 3922 votes – that the Board of Park Commissioners was established. It retained that name until becoming the Park and Recreation Board in 1967.[380]

Charles M. Loring (1833–1922), a Maine-born businessman and community benefactor, was the first President of the Board of Park Commissioners. Indeed it was Loring, as leader of the city's Improvement Society, who had invited H. W. S. Cleveland to visit Minneapolis in 1876 to address that Society. Cleveland's next return, however, was not until after the establishment of the Board of Park Commissioners when, in June 1883, he presented his *Suggestions for a System of Parks and Parkways for the City of Minneapolis* – the document on which the original planning and design of the Grand Rounds was based.

The first resolution of the Board of Trade at its January 1883 meeting was intended to 'give Minneapolis not only the finest and most beautiful system of Public Parks and Boulevards of any city in America . . . [which will] add many millions to the real estate value of our city'. Profit motives, as ever it seems, ran hand-in-hand with philanthropic motivations. The Board of Park Commissioners had the foresight to agree, at their meeting on 24 April 1883, that Loring should engage Cleveland. And it was Cleveland who suggested that the Board should 'lose no time in acquiring properties far ahead of the time of their actual need'. This advice became a cornerstone of the Board's policies. It is important to bear in mind that the main method, other than direct purchase, of acquiring land for the parks was by donation from landowners in exchange for tax deductions and a parkland setting for the development of their retained land.[381]

It was not until Cleveland's return to Minneapolis in 1883, then in his late sixties, and the presentation of his *Suggestions*, that he began to have a major impact in the cities of Minneapolis and St Paul. *Suggestions* was a radical and visionary document. It was probably inspired by the scope of Haussmann and Alphand's work in Paris; by the character of Olmsted's work on the Emerald Necklace in Boston (1878–95) and by the scale of redevelopment following the Great Fire in Chicago in 1871. It was produced, ironically enough, in the same year that the Northern Pacific Railroad linked Minneapolis with the West Coast. Cleveland's *Suggestions* were very much in tune with the aspirations of the New England flour and lumber mill owners who had established their businesses in the heart of the city near the St Anthony Falls on the Mississippi River.[382]

Cleveland's ideas for the parkway system were endorsed and expanded by a Special Committee on Park Enlargement in March 1891. That committee, chaired by William W. Folwell, stated that the city did not possess 'more than one-third of the park lands she ought now to own or to be in the way of acquiring'. The committee called for a general plan organizing the park system and, again for the system to be extended to encircle the whole city. It exhorted 'Minneapolis to aspire to be, what it is now in her power to become, THE BEAUTIFUL CITY of the land'. This sort of commitment gave the parks a remarkable early impetus. But problems inevitably arose. There were, for instance, conflicts over whether boulevards could be managed both as highways and as parkways, and recessions caused shrinkages in the tax base that paid for new park properties. Nevertheless, political will and professional endeavour have served Minneapolis well in the process of putting together an outstanding park system.[383]

Key Figures in the Establishment of the System

Newton stated that 'it is unforgivable that so little attention has been accorded by the profession to Cleveland, a completely dedicated early practitioner'. Cleveland was born in Lancaster, Massachusetts. He was the third son of a merchant navigator father, whose business eventually collapsed, and an active Unitarian mother with a keen interest in progressive education. Cleveland spent a number of years in Cuba during the 1830s while his father was a vice-consul in Havana. He subsequently trained as a surveyor and spent time with eastern intellectuals with a fascination for the 'West' and for 'Native Americans' – a fascination epitomized by the publication in 1854 of Henry Wadsworth Longfellow's epic poem, *The Song of Hiawatha*. Cleveland had made his first trips westward to Illinois in the 1830s, probably as a railroad surveyor. This experience seems to have provoked his dislike of the rectilinear pattern of new urban development in North America. As Neckar put it, he began 'to sense his first irritation with the sheer tyranny of this hard-edged organisation of a picturesque paradise'.[384]

During the early 1840s Cleveland, then in his late twenties, became a 'scientific farmer' near Burlington, New Jersey. He contributed material to Andrew Jackson Downing's (1815–52) *The Horticulturist* and, like contemporaries and fellow farmers Olmsted and Robert Morris Copeland, he turned gradually to 'landscape gardening'. In 1854 Cleveland moved to Boston and went into practice with Copeland, who had been a student of Longfellow's at Harvard. In 1855 they were commissioned to design Sleepy Hollow Cemetery in Concord, Massachusetts – with Ralph Waldo Emerson as a member of the Steering Committee. Neckar noted that, 'like Emerson, Cleveland saw the native landscape as the unplundered medium of American culture, a garden to be preserved and cultivated with artistic care and practical restraint'.[385]

Cleveland and Copeland did not carry the same influence in New York as Olmsted and Downing's former partner, the British-born architect Calvert Vaux (1824–95). Olmsted and Vaux's *Greensward* proposals won the competition for the design of Central Park in 1858. Cleveland and Copeland, the latter having submitted an unsuccessful entry to the competition for Central Park, continued to practise in New England until the American Civil War (1861–65) when Copeland enlisted in the Union Army. Cleveland left Massachusetts in 1867 to work in Tarrytown, New York and was eventually introduced to Olmsted and Vaux, becoming a field employee working on Prospect Park, where Olmsted and Vaux had been engaged since 1865. In 1869 Cleveland moved to Chicago to work, still with Olmsted and Vaux, on the South Park System. By 1870 Cleveland had parted ways with Olmsted and decided to stay in the Midwest but his 'early association with Olmsted led to their deep mutual respect and lasting friendship'.[386]

During the 1870s Cleveland went into business with civil engineer William French. Following the Great Fire in October 1871, they were appointed for some public reconstruction projects including new boulevards comparable with those being built by Haussmann in Paris. Earlier that year Cleveland had published *A Few Hints on Landscape Gardening in the West* in which he referred to 'twenty years experience in landscape gardening, during the last two of which I have been actively engaged in designing the arrangement of grounds for a variety of purposes, in Illinois, Indiana, Michigan, Wisconsin, Iowa and Kansas'. Cleveland and French also cultivated the latter's contacts in Minneapolis and St Paul. By 1872 Cleveland had begun 'urging the authorities of the two cities to be more aware of the area's unusually fine natural potentials for a system of public parks'. He gave public lectures in both cities and he and French obtained numerous projects there in addition to their continuing workload in Chicago. Among Cleveland's early projects in St Paul was the Oakland Cemetery, 'a masterpiece of topographic restraint intended, once again, to let nature's engineering control the mood of the landscape'.[387]

Cleveland's *Landscape Architecture As Applied to the Wants of the West* was published in 1873. The economic depression that year affected his business and precluded his return to Minneapolis until invited to do so by Loring in 1876. The book 'stressed the landscape architect's role in a region bustling with speculators, railroad construction, booming frontier towns and yeoman farmers stamping the relentless grid on the virgin prairies'. It was remarkable for the fact that 'in so early a treatise the aims and techniques of a new profession could be in such large part analysed and clearly enunciated'. In the book Cleveland described landscape architecture as 'the art of arranging land so as to adapt it most conveniently, economically and gracefully, to any of the varied wants of civilization'. He went on to criticize the 'laying out of towns' wherein 'no regard is paid to the topography of the ground; no reference is had to future interests or necessities of business or pleasure; no effort is made to secure the preservation of natural features which in time might be invaluable as a means of giving to the place a distinct and unique character'.[388]

Imaginative landscape architecture can only be achieved with imaginative clients. Strong professional support is also required for the implementation and management of proposals. Cleveland's proposals for the Minneapolis Park System clearly benefited from the support of Charles M. Loring, the first President of the Minneapolis Board of Park Commissioners. Loring took several years away from his own business to oversee the construction of the first parks. Indeed it appears that from 1883 to 1885 Loring performed most of the duties of the first Superintendent, Rufus Cook. Cook was dismissed in 1885 and replaced, apparently on Cleveland's recommendation, by

William Morse Berry who had been a construction superintendent for Cleveland on the South Parks in Chicago. In 1886 Cleveland himself moved his office from Chicago to Minneapolis.[389]

Cleveland's relocation and the installation of this team ensured that his proposals were supported both by energetic patronage and by capable site personnel. This enabled Cleveland to proceed swiftly with the creation of the parks on a design-build basis with the works being commenced according to schematic designs and finalized on site as a cooperative endeavour between the designer and superintendent. Their progress was so swift that in 1886 the Board, possibly feeling insecure about its work, invited Frederick Law Olmsted to visit Minneapolis and review its achievements. Olmsted appears not to have made any adverse comments but did observe that the system did not include 'an individual large park'. There is an interesting contrast here with Cleveland's opinion, from 1869, that 'Boston did not need a central park but should instead have a system of improvements over the surrounding country'.[390]

Olmsted's views notwithstanding, the momentum developed by the team of Loring, Cleveland and Berry provided a firm basis for the establishment of the Minneapolis Park System. Cleveland continued to work on the system until about five years before his death, aged 85, in December 1900. But the full realization of his ideas and the consolidation of the system were very much the work of Theodore Wirth, Superintendent of Parks from 1906 to 1935. Wirth was responsible for the completion of much of Cleveland's proposed system and for its expansion to include many neighbourhood parks. He also oversaw the creation of a number of major new elements in the system including the extension of Glenwood Park (renamed Theodore Wirth Park in 1938) and creation of the Victory Memorial Drive and Camden (now Webber) Park where Shingle Creek joins the Mississippi. The particular value of Wirth's additions is that they continued the Grand Rounds northward from Cedar Lake and back to the Mississippi River, north of downtown Minneapolis. Wirth noted that '95 per cent of our park lake areas are located in the south half of the city – and 80 per cent in the south-west quarter'. A large part of his energy was devoted to completion of the circuit. The final link in the circuit – the Great River Road – was completed in 1998.[391]

PLANNING AND DESIGN

In his *Suggestions* Cleveland urged the 'securing of the areas that are needed' for the parks 'before they become so occupied or acquire such value as to place them beyond reach'. He went on to suggest that the Board of Park Commissioners 'look forward for a century, to the time when the city has a population of a million, and think what will be their wants. They will have wealth enough to purchase everything that money can buy, but all their wealth cannot purchase a lost opportunity'. He may have developed this idea from his work on the South Park System in Chicago where land was acquired and the park and boulevard system was planned beyond that city's then developed area. Cleveland's proposals for boulevards, which he saw as barriers to the spread of fire, were also probably influenced by his knowledge of Haussmann's work in Paris and by his own time in Chicago.[392]

Cleveland advocated a master plan for the entire park system of Minneapolis. 'The plans for the general arrangement of the parks should be prepared as soon as may be', he wrote, 'so that the amount and character of each year's work may be predetermined and kept in progress, with the certainty that every step is towards the ultimate object, and the unity of design preserved throughout'. His proposals emphasized the role of the Mississippi as 'the grand natural feature which gives character to your city' proposing that 'a broad avenue be laid out on each side of the river'. He proposed that this parkway should be linked to the Minnehaha Falls to the south and that a system of contiguous lakefront parks and parkways should be created, incorporating many of the abundant existing water bodies along Minnehaha Creek. These included Lake Amelia (now Lake Nokomis), Rice Lake (now Lake Hiawatha), Lake Harriet, Lake Calhoun and, further north, the Lake of the Isles and Cedar Lake. This was the nucleus of the system to which Wirth secured the addition of the northern Parkways in 1921 and final acquisition of all of Minnehaha Creek in 1930. He then directed his planning and negotiation skills to the north-eastern sections of the system, acquiring land along Stinson and St Anthony's Boulevards. Wirth and his successors since the Second World War have concentrated on adding riverfront and downtown links to the Grand Rounds.[393]

Cleveland also proposed the small Central Park (now called Loring Park) close to downtown Minneapolis and a larger 'Driving Park' on the east bank of the river to the north of the city – never built but not far from the later Columbia Park, named for its commencement at the time of the 1893 World's Columbian Exposition. He proposed that these parks should be linked to one another and to the lakes by a system of boulevards following the gridiron road pattern. He expressed a preference for 'an extended system of boulevards, or

Detail of bridge by Siah Armajani between Loring Park and Walker Art Center (September 1998)

ornamental avenues, rather than a series of detached open areas or public squares'. Cleveland described his proposed system as comprising 'more than 20 miles of parkways completely encircling the central portions of the city'. More than three-quarters of his system was within 2 miles (3.2 kilometres) of the downtown and none of it was more than 4 miles (6.4 kilometres) away – 'the total amount of all the parks designed is less than one thousand acres'.[394]

This may not sound like a particularly ambitious set of proposals – until you remember that the population of Minneapolis in 1880 was less than 50,000 and that Cleveland was calling for the acquisition of land that was at that time well outside the developed area of the city. Its population has, in fact, never reached a million – in 1996 it was 368,383 – although nearly thre million people live in the Minneapolis/St Paul metropolitan area. Cleveland proposed significant works in the parks and parkways in the initial system. Each of these elements retains a strongly individual character derived from its natural attributes, from its location, from the works that have been done to it, and from the way that the system has been managed. Most of the water bodies in the system are fringed with parkways laid out on the principle of the least intrusive activity being closest to the amenity. This principle produces a detailed arrangement which might comprise, typically, water – marginal vegetation – sitting area – 8-foot (2.4 metres) wide walking/ jogging path – 1-foot (0.3 metres) wide buffer – 8-foot (2.4 metres) wide bike/skating path – buffer and 16-foot (4.8 metres) wide parkway (with or without 8-foot (2.4 metres) wide parking bays).[395]

Minnehaha Park

Minnehaha Park focuses on the 53-foot (16 metres) Minnehaha Falls on the Minnehaha Creek which runs from Lake Minnetonka, 22 miles (35 kilometres) to the west, into the nearby Mississippi River. The falls are thought to have been an important feature to the native Dakota people who lived in the area before being displaced, before the arrival of white settlers, by the Ojibway. The falls were celebrated by Henry Wadsworth Longfellow in his *The Song of Hiawatha* in 1853, although he never actually visited them . They became the centrepiece for the park in 1889. Walks, steps, bridges, picnic shelters and restrooms were built in the wooded areas near the falls and various additions, modifications, improvements and threats, particularly from proposals for the construction of highways, marked the park's history before 'restoration' proposals were drawn up in summer 1992. The site is a 172-acre (70 hectares) wedge-shaped piece of land between Hiawatha Avenue and the Mississippi. The falls are close to the corner of the wedge away from the river. The work rejuvenated many of the facilities provided in the original design and directed circulation within the park so as to reduce the physical impact of heavy usage. The work also increased the narrative content and dramatic effect of the approach to the falls. They plunge into an impressive – but unstable – bowl at the head of a wooded ravine. As they have eroded the ravine, they have exposed the layers of sedimentary rock that underlie the rest of the city. They can be less dramatic at times of low waterflow. It is creditable that attention has been paid to retaining the 'natural' qualities of the ravine – an enchanting place and an integral part of Longfellow's story.[396]

Lake Harriet, Lake Calhoun, Lake of the Isles, Cedar Lake

These four lakes, known as the Chain of Lakes, lie on the previous line of the Mississippi before it diverted to its current course some 25,000 years ago. They have a largely built-up watershed of about 7000 acres (2835 hectares). They were the most substantial part of Cleveland's proposals and remain a significant part of the Minneapolis Park System. The parkways with their biking/skating and walking/jogging tracks winding between housing areas and the lakes are an abiding image from Minneapolis – although each of these lakes is distinctive in its character and usage.

Lake Harriet, 353 acres (143 hectares), and Lake Calhoun, 520 acres (210 hectares), are sufficiently close to being circular that the whole of their shorelines are visible from any point on or within their banks. Lake Harriet, with its 'gingerbread castle' bandshell (reconstructed in 1988 to replace the original completed in 1904) is more sedate and domestic in character. The more gregarious Lake Calhoun reflects its proximity to the Uptown neighbourhood, Minneapolis's 'version of Greenwich

Victory Memorial Parkway (September 1998)

Village'. It has become a focus for sunners, surfers, in-liners and joggers. Between 1911 and 1925, 1.4 million cubic yards (1 million cubic metres) of material was dredged from Lake Calhoun and used, among other things, to create its beaches. Lake Harriet is 7 feet (2.1 metres) lower than Lake Calhoun and has never been linked to it. This is supposed to have maintained the purity of Lake Harriet's waters and, together with the fact that the horse-drawn trolley line was extended here in 1880, to have made it a popular picnic destination even by the time that Cleveland prepared his *Suggestions*.[397]

Lake of the Isles was the first major lake in the city to be reshaped by dredging and filling. Before the works commenced in 1889 it had comprised 100 acres (40 hectares) of water, 67 acres (27 hectares) of marsh and four islands. About half a million cubic yards (380,000 cubic metres) of

material was removed. Most of the surplus was carted to Columbia Park, leaving a lake with 120 acres (49 hectares) of water, no marshes and only two islands. These works created a landscape that became a focus for real estate development in much the way that Regent's Park or Central Park had become. The lake, with its bird sanctuary islands offering highly varied views and its shallow sinuous shoreline, has retained much of its intended romantic character and remains the peaceful focus of one of Minneapolis's wealthier residential areas. It has suffered, however, from raised water levels caused by a combination of greater precipitation and increased run-off from its catchment area. This has led, in turn, to the death of certain plant species that cannot tolerate such conditions. In essence, despite the channel that was completed in 1911 between the Lake of the Isles and Lake Calhoun, it naturally wants to be a wetland. Following flood conditions in spring 1997 which brought a water level of 145 feet (44.2 metres) compared with a normal level of 141.5 feet (43.1 metres), the Parks and Recreation Board commenced an exercise to restore the balance between ambient water levels, vegetation types, the appearance of the area and the activities that can occur on the shores of the lake.[398]

Cedar Lake, 190 acres (77 hectares), named for the Red cedars that used to stand on its shores, is the only one of the city's major lakes that is not entirely surrounded by public land. As a consequence it has a high proportion of unmanaged landscape including wooded promontories and shallow waters with lily pads and cattails, around its shores. This is a reflection of the conditions which, for practical reasons and because of current aesthetic preferences, the Board is seeking to achieve at Lake of the Isles. Development between 1991 and 1997 of the link from Cedar Lake westward to the suburb of St Louis Park and eastward to the Mississippi riverfront along the Cedar Lake Trail has created a significant addition to the park system. This was an outstanding example of public/private partnership in the acquisition and restoration of derelict land as a public park. The total area of the trail and associated parkland is 48 acres (19 hectares). Much of the land had been railyards and, unlike many such trails, an active single track continues to carry freight trains between the Twin Cities, the coalfields of the Dakotas and the Pacific ports of Portland and Seattle. In 1986, however, the railway company had started removing tracks and was preparing to sell the land for development. Residents from neighbouring suburbs started to campaign for its retention as parkland.

The Park and Recreation Board did not have the funds to acquire and restore the land and did not regard the project as one of its higher priorities. But neither did they wish to discourage a determined, articulate and imaginative group of citizens. In the event, two principal forces led to the Board and the residents being able to realize the project. First, in 1990, the railway company decided to put the 20-acre (8 hectares) corridor of land running eastward from Cedar Lake on the market in addition to the original 28 acres (11 hectares). This linked the original land to the suburbs of Hennepin County offering access to its extensive network of regional trails. It also brought the State Legislature as a funding body into the picture. Second, in early 1992, President George H. Bush signed the Intermodal Surface Transportation Efficiency Act (ISTEA) allowing, for the first time, expenditure of major sums on non-highway projects such as bikeways

and trails. From that point the project gathered momentum and has become another valuable link in the Minneapolis Park System. It is 'something unique amongst modern urban parks – a piece of public open space that is designed, managed, and overseen with as much care as if it were private'. Whether the Cedar Park Trail is a model that might be replicated in other cities is a moot point. It is, nevertheless, an object lesson in collaboration between determined citizens and an open-minded public administration.[399]

Theodore Wirth Park

At 743 acres (300 hectares), Theodore Wirth Park is the largest individual park in the Minneapolis park system and, unsurprisingly, its most diverse. Principal among its values are its varied terrain, including steep slopes which form part of the golf course in summer and provide downhill ski and sledding venues in winter. The park also contains a series of small lakes that form part of the Chain of Lakes. Unlike the lakes and associated parks and parkways in most of the rest of the Grand Rounds, Theodore Wirth Park is not a small-scale integral part of adjacent residential areas. It is a relatively large urban park with relatively standard urban park facilities and with the relatively familiar problems of highways and railways dissecting it. It is, however, exceptionally well maintained and makes an important contribution to the robustness of the Minneapolis park system in providing year-round outdoor facilities and landscape types not found in other parts of the system.

Loring Park and Links to the Downtown

Apart from breaks created by highways and railways, there are more or less direct links from Theodore Wirth Park via Bryn Mawr Meadows, the Parade and Minneapolis Sculpture Garden and from Cedar Lake along the Cedar Lake Trail to Loring Park. The 36-acre (15 hectares) park was one of the first parts of the park system to be designed by Cleveland. Works commenced in November 1883 under the name Central Park and under the direction of Charles Loring after whom it was renamed in 1890. By all accounts it was originally designed as an ornamental park incorporating an artificial lake in a figure of eight layout, a large central floral display area, gentle landform sloping towards the lake, and a series of sinuous and circuitous paths. This approach was only modified once the earthworks had begun, in order to include an island as a focus for the planting of native or 'wild' shrubs. The park also included a central shelter – a small cottage –

built in 1889 and a recreation pavilion built in 1906.[400]

In common with parks of its age, Loring Park has suffered a barrage of additions and amendments over time. Apart from the relatively brutal incorporation over time of basketball, tennis and shuffleboard courts, the park was severely disrupted in the 1960s by the construction of Interstate Highway 94 along its western edge – an edge that had taken the Board several years to purchase in small lots. The park has also been the recipient of two artworks in the last quarter of the twentieth century. The first, the Berger Fountain at the end of Loring Greenway, a spherical dandelion-head fountain installed in 1975. The second, a gazebo designed by Siah Armajani, who also designed the adjacent pastel-painted and poetically inscribed steel bridge (over the I-94) between the park and the Sculpture Garden, is an essay in understatement.[401]

Latterly Loring Park has been remodelled to designs by landscape architect and accomplished writer on urban parks, Diana Balmori. In effect she has attempted to re-establish the ideas of Cleveland at the same time as doing for Loring Park what Nash did for St James's Park in London – making its edges less permeable to hostile surroundings, particularly highways, and to use planting and landform to create an inner city sanctuary at the centre. Balmori was charged with incorporating an arm of the Cedar Lake Trail within the park – which she did by creating a perfect circle for it. It is not immediately apparent why she chose this form or why she recast some of Cleveland's circuitous pathways and planting beds literally as circles. It is also unclear why such a heavy and visible detail was chosen for railings around the horseshoe rink, the bridge and the fishing promontory into the lake. The replanted island, however, now looks as 'wild' as it might have been after its original planting.[402]

Loring Greenway

Loring Greenway, the link from Loring Park to the downtown, was designed by landscape architect Paul Friedberg. The Greenway begins at the Berger Fountain and, like the fountain, it is distinctly of its age – characterized more by brick-faced planters than by greenness. But, as a piece of urban open space planning, it is an excellent link between the park and Nicollet Mall, previously designed by Lawrence Halprin. The link incorporates Friedberg's far more successful Peavey Plaza. The Mall leads almost directly to the Warehouse District of the city and the post-industrial open spaces adjacent to the Mississippi where it flows past downtown Minneapolis.

Location

In terms of location, the Grand Rounds is integrated both with residential and downtown areas. It serves primarily as a highly accessible everyday adjunct to inner suburban areas. It is primarily a resource-based system with a predominantly linear form and a profusion of largely naturally occurring, water bodies. Cleveland's designs were based on 'the conviction that it is the original design and arrangement which confers upon any place its intrinsic expression of character, the want of which cannot be atoned for by any amount of subsequent dressing or decoration'. This conviction was allied to an intense dislike of gridiron urban layouts; an appreciation of the real estate value of urban parks and parkways and recognition of the visual and recreational value of the water bodies in the region.[403]

Cleveland's views were largely aesthetic in origin. This is evidenced by his statement that he 'would have the City itself such a work of art as may be the fitting abode of a race of men and women whose lives are devoted to a nobler end than money-getting and whose efforts shall be inspired and sustained by the grandeur and beauty of the scenes in which their lives are passed'. Cleveland's proposals were realized because of civic leaders who embraced the concept of public land. And, as Joan Nassauer noted, 'a century later, all the residents of the metropolitan area use the great connected Grand Round of parks along the river and lakes, and they assume the parks to be their rightful civic inheritance. Their pride of ownership helps to assure the stewardship of the public parks'.[404]

MANAGEMENT AND USAGE

In his account of development of the Cedar Lake Park and Trail, Harnik described the Minneapolis Park and Recreation Board as 'perhaps the nation's pre-eminent city park agency'. This accolade can be attributed to a number of factors. The Board itself identified three particular factors: first, that its members are directly elected rather than being appointees; second, that its capital budget is included in the city's property taxes and is directed specifically to the Board by the City Council and third, that the Board maintains a strong policy of involving local residents in the planning process for its projects.[405]

The Board consists of nine members who are elected for staggered four-year terms. Six are elected by district and the other three are elected by the city as a whole. The Board, rather than the

Minnehaha Creek
through Minnehaha Park
(October 1998)

Bridge at heart of Loring Park (September 1998)

city, owns the land and controls, maintains, polices and establishes the budget for the park system. Indeed, other than the electorate, there are only two significant controls on the normal activities of the Board – the Mayor who, since 1975, has been empowered to veto its actions on issues where the Board does not have a two-thirds majority; and the City Council, which provides most of the 30 per cent of the Board's revenues that are not derived from the dedicated property taxes.[406]

The Property Tax Levy directed to the Park and Recreation Board in the budget for 1998 was $25,425,438 out of a total city levy of $141,456,426. Property taxes provided 70 per cent of the Board's funds for 1998; 23 per cent came from Local Government Aid; 1 per cent came from fees and charges; and the remaining 6 per cent came from other sources, making a total about $36,400,000. This represents almost $100 per head of population in the City of Minneapolis or $14,000 per hectare of park land. The allocation of these funds for 1998 is given in Table 20.2.

Usage

Estimated figures for the total number of visits to the principal component parts of the Grand Rounds for 1995, 1997 and 1999 are given in Table 20.3.

Table 20.2 Minneapolis Parks and Recreation Board 1998 budget for expenditure by cost centre

Cost centre	$	%
Park rehabilitation	436,955	1.2
Parkway maintenance and improvements	1,019,424	2.7
Lake pollution control	543,988	1.5
Park maintenance	13,569,472	36.4
Park police	3,142,339	8.4
Administration	1,997,214	5.3
Unallocated	1,674,216	4.5
City-wide recreation	7,113,022	19.1
Planning	1,000,826	2.7
Teen teamworks and youthline	660,294	1.8
Forestry	6,102,194*	16.4
Credit for pension	(850,000)	–
Total	*36,409,944*	*100*

Source: Minneapolis Park and Recreation Board 1998 Budget
*Between 1973 and 1998 the city lost 126,000 trees from Dutch Elm Disease and planted 190,000 trees in compensation

Table 20.3 shows a steady rise from 1995 to 1997 and a highly significant increase from 1997 to 1999. Similarly a long-term pattern of increased usage is reflected in the estimated numbers of visits to the Minneapolis park system as a whole between 1982 and 1999. This is shown in Table 20.4.

PLANS FOR THE MINNEAPOLIS PARK SYSTEM

Understandably, a large park system with a large and reliably recurrent budget has a large ongoing programme of new works and improvements at any one time. The Superintendent's Annual Report for 1997 listed under the Planning Division's project involvement, eighteen completed projects – at a total cost of $2,086,900; twenty-eight projects in progress – at a total cost of $14,890,645, and eighteen pending projects – at a total cost of $3,817,000. It is significant that the approach to new works normally includes high levels of public consultation through the establishment of Citizen Advisory Committees. There is an 'up front' attitude towards informing residents about the availability of funding and possible sources of money for works, including private donations and a strong tendency to refer back to the precedents set by Cleveland and developed by Theodore Wirth. Wirth's *History of the Board of Park Commissioners*, published in 1945, still has a strong influence on the work of the Planning Division. It is noticeable, however, that recent

planting – like that on the island in Loring Park around the Lake of the Isles – is tending to favour the use of a higher proportion of native species, and that larger proportions of the parks – like the Glen in Minnehaha Park – are being planted and managed as wildlife habitat.[407]

The park system contains relatively few sculptural or art installations – apart, of course, from the Sculpture Garden at the Walker Art Center. This is a reflection of two factors. First, the need for all such installations to undergo in-house staff review, for them to meet Board policy and procedures, and for them to be approved by the Board; and second, the fact that the Board still adheres to the view put forward by Cleveland that 'the city itself should be a work of art'. One area in which the Board – and other agencies in the city – does have a very strong record is the hiring of 'name' landscape architects for the design of major open spaces. Among the accomplished practitioners undertaking projects there are Garret Eckbo – invited by the Board in 1971 to conduct a review of the parkway system; Lawrence Halprin – urban designer for the Nicollet Mall in the late 1960s; Paul Friedberg – designed Peavey Plaza and the Loring Greenway in the mid-1970s; Michael van Valkenberg who designed the extension to the Sculpture Park; Diana Balmori who was appointed for the reshaping of Loring Park, and Jones and

Table 20.3 Total number of visits to the Grand Rounds (1995–99)

Park facility	Total 1995	Total 1997	Total 1999
Cedar Lake Trail	–	165,700	538,500
Central Mississippi Riverfront	365,500	623,100	865,400
Chain of Lakes	2,222,100	2,307,100	5,524,300
Minnehaha Park	618,900	663,000	864,400
Minnehaha Parkway	456,500	728,300	2,701,300
Mississippi Gorge Park	469,100	708,100	2,399,000
Nakomis-Hiawatha Parkway	827,800	831,500	1,305,200
North Mississippi Park	25,900	32,100	61,300
Theodore Wirth Park	293,500	172,500	267,700
Wirth Memorial Parkway	339,400	321,700	1,000,000
Totals	5,618,500	6,555,000	15,527,200

Source: Annual Use Survey of Metropolitan Regional Recreation Open Space System/MN Office of Tourism

Table 20.4 Total number of visits to the Minneapolis Park System (1982–99)

1982	1988	1995	1997	1999
3,621,400	5,133,400	5,618,500	6,555,000	15,527,200

Source: Annual Use Survey of Metropolitan Regional Recreation Open Space System

*Peavey Plaza
(October 1998)*

Jones of Seattle (by competition) for the design of the Cedar Lake Trail. The federal government added to this list by having Martha Schwartz design the forecourt to the federal court building. Her characteristically controversial design, dominated by grassed drumlins, is directly overlooked from the offices of the Park and Recreation Board located in the adjacent Minneapolis Grain Exchange. Ironically it is one of the few public open spaces in the city that is not their direct responsibility.[408]

CONCLUSIONS

The robustness and effectiveness of the Minneapolis park system cannot be attributed to any single factor. It is the product of city elders with the foresight to establish an independent Board of Park Commissioners and to engage, trust, accept and act on the proposals of a visionary landscape architect. Since its inception the system has had the 'great good fortune' to have kept its finances substantially isolated from those for other government activities. It has maintained a strong sense of partnership between the Board, its employees and the citizens it serves, and it has maintained its dynamism by continuing to be a work in progress. As Wirth put it in 1945, 'the endowment of the city in the way of natural scenic attractions has been strikingly well preserved for the common use of all its people . . . for which all Minneapolitans may well be proud and very grateful'.

Just as the Minneapolis park system has been described as 'the best-located, best-financed, best-designed, best-maintained public open space in America', it is easy to agree, more than a century later, with the assertion in the Annual Report of the Board of Park Commissioners for 1898 that 'it was the great good fortune of Minneapolis to secure the services of one of the masters of American park design, Mr. H. W. S. Cleveland'. The Superintendent's Annual report for 1998 recorded that the Grand Rounds had been designated that year as a National Scenic Byway by the Federal Highway Commission – the nation's first totally urban scenic byway. The remarkable legacy of Cleveland, his visionary clients and their successors is an exceptional park system that continues to perform an invaluable role as an integral part of the physical structure and daily life of the city.[409]

*View from gazebo by
Siah Armajani, Loring
Park (September 1998)*

Reflections

Rapid population growth in European and North American cities in the nineteenth century made the provision of public parks a primary concern for national, state and city governments. In the United States land allocation was based on the principle of private ownership. The idea of public land was generally an alien concept and the role of government was seen – and to some extent, still is seen – as being to protect private property. The principle of land held in common was more familiar in Europe. Also, European cities had royal or private parks that could be made available for public use. There were therefore different approaches to park procurement between different countries. Equally, there were – and still are – different approaches to the design, management and funding of parks in different countries and in different cities. This is demonstrated by the three parks in Manhattan examined in this study – Paley Park is privately owned and privately managed; Bryant Park is publicly owned but privately managed and entirely privately funded, and Central Park is publicly owned, largely privately financed and managed by a trust. There are, however, many bases for the comparison of city parks – even if these demonstrate differences as well as similarities.[410]

The evolution of approaches to the design and management of parks is a major common strand. John Brinkerhoff Jackson noted that 'the picturesque park, open to the public . . . came to represent the impact of three distinct social forces: the urge to improve the living conditions of factory workers . . ., the urge to bring all classes in close contact with . . . "natural" environment, and the urge to improve the real estate value of areas surrounding the new parks'. Urban parks in Europe and North America have continued to serve as instruments of social engineering, urban land use planning and real estate development. Latterly they have also started to be revered as 'cultural heritage' – both in Europe and in North America. This has coincided with – and may even result from – an increase in the numbers of higher income residents living in inner cities. There has been a synchronous increase in the use of urban parks. This leads to the challenging question of how to mediate between demands for preservation of parks as cultural artefacts, demands for them to be managed in 'sustainable' ways, and demands for their use for active recreation – the recurrent triangle of art, ecology and society. The evolving relationship between 'culture' and 'nature' reflects the fact that parks, like cities, are never completed. Another constant in both continents is that 'the way that a society sees itself and its *joie de vivre* is expressed in the designing of public free space'.[411]

Differing versions of the nineteenth-century romantic park became the 'industry standard' on both sides of the Atlantic. This was widely seen as 'a facility aimed at counterbalancing the detrimental effects of the city' and was 'arranged with the cultured walker in mind'. It was a version of paradise – an escape from the city. The purposes for which parks have been planned and managed has changed over time but these original intentions have never been completely rejected. Galen Cranz chronicled four eras in the history of park politics in the United States: the Pleasure Ground (1850–1900), the Reform Park (1900–30), the Recreation Facility (1930–65) and the Open-Space System (after 1965). She subsequently identified a fifth era, or set of intended moral messages – the 'Sustainability' era. This era is characterized by calls for ecological integrity in planting design and for low energy inputs to park construction and maintenance. It has been followed by calls to treat older parks as 'works of landscape art' and to seek to restore them to their 'original' form. This leads to a situation where it is difficult for these parks to perform any role other than as places for 'a peaceful walk in pleasant surroundings'. During the 1990s there were also calls for more linear parks along natural and former transport routes, and for treating vegetated parks as one type of urban open space in an interconnected system.[412]

Recent research has added credibility to the 'pleasure ground' prototype. Olmsted argued that 'the beauty of rural scenery is a restorative antidote to the artificiality and oppression of urban conditions' – and that this view was 'too well established to need argument'. His view is supported by environmental psychologists Rachel and Stephen Kaplan. They found that 'peace, quiet, fascination, the chance to share with others and to do what one wishes are deeply important to human beings. The natural setting makes these satisfactions more available. Even the view of trees can lead to psychological gains'. Similarly, Baljon argued towards the end of *Designing Parks*, his review of the design competition for Parc de la Villette, that 'the openness of a grassy or scintillating space is the most important quality for the ordinary park: long sight lines to dream away in, the tranquillity of simple spaces in which to entertain one's thoughts, and the enchanting rhythms of the regularity and repetition of interconnected trees and hedges'.[413]

Nevertheless, there has been extensive debate about the continued need for parks. At a conference in 1992, Dutch landscape architect Adriaan Geuze, a principal of landscape consultancy West 8, stated that 'there is absolutely no need for parks any more, because all the nineteenth-century problems have been solved and a new type of city has been created. The park and greenery have become worn-out clichés'. Also in 1992, Michael Laurie questioned the need for large pastoral parks. Citing Golden Gate Park, San Francisco, Laurie argued that 'more important may now be village greens, town squares, flower gardens, and street trees, because they are closely associated with and in scale with residential neighbourhoods'. Equally, in 1997, Hans Ophius noted that 'parks are . . . cultural environments that express and explore vague notions about nature and communal space' whereas 'community recreation has now moved to the shopping mall, and society has become highly mobile and individualistic'. Ophius concluded that 'the park needs to be reinterpreted to suit contemporary cul-

tural demands'. He noted, however, that 'the powerful spiritual effect of nature should not be forgotten in the process' but that this 'should not be a mere return to immersion in greenery'.[414]

Nineteenth-century urban parks were primarily conceived as escapes into healthy, restorative, romantic, idyllic, pastoral settings. At the beginning of the twenty-first century, parks are widely seen as complementary parts of cities rather than as complete escapes from them. But few people now seek mystery (or even danger) in parks – if they ever did. There is a clearly apparent desire for safety and certainty. This is demonstrated by the 'restoration' of Bryant Park. It is also manifest in the baroque symmetry of Hamburg's Stadtpark and in the subdivision of a number of newer parks, like the Parc de Bercy, into intervisible, individual gardens. Their smaller scale and more cultivated character carry a clear message that they are safe places.

Many nineteenth-century parks were also intended to increase real estate values. The relationship between well-managed parks and higher real estate values remains strong. Garvin noted that parks 'stimulate private investment by attracting customers to an area' but that 'there are city parks that have now deteriorated so badly that they act as a depressant force to their surroundings'. Regent's Park and Birkenhead Park were models of the urban park as the focus of residential development. Properties overlooking Regent's Park continue to command high values. Birkenhead Park is in an economically depressed area and the decline of the local economy is reflected in the condition of the park. Regrettably its restoration was being predicated solely on the basis of its intrinsic value as 'cultural heritage' and not on the basis of its potential – even as 'cultural heritage' – as an economic catalyst. Olmsted, Vaux and Cleveland clearly understood the role of parks in raising real estate values. All four of the Paris parks examined in this study were intended to stimulate investment. So is the Landschaftspark Duisburg-Nord. The development of Freeway Park had a major business real estate dimension; Yorkville Park was seen as the focus of a Business Improvement District; the restoration of Bryant Park had a major impact on the value of adjacent property. In short, the value of parks to real estate development in most North American and many European cities is now taken almost for granted.[415]

The story of developer Donald Trump's 'Riverside South' project overlooking the Hudson River between 59th and 72nd Streets in New York City is germane. Trump proposed the creation of a park – now a widely adopted device for increasing real estate values and protecting views – between the development and the river. He anticipated benefiting from a federally funded proposal to relocate the elevated West Side Highway running between his development and the river. A protestor against the development, Representative Jerrold Nadler, managed to block the federal funds for the highway, thereby reducing Trump's apparent philanthropy. Parks on the model of Central Park have progressed from being an asset to real estate development to being, in more democratic days, a battle ground between developers and protestors.[416]

Sutton noted that land allocated for urban parks has often been 'some site undesirable for commercial or residential buildings, and in no way integral to established patterns of city life' and that 'officials adopted simplistic notions of a park, separating it in their minds from the activities of the city'. This was particularly true of Central Park – which was a major exercise in landscape creation – and a number of other parks covered in this study. This has tended to mean that park design has involved both the challenge of rehabilitation to 'naturalize' sites and the challenge of creating demand for their use. This sometimes causes landscape architects to take a pragmatic approach to park design.[417]

Many developments in park design have been made by designers who were not primarily landscape architects. Calvert Vaux, the principal designer of much of Central and Prospect Parks, originally trained as an architect. His death may even have been prompted by depression following public exposure of the fact that, although he held the post of New York City Landscape Architect in the 1890s, he had limited horticultural knowledge. Fritz Schumacher, whose work on the Hamburg Stadtpark pre-dated Leberecht Migge's work on the *Volkspark*, was also an architect. So too, of course, was Bernard Tschumi – designer of the idiosyncratic Parc de la Villette. There is evidence here of 'building' architects rather than landscape architects generating paradigm shifts in park design. Generally speaking, however, 'successful' park design and development are the product of team work. It is pertinent to consider here Baljon's comment that the design for Parc de la Villette was suitable for the involvement of other designers, and to recall the collaboration of the two architect/landscape architect teams in the design of Parc André-Citroën. Equally, Yorkville Park was a successful collaboration between California-based landscape architects and Toronto-based architects.[418]

The designs of nineteenth-century 'Pleasure Grounds' were strongly influenced by the pastoral/picturesque precedents established by Repton–Nash and Paxton, Lenné, Olmsted–Vaux,

Cleveland and Alphand. These designs were generally based on the principle of excluding the surrounding city as far as possible and creating balanced compositions of water, pasture and woodland – sweeping views of 'natural' scenery. In the early twentieth century, parks like Hamburg's Stadtpark continued to be comprised of these three elements – albeit in geometric layouts. Similarly, the Bos Park – designed in the 1930s – is composed of water, pasture and woodland – albeit in a distinctly Dutch model. These elements figure less in Grant Park – which, with its collection of Beaux-Arts 'rooms', is a permeable interface between the city and the lake. Similarly, Parque de María Luisa in Seville, with its grid of shaded *glorietas*, is prescient of later Parisian examples like the serial gardens at Parc André-Citroën or the parterres at Parc de Bercy.

The strongest point about the design of most of the parks in this study is the extent to which they are a direct response to their context. They reflect an approach based on comprehension, interpretation and expression of their unique and intrinsic natural and cultural characteristics. Even in the Bos Park, with its composition of conventional elements, the woodland was largely native species designed to appear 'natural' and to lower the water table. The circulation system and the scale of open spaces were designed to be experienced by bicycle or on horseback. Schumacher's design in the Stadtpark contained a wealth of locally derived imagery; Forestier interpreted Moorish garden traditions in the design of Parque de María Luisa; Huet *et al.* laid a new grid onto the older one at Bercy; the Latzs worked so closely with what they found at Duisburg-Nord that they were accused of 'doing nothing'. Nash, in his second design for Regent's Park; Paxton, making himself 'master of the locality'; Olmsted, introduced by Vaux into the competition for Central Park because of his intimate knowledge of the site – all worked closely with the intrinsic characteristics of their sites. So too did Lenné, Cleveland, Alphand, Provost and Clément, as did Zion at Paley Park, Smith at Yorkville Park and Danadjieva at Freeway Park. Successive managers of Stanley Park have eschewed master planning and relied heavily on the intrinsic qualities of the site as 'trapped wilderness'. Even Bennett's superimposition of Beaux-Arts geometry at Grant Park respected the pivotal role of that site in the larger context of the *Plan of Chicago*.

The one real exception to this approach was Tschumi's anti-contextual design for Parc de la Villette. He treated that park entirely as an opportunity to explore a theoretical deconstructivist approach to 'architecture'. Tschumi's writings about it are highly engaging. But the park itself has done relatively little for the development of what is essentially a context-driven art. Even the characteristically controversial landscape architect Martha Schwartz ensures that her work engages local context. In June 2000, the architect-dominated panel for the proposed Downsview Park in Toronto appointed architects Rem Koolhaas and his Office for Metropolitan Architecture – runners-up to Tschumi at la Villette – to design Canada's first federally sponsored urban park. Koolhaas, promoter of the concept of the 'Generic City' – a form of 'no-place' international metropolis – may prove to be as anti-contextual in his work in Toronto as Tschumi was in Paris. Regrettably technological developments are sometimes used to subdue local context rather than to understand it more fully and work with it more fruitfully.[419]

Although the Royal Parks in London are, effectively, National Parks, the emergence of new, nationally funded urban parks is a relatively recent phenomenon. Parc de la Villette and Downsview Park are new models. Their designation reflects the fact that many local government organizations struggle to fund their existing parks, let alone the creation of major new parks. In the United States the best maintained parks are in cities like Chicago and Minneapolis – where there are specifically dedicated property taxes, or in cities where high levels of direct private funding can be generated, as for Bryant Park and Central Park in New York. Parks that depend on general local government funds appear to fare worse those that have direct sources of dedicated income.

Garvin suggested that the funding and management system in Minneapolis might be used as a model by other cities in the United States, and that a 'National Urban and Suburban Park Development Program' should be established to sponsor similar local park boards. There were also calls – before the establishment of the Central Park Conservancy – for Central Park to become a National Park. Similarly, the United Kingdom House of Commons Environment Sub-Committee recommended in 1999 that a national government agency should be created to oversee urban parks. At that time the only source of national funds – other than for the Royal Parks – was the National Lottery. And that was only available for the restoration of 'historic parks' as items of National Heritage. Funding of the other European parks covered by this study is largely from local government sources. The German examples have the advantages (and disadvantages) of two levels of government – *Land* and city – providing funds (and plans) for them; the Amsterdam, Paris and Seville examples are all

directly funded by city authorities with minor income from the staging of events and the provision of services to users.[420]

Use levels in most of the parks in the study rose significantly – and in cases like Minneapolis, astronomically – during the 1990s. Peter Latz suggests that nowadays everyone goes to parks alone. Although certain user figures – for instance for Central Park in 1995 – support Latz's argument, there are still significant numbers who visit parks in groups. This is particularly true of racial minorities – for instance, Turkish residents in Berlin using the Tiergarten. Rises in the proportion of visitors going to parks on their own, and in the proportion of women visiting parks probably reflect a perception of higher levels of safety. Also, there is little evidence to support Catharine Ward Thompson's statement that 'in today's multicultural society, just as in Olmsted's time, the urban park is one of the few places where strangers come together regardless of economic, ethnic, or social status'. There is more evidence of cautious co-existence and of people taking the opportunity to observe different social groups rather than to mix with them.[421]

User surveys at Parc de la Villette suggested a pattern of older, richer, suburban dwellers using the cultural facilities there while poorer, local residents used the outdoor spaces. This reflects recurrent evidence that a relatively high proportion of users live or work close to the parks; that a high proportion of users are regular visitors, and that a high proportion of visitors go there on foot. A number of the parks have introduced restrictions on car usage and/or higher parking charges. This pattern of local usage supports Christopher Alexander's assertion that 'people need green open spaces to go to; when they are close they use them. But if the greens are more than three minutes away, the distance overwhelms the need'. It supports Laurie's argument that more resources should be devoted to smaller, more local parks than to large pastoral parks.[422]

There are clear indications that most parks – and particularly large pastoral parks – are using their historic status as a lever to generate funds for their physical rehabilitation. Ian Grandison, commenting on 'the rise of cultural landscape preservation in America', noted that 'in historic preservation, as is still often the case in the disciplines of architecture and landscape architecture, the focus remains on individuals as isolated creative impulses'. This is borne out in Ward Thompson's survey of seven large pastoral parks in the north-east United States – including Prospect Park and Central Park. Each plan she studied claimed 'to maintain the original philosophy or design intent of the park, but to adapt the detail'. Equally, the principal argument for restoration of Birkenhead Park was its value 'as a major work of art'. Even the innovatory Ville de Paris began the twenty-first century by proposing the restoration of the Parc des Buttes-Chaumont. There are often two principal areas of departure from completely faithful restoration of such parks. The first is to try and redress the lack of ecological integrity in the design of most of their original woodland; the second is to acknowledge current user demands — particularly for active recreation facilities. This is demonstrated by management policies for Prospect Park. There is, however, a high level of cautiousness about new art installations. This is typified by the view of the Bryant Park Art Committee that people will only come to see 'legendary' pieces.[423]

Parks change through the forces of nature, through the effects of usage and through the decisions and actions (or inaction) of their managers. Christopher Leinberger and Gayle Berens noted that

'it is easy to forget that each generation has different open space needs. Like fashion and music, parks and park design become passé . . . maintaining a continuous connection to market preferences is critical to success . . . parks have never had as many visitors as they have now, and many suffer from overuse and insufficient funding'. In a chapter on the 'Past and Future Park', Jackson noted that failure of parks to adapt has contributed to a situation in which the park 'is becoming merely one space out of many, now serving an invaluable function primarily for children, older people, and the dedicated student of nature, while the more mobile, more gregarious elements seek recreation in shopping malls, in the street, on the open road, and in sports arenas'.[424]

Bryant Park is probably the most extreme example of the trend in the United States towards private funding and private management of public parks. Bryant Park also demonstrates measures that have

Brockton Point, Stanley Park, Vancouver (June 1998)

been called for by a number of critics. These revolve around issues of safety, legibility, simplicity, calmness and ease of use – interspersed with moments of vitality and a tendency towards 'the-meing'. Park designers are likely to continue to develop approaches that deal more overtly with human experience – the lessons of Repton, Olmsted–Vaux and Disney coming full circle – on the one hand, while adopting a stance on the relationship between 'culture' and 'nature'. The serial gardens at Parc André-Citroën are an example of the former approach; the Landschaftspark Duisburg-Nord is an example of the latter approach. Both of them demonstrate a continuing role for parks as recreational settings for the relaxation and entertainment of urban dwellers – settings that display current knowledge and values in the fields of horticulture and ecology.

The parks covered by this study demonstrate, above all, that:

- vegetated parks are now seen as complementary parts of post-industrial cities rather than as complete escapes from them
- park locations have a stronger influence on the character of the parks than the parks have on the character of their locations
- park designs reflect politicians', planners' and designers' attitudes to human intervention in natural processes and often seek to play a didactic role in this respect
- calls for 'sustainable', ecology-driven approaches to park design and management increased in the latter part of the twentieth century
- calls for 'faithful' restoration of urban parks as historic artefacts became increasingly prevalent in the 1990s
- recent park designs are tending towards subdivision into relatively small individual gardens
- 'successful' park design tends to be context-driven and to be directed towards the quality of user experience rather than towards the formal or theoretical content of the design

- parks occupy often large and generally valuable land areas. They continue to occupy that land because they are perceived as providing worthwhile public services. Regular user surveys are an important method of ensuring that parks continue to provide worthwhile services
- 'successful' parks continue to have the effect of raising/maintaining the market value of adjacent real estate
- the management and maintenance of parks are most effective when they are funded from reliable, dedicated income sources rather than from general government revenues
- there is a growing trend towards event-driven, business-derived management regimes – like those at Bryant Park and the Landschaftspark Duisburg-Nord
- there is an emerging pattern of central or federal government sponsorship of major city parks
- levels of park use rose significantly in most Western European and North American parks during the 1990s. The proportion of visitors going to parks on their own also increased. Both these patterns probably reflect generally lower crime levels and higher levels of perceived safety in parks
- parks continue to perform a significant role as meeting and recreation places for members of ethnic minorities who tend to use them in relatively large groups
- the majority of visitors to even the largest parks tended to live or work relatively close to them and to travel to them on foot.

No single park can be deemed 'successful' in every respect. But each example in this study demonstrates 'successful' approaches to different aspects of the planning, design and management of urban parks. As a collection they give a clear picture of why urban parks have been created, how they have been designed, how they are managed, and what plans are being made for them at the beginning of the twenty-first century.

Endnotes

INTRODUCTION

1 One example of this definition of parks is *Chambers Twentieth Century Dictionary* (1972). Edinburgh, W. & R. Chambers, p. 965; Newton, Norman T. (1971). *Design on the Land*. Cambridge, MA, Belknap, p. 273 suggested that 'the first *official* use of the title Landscape Architect' was a reference to Olmsted and Vaux by the Commissioners of Central Park in May 1863. Alex, William (1994). *Calvert Vaux: Architect and Planner*. New York, Ink, p. 10 suggested that the New York State Legislature used the title when referring to them in April 1860; Rybczynski, Witold (1999). *A Clearing in the Distance: Frederick Law Olmsted and North America in the Nineteenth Century*. Toronto, HarperCollins Canada, p. 261 suggested that Vaux used the title first in correspondence with Olmsted in 1865, but that John Dixon Hunt had noted that John Claudius Loudon published *The Landscape Gardening and Landscape Architecture of the Late Humphry Repton Esq.* in 1840.

2 Cranz, Galen (1982). *The Politics of Park Design*. Cambridge, MA, MIT Press. Cranz's study was organized on the basis of four eras of park design and management in America: the Pleasure Ground (1850–1900), the Reform Park (1900–30), the Recreation Facility (1930–65) and the Open-Space System (from 1965).

3 Jacobs, Jane (1961). *The Death and Life of Great American Cities*. New York, Vintage, p. 90.

4 Main sources in the early 1980s were either historical – like George F. Chadwick's *The Park and the Town* (1966) or Norman T. Newton's *Design on the Land* (1971) – or covered restricted locations. Other references included Jacobs' observations on parks in *The Death and Life of Great American Cities*; Geoffrey and Susan Jellicoe's sweeping *The Landscape of Man* and August Heckscher and Phyllis Robinson's *Open Spaces: The Life of American Cities* (1977) – a comprehensive but exclusively US-based study. Sha Tin Town Park was documented in *Architectural Review*, Volume 189, No. 1130 (1991), pp. 63–7.

5 Regrettably, the chapters on Park Güell, Barcelona; St James's Park, London; Luisenpark, Mannheim, Golden Gate Park, San Francisco and the Emerald Necklace, Boston had to be held back.

1 PALEY PARK, NEW YORK

6 Kayden, Jerold (2000). 'Plaza Suite' in *Planning*, Volume 66, No. 3, p. 18; Johnson, Jory (1991). *Modern Landscape Architecture: Redefining the Garden*. New York, Abbeville, pp. 191, 194; *Architectural Record* (1967), Volume 142, No. 9, p. 117; Kim, Mik Young in Bennett, Paul (1999). 'Playtime in the City' in *Landscape Architecture*, Volume 89, No. 9, p. 88.

7 Seymour, Whitney North, Jr (1969). 'An Introduction to Small Urban Spaces' in *Small Urban Spaces*. New York, New York University Press, pp. 2–6; Tamulevich, Susan (1991). 'Mr. Zion Finds Utopia' in *Process Architecture*, No. 94, p. 7; Seymour, Whitney North, Jr (1969), ibid., p. 5.

8 Undated 'Statement by William S. Paley' provided by Philip J. Boschetti, Assistant Secretary of the Greenpark Foundation with letter to author dated 25 August 1989.

9 Blumenthal, Ralph (2000). *Stork Club*. New York, Little, Brown documented the life of the Club.

10 *Macleans* magazine (1990), Volume 103, No. 45, p. 58 from website kcmetro.cc.mo.us (accessed 10 May 2000).

11 Decker, Andrew (1991). 'Country Gentleman' in *Process Architecture*, No. 94, pp. 20–3; Seymour, Whitney North, Jr (1969), op. cit., pp. xix–xx; Muschamp, Herbert. Obituary in *New York Times* (28 April 2000).

12 Landau, Ian (1999). 'Midtown' in Dahl, Shawn (Editor). *Time Out New York* (seventh edition). Harmondsworth, Penguin, p. 56; Zion and Breen also worked with architect Philip Johnson on the courtyard of the Museum of Modern Art.

13 Abercrombie, Stanley (1991). 'Evaluation: A Prototype Left Unreplicated' in *Process Architecture*, op. cit., pp. 38–9; and Zion, Robert L. (1969). 'Parks Where the People Are – The Small Midtown Park' in Seymour, Whitney North, Jr, op. cit., pp. 73–8; Whyte, William H. (1980). *The Social Life of Small Urban Spaces*. Washington, DC, Conservation Foundation, p. 53.

14 Jacobs, Jane (1961). *The Death and Life of Great American Cities*. New York, Vintage, pp. 103–6 noted that enclosure, intricacy, centring and sun are the principal

requirements for the success of neighbourhood parks; noted at author's meeting with Phillip A. Raspe, Jr of the Paley Foundation on 24 April 2000 that yellow tulips form part of cycle because, at the time of opening, Paley's wife, Barbara Cushing Paley, said that they should always be displayed in spring.

15 Birnie, William A. H. (January 1969). 'Oasis on 53rd Street' in *Reader's Digest*. Pleasantville, Reader's Digest Association; Whyte, William H. (1980), op. cit., p. 73.

16 The City of New York, owners of the sidewalk, refused consent for replacement of the trees.

2 VILLAGE OF YORKVILLE PARK, TORONTO

17 The competition was run under the name Cumberland Park, after the street along its north side, and the park was referred to by that name until September 1992; website *city.toronto.on.ca* (accessed 31 October 1999) noted Toronto's population at 2.4 million; Ken Smith of landscape architects Schwartz/Smith/Meyer kindly provided a file of newspaper articles about the project from the period April 1992 to August 1996. The cost of the rock was widely reported as C$282,933. In September 1999 it was dedicated to the People of the First Nations in Canada.

18 Principal sources for this history are Parks and Recreation Department, City of Toronto's documents *Cumberland Park Design Competition* (July 1991) and *A Walk through the Village of Yorkville Park* (June 1994). Farm Lots were 80 hectare agricultural plots. The village developed on parts of five of them.

19 Website *toronto.com* (accessed 28 October 1999) noted that BIAs were established across Canada to 'fight back against economic stagnation and physical decay' in downtown areas; that there were over 200 BIAs in Ontario including thirty-nine in Toronto, of which Bloor–Yorkville, representing over 2500 businesses, was the largest.

20 City of Toronto. *Cumberland Park Design Competition* (July 1991), p. 6 suggested that five would be shortlisted; ibid., p. 22.

21 Ibid., p. 26.

22 Other jurors were journalist (later Governor General of Canada) Adrienne Clarkson, architect Carol Kleinfeldt and Professors of Landscape Architecture, Walter Kehm and Moura Quayle.

23 Berton, Pierre (11 September 1993). 'The Archer & The Rock: What have we Learned?' in *The Toronto Star*, p. F3; Vaughan, Colin (9 August 1993). 'Myth, Merits of the Rock' in *The Globe and Mail*.

24 Author's correspondence with Ken Smith in April and August 1999 and meeting with Stephen O'Bright of Toronto Department of Parks and Recreation and David Oleson of Oleson Worland Architects on 12 October 1999.

25 Comment noted at author's meeting with Stephen O'Bright and David Oleson on 12 October 1999 (note 24); City of Toronto. *Cumberland Park Design Competition* (July 1991), p. 18.

26 Competition juror Walter Kehm noted, 'when we talk of ecosystem we must in an urban context think in terms of metaphor'; statement of objectives derived from *Project Fact Sheet* provided by Ken Smith in correspondence with author in April 1999.

27 Griswold, Mac (1993). 'Box Set: Cumberland Park' in *Landscape Architecture*, Volume 83, No. 4, p. 68; the rock derives from an outcrop of Muskoka granite near Gravenhurst, Ontario. It was removed in 135 pieces each weighing between 225 and 900 kilograms and transported on flatbed trailers for re-assembly on site. This caused extensive, and not altogether supportive, comment in the local and national press throughout 1993. The water/ice curtain comprises a stainless steel frame suspending a series of taut, vertically aligned stainless steel cables. These create a water wall for most of the year and an ice wall in winter when warm water from the overhead trough freezes as it runs down the cables.

28 Similar comments were contained in some early reviews of the design. Deirdre Hanna in *Now* magazine (18–24 November 1993) described the design as 'too self-conscious to be truly relaxed . . . too clever for its own good' and as not offering 'any more of a break from urban, everyday life than the parking lot it replaces'.

29 Powell, Elizabeth Anne (1996). 'Northern Exposure' in *Landscape Architecture*, Volume 86, No. 11, p. 71; Monsebraaten, Laurie (29 January 1993). 'Between a Rock and a Green Space' in *The Toronto Star*.

3 FREEWAY PARK, SEATTLE

30 Halprin, Lawrence (1966). *Freeways*, New York, Reinhold, in which he stated that 'often depressed roadways form great ditches through the closely built-up, fine-grained texture of old neighborhoods and completely obliterate their fine urban qualities' (p. 24) but that 'of all the side-by-side freeways, however, this is the best because its visual impact is ameliorated by being depressed and the volume of noise is somewhat softened' (p. 66); and that 'we must reorder our thinking and realize that freeways must also be designed to carry their own built-in amenities with them' (p. 134); Halprin, Lawrence (1972). *Cities*. Cambridge, MA, MIT Press (revised paperback edition), p. 233.

31 Marshall, Margaret (1977). 'How the Impossible Came to Be' in *Landscape Architecture*, Volume 67, No. 5, pp. 399–403.

32 Figures from press handout dated 16 July 1976 and received on 5 November 1999 from Seattle Department of Parks and Recreation and Marshall, Margaret (1977), op. cit., p. 400.

33 Moore, Charles (1986). 'Still Pools and Crashing Waves' in *Lawrence Halprin: Changing Places*. San Francisco, San Francisco Museum of Modern Art, p. 25; Walker, Peter and Simo, Melanie (1994). *Invisible Gardens: The Search for Modernism in the American Landscape*. Cambridge, MA, MIT Press, pp. 146–7, 158.

34 Thompson, William J. (1992). 'Master of Collaboration' in *Landscape Architecture*, Volume 82, No. 7, pp. 64, 68; 'People' in *Landscape Architecture* (1977), Volume 67, No. 5, p. 383.

35 Halprin, Lawrence (1966), op. cit., p. 49; author's telephone conversation on 22 November 1999 with Kerry Lasko of Seattle Department of Parks and Recreation.

36 Danadjieva, Angela (1977). 'Seattle's Freeway Park II: Danadjieva on the Creative Process' in *Landscape Architecture*, Volume 67, No. 5, p. 406.

37 Ibid., pp. 404–5.

38 Author's telephone conversation with Kerry Lasko on 22 November 1999, op. cit.

39 Hinshaw, Mark (1999). 'Two Urban Parks' in *Landscape Architecture*, Volume 89, No. 10, p. 124.

40 Futagawa, Yukio (Editor) (1982). *Seattle Freeway Park* in *GA (Global Architecture)* Document Special Issue 1970–80. Tokyo, ADA EDITA Tokyo; Lyall, Sutherland (1991). 'Seattle Freeway Park' in *Designing the New Landscape*. London, Thames & Hudson, p. 37; Walker, Peter and Simo, Melanie (1994), op. cit., pp. 158–60.

41 Website *ci.seattle.wa.us/parks/parkboard* (accessed 22 November 1999).

42 Roberts, Paul (1993). 'Freeway Park: Still an Icon, but a Few Glitches at `25`' in *Landscape Architecture*, Volume 83, No. 2, p. 56; CPTED is an approach to deterring crime by, *inter alia*, increasing surveillance through better lighting, visibility and programming of activities in public open space. It is endorsed by the Conference of US Mayors.

43 Hinshaw, Mark (1999), op. cit., p. 124.

44 Author's telephone conversation with Kerry Lasko on 22 November 1999, op. cit.; noted that the canyon waterfall is shut off in the fall when leaf litter can clog the pumps.

45 Marshall, Margaret (1977), op. cit., p. 402; Roberts, Paul (1993), op. cit., p. 57.

4 BRYANT PARK, NEW YORK

46 Whyte, William H. (1980). *The Social Life of Small Urban Spaces*. Washington, DC, Conservation Foundation, p. 58; use of words like 'restoration' and 'rehabilitation' to describe the work done to Bryant Park can cause confusion. The organization charged in 1980 with revitalizing the park called itself a Restoration Corporation. Landscape architect Charles A. Birnbaum, author of the US Secretary of the Interior's *Guidelines for the Treatment of Cultural Landscapes* (1996), adopted the words 'preservation', 'rehabilitation', 'restoration' and 'reconstruction' to define different treatments of historic landscapes. In brief, restoration involves maintaining a property as it was at a particular point in time; rehabilitation aims to 'convey historical values'. In his review of Thompson, J. William (1997). *The Rebirth of New York City's Bryant Park*. Washington, DC, Spacemaker, in *Land Forum* magazine (also Spacemaker), Issue 03, Birnbaum criticized the description by landscape architect Laurie Olin of his work on Bryant Park as

'restoration' and described it as a 'successful *reha-bilitation*'. Olin was invited to respond in the same issue and produced a long tirade against restoration as defined by Birnbaum. 'Restoration' is only used here in the name of the Corporation or in the sense proposed by Birnbaum.

47 Berens, Gayle. 'Bryant Park, New York City' in Garvin, Alexander and Berens, Gayle (1997). *Urban Parks and Open Space*. Washington, DC, Urban Land Institute, pp. 45–7; Thompson, J. William (1997), op. cit., pp. 18–21; website *www.bryantpark.org/history* (accessed on 12 May 2000).

48 Khan, Eve (1992). 'Panacea in Needle Park' in *Landscape Architecture*, Volume 82, No. 12, p. 61.

49 Thompson, J. William (1997), op. cit., p. 23 lists Whyte's recommendations.

50 Ibid., p. 23; Berens, Gayle in Garvin, Alexander and Berens, Gayle (1997), op. cit., p. 48. Berens also noted that 'while the initiative for a BID comes from . . . business owners seeking common services, the city . . . must approve the BID's boundaries, annual budget, financing strategy, and the services to be provided'. In 1999 and 2000, the levy was $0.1261795 per square foot.

51 Berens, Gayle in Garvin, Alexander and Berens, Gayle (1997), op. cit., p. 50 credited Marshall Rose, Chair of the Library's Building Committee with this idea. Thompson, J. William (1997), op. cit., p. 27 noted that Olin claimed credit for it. Berens, Gayle., ibid., p. 56 noted that the total cost comprised basic park rehabilitation – $5.95 million; concessions, monuments and horticulture – $9.76 million; fees – $1.98 million.

52 Thompson, J. William (1997), op. cit., p. 22; Goldberger, Paul (8 November 1999). 'Face-Lift Department' in *The New Yorker*, p. 34; noted at author's meeting with Daniel Biederman on 25 April 2000. Biederman stressed that young designers are inured to plan views and bird's eye views of sites and do not recognize that 'design is for people who's average eye-level is less than 5 foot 7 inches above ground level'.

53 Berens, Gayle in Garvin, Alexander and Berens, Gayle (1997), op. cit., p. 56.

54 Rosenzweig, Roy and Blackmar, Elizabeth (1992). *The Park and the People: A History of Central Park*. Ithaca, Cornell University Press (paperback edition 1998), pp. 382–3 recounted events in 1901 when the Manhattan Park Commissioner licensed a chair rental operator in Madison Square Park. It resulted in boycotts and civil disobedience referred to as 'Chair Sunday'. BPRC does not charge for use of the movable chairs.

55 Birnbaum, Charles A. (1999). Review of Thompson, J. William (ibid.) in *Land Forum*, Issue 03; Thompson, J. William (1997), op. cit., p. 30; Berens, Gayle in Garvin, Alexander and Berens, Gayle (1997), op. cit., p. 46 noted Whyte's thesis that 'a park's success can be measured in part by the percentage of female users. When women feel safe in a space, they are likely to use it more frequently'. This was balanced against Whyte and Biederman's recognition of Jane Jacobs' four fac-tors for the success of neighbourhood parks – enclosure, intricacy, centring and sun.

56 Thompson, J. William (1997), op. cit., pp. 19, 29 noted that twelve of the original 240 plane trees were removed to facilitate the redesign and six because they were dead or dying. The remaining trees are root-fed every other year (at a cost, in 2000, of $80 per tree).

57 Noted at author's meeting with Daniel Biederman on 25 April 2000; website *www.bryant-park.org/bprc* (accessed 12 May 2000); Goldberger, Paul (1999), op. cit., p. 34 noted that Biederman was delighted that the new users of Herald and Greeley Squares were 'mostly black, Hispanic and Asian' and included 'plenty of women and families'. This validated his belief that the BPRC approach was not dependent on well-heeled office workers for its success.

58 Noted at author's meeting with Daniel Biederman on 25 April 2000; Berens, Gayle in Garvin, Alexander and Berens, Gayle (1997), op. cit., p. 46; 'quality of life enforcement' involves issues like drug and alcohol use, amplified music, panhandling, dogs on the lawn, organized ball games, etc.

59 Noted at meeting with Daniel Biederman on 25 April 2000.

60 BPRC has an Art Committee including representatives from the Metropolitan Museum and the *Wall Street Journal*, the film critic of *The New Yorker*, a sculptor and an arts lawyer.

61 Carr, Stephen; Francis, Mark; Rivlin, Leanne and Stone, Andrew M. (1992). *Public Space*. Cambridge, Cambridge University Press, p. 149; Goldberger, Paul (3 May 1992). 'Bryant Park, an Out-of-Town Experience' in *The New York Times*, Section 2, p. 34 quoted in Thompson, J. William (1997), op. cit., p. 33; Khan, Eve (1992), op. cit., p. 61.

5 PARC DE BERCY, PARIS

62 The area within the Boulevard Périphérique – the ring road on the line of nineteenth-century fortifications around Paris. It is effectively the area included in the Ville de Paris – the City of Paris administrative area established in 1977. The population of this area in the 1990s was about 2.1 million; the population of metropolitan Paris was about 10.6 million.

63 This history of the site and of the project is drawn from three main sources: Micheloni, Pierre (1993). 'Le Parc de Bercy et son Quartier' in *Paris Projet Numéro 30–31: Éspaces Publics*. Paris, BRES, pp. 122–9; Mairie de Paris (1999). 'Bercy en Trois Siècles' [Bercy over Three Centuries] in *Expositions: Bercy – la Genèse d'un Grand Parc* [Exhibitions: Bercy – the Genesis of a Great Park], Exhibition Report, unpaginated; and Diedrich, Lisa (September 1994). 'Le Jardin de la Mémoire: Out of Budget, Out of Mind?' in *Topos European Landscape Magazine*, No. 8, pp. 74–80.

64 Mairie de Paris (1999), ibid., unpaginated.

65 Diedrich, Lisa (1994), op. cit., p. 74; Micheloni, Pierre (1993), op. cit., p. 122;

66 Starkman, Nathan (1993). 'Deux Nouveaux Parcs à Paris' in *Paris Projet Numéro 30–31: Éspaces Publics*. Paris, BRES, p. 88.

67 Ferrand, Marilène, Feugas, Jean-Pierre, Huet, Bernard, Le Caisne, Ian and Le Roy, Bernard (1993). 'Remémoration' [Recollection] in *Paris Projet Numéro 30–31: Éspaces Publics*. Paris, BRES, p. 150.

68 Mairie de Paris (1999), op. cit., 'Zonage: les Éspaces Publics' [Zoning: The Public Spaces], unpaginated.

69 Huet, Bernard. 'Park Design and Urban Continuity' in Knuijt, Martin, Ophius, Hans and van Saane, Peter (Editors) (1993). *Modern Park Design – Recent Trends*. Amsterdam, THOTH, pp. 18–27; 'A park est un parc is een park ist ein Park' in ibid., p. 28.

70 Mairie de Paris (1999), op. cit., 'Paris, un programme d'urbanisme – un programme de grands parcs' [Paris, a Planning Programme – a Programme of Major Parks], unpaginated; Étude APUR (1981), 'Les éspaces verts de Paris, situation et projets'.

71 In 1985 the Bercy area was divided into two ZACs – ZAC Corbineau Lachambeaudie adjacent to the railway lines and ZAC Bercy covering 51 hectares between Rue de Bercy and Rue de Pommard and the river, including the remaining wine warehouses and the POPB; the high running costs of the American Center prompted its closure in the mid-1990s; Rebois, Didier (1994). 'Bercy: un morceau policé' in *L'Architecture d'Aujourd'hui*, No. 295. pp. 69–71 examined the result of Buffi's proposals.

72 Holden, Robert (1989). 'New Parks for Paris' in *Architects' Journal*, Volume 190, No. 2, p. 57; Dumont, Marie-Jeanne (1994), op. cit., p. 66; 'Le Parc de Bercy: Concours Européen 1987' [European Competition for the Parc de Bercy] in *Paris Projet Numéro 30–31*, op. cit., pp. 132–3.

73 Micheloni, Pierre (1993), op. cit., p. 128; Mairie de Paris (1999), op. cit., 'Le projet lauréat: les idées clés' [The Winning Scheme: The Key Ideas], unpaginated; Huet, Bernard in Knuijt, Martin, Ophius, Hans and van Saane, Peter (Editors) (1993), op. cit., p. 26.

74 For instance, Holden, Robert (1998). 'Where Landscape Comes First' in *Architects' Journal*, Volume 207, No. 22, pp. 37–9; Arnold, Françoise (March 1998). 'Parc de Bercy in Paris' in *Topos European Landscape Magazine*, No. 22, pp. 87–93; or Diedrich, Lisa (1994), op. cit., pp. 74–80.

75 Noted at author's meeting with Marie-Joseph Gambard and Sophie Dobler of the Projects Section of the Direction des Parcs, Jardins et Éspaces Verts of the City of Paris on 14 June 1999; Diedrich, Lisa (1994), ibid., p. 78.

76 Website *www.paris-france.org/parisweb/en* (accessed 11 January 2000).

77 Huet, Bernard in Knuijt, Martin, Ophius,

Dumont, Marie-Jeanne (1994). 'L'époque Apur, vingt-cinq ans d'histoire' [The APUR Epoch: 25 Years of History] in *L'Architecture d'Aujourd'hui*, No. 295, pp. 64, 66.

Hans and van Saane, Peter (Editors) (1993), op. cit., p. 25.

6 PARC ANDRÉ-CITROËN, PARIS

78 Provost, Alain (1991). 'Parc André-Citroën à Paris' in *La Feuille du Paysage*, No. 10, p. 2.

79 Bédarida, Marc (1995). 'French Tradition and Ecological Paradigm' in *Lotus International*, No. 87, pp. 12–13; *Parc André-Citroën: From a hamlet to a factory* on website *www.paris-france.org/parisweb/en* (accessed 11 January 2000); bleach was invented at the chemical factory – giving rise to its French name – Eau de Javel.

80 Bédarida, Marc (1995), op. cit., p. 12; Starkman, Nathan (1993). 'Deux Nouveaux Parcs à Paris' in *Paris Projet Numéro 30–31: Éspaces Publics*. Paris, BRES, p. 88.

81 Bédarida, Marc (1995), ibid., p. 12; Ellis, Charlotte (1993). 'Parc André-Citroën: The Rage in Paris', *Landscape Architecture*, Volume 83, No. 4, p. 64.

82 Rosen, Miriam (February/March 2000). '*Terra Infirma*' in *Metropolis*, p. 110; Provost, Alain (1998). 'Dans la pente/On the Slope' in *Pages Paysages*, No. 7. Versailles, Association Paysage et Diffusion, pp. 132–7 documented the Parc Diderot; 'Le Champ/The Field', pp. 150–9 reflected Clément's horticultural interests; Garcias Jean-Claude (1993). 'Un Lustre Après, Le Concours Citroën Revisité' [Afterglow – The Citroën Competition Revisited] in *Paris Projet Numéro 30–31: Éspaces Publics*. Paris, BRES, pp. 111–14 concluded that 'the winning entries were incontestably the best. But was it necessary to have such flowering rhetoric to justify them?'.

83 Milliex, Jean-Michel (1993). 'Le Parc André-Citroën et son Quartier' in *Paris Projet Numéro 30–31: Éspaces Publics*. Paris, BRES, p. 93; Bédarida, Marc (1995), op. cit., p. 13. Bédarida also noted that, apart from the embankments of the river, the park has seventeen different sides or directions; Provost, Alain (1991), op. cit., p. 2.

84 Starkman, Nathan (1993). 'Deux Nouveaux Parcs à Paris' in *Paris Projet Numéro 30–31*, op. cit., p. 88; 'Concours pour le Parc André-Citroën' [Competition for the Parc André-Citroën] in *Paris Projet Numéro 30–31*, op. cit., p. 99; Garcias Jean-Claude (1993), op. cit., p. 100. The reference to a 'neo-constructivist fairground' is, of course, another dig at the selected design for la Villette; Bédarida, Marc (1995), op. cit., p. 14.

85 Garcias (1993), op. cit., pp. 101, 115 contained colour reproductions of the two original schemes; Bédarida, Marc (1995), op. cit., p. 14; Provost, Alain (1991), op. cit., p. 2.

86 Provost, Alain (1991), op. cit., p. 2.

87 Baljon, Lodewijk (June 1997). 'Paris as a Laboratory for the Park of the Twenty-first Century' in *Topos European Landscape Magazine*, No. 19, p. 81.

88 'Entretien avec les Lauréats' [Discussion with the Winners] in *Paris Projet Numéro 30–31: Éspaces Publics*. Paris, BRES, p. 116; Provost, Alain (1991), op. cit., p. 2.

89 Clément, Gilles (1995), op. cit., p. 87; Andersson, Thorbjörn (1996). 'Parks – The Urban Countryside' in *Lutblick Landskap*, Stockholm, Volume 13, No. 1, p. 60.

90 Clément, Gilles (1995). 'Identity and Signature' in *Topos European Landscape Magazine*, No. 11, p. 88; Treib, Marc (1995). 'Must Landscapes Mean? Approaches to Significance in Recent Landscape Architecture' in *Landscape Journal*, Volume 14, No. 1, p. 54.

91 Schäfer, Robert (January 1993). 'Parc André-Citroën, Paris' in *Topos European Landscape Magazine*, No. 11, p. 79.

92 Vonier, Thomas (1993). 'Non-Parallel Parking' in *Progressive Architecture*, Volume 10, p. 68 noted that 'on cool or wet, gray days, one may find André-Citroën completely deserted'.

93 Website   *www.paris-france.org/parisweb/en* (accessed 11 January 2000).

7 PARC DES BUTTES-CHAUMONT, PARIS

94 'Sublime' is used here in the sense of Edmund Burke's definition of 'whatever excites 'ideas of pain and danger' rather than Uvedale Price's sense of 'creation of the sublime being above our powers'; Robinson, William (1883). *The Parks and Gardens of Paris* (third edition), London, John Murray, p. 66 described it as 'the most distinct and interesting garden in Paris'; Russell, John (1960). *Paris*, London, B. T. Batsford, p. 158 stated that 'the metamorphosis of the Buttes-Chaumont was not less remarkable' than the better known Bois de Boulogne; von Joest, Thomas (1991). 'Haussmann's Paris: A Green Metropolis?' in Teyssot, Georges and Mosser, Monique (Editors) (1991). *The History of Garden Design*. London, Thames & Hudson, p. 392 described it as 'certainly the finest and most exciting . . . of all the parks within the city walls'.

95 Vernes, Michel (1989). 'Au Jardin comme à la Ville: 1855–1914 – le Style Municipal' in *Parcs & Promenades de Paris*. Paris, Demi-Cercle, p. 15 noted that London's parks and squares were a strong influence on Napoléon III's plans for parks in Paris – but that they did not form a model for the 'system' put in place by Alphand; Loyer, François (1989). 'Le Paris d'Haussmann' in Cohen, Jean-Louis and Fortier, Bruno (Exhibition Directors), *Paris: La Ville et ses Projets*. Paris, Babylone/Pavillon de l'Arsenal, p. 150 noted that when Napoléon III sent for Haussmann to undertake the transformation of the capital, everything was in place for the project to be realized; response of 28 September 1987 to author's questionnaire from Direction des Parcs, Jardins et Éspaces Verts, Ville de Paris; *Hôtel de Ville Communiqués Conférence de presse du 05 Novembre 1999: La restauration du parc des Buttes-Chaumont* from website *www.paris-france.org* (accessed 11 January 2000) noted that the park was 'born from the will of Napoléon III'.

96 Chadwick, George F. (1966). *The Park and the Town*. London, Architectural Press, p. 152; Russell, John (1960), op. cit., p. 155 noted that the population of Paris 'nearly doubled in the first thirteen years of Haussmann's prefecture – from 1853 to 1866'; Marceca, Maria Luisa (1981). 'Reservoir, circulation, residue: JCA Alphand, Technological Beauty and the Green City' in *Lotus International*, No. 30, p. 61.

97 Robinson, William (1883), op. cit., p. 66; Alphand, A. (1867–73). *Les Promenades de Paris*. Paris, J. Rothschild; Princeton, Princeton Architectural Press (1984 edition), pp. 200–3; response of 28 September 1987 to author's questionnaire; *Hôtel de Ville Communiqués Conférence de press du 05 Novembre 1999*, op. cit.

98 Vernes, Michel (1989), op. cit., p. 15. Saint-Simon (1760–1825) was a French social reformer and philosopher who argued that society should be organized by leaders of industry and given spiritual direction by scientists; Fleming, John; Honour, Hugh and Pevsner, Nikolaus (1999). *The Penguin Dictionary of Architecture and Landscape Architecture* (fifth edition). Harmondsworth, Penguin, p. 254; Russell, John., op. cit., pp. 152–4 noted that Haussmann 'had broken the back of socialism in the Var, and of Republicanism in the region around Auxerre. Even the working-class centre of Ancy-le-Franc bowed to his will . . .'.

99 von Joest, Thomas (1991), op. cit., p. 390; Garvin, Alexander (1996). *The American City – What Works, What Doesn't*. New York, McGraw-Hill, p. 429 noted that 'before Haussmann began his work only one of every five buildings was supplied with running water, fewer than 150 pumped it above ground level, and none could depend on a steady supply of potable water'; Russell, John (1960), op. cit., p. 155 noted that 1253 registered water carriers were still working in 1860; Vernes, Michel (1989), op. cit., p. 15 noted that all streets wider than 26 metres were planted with rows of trees; Chadwick, George F. (1966), op. cit., p. 152; Loyer, François (1989), op. cit., pp. 144, 152.

100 Russell, John (1960), op. cit., pp. 162–3; Marceca, Maria Luisa (1981), p. 66; Vernes, Michel (1989), op. cit., p. 16.

101 Vernes, Michel (1984). 'Cities and Parks in Opposition' in *Architectural Review*, Volume 175, No. 1048, p. 59/6; von Joest, Thomas (1991), op. cit., p. 397; Marceca, Maria Luisa (1981), op. cit., p. 63; Merivale, John (1978). 'Charles-Adolphe Alphand and the Parks of Paris' in *Landscape Design*, Number 123, p. 32; Vernes, Michel (1989), op. cit., p. 16.

102 Vernes, Michel (1989), ibid., p. 15; von Joest, Thomas (1991), op. cit., pp. 392, 397.

103 Vernes, Michel (1989), ibid., pp. 15–17.

104 Marceca, Maria Luisa (1981), op. cit., p. 59; Tschumi, Bernard (1987). *Cinégram Folie: Le Parc de la Villette*. Princeton, Princeton Architectural Press, p. 1; and Meyer, Elizabeth K. (1991). 'The Public Park as Avante-garde (Landscape) Architecture: A Comparative Interpretation of Two Parisian Parks, Parc de la Villette (1983–1990) and Parc des Buttes-Chaumont (1864–1867)' in *Landscape Journal*, Volume 10, Number 1, p. 21. Tschumi's comments might have applied to Olmsted–Vaux parks in North America but were not applicable to Buttes-Chaumont.

105 Vernes, Michel (1989), op. cit., pp. 15–17.

106 Merivale, John (1978), op. cit., p. 34.

107 Chadwick, George (1966), op. cit., p. 151 noted this style of planting and (on p. 161) Olmsted's view of it.

108 Robinson, William (1883), op. cit., p. 70; Marceca, Maria Luisa (1981), op. cit., p. 61; Meyer, Elizabeth K. (1991), op. cit., p. 20. The park restoration programme announced in November 1999 envisaged the barring of private vehicles from the park.

109 Noted at author's meeting with Marie-Joseph Gambard and Sophie Dobler of the project section of the *Direction des Parcs, Jardins et Éspaces Verts* of the City of Paris on 14 June 1999.

8 PARC DE LA VILLETTE, PARIS

110 Barzilay, Marianne, Hayward Catherine and Lombard-Valentino, Lucette (1984). *L'Invention du Parc*. Paris, Graphite/Établissement Public du Parc de la Villette (EEPV), p. 6. The EEPV registered 805 expressions of interest from forty-one countries; Tschumi, Bernard (1987). *Cinégram Folie: Le Parc de la Villette*. Princeton, Princeton Architectural Press contained Tschumi's explanation of the design. Parts of this book were reproduced in revised form as 'Abstract Mediation and Strategy' in Tschumi, Bernard (1996). *Architecture and Disjunction*. Cambridge, MA, MIT Press; Lechte, John, '(Not) Belonging in Postmodern Space' in Watson, Sophie and Gibson, Katherine (Editors) (1995). *Postmodern Cities and Spaces*. Oxford, Blackwell, p. 109 noted that Tschumi's 'key terms are "superimposition", "dissociation" and "dispersion", rather than unity or harmony. Influenced by Derrida and Joyce, as well as by Calvino, Bataille, Kafka and Poe, Tschumi aimed . . . to emphasise the heterogeneous non-relation between elements. Through programmatic disjunctions at the planning stage, Tschumi breaks up the surface . . . into fragments' and reassembles them 'according to a principle selected at random'; Tschumi, Bernard (1987), op. cit., p. VII stated that the 'La Villette project . . . attempts to dislocate and de-regulate meaning, rejecting the "symbolic" repertory of architecture as a refuge of humanist thought. For today the term "park" (like "architecture", "science" or "literature") has lost its universal meaning; it no longer refers to a fixed absolute, nor to an ideal'. On p. VIII he continued 'most importantly, the Park calls into question the fundamental or primary signified of architecture – its tendency (as Derrida remarks in *La Case Vide*) to be "*in service*, and *at service*," obeying an economy of meaning premised on functional use'.

111 Ibid., p. 1; p. VII stated that the project 'subverts a number of ideals that were sacrosanct to the Modern period and, in this manner, it can be allied to a specific vision of postmodernity'; Meyer, Elizabeth K. (1991). 'The Public Park as Avante-garde (Landscape) Architecture: A Comparative Interpretation of Two Parisian Parks, Parc de la Villette (1983–1990) and Parc des Buttes-Chaumont (1864–1867)' in *Landscape Journal*, Volume 10, Number 1, p. 26 stated that Tschumi's design 'is not an avant-garde piece of landscape design'. She continued that 'it may expand architecture's boundaries to include the park, but it does not expand the boundaries of landscape design. Nonetheless, La Villette is an important criticism of architecture and landscape architecture that assumes an a priori, ideal order of hierarchical parts. La Villette is also a substantial critique of landscape design that is wallowing in kitsch and in the image of the Picturesque'; Holden, Robert (1983). 'An Urban Park for the Twenty-first Century' in *Landscape Architecture*, Volume 73, No. 4, p. 66 declared a one-stage competition 'for a park and brief so complex' as a 'daft idea'; Hunt, John Dixon (1992). *Gardens and the Picturesque: Studies in the History of Landscape Architecture*. Cambridge, MA, MIT Press, p. 299 described Chemetoff's bamboo grove as 'the one successful moment in the otherwise silly Parc de la Villette'; Jellicoe, Geoffrey (1983). 'Park Futures' in *Architects' Journal*, Volume 178, Nos 51 and 52, p. 56. Similarly, Ralph Neale noted in 'The Significance of Parc de la Villette', the editorial to *Landscape Australia*, No. 4/1991, Melbourne, p. 312 that 'had such a plan been submitted as a proposal for a city park by a third year landscape architecture student in Australia, ignoring as it does historical context, showing no respect for topographical features, deaf to the effects of traffic noise and disregarding the needs of the local people . . . the student would have received very poor marks indeed'; Gough, Piers (1989). 'Gough in Paris' in *Architects' Journal*, Volume 192, No. 2, p. 28.

112 Barzilay, Marianne, Hayward Catherine and Lombard-Valentino, Lucette (1984), op. cit., pp. 11–13, 246–7; Baljon, Lodewijk (1992). *Designing Parks*. Woodbridge, Garden Art and Amsterdam, Architectura & Natura, pp. 25–30; Cadoret, Anne-Valérie and Lagrange, Florence (Editors) (1996). *Guides Gallimard Paris La Villette*. Paris, Nouveaux-Loisirs, pp. 4–7.

113 Baljon, Lodewijk (1992), ibid., p. 29; *Le Site de la Villette: Repères Chronologiques 1970–1997* provided by the Établissement Public du Parc et de la Grande Halle de la Villette (EPPGHV).

114 Ibid., p. 32.

115 Tschumi, Bernard (1987). op. cit., pp. 4, VII, 1; Meyer, Elizabeth (1991), op. cit., p. 24.

116 Sudjic, Deyan (1992). *The 100 Mile City*. London, André Deutsch, pp. 77–80; Bailly, Jean-Christophe. 'Paris, Memory in Progress' in Cohen, Jean-Louis and Fortier, Bruno (1989) (Exhibition Directors), *Paris: La Ville et ses Projets*. Paris, Babylone/Pavillon de l'Arsenal, p. 27.

117 Tschumi, Bernard (1987), op. cit., p. VII; p. 1 contained comments such as 'the park forms part of the vision of the city'. This seems to be a milder version of Galen Cranz's concluding statement in *The Politics of Park Design* (1982) that 'Those with an interest in the character of urban life should seize on parks as one of the vehicles for the realization of their particular visions, and debate about parks should revolve around those visions'. Cranz was, of course, a member of Tschumi's team for the first stage of the competition. Similarly, Tschumi only addressed Olmsted's nineteenth-century vision of the urban park in a brief and dismissive way. He did not take the opportunity to compare and contrast his vision for the next century with Olmsted's vision for the preceding century; Girot, Christophe (1996). 'Some Thoughts about Landscape Education at Versailles' in Goldhoorn, Bart (Editor). *Schools of Architecture*. Rotterdam, NAi, pp. 28–9; Jellicoe, Geoffrey and Jellicoe, Susan (1975). *The Landscape of Man* (third edition). London, Thames & Hudson, p. 373 noted that the park 'will only properly be comprehended in reality after some twenty years'.

118 Baljon, Lodewijk (1992), op. cit., p. 30; Tiévant, Sophie (December 1996). *Pratique et Image du Site de la Villette* [Use and Image of the Site of la Villette]. Paris, Centre d'Étude et de Récherche sur les Pratiques de l'Éspace (CEPRE), p. 48.

119 Baljon, Lodewijk (1992), op. cit., pp. 37–47; Barzilay, Marianne, Hayward Catherine and Lombard-Valentino, Lucette (1984), op. cit., p. 240.

120 Tschumi, Bernard (1996), op. cit., pp. 174, 179, 12, IV, 5.

121 This matches the observation of Peter Latz that 'nowadays everyone goes alone to urban parks' (see Chapter 14 'Landschaftspark, Duisburg-Nord').

122 Jellicoe, Geoffrey (1983), op. cit., p. 59; address by Marc Treib to the 'Thinking about Landscape: Interdisciplinary Contributions of the 1990s' Conference at the Graduate School of Design, Harvard University on 9–10 April 1999.

123 Lyall, Sutherland (1991). *Designing the New Landscape*. London, Thames & Hudson, pp. 118–21; Treib, Marc (1995). 'Must Landscapes Mean? Approaches to Significance in Recent Landscape Architecture' in *Landscape Journal*, Volume 14, Number 1, pp. 47–62; Berrizbeitia, Anita and Pollak, Linda (1999). *Inside Outside: Between Architecture and Landscape*. Gloucester, MA, Rockport, p. 62.

124 Cadoret, Anne-Valérie and Lagrange, Florence (Editors) (1996). *Guide Gallimard to la Villette*, p. 8.

125 Tiévant, Sophie (1996), op. cit., pp. 10, 22, 44–5, 50.

126 Treib, Marc (1995), op. cit., summarized this dichotomy in his characteristically wry way: 'the ideas used to conceive the park are rich and evocative; the experience on site is limited and spatially uninteresting'. This view was amplified in a lecture (op. cit., 9 April 1999) in which he commended the fascination of the story but characterized the park as a 'dull' place full of 'zippy' metal; Meyer, Elizabeth K. (1991), op. cit., p. 26; Tschumi, Bernard (1996), op. cit., p. 201.

127 Baljon, Lodewijk (1992), op. cit., p. 212; Barzilay, Marianne, Hayward Catherine and Lombard-Valentino, Lucette (1984), op. cit., p. 19.

9 PARQUE DE MARÍA LUISA, SEVILLE

128 Imbert, Dorothée (1993). *The Modernist Garden in France*. New Haven and London, Yale University Press, p. 213 noted that the exposition changed from being Hispano-American to Ibero-American in 1922 when it was agreed that Portugal would also participate in the event.

129 García-Martin, Manuel (1992). *El Parque de María Luisa de Sevilla*. Barcelona, Gas Natural SDG, pp. 38, 37; although much of Spain suffered economic decline in the eighteenth and nineteenth centuries and industrialization came later than in much of the rest of Europe, urban populations still grew relatively quickly. It was noted on p. 37 that by 1869 Seville had a population of 120,000; the Parque del Retiro in Madrid, for instance, was opened for public access when Isabella II lost her throne in 1868 – but with less redesign than the Parque de María Luisa.

130 Ibid., p. 38.

131 Baird, David, Symington, Michael and Tisdall, Nigel (1999). *Eyewitness Travel Guide to Seville and Andalusia*. London, Dorling Kindersly, pp. 39–51.

132 García-Martin, Manuel (1992), op. cit., p. 34; Fleming, John, Honour, Hugh and Pevsner, Nikolaus (1999). *The Penguin Dictionary of Architecture and Landscape Architecture* (fifth edition). Harmondsworth, Penguin, p. 191.

133 Figure given at author's meeting with José Elías Bonells of the Servicio de Parques y Jardines of the Ayuntamiento de Sevilla on 31 May 1999; Gimeno, José Antonio Mejías, Camacho, Cristina Andrés and Martin, Angel (1999). *Guia de los Parques y Jardines de Sevilla*. Seville, Ayuntamiento de Sevilla, pp. 35–40 noted that Lecolant designed the Monte Gurugu and the Duck Island; Lejeune, Jean-François and Gelabert-Navia, José (fall 1991). 'Jean-Claude Nicolas Forestier: The City as Landscape' in *The New City Foundations*, University of Miami School of Architecture, p. 53 also noted the involvement of Lecolant.

134 García-Martin, Manuel (1992), op. cit., pp. 32–3; Imbert, Dorothée (1993), op. cit., pp. 17–19; Forestier, J. C. N. (1924). *Gardens: A Notebook of Plans and Sketches*, translated from the French by Fox, Helen Morgenthau. New York, Charles Scribner's Sons, pp. 185–6; García-Martin, Manuel (1992), op. cit., pp. 55–7; ibid., p. 47 quoted from a report in the newspaper *El Liberal* of 27 January 1911; Imbert, Dorothée (1993), op. cit., p. 17 gave the date of Forestier's appointment as 1 April 1911.

135 Assassin, Sylvie (1992). *Séville: l'exposition ibéro-américaine 1929–30*. Paris, Institut Français d'Architecture/NORMA – chronology; Goode, Patrick and Lancaster, Michael (1986). *The Oxford Companion to Gardens*, Oxford, Oxford University Press, p. 195; and Fleming, John; Honour, Hugh and Pevsner, Nikolaus (1999), op. cit., p. 198; Imbert, Dorothée (1993), ibid., p. 211 noted that Forestier had originally intended to join the navy but suffered paralysis of the right arm as a result of a horse-riding accident.

136 García-Martin, Manuel (1992), op. cit., p. 48 quoted him as being regarded as 'small in stature and stout, with a greying beard – but a vivacious appearance'; Casa Valdés, Marquesa de (1973). *Spanish Gardens – English Language Edition 1987*. London, Antique Collector's Club, p. 251; Lejeune, Jean-François and Gelabert-Navia, José (1991), op. cit., p. 58.

137 Imbert, Dorothée (1993), op. cit., pp. 12, 15.

138 Gromort, Georges (1953). *L'Art des Jardins: Volume II – Deuxième Édition*. Paris, Vincent, Fréal & Cie, p. 140; Casa Valdés, Marquesa de (1973). *Spanish Gardens – English Language Edition 1987*. London, Antique Collector's Club, p. 250; Forestier, J. C. N. (1924), op. cit., p. vi.

139 Gimeno, José Antonio Mejías, Camacho, Cristina Andrés and Martin, Angel (1999), op. cit., pp. 35–41.

140 Chadwick, George F. (1966). *The Park and the Town*. London, Architectural Press, p. 301; Imbert, Dorothée (1993), op. cit., p. 25.

10 BIRKENHEAD PARK, MERSEYSIDE

141 Noted at author's meeting with Jim Lester of the Leisure Services and Tourism Department of the Metropolitan Borough of Wirral on 30 July 1999 that the area has 'European Priority 1 Status'.

142 Goode, Patrick and Lancaster, Michael (1986). *The Oxford Companion to Gardens*. Oxford, Oxford University Press, p. 56 suggested that Olmsted 'reproduced its circulation system in a modified form at Central Park'; Chadwick, George F. (1966). *The Park and the Town*. London, Architectural Press, pp. 121–2 noted that Victoria Park in the East End of London was designated in 1842 as a public park at the centre of a state-financed, profit-oriented, residential development but that enclosure of the park did not begin until 1844; Smith, Allan (1983). 'Paxton's Park' in *Architects' Journal*, Volume 178, Nos 51 and 52, p. 50.

143 Thornton, Clifford E. (1983). *The People's Garden: A History of Birkenhead Park*. Metropolitan Borough of Wirral, Department of Leisure Services and Tourism, Libraries and Arts, p. 2; Liverpool, by all accounts, had already rejected the idea of a park there on the grounds that the city had expanded rapidly and even marginal land had become too expensive; Chadwick, George F. (1966), op. cit., p. 68; and Newton, Norman T. (1971). *Design on the Land: The Development of Landscape Architecture*. Cambridge, MA, Belknap, p. 227 both cited this as the Third Birkenhead Improvement Act. Thornton, Clifford E. (1983), op. cit., p. 4 referred to it as the Second Birkenhead Improvement Act.

144 Goode, Patrick and Lancaster, Michael (1986), op. cit., p. 55; Metropolitan Borough of Wirral (1991). *Birkenhead Park Management Plan*. Department of Leisure Services and Tourism, p. 7; Parklands Consortium (1999). *Birkenhead People's Park Restoration and Management Plan: Volume I – Survey and Analysis*. Metropolitan Borough of Wirral, p. 8; Thornton, Clifford E. (1983), op. cit., p. 5 quoting from a letter contained in the Markham Papers, Chatsworth; Parklands Consortium (1999), op. cit., pp. 29, 14.

145 Ibid., pp. 19–20.

146 Ibid., pp. 21–2; Chadwick, George F. (1966), op. cit., pp. 66–94; Goode, Patrick and Lancaster, Michael (1986), op. cit., p. 426; Smith, Allan (1983), op. cit., p. 50 noted that railways were 'a popular activity, not an elitist one'; Parklands Consortium (1999), op. cit., p. 2; Fleming, John; Honour, Hugh and Pevsner, Nikolaus (1999). *The Penguin Dictionary of Architecture and Landscape Architecture* (fifth edition). Harmondsworth, Penguin, p. 427.

147 Smith, Allan (1983), ibid., p. 50. In an exchange of faxes on 4 April 2000 the Royal Institute of British Architects (RIBA) confirmed that the Institute was formed in 1834 but that it was not until May 1882 that candidates for Associateship had to have passed the 'RIBA Obligatory Examination'; Parklands Consortium (1999), op. cit., p. 18; and Fleming, John, Honour, Hugh and Pevsner, Nikolaus (1999), ibid., p. 427.

148 Paragraph based on Thornton, Clifford E. (1983), op. cit., p. 23; and Parklands Consortium (1999), op. cit., pp. 12–13.

149 Ibid., p. 6 noted that land sales were held in 1845, 1859 and 1861 – and that by 1861 less than forty houses had been built; chronologies for the park in Thornton, Clifford E. (1983), ibid., pp. 15–19; Metropolitan Borough of Wirral (1991), op. cit., pp. 9–11; and Parklands Consortium (1999), op. cit., pp. 2–46 noted the erection and removal of two bandstands in the lower park, the erection and removal after bomb damage in the Second World War of a Palm House in the upper park, and the planting in 1952 of trees along the Coronation Walk in the southeast of the lower park; Beckett, Penny and Dempster, Paul (1989). 'Birkenhead Park' in *Landscape Design*, No. 185, pp. 24–7 gave a lucid account of the forces that had shaped the park to that date. Compulsory Competitive Tendering (CCT) for the provision of government services was instituted throughout Britain in the early 1990s. This led, according to park managers, to 'up to 50 per cent being sucked out of the parks budget' for the Borough of Wirral.

150 Ibid., p. 24; noted at author's meeting with Jim Lester on 30 July 1999, op. cit.; Jacobs, Jane (1961). *The Death and Life of Great American Cities*. New York, Vintage, p. 98.

151 Chadwick, George F. (1966), op. cit., pp. 68, 71, 91; Smith, Allan (1983), op. cit., p. 50; Parklands Consortium (1999), op. cit., pp. 10–11, 25. There is, of course, a corollary argument that this is outdated jingoistic nonsense about an era that did not have, for instance, universal suffrage; ibid., pp. 7–12 noted that Paxton required the styles for the design of the houses 'to be sourced from the history and materials of Britain (mainly England) itself'; Newton, Norman T. (1971), op. cit., pp. 229–30.

152 Ibid., pp. 229–30; Olmsted, Frederick Law

(1859). *Walks and Talks of an American Farmer in England*. Ann Arbor, University of Michigan Press (1967 edition). p. 53; Chadwick, George F. (1966), op. cit., p. 69.

153 Parklands Consortium (1999), op. cit., p. 33 noted that 'there was great pressure on Paxton and Kemp to achieve a mature layout in the park very quickly'.

154 Beveridge, Charles E. and Hoffman, Carolyn F. (Editors) (1997). *The Papers of Frederick Law Olmsted: Supplementary Series, Volume 1 – Writings on Public Parks, Parkways, and Park Systems*. Baltimore, Johns Hopkins University Press, p. 70.

155 Parklands Consortium (1999), op. cit., p. 16; Metropolitan Borough of Wirral (1991), op. cit., pp. 51–2.

156 Noted at author's meeting with Jim Lester on 30 July 1999, op. cit.; Beckett, Penny and Dempster, Paul (1989), op. cit., p. 27.

157 North West Tourist Board (November 1992). *Visitor Survey 1992*.

158 Parklands Consortium (1999). *Birkenhead People's Park Restoration and Management Plan: Volume II – Recommendations*. Metropolitan Borough of Wirral, p. 1.

159 Noted at author's meeting with Jim Lester on 30 July 1999, op. cit.

160 Newton, Norman T. (1971), op. cit., p. 232; Chadwick, George F. (1966), op. cit., p. 70.

11 REGENT'S PARK, LONDON

161 As Prince of Wales, George had ordered the remodelling in 1783 of Carlton House, adjacent to St James's Park, as his London residence. As Prince Regent he had developed the Royal Pavilion in Brighton, largely designed by Nash, and a series of adjacent terraces, squares and crescents. As King George IV, he went on to order the demolition of Carlton House in 1825 and the rebuilding of Buckingham House; Summerson, John (1980). *The Life and Work of John Nash*. Cambridge, MA, MIT Press, p. 166 noted that Nash himself used this description of George IV in 1828; 104 hectares of park are freely open to the public and 3 hectares are allocated to management and maintenance functions; Chadwick, George F. (1966). *The Park and the Town*. London, Architectural Press, p. 31; Regent's Park was not the first Royal Park to be open to the public. Hyde Park had been opened by King Charles I (reigned 1625–49) in about 1635.

162 Regency architecture in Britain refers to the style of building design from 1811 to 1820 when George, Prince of Wales was Prince Regent before becoming King George IV. In France, Regency architecture refers to the preiod from 1715 to 1723 during the reign of Louis XV when Philip, Duke of Orleans was Regent.

163 A circle, of course, provides the highest ratio of land area to perimeter of any geometric form (a little over 25% more than a square) and is therefore the most cost-efficient land area to enclose.

164 Summerson, John (1980), op. cit., p. 60.

165 Ibid., p. 61.

166 Saunders, Ann (1969). *Regent's Park*. New York, Augustus M. Kelley, p. 89; Summerson, John (1980), ibid., pp. 65, 70.

167 The canal, eventually constructed and named the Regent's Canal, was being mooted as a link between the Grand Union Canal to the west and the London docks to the east. Its construction was proposed as a means of avoiding growing congestion on the streets of London. Nash saw it as a visual bonus to his scheme; Saunders, Ann (1969), ibid., p. 203.

168 Summerson, John (1980), op. cit., p. 66; Saunders, Ann (1969), op. cit., p. 72 suggested that Nash adopted this from White's proposals without giving him any credit. This is not out of character – but could also have been inspired by his work with Humphry Repton (whose son George Stanley was still working with Nash).

169 Chadwick, George F. (1966), op. cit., pp. 20–34; and Goode, Patrick and Lancaster, Michael (1986). *The Oxford Companion to Gardens*. Oxford, Oxford University Press, pp. 467–9; Summerson, John (1980), ibid., p. 36 noted that this raised Nash's fees to these clients to 7 per cent of the cost of the works (4.5 per cent for him and 2.5 per cent for Repton) compared with Nash's normal rates of 4.5 or 5.0 per cent.

170 Ibid., p. 36; Chadwick, George F. (1966), op. cit., p. 29; Repton's theories of landscape design were expressed in, for example, *Sketches and Hints on Landscape Gardening* (1795) and *Theory and Practice of Landscape Gardening* (1803); his essay *An Inquiry into the Changes in Taste in Landscape Gardening* (1806) and his last published work *Fragments on the Theory and Practice of Landscape Gardening* (1816). Repton's *Sources of Pleasure in Landscape Gardening*, Chapter IX of *Sketches and Hints*, included a timeless summary of the essence of his approach. He presented this under the headings 'congruity; unity; order; symmetry; picturesque effect; intricacy; simplicity; variety; novelty; contrast; continuity; association; grandeur; appropriation; animation; and the seasons and times of day'.

171 The Whigs (a title derived from the nickname for a group of Presbyterian alleged terrorists from south-west Scotland) was a generally liberal eighteenth and early nineteenth century English political group that sought to limit the power of the monarchy; Burke quoted in White R. J. (1967). *A Short History of England*. Cambridge, Cambridge University Press, p. 224.

172 Hunt, John Dixon (1992). *Gardens and the Picturesque*. Cambridge, MA, MIT Press, p. 186; and Chadwick, George F. (1966), op. cit., p. 21 quoted from Uvedale Price's *Essays on the Picturesque* (1794), that 'the study of pictures can only produce any real advantage if we use it as a school in which we may learn to enlarge, correct, and refine our views of Nature and by that route become good judges of scenery'; Repton, Humphry (1795). *Sketches and Hints on Landscape Gardening* and *Theory and Practice of Landscape Gardening* in Nolen, John. Boston, Riverside (1907 edition), op. cit., p. 36.

173 Repton, Humphry (1803). *Theory and Practice of Landscape Gardening* in Nolen, John, ibid., p. 79; Chadwick, George F. (1966), ibid., pp. 22, 33; Hunt, John Dixon (1992), op. cit., p. 152; Jellicoe, G. A. (1970). *Studies in Landscape Design*, Volume 3. London, Oxford University Press, p. 71.

174 Slavid, Ruth (1999). 'Staging Open Air's Renewal' in *Architects' Journal*, Volume 210, No. 8, p. 8.

175 Summerson, John (1980), op. cit., pp. 116–17 quoted from 2nd Report of the Commissioners of Woods, Forests and Land Revenues (1813); Jacobs, Jane (1961). *The Death and Life of Great American Cities*. New York, Random House, p. 95.

176 Summerson, John (1980), ibid., p. 66; Chadwick, George F. (1966), p. 31.

177 In the Royal Parks Review Group report on Regent Park (April 1993) architect Terry Farrell recommended that a pedestrian link should be created on the line of Portland Place through the centre of Park Square to Avenue Gardens and the Broad Walk.

178 Darley, Gillian (1985). 'The Plight of the Royals' in *Architects' Journal*, Volume 182, No. 50, pp. 22–5.

179 They also close the road gates to the park at midnight and re-open them at 7.00 a.m. each day.

180 Reported in *Landscape Design* (1999), No. 278, p. 9; and author's telephone conversation with Jenny Adams, Head of Inner Royal Parks on 23 July 1999.

181 Repton, Humphry (1803), op. cit., p. 100.

182 The London Zoo, like many others around the world, is now playing an increasingly significant role in the conservation as well as the display of rare and exotic animal species.

12 GRANT PARK, CHICAGO

183 Sniderman, Julia (October 1994) noted at the *City Parks 2000* Conference in Glasgow, Scotland, that 24 miles (38 kilometres) of the 32 miles (51 kilometres) of Lake Michigan shoreline in Chicago were open parkland.

184 Wille, Lois (1991). *Forever Open, Clear and Free: The Struggle for Chicago's Lakefront* (second edition). Chicago, University of Chicago Press, p. 23 quoted these words as being written on a map of the Chicago lakefront in 1836 by the Commissioners from the State of Illinois who were selling 'unsettled areas to pay for a new shipping canal'. The *National Register of Historic Places Form for Grant Park* quoted from Fink, Theodore J. (1979) in *Grant Park Tomorrow, Future of Chicago's Front Yard* (Chicago, Open Lands Project), p. 17 that the words were 'public ground to remain free of buildings'.

185 Wille, Lois (1991), op. cit., pp. 4–70 and Chicago Park District documents including *Grant Park Design Guidelines* (1992); *National Register of Historic Places Form for Grant Park* (1992); *Cityspace: An Open Space Plan for Chicago* (1998); *Welcome to Grant Park* (1999) and *Request for Professional Planning*

Services for the Grant Park Framework Plan (2000).

186 The perceived danger to settlers had virtually disappeared and the land was to be sold by the federal government; Wille, Lois (1991), ibid., p. 30.

187 Chicago Park District (1992). *Grant Park Design Guidelines*, p. 9.

188 The Supreme Court ruled in 1892 that it did not have the right to grant the IC title because a) the land had been confirmed to be public held free of development in 1861 and b) the land had been transferred to the City of Chicago in 1863.

189 Wille, Lois (1991), op. cit., pp. 52–4 noted that 'in the first 20 years after the fire, the three park commissions spent $24,000,000 . . . on a system of eight big parks, twenty-nine little ones and 35 miles of broad boulevards'.

190 Ibid., pp. 71–81; Chicago Park District's *Grant Park Design Guidelines* (1992), pp. 10–12; and *National Register of Historic Places Form for Grant Park* (1992), pp. 27–30.

191 Ward had already agreed to construction of the Art Institute.

192 Wille, Lois (1991), op. cit., p. 81 from Ward's sole interview with the *Chicago Tribune*.

193 Fleming, John; Honour, Hugh and Pevsner, Nikolaus (1999). *The Penguin Dictionary of Landscape Architecture* (fifth edition). Harmondsworth, Penguin, pp. 80, 489; Wille, Lois (1991), op. cit., p. 84 noted that Burnham undertook most of his planning studies – including work on the McMillan Plan for Washington (1901–02), Cleveland (1903), Manila (1905) and San Francisco (1905–06) – for no fee . . . because he could afford to; and as a way to generate architectural work; Chicago Park District (1992). *Grant Park Design Guidelines*, p. 11.

194 Wille, Lois (1991), op. cit., p. 84; Hasbrouk, Wilbert R. (1970). *Plan of Chicago by Daniel H. Burnham and Edward H. Bennett*. reprint New York, Da Capo, Introduction, p. VI.

195 Ibid., p. V quoted this statement and noted that it was from 'an otherwise long forgotten speech; Garvin, Alexander (1996). *The American City – What Works, What Doesn't*. New York, McGraw-Hill, p. 428 stated that it was quoted in a 1918 Christmas card from Willis Polk to Edward Bennett as being a statement from 1907; Hasbrouk, Wilbert R. (1970), op. cit., p. 118 stated that 'the intellectual life of the city will be stimulated by institutions grouped in Grant Park; and in the center of all the varied activities of Chicago will rise the towering dome of the civic center, vivifying and unifying the entire composition'; Garvin, Alexander (1996), ibid., p. 429 noted that 'the single most important contribution . . . came from a non-participant: Baron Georges-Eugène Haussmann' and Guinther, John (1996). *Direction of Cities*. Harmondsworth, Penguin, p. 54 noted that 'Burnham was more directly influenced by . . . Haussmann' than by the City Beautiful Movement; Wilson, William H. (1989). *The City Beautiful Movement*. Baltimore, Johns Hopkins University Press (paperback edition 1994), pp. 281–3; Chadwick, George F. (1966).

The Park and the Town. London, Architectural Press, p. 216; Hasbrouk, Wilbert R. (1970), ibid., Introduction, p. VIII.

196 Chicago Park District (1992). *National Register of Historic Places Form for Grant Park*, p. 36.

197 Wolfe, Gerard R. (1996). *Chicago in and Around the Loop*. New York, McGraw-Hill, p. 102; Chicago Park District (1999). *Welcome to Grant Park* (unpaginated).

198 Chicago Park District's *National Register of Historic Places Form for Grant Park* (1992), pp. 39–42; *Grant Park Design Guidelines* (1992), p. 16.

199 Wolfe, Gerard R. (1996), op. cit., p. 296; Chicago Park District (1992). *Grant Park Design Guidelines*, p. 18.

200 Bennett, Paul (1999). 'The *Un* Motor City' in *Landscape Architecture*, Volume 89, No. 3, pp. 68–75, 100–2 described establishment of the Museum Campus; the Millennium Park attracted Gehry as an opportunity to build his first bridge – spanning from there to the Bicentennial Plaza.

201 Hasbrouk, Wilbert R. (1970), op. cit., *Plan of Chicago*, p. 114 stated that 'Congress Street stands in such relations to Grant Park that its use as a central axis of the city allows park and avenue to sustain reciprocal relations . . .'; Hinchliff, William B. in Sinkevitch, Alice (Editor) (1993). *AIA Guide to Chicago*. San Diego, Harcourt Brace, p. 98; noted at author's meeting on 14 April 2000 with Ed Uhlir, Project Director for Millennium Park, that the park had been instrumental in attracting conversions of overlooking buildings to condominiums – particularly on its south-west side; Chicago Park District (1998). *Cityspace: An Open Space Plan for Chicago*, p. 85.

202 Chicago Park District (1992). *National Register of Historic Places Form for Grant Park*, p. 13.

203 Chicago Park District (1992). *Grant Park Design Guidelines*, pp. 10–11, 29; Chicago Park District (1992). *National Register of Historic Places Form for Grant Park*, p. 36.

204 Chicago Park District (1992). *Grant Park Design Guidelines*, p. 31; Hutchinson Field was built three blocks wide – as Bennett intended – whereas Butler Field is only two blocks wide; path layouts that pay no attention to desire lines and the use of fences rather than hedges add to the disappointment of the Bicentennial Plaza – particularly in a city that is renowned for its construction detailing.

205 Noted at author's meeting with John Henderson, Research and Policy Manager with Chicago Park District on 14 April 2000 that the State Legislature had money set aside for the construction of an underpass from Buckingham Fountain to the lakefront; Kamin, Blair (29 October 1998). 'Grant Park's Double Life' in the *Chicago Tribune* noted that Grant Park had 1.5 benches per acre compared with 5.3 per acre in Central Park, New York.

206 Wille, Lois (1991), op. cit., pp. 99–148 gave an account of the management of the Park District from 1934 to 1970; Ward Thompson, Catharine (1998). 'Historic Parks and Contemporary Needs' in *Landscape Journal*, Volume

17, Number 1, p. 5; Friends of the Parks (who are 'not necessarily Friends of the Park District') are represented at all Board Meetings and regularly get to speak to the press before the Board does.

207 Noted at author's meetings with John Henderson and Ed Uhlir on 14 April 2000; reported comments in the *Chicago Tribune* of 29 January 1999.

208 Chicago Park District (1992). *Grant Park Design Guidelines*, p. ii.

209 Garvin, Alexander (1996), op. cit., p. 52.

13 STADTPARK, HAMBURG

210 De Michelis, Marco. 'The Green Revolution: Leberecht Migge and the Reform of the Garden in Modernist Germany' in Teyssot, Georges and Mosser, Monique (Editors) (1991). *The History of Garden Design*. London, Thames & Hudson, p. 409 in which De Michelis quoted from Ludwig Lesser, founder of the Deutscher Volksparkbund (German Volkspark Alliance) in 'Die Volksparks der Zukunft (Vortrag von L. Lesser)' in *der Städtebau*, No. 9 (1912), p. 60.

211 Sperber's first name is variously given as Fritz, Freidrich and Alfred. Fritz – the name given in Goecke, Michael (August 1980), *70 Jahre Hamburger Stadtpark* in an offprint of *Das Gärtenamt*, No. 29, Patzer, Hannover, pp. 543–73 is used here; there are larger areas of public woodland on the fringes of the city and the nearby Ohlsdorf Cemetery is more than twice the size of the Stadtpark. The Aussenalster – between the Stadtpark and the city centre to the south – is a water body of about 200 hectares used largely for recreational sailing and with parkland on its shores; the *Porträt* of Alfred Lichtwark in *Gärten & Landschaft*, February 1996, p. 40 gave the height of the water tower as 38 metres. Venier, Arnalda (1981) in 'Milk, Meadow, Water, Brick: Story of the Hamburg Stadtpark' in *Lotus International*, No. 30, p. 101 gave the height as 50 metres. Whichever, the structure is sufficiently high that it has accommodated a planetarium since 1929; Grout, Catherine (June 1997). 'Der Stadtpark als politisches Symbol/The City Park as Political Symbol' in *Topos European Landscape Magazine*, No. 19, p. 17; Pohl, Norfried (1993). 'In which the spirit of the *Volkspark* also . . .' in Knuijt, Martin, Ophius, Hans and van Saane, Peter (Editors) (1993). *Modern Park Design – Recent Trends*. Amsterdam, THOTH, p. 74; Chadwick, George F. (1966). *The Park and the Town*. London, Architectural Press, pp. 255–6.

212 Goecke, Michael (1980), op. cit., p. 4 (of offprint).

213 Maass, I. (1981). 'People's Parks in Germany' in *Lotus International*, No. 30, p. 124; internal account (dated 1999) of the history of the park from the Amt für Naturschutz und Landschaftspflege (Office for Nature Conservation and Landscape Management) of the Hamburg Umweltbehörde (Environmental Authority) supplied at author's meeting with Heino Grunert and Andrea Zörning of that Office

on 5 July 1999; *Parkpflegewerk* (Park Management Plan) – prepared for that authority by Büros Müller-Glassl & Partner (Bremen) and Schaper-Steffen-Runtsch (Hamburg) and adopted in November 1997 – Section 4.2, pp. 6–9; response to author's questionnaire by Herr Schaake of Bezirksamt Hamburg-Nord (Hamburg-Nord District government) in June 1987.

214 Gothein, Marie Luise (1928). *A History of Garden Art, Volume II.* repr. New York, Hacker Art Books (1979), p. 357; Chadwick, George F. (1966), op. cit., p. 255.

215 Venier, Arnalda (1981), op. cit., p. 101.

216 Pogacnik, Marco. 'The Heimatschutz Movement and the Monumentalization of the Landscape' in Teyssot, Georges and Mosser, Monique (Editors) (1991), op. cit., pp. 463–4; Venier, Arnalda (1981), op. cit., p. 103.

217 This would have been 'old' marks before the revaluation of the currency in 1923; Venier, Arnalda (1981), op. cit., p. 101.

218 *Porträt* of Fritz Schumacher in *Gärten & Landschaft*, May 1996, p. 39. Regrettably, in July 1999, the RIBA had no copy of the citation for his election.

219 Chadwick, George F. (1966), op. cit., p. 255.

220 Maass, I. (1981), op. cit., p. 125 quoting from Schumacher's *Ein Volkspark* (1928), Munich; Steenbergen, Clemens. 'Teatro Rustico: The Formal Strategy and Grammar of Landscape Architecture' in Knuijt, Martin, Ophius, Hans and van Saane, Peter (Editors) (1993), op. cit., p. 122; Baljon, Lodewijk (1992). *Designing Parks.* Woodbridge, Garden Art, and Amsterdam, Architectura & Natura, p. 194.

221 Pohl, Norfried (1993), op. cit., pp. 72–3; Chadwick, George F. (1966), op. cit., p. 255; Frank, Harmut (1991). *Lo Stadtpark* in *Abitare*, No. 298, p. 146.

222 Noted at author's meeting with Heino Grunert and Andrea Zörning on 5 July 1999, op. cit.

223 Comment noted at author's meeting with Heino Grunert and Andrea Zörning on 5 July 1999, op. cit.

224 De Michelis, Marco (1981). *'Il verde e il rosso*/The Red and the Green – Park and City in Weimar Germany' in *Lotus International*, No. 30, p. 109.

225 Chadwick, George F. (1966), op. cit., p. 254; Maass, I. (1981), op. cit., pp. 123, 127.

14 LANDSCHAFTSPARK DUISBURG-NORD

226 Weilacher, Udo (1996). *Between Landscape Architecture and Land Art*, Basel, Birkhäuser, p. 122 described it as 'the park of the twenty-first century'; Pehnt, Wolfgang (March 1999). 'Changes Have to Take Place in People's Heads First' in *Topos European Landscape Magazine*, No. 26, p. 20; Dahlheimer, Achim (1999). *IBA '99 Finale: Short Information* (in English). IBA Emscher Park, unpaginated.

227 Fleming, John; Honour, Hugh and Pevsner, Nikolaus (1999). *The Penguin Dictionary of Landscape Architecture* (fifth edition). Harmondsworth, Penguin, p. 335 noted the connection with Gasworks Park; Steenbergen, Clemens. 'Teatro Rustico: The Formal Strategy and Grammar of Landscape Architecture' in Knuijt, Martin, Ophius, Hans and van Saane, Peter (Editors) (1993). *Modern Park Design – Recent Trends.* Amsterdam, THOTH, p. 129 described decomposition as 'the process whereby the active composition elements are freed from their existing context so that they can be applied in a new staging'. Fleming, John, Honour, Hugh and Pevsner, Nikolaus (1999), ibid., p. 149 described 'Deconstructivism or Deconstructionism' as 'terms used in, respectively, the United States and Europe for a development in architectural theory and practice in the 1980s . . . Deconstructivism alludes to Russian Constructivism as a point of departure, Deconstructionism to the literary theory and critical methodology of the French philosopher Jacques Derrida (b. 1930)'. Fleming *et al.* go on to cite the Deconstructivism exhibition at the MoMA in New York in 1988 where the catalogue talked in terms of 'disruption, dislocation, deflection, deviation and distortion, and was not concerned in any simple sense with fragmentation or the taking apart of constructions' whereas 'Deconstructionism is based on the assumption that architecture is a language, amenable to the methods of linguistic philosophy'; Tschumi, Bernard (1987). *Cinégram Folie: Le Parc de la Villette.* Princeton, Princeton Architectural Press, p. VI talked about his points, lines and surfaces 'refusing ascendancy of any privileged systems or organizing element'. He called them 'calculated discontinuity' and 'disintegration'.

228 Reiss-Schmidt, Stephan (1999). 'The Ruhr Region and the Siedlungsverband Ruhrkohlenbezirk (SVR)' in *Planning in Germany*, Special Bulletin '99 for the 35th Congress of the International Society of City and Regional Planners (ISOCARP), pp. 32–43 is the principal source for this section.

229 Karl Gansler, Managing Director of the IBA in 'Emscher Park Building Exhibition: A Motor for Structural Change' in *Topos European Landscape Magazine*, No. 26, op. cit., p. 14 commented that the SVR was 'the oldest regional organization in the world'. It was succeeded in 1979 by the Kommunalverband Ruhrgebiet (KVR). The KVR took over the role of the IBA after its completion in 1999.

230 Zlonicky, Peter (1999). 'The Emscher Park International Building Exhibition – Goals, Changes, Achievements' in *Planning in Germany*, Special Bulletin '99 for the 35th Congress of the International Society of City and Regional Planners (ISOCARP), p. 44.

231 Weilacher, Udo (1996), op. cit., p. 122; noted at author's meeting with Ellen Hein, Dominique Neuhauss and Günter Zieling of Landschaftspark Duisburg-Nord GmbH and Claus Heimann and Philip Kühnel of the Duisburg office of Latz + Partner on 28 June 1999.

232 Quoted in Diedrich, Lisa (1999). 'No Politics, No Park: The Duisburg-Nord Model' in *Topos European Landscape Magazine*, No. 26, op. cit., pp. 72–3; IBA Emscher Park GmbH (1990), Position Paper *Ecological Construction*, p. 1.

233 Schwarze-Rodrian, Michael (1999). 'Intercommunal Co-operation in the Emscher Landscape Park' in *Topos European Landscape Magazine*, No. 26, p. 57.

234 Diedrich, Lisa (1999), op. cit., p. 72; Schmidt, Arno Sighart (1994). 'The Role of the Landscape Architect in the Emscher Park', translated summary in *Gärten + Landschaft*, Volume 7, p. 39.

235 Linne, Martin (1994). 'Duisburg North Landscape Park', translated summary in *Gärten + Landschaft*, Volume 7, p. 40; Diedrich, Lisa (1999), op. cit., p. 69; Weilacher, Udo (1996), op. cit., p. 110 included a small-scale version of the Lassus scheme; ibid., pp. 121–4.

236 Weilacher, Udo (1996), ibid., pp. 125–36; Geuze, Adrian 'Theme: Dynamic Modern Times' in Knuijt, Martin, Ophius, Hans and van Saane, Peter (Editors) (1993), op. cit., p. 48.

237 Dettmar, Jörg (1999). 'Wilderness or Park?' in *Topos European Landscape Magazine*, No. 26, op. cit., p. 35; Poblotzki, Ursula (1999). 'Transformation of a Landscape' in *Topos European Landscape Magazine*, No. 26, op. cit., pp. 47, 50; Linne, Martin (1994), op. cit., p. 40.

238 From a lecture by Peter Latz at Harvard University in April 1998; Diedrich, Lisa (1999), op. cit., p. 74 attributed these statements to Latz; Weilacher, Udo (1996), op. cit., p. 122 also noted that Latz's use of grids in earlier projects 'provided a framework for individual action on the part of the individual user'. Equally Jackson, John Brinkerhoff (1994). *A Sense of Place, A Sense of Time*, New Haven and London, Yale University Press, p. 157 stated 'we also, I think, feel a deep and persistent need for privacy and independence in our domestic life'.

239 Parker, Angus (1996). 'The Beast Breathes Again' in *Landscape Design*, Number 254, p. 13; Latz, Peter, '"Design" by handling the existing' in Knuijt, Martin, Ophius, Hans and van Saane, Peter (Editors) (1993), op. cit., p. 91.

240 For instance, Latz (1993) op. cit., and his lecture at Harvard University in April 1998; Diedrich, Lisa (1999), op. cit., and Weilacher, Udo (1996), op. cit.; the Piazza Metallica is a multipurpose square stage comprising forty-nine steel plates that had lined the foundry pits in the works; Cowperplatz has been planted with a grid of standard trees; a series of gardens composed largely of elements found on site has been created in the former sintering bunkers.

241 Schwarze-Rodrian, Michael (1999), op. cit., p. 53; noted at author's meeting with Ellen Hein, Dominique Neuhauss and Günter Zieling on 28 June 1999, op. cit.

242 Diedrich, Lisa (1999), op. cit., p. 73; lecture by Latz at Harvard University in April 1998; noted at author's meeting with Ellen Hein, Dominique Neuhauss and Günter Zieling on 28 June 1999.

243 The lighting scheme was designed by London-based Jonathan Park whose Studio Park has, with Mark Fisher, designed substantial stage sets for rock bands like Pink Floyd and the Rolling Stones. See, for instance, 'Industrial Manoeuvres in the Dark' in *Building Design*, 17 January 1997, pp. 12–13.

244 Treib, Marc (1995). 'Must Landscapes Mean? Approaches to Significance in Recent Landscape Architecture' in *Landscape Journal*, Volume 14, Number 1, p. 58.

15 PROSPECT PARK, BROOKLYN, NEW YORK

245 Simpson, Jeffrey (1981). 'Prospect Park' in *Art of the Olmsted Landscape: His Works in New York City*. New York, New York Landmarks Preservation Commission, p. 23 described Prospect Park as a 'masterpiece' where 'the disciplined shaping of landscape for public recreational spaces which they virtually invented in . . . Central Park was realized most fully'; Zaitzevsky, Cynthia (1982). *Frederick Law Olmsted and the Boston Park System*. Cambridge, MA, Belknap, pp. 31, 30 noted that although 'it is only about half the size of Central Park, Prospect Park conveys more of a sense of spaciousness' and is 'a more satisfying aesthetic whole'; Schuyler, David (1986). *The New Urban Landscape*. Baltimore, Johns Hopkins University Press, p. 124 quoted Charles Sprague Sargent's 1888 assessment of the park as 'one of the great artistic creations of modern times'.

246 Noted at author's meeting with Prospect Park Administrator Tupper Thomas on 25 April 2000.

247 Schuyler, David (1986), op. cit., p. 115; Carr, Ethan (1988). *Three Hundred Years of Parks: A Timeline of New York City Park History*. New York, City of New York Parks and Recreation, p. 16. Brooklyn remains the most populous of the five boroughs that now make up New York City; its populousness in the 1850s is reflected in the 'hundreds and hundreds' in Walt Whitman's poem *Crossing Brooklyn Ferry* (1856).

248 Graff, M. M. (1985). *Central Park – Prospect Park: A New Perspective*. New York, Greensward Foundation, p. 112 quoted Stranahan as having stated that 'the park will hold strong inducements to the affluent to remain in our city, who are now too often induced to change their residences by the seductive influences of the New York park'; Lancaster, Clay (1967). *Prospect Park Handbook* (1988 edition). New York, Greensward Foundation, p. 21.

249 Sauer, Leslie Jones and Andropogon Associates (1998). *The Once and Future Forest: A Guide to Forest Restoration Strategies*. Washington, DC, Island, p. 220; Zaitzevsky, Cynthia (1982), op. cit., p. 31. Manhattan had been completely covered by the Wisconsin Glacier.

250 Toth, Edward and Sauer, Leslie (1994). *Saving Brooklyn's Last Forest: The Plan for Prospect Park*. New York, Prospect Park Alliance, p. 8 quoting from Annual Report of 1861; Alex, William (1994). *Calvert Vaux: Architect and Planner*. New York, Ink, p. 131 contained a clear print of Viele's 'Plan for the Improvement of Prospect Park' of 1861.

251 Schuyler, David (1986), op. cit., p. 117.

252 The background to how Olmsted and Vaux came to work together on Central Park is discussed in Chapter 17; Graff, M. M. (1985), op. cit., pp. 29–30; and Kelly, Bruce, Guillet, Gail Travis and Hern, Mary Ellen W. (1981). *Art of the Olmsted Landscape*. New York, New York Landmarks Preservation Commission, pp. 69–70.

253 Fleming, John; Honour, Hugh and Pevsner, Nikolaus (1999). *The Penguin Dictionary of Architecture and Landscape Architecture* (fifth edition). Harmondsworth, Penguin, p. 158; Alex, William (1994), op. cit., pp. 1–3; Kelly, Bruce, Guillet, Gail Travis and Hern, Mary Ellen W. (1981), op. cit., p. 64.

254 Beveridge, Charles E. and Rocheleau, Paul (1998). *Frederick Law Olmsted: Designing the American Landscape*. New York, Universe (revised edition of 1995 publication under same name), pp. 10–26.

255 Rybczynski, Witold (1999), op. cit., pp. 259, 281; Graff, M. M. (1985), op. cit., pp. 112–13; and Lancaster, Clay (1967), op. cit., p. 23. Stranahan's reputation for altruism and incorruptibility is reflected in two particular stories. First, that he supported construction of the Brooklyn Bridge despite his interests in the competing ferry system; second, that although he had served as President of the Commission without remuneration, when he retired he presented the city with a cheque for $10,604.42 to cover a shortfall in the books during his administration.

256 Graff, M. M. (1985), ibid., p. 114; Garvin, Alexander (1996). *The American City – What Works, What Doesn't*. New York, McGraw-Hill, pp. 48–9.

257 Quoted by Schuyler, David (1986), op. cit., p. 120 and Rybczynski, Witold (1999), op. cit., p. 271; quoted by Kelly, Bruce, Guillet, Gail Travis and Hern, Mary Ellen W. (1981), op. cit., p. 64.

258 Hiss, Tony (1990). *The Experience of Place*. New York, Vintage, pp. 28–36; Garvin, Alexander (1996), op. cit., p. 48; Simpson, Jeffrey (1981), op. cit., p. 24.

259 Newton, Norman T. (1971), op. cit., p. 284; Beveridge, Charles E. and Rocheleau, Paul (1998), op. cit., pp. 66–7.

260 Toth, Edward and Sauer, Leslie (1994), op. cit., p. 11. It must be remembered, however, that Olmsted and Vaux were accustomed to the availability of a large workforce.

261 Rybczynski, Witold (1999), op. cit., p. 412.

262 Ibid., pp. 312–13. Vaux and Olmsted continued to work together on uncompleted commissions until 1874 and collaborated again in 1887 on Morningside Park, New York.

263 Lancaster, Clay (1967), op. cit., p. 115.

264 Carr, Ethan (1988), op. cit., p. 42; Prospect Park Alliance Report (1997), p. 16; Sauer, Leslie Jones and Andropogon Associates (1998), op. cit., p. 201 noted that volunteer labour is valuable not purely because it can save money, but because it builds positive use and educates users; workforce numbers noted at author's meeting with Prospect Park Administrator Tupper Thomas on 25 April 2000.

265 Noted at author's meeting with Prospect Park Administrator Tupper Thomas on 25 April 2000; response to author's questionnaire in August 1989.

266 Toth, Edward and Sauer, Leslie (1994), op. cit., p. 4.

267 Ibid., p. 12.

268 Beveridge, Charles E. and Rocheleau, Paul (1998), op. cit., p. 44; Scott, A. O. (August/September 1999). 'American Pastoral': a review of Witold Rybczynski's *A Clearing in the Distance*, in *Metropolis*, p. 101.

16 TIERGARTEN, BERLIN

269 Balfour, Alan. 'Octagon' in Corner, James (Editor) (1999), *Recovering Landscape*. Princeton, Princeton Architectural Press, p. 88.

270 Ladd, Brian (1997). *The Ghosts of Berlin: Confronting German History in the Urban Landscape*. Chicago, University of Chicago Press, pp. 98, 74.

271 Rimmer, David (Editor) (1998). *Time Out Berlin Guide*. London, Penguin/Time Out, p. 60 dubs Berlin 'the world's fifth-largest Turkish city'.

272 Ladd, Brian (1997), op. cit., pp. 134–41 described Hitler and Speer's proposals for *Germania*, their proposal 'to make Berlin into a new city'; Strasse des 17 Juni ('Street of the 17 June') is the name given by the West to the 3.2-kilometre-long Charlottenburger Chaussee, the westward extension of Unter den Linden created in 1695 through the Tiergarten. The 17 June was the date in 1953 of a failed uprising against the East German government. Unter den Linden (literally 'Under the Limes') is the boulevard built in 1648 from the royal palace to the eastern edge of the Tiergarten by Friedrich Wilhelm (ruled 1640–88) the 'Great' Elector. The name Elector refers to the rulers' participation in the election of the Holy Roman Emperor.

273 Ladd, Brian (1997), op. cit., pp. 47–81; Balfour, Alan in Corner, James (Editor) (1999), op. cit., pp. 87–9 and Studemann, Frederick in Rimmer, David (Editor) (1998), op. cit., pp. 5–23.

274 Von Krosigk, Klaus (1995). *Garden Guide – Grosser Tiergarten (English)*, Berlin, Museumspädagogischer Dienst (Museum Education Service) Berlin and Senatsverwaltung für Stadtentwicklung und Umweltschutz (Department of City Planning and Environmental Protection) Berlin (unpaginated); Wörner, Rose and Wörner, Gustav, 'Das Parkpflegewerk für de Tiergarten' [Park Management for the Tiergarten] in *Landesdenkmalamt Berlin*. Berlin, Monuments Office of the State of Berlin (1996), *Der Berliner Tiergarten – Vergangenheit und Zukunft* (An Item of the Past and Future), *Landesdenkmalamt Berlin* and Schelzky & Jeep, Berlin, pp. 63–4; Goode, Patrick and Lancaster, Michael (1986). *The Oxford Companion to Gardens*, Oxford, Oxford University Press, pp. 555–6 are principal sources for this

account of establishment of the Tiergarten.

275 Wendlan, Folkwin in *Landesdenkmalamt Berlin*. Berlin, Monuments Office of the State of Berlin (1996), op. cit., p. 8.

276 Wendlan, Folkwin, ibid., p. 10 showed a plan from 1765 illustrating Knobelsdorff's layout; Goode, Patrick and Lancaster, Michael (1986), op. cit., p. 555. This conflicts with the statement in Fleming, John; Honour, Hugh and Pevsner, Nikolaus (1999). *The Penguin Dictionary of Architecture and Landscape Architecture* (fifth edition). Harmondsworth, Penguin., p. 322, which stated that in 1746 Knobelsdorff 'quarrelled with the king, who dismissed him and thus ended his architectural career'.

277 Enke, Roland (1999). Berlin: *Open City. The City on Exhibition*. Berlin, Nicholaische Verlagsbuchhandlung, p. 14 credits Phillipp Daniel Boumann as architect for the Bellevue Palace.

278 Fleming, John; Honour, Hugh and Pevsner, Nikolaus (1999), op. cit., pp. 511, 343; Ladd, Brian (1997), op. cit., p. 98.

279 Schmidt, Hartwig (1981) 'Plans of Embellishment: Planning of Parks in 19th Century Berlin' in *Lotus International*, No. 30, pp. 81–3; von Krosigk, Klaus (1995), op. cit., unpaginated; Fleming, John; Honour, Hugh and Pevsner, Nikolaus (1999), ibid., pp. 344, 262.

280 Von Krosigk, Klaus (1995), op. cit., unpaginated; Enke, Roland (1999), op. cit., p. 237.

281 Ladd, Brian (1997), op. cit., pp. 96–100.

282 Ibid., p. 138; and Enke, Roland (1999), op. cit., pp. 237–8; Studemann, Frederick in Rimmer, David (Editor) (1998), op. cit., p. 17; Wörner, Rose and Wörner, Gustav (1996), op. cit., p. 63.

283 Enke, Roland (1999), op. cit., p. 237; Wörner, Rose and Wörner, Gustav (1996), op. cit., p. 40; von Krosigk, Klaus (1995), op. cit., unpaginated.

284 Inevitably the Englischer Gärten was dubbed the 'Garden of Eden'.

285 Ladd, Brian (1997), op. cit., p125.

286 Studemann, Frederick in Rimmer, David (Editor) (1998), op. cit., p. 5.

287 Fleming, John,; Honour, Hugh and Pevsner, Nikolaus (1999), op. cit., p. 343; Goode, Patrick and Lancaster, Michael (1986), op. cit., p. 333; Chadwick, George F. (1966). *The Park and the Town*. London, Architectural Press, pp. 249–50; Gothein, Marie Luise (1928). *A History of Garden Art*, Volume II. repr. New York, Hacker Art Books (1979), p. 345.

288 Schmidt, Hartwig (1981), op. cit., p. 83.

289 Ibid., p. 85.

290 Von Buttlar, Florian (1985). *Parks in the City* in *Gärten + Landschaft*, Volume 4, p. 47; von Krosigk, Klaus (1995), op. cit., unpaginated.

291 Schmidt, Hartwig (1981), op. cit., p. 83 quoted this from Hinz, Gerhard (1937). *Peter Josef Lenné und seine bedeutendsten Schöpfungen in Berlin und Potsdam*, Berlin, p. 184, in which Lenné was explaining his proposal for the park in the north of Berlin subsequently designed by Gustav Meyer and named Friedrichshain; von Krosigk, Klaus (1995), op. cit., unpaginated; Schmidt, Hartwig (1981), ibid., p. 83 quoted this from Hennebo, D. and Hoffmann, A. (1963). *Geschichte der deutschen Gärtenkunst*, Volume 3, p. 81.

292 At author's meeting with Klaus von Krosigk, Deputy Director of the Berlin Department for the Preservation of Historical Buildings, Gardens and Landscapes on 2 July 1999, he expressed his optimism that when building work directly south of the park was completed, there would be a call for the re-establishment of avenue planting along that edge of the park.

293 Schäfer, Robert (September 1999). 'Berlin Planning Departments Restructured' in *Short Cuts* in *Topos European Landscape Magazine*, No. 28, p. 107.

294 Von Buttlar, Florian, op. cit., p. 49.

295 Von Krosigk, Klaus (1995), op. cit., unpaginated; Wörner, Rose and Wörner, Gustav in *Landesdenkmalamt Berlin* – Monuments Office of the State of Berlin (1996), op. cit., pp. 63–6.

296 Von Krosigk, Klaus (1999). *Gärtenkunst Berlin – 20 Jahre Gärtendenkmalpflege in der Metropole* (Garden Art of Berlin – 20 Years of Conservation of Historic Gardens and Parks in the Capital) [bilingual]. Berlin, Landesdenkmalamt and Schelzky & Jeep, p. 42.

297 Kramer, Jane. 'Living with Berlin' in *The New Yorker*, 5 July 1999, p. 55; Ladd, Brian (1997), op. cit., p. 68.

17 CENTRAL PARK, NEW YORK

298 Chadwick, George F. (1965). *The Park and the Town*. London, Architectural Press, p. 184.

299 Rosenzweig, Roy and Blackmar, Elizabeth (1992). *The Park and the People: A History of Central Park*. Ithaca, Cornell University Press (paperback edition 1998), pp. 15–17; Graff, M. M. (1985). *Central Park – Prospect Park: A New Perspective*. New York, Greensward Foundation, pp. 4–6; Stewart, Ian R. (1981). 'The Fight for Central Park' in Kelly, Bruce, Guillet, Gail Travis and Hern, Mary Ellen W. (1981). *Art of the Olmsted Landscape*. New York, New York City Landmarks Preservation Commission, p. 89; Tatum, George B. (1991). Introduction to Downing, A. J. (1865). *Landscape Gardening and Rural Architecture*. New York, Orange Judd (seventh edition); repr. New York, Dover, p. v, noted that this was followed in 1842 by *Cottage Residences* and, in 1850, *The Architecture of Country Houses*.

300 Garvin, Alexander (1996). *The American City – What Works, What Doesn't*. New York, McGraw-Hill, p. 31; Kelly, Bruce (August 1982). 'The Rehabilitation of Central Park, New York' in *Landscape Design*, Number 139, p. 32; Stewart, Ian R. (1981), op. cit., p. 92.

301 Stewart, Ian R. (1981), op. cit., pp. 95, 87; Sutton, S. B. (1971). *Civilizing American Cities: Frederick Law Olmsted Writings on City Landscapes*. Da Capo, New York (1997 edition), p. 86 quoted Olmsted's address 'Public Parks and the Enlargement of Towns' to the Lowell Institute in February 1870, in which he stated his belief that the site was selected because it appeared 'to be about the middle of the island, and therefore . . . one which would least excite local prejudices'. He went on to note that 'it would have been difficult to find another body of land of six hundred acres upon the island . . . which possessed less of . . . the most desirable characteristics of a park'.

302 Figures from memo dated 12 June 1997 from Central Park Historian Sara Cedar Miller; Central Park Conservancy (1985). *Rebuilding Central Park: A Management and Restoration Plan*, pp. 22–3; Beveridge, Charles E. and Rocheleau, Paul (1998). *Frederick Law Olmsted: Designing the American Landscape*. New York, Universe (revised edition of 1995 publication), p. 51; Carr, Ethan (1988). *Three Hundred Years of Parks: A Timeline of New York City Park History*. New York, City of New York Parks and Recreation, p. 14.

303 Stewart, Ian R. (1981), op. cit., p. 97 noted that 'much credit . . . must be given to the vision, tenacious support and leadership of individuals such as Bryant, Downing, Kingsland and other public figures'; Tatum George B. in Alex, William (1994). *Calvert Vaux: Architect and Planner*. New York, Ink, p. 11; Chadwick, George F. (1966), op. cit., p. 181 and Beveridge, Charles E. and Rocheleau, Paul (1998), p. 50; Graff, M. M. (1985), op. cit., p. 13; Chadwick, George F. (1966), op. cit., p. 164.

304 Alex, William (1994), op. cit., p. 107; Scott, A. O. (August/September 1999). 'American Pastoral': a review of Witold Rybczynski's *A Clearing in the Distance*, in *Metropolis*, p. 103.

305 Mann, William A. (1993). *Landscape Architecture: An Illustrated History in Timelines, Site Plans and Biography*. New York, Wiley, p. 357 noted that the requirements for the competition were '1. four transverse roads running east–west through the park; 2. a parade ground for the militia; 3. a fountain; 4. three playgrounds; 5. a concert hall; 6. a flower garden; 7. a site for ice-skating; 8. plans to be in India ink or sepia ink at the scale of 1" = 100'; 9. a written description of the proposed park; 10. all work due on April 1, 1858'; Rosenzweig, Roy and Blackmar, Elizabeth (1992), op. cit., p. 120.

306 Tatum, George B. in Alex, William (1994), op. cit., p. 12. Although Olmsted sought to redress this in subsequent correspondence between the two of them, he remained keen to ensure that public awareness of his work was maintained; Walmsley, Anthony (1975). *Made Landscapes from Prehistory to the Present. A Selection of Models Prepared by Students of the Graduate School of Fine Arts at the University of Pennsylvania, Philadelphia, Pa, USA from 1968–74 with an Introduction and Commentary by Anthony Walmsley*. Philadelphia, author, #15, p. 38; Graff, M. M. (1985), op. cit.. pp. 33–7, 46–51, 73–5; Tatum George B. in Alex, William (1994), op. cit., p. 15. Mould is noted for his design of the now demolished red brick and yellow limestone First Congregational Church in New York – referred to as the 'Church of the Holy Zebra'; Rybczynski, Witold (1999). *A Clearing in the Distance: Frederick Law Olmsted and North America in the*

Nineteenth Century. Toronto, HarperCollins Canada, p. 169.

307 Downing, Andrew J. *Rural Essays* quoted in Stewart, Ian R. (1981), op. cit., p. 94; Sutton, S. B. (1971), op. cit., p. 88. Olmsted quoted the Editorial: 'When we open a public park Sam will air himself in it. He will take his friends whether from Church Street, or elsewhere. He will knock down any better dressed man who remonstrates with him. He will talk and sing, and fill his share of the bench, and flirt with the nursery maids in his own coarse way. Now we ask what chance have William B. Astor and Edward Everett against this fellow citizen of theirs? Can they and he enjoy the same place?'; and ibid., p. 92.

308 Beveridge, Charles E. and Hoffman, Carolyn F. (Editors) (1997). *The Papers of Frederick Law Olmsted: Supplementary Series, Volume 1 – Writings on Public Parks, Parkways, and Park Systems.* Baltimore, Johns Hopkins University Press, pp. 474–7.

309 Rybczynski, Witold (1999), op. cit., p. 177 quoted this from a communication dated 31 May 1858 from Olmsted to the Central Park Commissioners; Beveridge, Charles E. and Rocheleau, Paul (1998), p. 52.

310 Zaitzevsky, Cynthia (1982). *Frederick Law Olmsted and the Boston Park System.* Cambridge, MA, Belknap, pp. 23–4; Chadwick, George F. (1966), op. cit., p. 185.

311 Rosenzweig, Roy and Blackmar, Elizabeth (1992), op. cit., p. 150 noted that in the first five years, labourers excavated, moved or brought into the site nearly 2.5 million cubic yards of stone and earth; used 166 tons of gunpowder to move more than 300,000 cubic yards of rock, crushing about 25,000 cubic yards into paving aggregate; Chadwick, George F. (1966), ibid., pp. 184–5; Lippard, Lucy R. (1997). *The Lure of the Local.* New York, The New Press, p. 250; Wilson, Alexander (1991). *The Culture of Nature: North American Landscape from Disney to the Exxon Valdez.* Toronto, Between the Lines, p. 95.

312 They underestimated the extent to which the value placed on a view of the park would eventually result in high-priced high-rise building, well above the tree canopy, all along its edges.

313 Alex, William (1994), op. cit., p. 111; Kelly, Bruce, Guillet, Gail Travis and Hern, Mary Ellen W. (1981). *Art of the Olmsted Landscape.* New York, New York City Landmarks Preservation Commission, p. 28; Graff, M. M. (1985), op. cit., pp. 88–9; Kelly, Bruce, Guillet, Gail Travis and Hern, Mary Ellen W. (1981), ibid., p. 39.

314 Alex, William (1994), op. cit., p. 234; Beveridge, Charles E. and Rocheleau, Paul (1998), pp. 22–5; Carr, Ethan (1988), p. 18.

315 Graff, M. M. (1985), op. cit., pp. 55–62; Rosenzweig, Roy and Blackmar, Elizabeth (1992), op. cit., pp. 186–7, 192–6, 273–4, 350; Rybczynski, Witold (1999), op. cit., pp. 184–6, 311. The Beaux-Arts Fifth Avenue wing of the Metropolitan Museum was designed by Richard Morris Hunt in 1895; Schuyler, David (1986). *The*

New Urban Landscape. Baltimore, Johns Hopkins University Press, p. 100.

316 Rosenzweig, Roy and Blackmar, Elizabeth (1992), ibid., pp. 307, 289, 294, 381; Graff, M. M. (1985), op. cit., pp. 62–8; Carr, Ethan (1988), op. cit., pp. 29, 31.

317 Rosenzweig, Roy and Blackmar, Elizabeth (1992), ibid., pp. 375, 410, 399, 400, 402, 435, 439; Carr, Ethan (1988), op. cit., p. 29.

318 Rosenzweig, Roy and Blackmar, Elizabeth (1992), ibid., p. 449; Buford, Bill. 'Lions and Tigers and Bears: Camping in Central Park' in *The New Yorker*, 23 and 30 August 1999, p. 106; Kelly, Bruce (1982), op. cit., p. 32; Central Park Conservancy (1985), op. cit., p. 40.

319 Carr, Ethan (1988), op. cit., p. 37; Rosenzweig, Roy and Blackmar, Elizabeth (1992), op. cit., pp. 462–3, 470, 476.

320 Ibid., p. 502.

321 Harden, Blaine. 'Neighbors Give Central Park a Wealthy Glow', *New York Times*, 22 November 1999, p. B6.

322 Rogers, Elizabeth Barlow (1987). *Rebuilding Central Park: A Management and Restoration Plan.* Cambridge, MA, MIT Press, p. 153. Also recorded at author's meeting with Bruce Kelly on 14 May 1991 that 'Central Park is viewed as a National Park even though it is not managed by the National Park Service'.

323 'Central Park Conservancy' in *Landscape Architecture*, Volume 82, No. 11 (1992), p. 55.

324 Figures from a response to author's questionnaire in August 1989; website *www.centralparknyc.org* (accessed 28 April 2000); Central Park Conservancy Annual Report 1999.

325 Figures from Central Park Conservancy Annual Report 1999.

326 Harden, Blaine (1999), op. cit., p. B6.

327 Domosh, Mona (1996). *Invented Cities – The Creation of Landscape in Nineteenth Century New York and Boston.* New Haven and London, Yale University Press, p. 24; information sheet from City of New York Parks and Recreation Librarian; Rybczynski, Witold (1999), op. cit., p. 183; Sutton, S. B. (1971). *Civilizing American Cities: Frederick Law Olmsted Writings on City Landscapes.* Da Capo, New York (1997 edition), p. 111 quoted Olmsted's report 'Public Pleasure Grounds for the City of San Francisco' 1866; Chadwick, George F. (1966), p. 188.

328 Rosenzweig, Roy and Blackmar, Elizabeth (1992), op. cit., pp. 307–10.

329 Fitch, Marston James (1981). 'Design and Designer: 19th Century Innovation' in Kelly, Bruce, Guillet, Gail Travis and Hern, Mary Ellen W. (1981). *Art of the Olmsted Landscape.* New York, New York City Landmarks Preservation Commission, p. 77; Central Park Market Survey 1995.

330 Rybczynski, Witold (1999), op. cit., p. 179; Buford, Bill (1999), op. cit., p. 106; Rosenzweig, Roy and Blackmar, Elizabeth (1992), op. cit., pp. 474–80. The 'wilding' incident led to the establishment by the Conservancy of a Citizens Task Force on the Use and Security of

Central Park – nevertheless, another jogger was murdered in 1995; Buford, Bill (1999), ibid., p. 102; *International Herald Tribune*, 13 June, p. 3; 14 June, p. 2; 23 June, p. 7; 27 June 2000, p. 9.

331 Central Park Conservancy (1985). *Rebuilding Central Park: A Management and Restoration Plan*, p. 5; Sauer, Leslie Jones and Andropogon Associates (1998). *The Once and Future Forest: A Guide to Forest Restoration Strategies.* Washington, DC, Island, pp. 195–209 described the work in the North Woods.

332 Central Park Conservancy Annual Report 1999.

333 Schuyler, David (1986). *The New Urban Landscape.* Baltimore, Johns Hopkins University Press, p. 78; Chadwick, George F. (1966), op. cit., p. 190; Wilson, William H. (1989). *The City Beautiful Movement.* Baltimore, Johns Hopkins University Press (paperback edition 1994), p. 9 suggested that 'the taproot of the City Beautiful movement lies in nineteenth-century landscape architecture, personified by Frederick Law Olmsted'; Legates, Richard T. and Stout, Frederic (Editors) (1996). *The City Reader.* London, Routledge, p. 337 suggested that 'behind the somewhat convoluted Victorianisms of his prose lies a strikingly modern mind'; Rosenzweig, Roy and Blackmar, Elizabeth (1992), op. cit., p. 415 gave this quote from architect Ernest Flagg.

334 Harden, Blaine (1999), op. cit., p. A1; Garvin, Alexander (1996), op. cit., p. 41; Rosenzweig, Roy and Blackmar, Elizabeth (1992), op. cit., p. 529.

18 STANLEY PARK, VANCOUVER

335 Quoted by Paterson, Douglas (1994) 'Regional Design: Some Principles' in *Landscape Architecture*, Volume 84, No. 4, p. 73 and attributed by him, in a telephone conversation with author on 17 November 1999, to Harlem Bartholomew – author of the 1928 plan for Vancouver; Steele, Richard M. (1993). *Stanley Park.* Surrey, British Columbia, Heritage House, p. 13 quoted the population in June 1886 as 2600; Martin, Linda and Seagrave, Kerry (1983). *City Parks of Canada*, Oakville, Mosaic, p. 106 quoted the population when the park was opened in September 1888 as 'about 6,000'; Wershler, Terri and Lees, Judi (1996). *Vancouver, The Ultimate Guide*, Vancouver, Greystone, p. 7 quoted the population of Granville, when it became the City of Vancouver in 1886, as 1000.

336 Steele, Richard M. (1993), op. cit., pp. 14–15.

337 Martin, Linda and Seagrave, Kerry (1983), op. cit., p. 105.

338 Conn, Heather (1998), quoted in *The Origins of Stanley Park* from *The Greater Vancouver Book – An Urban Encyclopaedia.* Linkman; website *discovervancouver.com* accessed December 1998.

339 MacMillan Bloedel Ltd Woodland Services (July 1989). *Stanley Park Regeneration Program Folio 1: Forest Management Plan* for Vancouver Board of Parks and Recreation, pp. 2–4; the Lost

Lagoon was named after a poem by Pauline Johnson, Ontario-born daughter of a Mohawk Chief and English mother.

340 Johnston, Elizabeth (Editor) (January 1982). 'Great Parks of the World: Stanley Park: Part II', *Parks and Recreation Resources* magazine, p. 51; Steele, Mike (1993), op. cit., p. 21. Terri Clark, Public Information Officer for the Board since the mid-1970s, also has an impressive record of unbroken involvement with the park.

341 Noted from author's telephone conversation with Paterson on 17 November 1999.

342 Stanley Park Transportation Management Plan Public Process Document (March 1996), p. 7.

343 Population and estimated residential capacity figures noted from author's telephone conversation with Paul Nolan of City of Vancouver Planning Department on 30 March 1999; Stanley Park *Transportation and Recreation Report* (1996), p. 8.

344 'Stanley Park – A Sense of Place', Volume 1, Issue 1 (1991), p. 1. Interestingly, MacLaren Plansearch suggested the slogan 'sense of place' as the theme for the 1985 Stanley Park Master Plan. They described this as meaning 'the relationship between the people and their overall environment as expressed in Stanley Park'.

345 Stanley Park *Task Force Final Report* (May 1992), p. 10.

346 *About the Board of Parks and Recreation* from the City of Vancouver Board of Parks and Recreation website (accessed December 1998).

347 Noted from author's telephone conversation with Terri Clark in September 1998.

348 Stanley Park *Task Force Final Report* (May 1992), p. 8; Belyea, Sorensen and Associates (January 1992), *Stanley Park Technical Report* for Stanley Park Task Force, p. 21.

349 Newton, Norman T. (1971). *Design on the Land: The Development of Landscape Architecture.* Cambridge, MA, Belknap, p. 299.

350 Stanley Park *Transportation and Recreation Report* (1996), p. 28.

351 MacMillan Bloedel Ltd Woodland Services (1989), op. cit., p. iv; park managers in other countries might be consoled by the fact that Canada's most revered public park also suffers the ravages of an excessive population of Canada geese; Stanley Park *Task Force Final Report* (May 1992), p. 20.

352 Vancouver Greenways Plan, City of Vancouver (October 1995), p. 5; Landscape architects Philips Wuori Long were involved with integration of Coal Harbour and the park, and on the restoration of disturbed areas following the removal of the zoo; landscape architects R. Kim Perry and Associates were engaged by Vancouver City Council to design the bikeway along English Bay.

353 Sublime is used here in the sense that Uvedale Price used it in his *Essay on the Picturesque* (1794) – in that 'to create the sublime is above our powers'.

354 Cranz, Galen (1982). *The Politics of Park Design.* Cambridge, MA, MIT Press, p. 253.

355 Valpy, Michael. *Toronto Globe and Mail*, 12 July 1996, described the Seawall as 'a beautiful creation whose value has been debased horrendously by both overuse and conflicting use'. His somewhat negative conclusion was that extending the wheel and walkways adjacent to the park were 'nice ideas' but 'the problem is too many people'.

19 AMSTERDAMSE BOS, AMSTERDAM

In The Netherlands the park is called 'Het Amsterdamse Bos', literally 'the Amsterdam Forest (or Woodland) Park'. For ease of reference it has been called the Bos Park in this chapter.

356 Daalder, Remco (1999). *Het Amsterdamse Bos – Bos voor de Toekomst* in *StadenGroen*, Amsterdam, Volume 2, Number 1, p. 19.

357 Jury Report for the International Open Competition of 1995 for *Designing the Inner Fringes of Green Heart Metropolis.*

358 Jellicoe, Geoffrey and Jellicoe, Susan (1987). *The Landscape of Man.* London, Thames & Hudson, p. 302; Stedelijk Beheer Amsterdam (1994). *Amsterdamse Bos: Visitors' Information on Forestry Practice.*

359 Chadwick, George F. (1965). *The Park and the Town.* London, Architectural Press, pp. 302–3.

360 Polano, Sergio. 'The Bos Park, Amsterdam, and Urban Development in Holland' in Teyssot, Georges and Mosser, Monique (Editors) (1991). *The History of Garden Design.* London, Thames & Hudson, pp. 507–9.

361 Chadwick, George F. (1965), op. cit., p. 256 quoting from Schumacher's paper 'Grünpolitik der Grosstadt-Umgebung'.

362 Balk, J. Th. (1979). *Een Kruiwagen vol Bomen.* Amsterdam, Stadsdrukkerij van Amsterdam, p. 59 gave the figure for the original area; 'The Amsterdam Boschplan' in *Journal of the Royal Institute of British Architects*, Volume 45, Third Series, No. 14, p. 3 acknowledged that it made free use of an article by Dr Ing. T. P. Byhouwer (1937) in *de 8 en Opbouw*, No. 2.

363 Balk, J. Th. (1979), ibid., p. 29; Berrizbeita, Anita. 'The Amsterdam Bos: The Modern Park and the Construction of Collective Experience' in Corner, James (Editor) (1999). *Recovering Landscape.* New York, Princeton Architectural Press, p. 189; Public Parks Service of Amsterdam – Dienst Publieke Werken (undated Guidebook). *het Amsterdamse Bos – The Amsterdam Forest Park*, p. 6.

364 *RIBA Journal*, 23 May 1938, op. cit., p. 5 stated that the cost of acquisition was Hfl5.4 million.

365 Berrizbeita, Anita in Corner, James (Editor) (1999), op. cit., pp. 188–9; *RIBA Journal*, 23 May 1938, op. cit., p. 8.

366 Noted at author's meeting with Mrs R. L. A. van Oosten, Director of the Amsterdamse Bos, on 25 June 1999 and from information supplied by her including excerpts from Dienst Ruimtelijke Ordening, City of Amsterdam (1994). *Growth and 'green'* in *Amsterdam Present*, pp. 153–9; it was also noted that the Natuurmonumenten, twelve regionally based semi-private, semi-public nature organizations, with about 900,000 members, is a powerful lobby for nature conservation in the *Staatsbosbeheer* (state forests) and other nature reserves.

367 *het Amsterdamse Bos – the Amsterdam Forest Park*, op. cit., p. 6.

368 Ibid., p. 6.

369 Stedelijk Beheer Amsterdam (1994), op. cit.

370 City of Amsterdam (1994), op. cit., p. 155; *RIBA Journal*, 23 May 1938, op. cit., p. 8; Chadwick, George F. (1965), op. cit., p. 306; Polano, Sergio (1991) in Teyssot, Georges and Mosser, Monique (Editors) (1991), op. cit., p. 508; Berrizbeita, Anita in Corner, James (Editor) (1999), op. cit., pp. 192, 195.

371 Hunt, John Dixon (1992). *Gardens and the Picturesque: Studies in the History of Landscape Architecture.* Cambridge, MA, MIT Press, pp. 140, 152; *RIBA Journal*, 23 May 1938 ibid., p. 8.

372 Lootsma, Bart. 'Synthetic Regionalization: The Dutch Landscape Toward a Second Modernity' in Corner, James (Editor) (1999), op. cit., p. 260; Koolhaas, Rem and Mau, Bruce (1995). *S, M, L, XL.* New York, Monacelli (second edition 1998), p. 934; Daalder, Remco (1999), op. cit., p. 19; Lootsma, Bart (1999), op. cit., p. 273.

373 Noted at author's meeting with Mrs R. L. A. van Oosten on 25 June 1999 op. cit.

374 *RIBA Journal*, 23 May 1938, op. cit., pp. 7–8; visitor figures for 1985 from a response by Mr J. W. Butterman at the Amsterdamse Bos to author's questionnaire in August 1987; other information provided at meeting with Mrs R. L. A. van Oosten on 25 June 1999, op. cit.

375 City of Amsterdam (1994), op. cit., pp. 153–9; dRO, Amsterdam (1994). *Een groenstructuur met een hoofdletter.* Volume 12, Number 113, p. 13.

376 Stedelijk Beheer Amsterdam (1994), op. cit.; text for an address by Dr Remco Daalder to a conference in the United Kingdom in 1998 and the meeting with Mrs R. L. A. van Oosten, Director of the Amsterdamse Bos, on 25 June 1999, op. cit.

20 THE MINNEAPOLIS PARK SYSTEM

377 Garvin, Alexander (1996). *The American City – What Works, What Doesn't.* New York, McGraw-Hill, p. 63; Wirth, Theodore (1945). *Minneapolis Park System 1883–1944: Retrospective Glimpses into the History of the Board of Park Commissioners of Minneapolis, Minnesota and the City's Park, Parkway and Playground System.* Minneapolis, Board of Park Commissioners, p. 113 explained the origin of the title 'Grand Rounds'. The Park and Recreation Board has recently revived that title although the main lakes – Harriet, Calhoun, Lake of the Isles and Cedar – are called the 'Chain of Lakes' or simply 'the lakes'.

378 Minneapolis Park and Recreation Board (1999). *Superintendent's Annual Report for 1998*, p. 7; Hill Nettleton, Pamela (1998). *Access*

Minneapolis/St. Paul. New York, Access, p. 124;
Wirth, Theodore (1945), op. cit., Foreword.

379 Ibid., p. 15.

380 Ibid., p. 21, cited the *Minneapolis Tribune* as being particularly outspoken in its support for parks. They were probably articulating and playing to the views of 'improvement-minded' mill owners, other business leaders and their wives.

381 Ibid., pp. 19, 26.

382 Tishler, William H. 'H. W. S. Cleveland' in Tishler William H. (Editor) (1989). *American Landscape Architecture: Designers and Places.* Washington, DC, Preservation Press, p. 24.

383 Wirth, Theodore (1945), op. cit., pp. 114–16.

384 Newton, Norman T. (1971). *Design on the Land: The Development of Landscape Architecture.* Cambridge, MA, Belknap, pp. 309–15; Haglund, Karl (January 1976). 'Rural Tastes, Rectangular Ideas, and the Skirmishes of H. W. S. Cleveland', *Landscape Architecture*, Volume 75, p. 68; Neckar, Lance M. 'Fast-Tracking Culture and Landscape: Horace William Shaler Cleveland and the Garden in the Midwest' in O'Malley, Therese and Treib, Marc (Editors) (1995). *Regional Garden Design in the United States.* Washington, DC, Dumbarton Oaks Trustees for Harvard University, p. 72.

385 Newton, Norman T. (1971), ibid., p. 309; Neckar, Lance M. in O'Malley, Therese and Treib, Marc (Editors) (1995), ibid., pp. 73–5.

386 Haglund, Karl (1976), op. cit., p. 68; Tishler, William H. (1989), op. cit., p. 24.

387 Newton, Norman T. (1971), op. cit., pp. 311, 314; Haglund, Karl (1976), op. cit., p. 69; Neckar, Lance M. in O'Malley, Therese and Treib, Marc (Editors) (1995), p. 83.

388 Tishler, William H. (1989), op. cit., p. 24; Newton, Norman T. (1971), op. cit., p. 312; Cleveland, H. W. S. (1873). *Landscape Architecture as Applied to the Wants of the West* originally published in Chicago, Jansen, McLurg & Co. and repr. Lubove, Roy (Editor) (1965), Pittsburgh, University of Pittsburgh Press, p. 5; Cleveland, H. W. S. (1873), ibid., p. 50.

389 Neckar, Lance M. in O'Malley, Therese and Treib, Marc (Editors) (1995), op. cit., p. 89. Berry is credited by Wirth as having been Superintendent of Parks from April 1884 to December 1905.

390 Neckar, Lance M. in O'Malley, Therese and Treib, Marc (Editors) (1995), ibid., p. 90. Neckar referred here to Olmsted's letter of 6 October 1886 in which he stated that 'the kind of recreation that these large parks supply . . . is that which a man [sic] insensibly obtains when he [sic] puts the city behind him [sic] and out of his [sic] sight and goes where he [sic] will be under the undisturbed influence of pleasing natural scenery', Zaitzevsky, Cynthia (1982). *Frederick Law Olmsted and the Boston Park System.* Cambridge, MA, Belknap, p. 35 quoting from Cleveland's *The Public Grounds of Chicago: How to Give Them Character and Expression.* Chicago, Charles D. Lakey (1869).

391 Wirth, Theodore (1945), op. cit., p. 79;

Minneapolis Park and Recreation Board (1999), op. cit., p. 8.

392 Cleveland, H. W. S. (1883) *Suggestions for a System of Parks and Parkways for the City of Minneapolis* in Wirth, Theodore (1945), ibid., pp. 28–9; Cranz, Galen (1982). *The Politics of Park Design.* Cambridge, MA, MIT Press, p. 30.

393 Cleveland, H. W. S. (1883), op. cit., in Wirth, Theodore (1945), op. cit., p. 29.

394 Ibid., pp. 29, 32.

395 Heckscher, August Robinson, Phyllis (1977). *Open Space: The Life of American Cities.* New York: Harper & Row, p. 206; Hill Nettleton, Pamela (1998), op. cit., p. 243.

396 Sanders Wacker Wehrman Bergly, Inc. (1992). *The Minnehaha Park Renovation Plan* for The Minneapolis Park and Recreation Board; Longfellow's *The Song of Hiawatha* addressed 'Ye who loved the haunts of Nature, Love the Sunshine of the meadow, Love the shadow of the forest, Love the wind among the branches . . .'.

397 Hill Nettleton, Pamela (1998), op. cit., p. 80; Wirth, Theodore (1945), op. cit., p. 84; Hagen, Kai (1989). *Parks and Wildlands,* Minneapolis, Nodin, p. 23. The levels of Lake Calhoun and Lake of the Isles were lowered in 1905 and they were connected by a canal opened in July 1911. The water link between Cedar Lake and Lake of the Isles was completed in 1913, lowering the level of Cedar Lake by about 5 feet (1.5 metres).

398 Cleveland had noted in his *Suggestions for a System of Parks and Parkways for the City of Minneapolis* that 'in the ten years succeeding the commencement of work on Central Park in New York, the increased valuation of taxable property in the wards immediately surrounding it was no less than $54,000,000, affording a surplus . . . sufficient to pay for the entire cost of the park in less time than was required for its construction' in Wirth, Theodore, op. cit., p. 28.

399 Harnik, Peter. 'Cedar Lake Park and Trail' in Garvin, Alexander and Berens, Gayle (1997). *Urban Parks and Open Space.* Washington, DC: Urban Land Institute, pp. 58–69 gave a full account of the acquisition and development of the park and trail.

400 Neckar, Lance M. in O'Malley, Therese and Treib, Marc (Editors) (1995), op. cit., p. 90.

401 The Berger Fountain looks misplaced and dated. It is understood that installation was arranged as a holiday souvenir by a former Parks Superintendent, Benjamin Berger, who had seen the original, designed by Robert Woodward, designer of the later and quite outstanding 'Ashtray' at Darling Harbour, Sydney, during a vacation in Australia.

402 *Landscape Objectives* on Planting Plan dated 14 December 1994 by Balmori Associates, Inc. and Brauer and Associates for Minneapolis Park and Recreation Board; *Process Architecture*, No. 133 (1998), p. 26 *et seq.* described Balmori's design. The somewhat clumsy flower motif cast into Balmori's railings appears to be derived from the form of the window on the façade of the recreation pavil-

ion. Cleveland's original layout – without the island – was reproduced in Wirth, Theodore (1945), op. cit., p. 43.

403 Cleveland, H. W. S. (1883) in Newton, Norman T. (1971), op. cit., p. 312.

404 Cleveland, H. W. S. 'Aesthetic Development' in Neckar, Lance M. in O'Malley, Therese and Treib, Marc (Editors) (1995), op. cit., p. 93; Nassauer, Joan Iverson in Nassauer, Joan Iverson (Editor) (1997). *Placing Nature: Culture and Landscape Ecology.* Washington, DC, Island, p. 69.

405 Harnik, Peter in Garvin, Alexander and Berens, Gayle (1997), op. cit., p. 62; response to author's questionnaire to Minneapolis Park and Recreation Board, October 1998.

406 Garvin, Alexander (1996), op. cit., p. 66.

407 *Lake of the Isles Fact Sheet* (1998) produced by Minneapolis Park and Recreation Board.

408 Noted from author's meeting with Robert Mattson, Landscape Architect at Park and Recreation Board on 13 July 1989; Halprin, Lawrence (1972). *Cities.* Cambridge, MA, MIT Press, pp. 224–7; Bennett, Paul (1999). 'Dance of the Drumlins' in *Landscape Architecture*, Volume 89, No. 8, gave an account of Schwartz's forecourt. He commented that the city lacks a 'landscape of such presence that it imparts an identity' – re-echoing (perhaps unwittingly) Olmsted's comment in 1886 about the lack of individual large park in Minneapolis. Bennett noted that Schwartz felt that the city lacks 'civic identity discernible in built form'. He also noted that the drumlins are proving to be a 'maintenance nightmare' and that Minneapolis architecture critic Linda Mack called the design 'cheeky' and suggested that it is inappropriate. Schwartz, Bennett recorded, believed that 'the city needs strategies for building public space . . .'.

409 Wirth, Theodore (1945), op. cit., p. 168.

REFLECTIONS

410 Boston Common, established in 1634, is regarded as the first public park in the United States.

411 Jackson, John Brinkerhoff (1994). *A Sense of Place, A Sense of Time,* New Haven and London, Yale University Press, p. 114; Strieder, Peter (1998) in Foreword of Meyer, Gustav (1860). *Lehrbuch der Schönen Gärtenkunst.* repr. Berlin, Riegel.

412 Baljon, Lodewijk (1992). *Designing Parks.* Woodbridge, Garden Art, p. 10; Cranz, Galen (1982). *The Politics of Park Design.* Cambridge, MA, MIT Press. Cranz's book was organized around the first four eras. She identified the fifth era in conversation with author at the *City Parks 2000 Conference* in Glasgow in October 1994 and subsequently in Winnipeg in February 1999; Blume, Mary. 'The New City Park: A Pathway Instead of a Place' in *International Herald Tribune*, 22–23 October 1994 publicized landscape architect Diana Balmori's advocacy of linear parks; London-based academic Tom Turner has written and spoken widely about his concept of harlequin-coloured urban open spaces.

413 Beveridge, Charles E. and Hoffman, Carolyn F. (Editors) (1997). *The Papers of Frederick Law Olmsted: Supplementary Series, Volume 1 – Writings on Public Parks, Parkways, and Park Systems.* Baltimore, Johns Hopkins University Press, pp. 474–7; Kaplan, Rachel and Kaplan, Stephen (1989). *The Experience of Nature: A Psychological Perspective.* Cambridge, Cambridge University Press, pp. 172–3. They go on to state that 'the immediate outcomes of contacts with nearby nature include enjoyment, relaxation, and lowered stress levels . . . well-being is affected by such contacts. People with access to nearby-natural [sic] settings have been found to be physical healthier than other individuals'; Baljon, Lodewijk (1992), op. cit., p. 236.

414 Knuijt, Martin, Ophius, Hans and van Saane, Peter (Editors) (1993). *Modern Park Design – Recent Trends.* Amsterdam, THOTH, p. 38. Ironically, in Booth, Robert (2000), 'People' column of *Architects' Journal*, Volume 211, No. 23. p. 24 Geuze is quoted as saying 'I really respect the Anglo-Saxon romantic park and Jubilee Gardens will be at least 70 per cent grass with large trees that evoke park design from a century ago'; Laurie, Michael (December 1992). 'The Urban Mantlepiece' in *Landscape Design*, No. 216, pp. 21–2; Ophius, Hans (June 1997). 'Brauchen wir noch Parks?: Do We Still Need Parks?' in *Topos European Landscape Magazine*, No. 19, pp. 90–5.

415 Garvin, Alexander (1996). *The American City – What Works, What Doesn't.* New York, McGraw-Hill, p. 69.

416 Goldberger, Paul (1999). 'Zone Defense – Is Donald Trump Unstoppable?' in *The New Yorker*, 22 February and 1 March 1999, pp. 178–9.

417 Sutton, S. B. (1971). *Civilizing American Cities: Frederick Law Olmsted Writings on City Landscapes* (1997 edition). Da Capo, New York, p. 11.

418 Greenbie, Barrie (1985). 'Restoring the Vision' in *Landscape Architecture*, Volume 75, No. 5, writing about differences in character between landscape architects and building architects, observed that landscape architects tend to look at sites in terms of 'what is there already' whereas building architects tend to look at them in terms of 'what they can put there'. Greenbie suggested that landscape architects' approach can be characterized as humility – and that humility is not a common characteristic of strong leaders. It certainly wasn't one of Olmsted's principal characteristics.

419 Bennett, Paul (1999). 'Dance of the Drumlins' in *Landscape Architecture*, Volume 89, No. 8, p. 67 noted Schwartz's view that 'designing for the public realm is a matter less of art than of politics – not the politics of campaigns and soft money, but the politics of public dialogue, concensus, and group action'; OMA teamed up for the Downsview Park competition with the same Toronto-based architects – Oleson Worland – that Schwartz Smith and Meyer worked with on Yorkville Park.

420 Garvin, Alexander (1996), op. cit., p. 70.

421 Latz, Peter in Diedrich, Lisa (1994). 'Le Jardin de la Mémoire: Out of Budget, Out of Mind?' in *Topos European Landscape Magazine*, No. 8, p. 74; User surveys conducted by the Chicago Park District for Lincoln Park in 1991 concluded that 'whites tend to come alone or in small groups, with an average group size of 1.6 persons. More than 10% of Hispanics and Asians come in groups of 10 or more. Average group size for African Americans is 3.7; for Hispanics, 4.4; and for Asians, 5.5'. That survey also found that 'minorities visit from farther away than do whites, with 20% of Asians coming from the suburbs and 80% arriving by car'; Ward Thompson, Catharine (spring 1998). 'Historic Parks and Contemporary Needs' in *Landscape Journal*, Volume 17, Number 1, p. 19. Whereas Beveridge, Charles E. and Rocheleau, Paul (1998). *Frederick Law Olmsted: Designing the American Landscape.* New York, Universe, p. 46 noted that 'Olmsted fervently hoped that the great urban park would become a place where all classes would meet and mix'; Rosenzweig, Roy and Blackmar, Elizabeth (1992). *The Park and the People: A History of Central Park.* Ithaca, Cornell University Press (paperback edition 1998), p. 334 noted that even towards the end of the nineteenth century 'self-segregation had a temporal as well as a spatial dimension: fashionable women on the East Drive on weekday afternoons, gentlemen's riding clubs on the bridle paths on weekday mornings, working-class families at the menagerie on Sunday afternoons, sporting men at McGown's Pass Tavern in the evenings'.

422 Alexander, Christopher *et al.* (1977). *A Pattern Language.* New York, Oxford University Press, p. 305. Greenhalgh, Liz and Worpole, Ken (Comedia – 1996). *People, Parks and Cities.* London, HMSO, pp. 32–3 noted the same pattern in the United Kingdom; Laurie, Michael (1992), op. cit., pp. 21–2.

423 Grandison, Kenrick Ian (spring 1999). 'Challenging Formalism: The Implications of Contemporary Cultural Theory for Historic Preservation' in *Landscape Journal*, Volume 18, Number 1, p. 37; Ward Thompson, Catharine (spring 1998), op. cit., p. 23; Parklands Consortium (1999). *Birkenhead People's Park Restoration and Management Plan: Volume II – Recommendations.* Metropolitan Borough of Wirral, p. 1.

424 Leinberger, Christopher and Berens, Gayle. 'Executive Summary: Creating Better Urban Parks and Open Space' in Garvin, Alexander and Berens, Gayle (1997). *Urban Parks and Open Space.* Washington, DC, Urban Land Institute, p. 26; Jackson, John Brinkerhoff (1994), op. cit., p. 116.

Backword

The author thanks the staff at Spon Press, Routledge, Taylor & Francis and their project managers, M Rules, for their commitment to the publication of this book. Particular thanks are due to Rebecca Casey and Caroline Mallinder at Spon Press for their responsive guidance.

Representatives of the various parks who answered questionnaires, who kindly provided background information and/or agreed to be interviewed and to comment on draft scripts for the individual parks, were:

* Paley Park – Phillip Raspe Jr (The Paley Foundation), Philip Boschetti (The Greenpark Foundation)
* Yorkville Park – Ken Smith (Ken Smith Landscape Architect, New York), Stephen O'Bright (Toronto Department of Parks and Recreation), David Oleson (Oleson Worland Architects, Toronto)
* Freeway Park – Kerry Lasko (Seattle Department of Parks and Recreation)
* Bryant Park – Daniel A. Biederman, Jerome Barth and Ethan Lurcher (34th Street Partnership)
* Parcs de Bercy, André-Citroën and Buttes-Chaumont – Marie-Joseph Gambard and Sophie Dobler (Direction des Parcs et Éspaces Verts, Ville de Paris)
* Parc de la Villette – Carine Deschênes (Établissement Public du Parc et de la Grande Halle de la Villette)
* Parque de María Luisa – José Elía Bonels (Servicio de Parques y Jardines, Ayuntamiento de Sevilla).
* Birkenhead Park – Jim Lester and Mike Garbutt (Metropolitan Borough of Wirrall)
* Regent's Park – Jenny Adams and David Castleton (Royal Parks Agency), David McQuitty (Colvin and Moggeridge)
* Grant Park – Julia Sniderman Bachrach, John Henderson and Ed Uhlir (Chicago Park District)
* Stadtpark, Hamburg – Heino Grunert and Andrea Zörning (Hamburg Umweltbehörde)
* Landschaftspark Duisburg-Nord – AnneLiese Latz, Claus Heimann and Philip Kühnel (Latz + Partner, Duisburg), Ellen Hein, Dominique Neuhauss and Günter Zieling (Landschaftspark Duisburg-Nord GmbH)
* Prospect Park – Tupper Thomas, Barbara McTiernan and Lucy Gentile (Prospect Park Alliance)
* Tiergarten – Klaus von Krosigk (Landesdenkmalamt Berlin)
* Central Park – Kate Clark (Librarian, City of New York Department of Parks and Recreation), Rick Lepkowski and Erna Stennet (Central Park Conservancy), Bruce Kelly (Bruce Kelly and David Varnell, Landscape Architects, New York)
* Stanley Park – Terri Clark and Dana Walker (Vancouver Board of Parks and Recreation), Michael von Hausen (City of Vancouver Planning Department)
* Bos Park – Roos van Oosten and Jenny Hofman (Amsterdamse Bos)
* Minneapolis – Robert Mattson, Sandra Welsh and Mary (Mitzi) Patterson (Minneapolis Park and Recreation Board).

Each person was extraordinarily helpful and I am extremely grateful for their time and assistance.

A number of employers and colleagues have given generous support to the project. These include Brian Clouston, Annie Coombs, Wendy Lui, Henry Steed, Jennifer Steed and Stanley Yip at Brian Clouston and Partners Hong Kong Limited; Jacob Rothschild, Robert Holden and John Hopkins at Clifton Design; John Hopkins and Justine Dudley at Tate Hopkins and, latterly, EDAW; Michael Cox – Dean, Charles Thomsen – Associate Dean, and Mary Lochhead – Head Librarian, Richard Perron and Terry Walker – Directors of the CadLab, and their respective staff in the Faculty of Architecture at the University of Manitoba.

Friends and colleagues who have given advice and comments on the project overall include, in roughly chronological order, Brian Clouston, Henry Steed, Ian Laurie, Michael Ellison, Adrian Forty, Jean Wetherburn, Jan Green, Geoffrey Jellicoe, John Stoddart, Dimon Liu, Christine Wilson, Sandra Donaldson, Michael Laurie, Alan Barber, Leonard Lynch, Jere S. French, Lance Neckar, James Corner, Raphael Gomez-Moriana and Charlie Thomsen. Friends, colleagues and relatives who have assisted or advised on specific aspects of the project include Philip Tate, Lise Attia, Corinne Cassé, Aymara Izquiel, Eva Smazal and Natasha Angus – translations; Martin Tate – political history; Sheila Harvey at the Landscape Institute Library – sourcing information; Ian White – questionnaire design; David Van Vliet – German parks; Doug Paterson – Stanley Park; Lance Neckar – H. W. S. Cleveland and Minneapolis parks; Mireia Fernandez – Spanish parks; Daniel Roehr – Berlin parks; and Ursula Wieser – Paris parks.

I am also grateful to Peter William Siry, a graduate student in landscape architecture at the University of Manitoba, for drawing the plans of the parks. Funding was received from The Landscape Design Trust for Martin Jones' photographs of the parks in New York and Paris. Martin , who was involved with the project since 1987, took many of the photographs for the book and many more of parks that are not covered in this volume. Sadly, Martin died shortly before the book was printed. I am glad he knew that one of his photographs would be on the cover. And I hope that his wife Nina and their son Ben and her daughter Emily regard this book as a fitting tribute to Martin's work.

I must thank my parents – Malcolm, who died before the book was written, and Margaret – for supporting my decision to become a landscape architect and for their contributions to the project.

The most important contribution was from my wife and colleague Dr Marcella Eaton. She was a constantly supportive companion and thoughtful critic during visits to the parks, during meetings with their managers and in her reading and re-reading of the drafts for the text. I could not have completed this book without her.

ILLUSTRATION CREDITS

Dr Marcella Eaton

p.8 bottom (April 2000); pp.11, 16 (October 1999); p.28 top (April 2000); pp.34, 36, 45 top (June 1999); p. 71 (May 1999); pp.79–80 (July 1999); p. 101 (April 2000); p.104 (April 2000); pp.111–12 (July 1999); pp.116, 119, 120 left (June 1999); p.149 (April 2000); p.165 (June 1998); pp.184, 192 (September 1998)

Martin Jones

pp.5, 8 top, 26, 28 bottom, 29, 30 (October 1999); pp.37–8 (June 2000); pp.41,43–4, 49, 51, 52–3 (May 2000); pp.49, 51, 52–3, 61, 63 (June 2000); p.88 (July 1996); p.90 (May 1993); p.92 top (June 1993); p.92 bottom (October 1993); p.93 (May 1993); pp.109, 113 (July 1987); pp.128–9, 132 bottom (October 1999); p.144, 148, 150, 153, 156 (October 1999)

Jonathan Park

p.121 (October 1996)

Alan Tate

p.9 (July 1989); pp.13–14 (October 1999); p.17 (November 1999); p.20 (June 1997); pp.21–2 (November 1999); p.45 bottom (June 1999); p.60 (June 1999); p.65 (June 2000); pp.68–70, 72 (May 1999), pp.76–7 (July 1999); p.97 (April 2000); p.100 (September 1990); p.103 (April 2000); pp.117, 120 right (June 1999); p.126 (April 2000); p.132 top (October 2000); pp.136–41 (July 1999); p.152 (April 2000); pp.160–1 (June 1998), p.163 (June 1987); p.164 (November 1999); pp.172–7 (June 1999); p.185 (September 1998); p.188 (October 1998); p.189 (September 1998), p.191 (October 1998); p.197 (June 1998)

Index